THE

Healthy Slow Cooker

SECOND EDITION

135 Gluten-Free Recipes
for Health and Wellness

Judith Finlayson

Robert
ROSE

The Healthy Slow Cooker, Second Edition
Text copyright © 2014 Judith Finlayson
Photographs copyright © 2014 Robert Rose Inc.
Cover and text design copyright © 2014 Robert Rose Inc.

Some of the recipes in this book appeared in the following books, often in a slightly different form: *Slow Cooker Comfort Food* (2009), *The Vegetarian Slow Cooker* (2010), *The 150 Best Slow Cooker Recipes* (2011), *The Complete Gluten-Free Whole Grains Cookbook* (2013) and *The 163 Best Paleo Slow Cooker Recipes* (2013).

For complete cataloguing information, see page 343.

Design and Production: Kevin Cockburn/PageWave Graphics Inc.
Editor: Carol Sherman
Copy Editor: Karen Campbell-Sheviak
Indexer: Gillian Watts
Nutritional Consultant: Doug Cook, RD, MHSc

Photography: Colin Errison
Associate Photographer: Matt Johannsson
Food Styling: Kathryn Robertson
Prop Styling: Charlene Errison
Photography on pages 32, 44, 135, 187: Mark T. Shapiro
Food Styling: Kate Bush
Prop Styling: Charlene Errison

Additional photos: page 3 @iStockphoto.com/kcline, page 9 @iStockphoto.com/loops7, page 14 @iStockphoto.com/kazoka30, page 25 @ iStockphoto.com/Juanmonino, page 29 @iStockphoto.com/Elenathewise, page 31 @iStockphoto.com/deymos, page 37 @iStockphoto.com/Floortje, page 47 @iStockphoto.com/DGM007, page 49 @iStockphoto.com/Ekaterina_Lin, page 57 @iStockphoto.com/JonnyJim, page 59 @iStockphoto.com/PoppyB, page 63 @iStockphoto.com/SilviaJansen, page 67 @iStockphoto.com/archives, page 76 @iStockphoto.com/dantok, page 83 @iStockphoto.com/filonmar, page 87 @iStockphoto.com/tastymorsels, page 91 @iStockphoto.com/jurgakarosaite, page 97 @ iStockphoto.com/ROTTSTRA, page 99 @iStockphoto.com/DOUGBERRY, page 101 @iStockphoto.com/magdasmith, page 103 @ iStockphoto.com/fcafotodigital, page 105 @iStockphoto.com/small_frog, page 108 @iStockphoto.com/PoppyB, page 111 @iStockphoto.com/rudisill, page 125 @iStockphoto.com/ozdigital, page 127 @iStockphoto.com/Alejandro Rivera, page 131 @iStockphoto.com/adel66, page 136 @ iStockphoto.com/Funwithfood, page 141 @iStockphoto.com/lightshows, page 143 @iStockphoto.com/Gimmerton, page 145 @iStockphoto.com/YinYang, page 147 @iStockphoto.com/DebbiSmirnoff, page 155 @iStockphoto.com/wragg, page 167 @iStockphoto.com/milanfoto, page 171 @iStockphoto.com/WoodyUpstate, page 188 @iStockphoto.com/Juanmonino, page 202 @iStockphoto.com/eddieberman, page 207 @iStockphoto.com/Floortje, page 209 @iStockphoto.com/Mantonature, page 211 @iStockphoto.com/Tokle, page 217 @iStockphoto.com/duckycards, page 221 @iStockphoto.com/Erickson Photography, page 229 @iStockphoto.com/Chris Gramly, page 233 @iStockphoto.com/esseffe, page 245 @iStockphoto.com/chang, page 250 @iStockphoto.com/Jamesmcq24, page 253 @iStockphoto.com/Elenathewise, page 255 @iStockphoto.com/CaroleGomez, page 257 @iStockphoto.com/MKucova, page 259 @iStockphoto.com/wragg, page 265 @iStockphoto.com/FotografiaBasica, page 267 @iStockphoto.com/Alasdair Thomson, page 273 @iStockphoto.com/matka_Wariatka, page 277 @iStockphoto.com/FotografiaBasica, page 283 @iStockphoto.com/robynmac, page 288 @iStockphoto.com/FotografiaBasica, page 295 @iStockphoto.com/arnowssr, page 297 @iStockphoto.com/DebbiSmirnoff, page 299 @iStockphoto.com/ballycroy, page 305 @iStockphoto.com/johnnyscriv, page 313 @iStockphoto.com/leeser87, page 315 @iStockphoto.com/JLVarga, page 317 @iStockphoto.com/john shepherd, page 319 @iStockphoto.com/Alasdair Thomson, page 327 @iStockphoto.com/republica, page 329 @iStockphoto.com/letty17, page 331 @iStockphoto.com/BurAnd, page 333 @iStockphoto.com/ratmaner, page 335 @iStockphoto.com/baibaz

Cover: Moroccan-Style Lamb with Raisins and Apricots (page 227)
Page 6: Two-Bean Turkey Chili (page 146)
Page 10: Braised Veal with Pearl Onions and Sweet Peas (page 212)

The publisher gratefully acknowledges the financial support of our publishing program by the Government of Canada through the Canada Book Fund.

Published by Robert Rose Inc.
120 Eglinton Avenue East, Suite 800, Toronto, Ontario, Canada M4P 1E2
Tel: (416) 322-6552 Fax: (416) 322-6936
www.robertrose.ca

Printed and bound in Canada

1 2 3 4 5 6 7 8 9 TCP 22 21 20 19 18 17 16 15 14

Contents

Acknowledgments

A cookbook is never just a one-person production. There are so many facts (consider the lines of recipe ingredients alone) and components (photographs and food styling among them) that it requires a community of people working together to create a book that will meet the demanding criteria of today's marketplace. Basically, I've been working with the same terrific team for more than 10 years. They are consummate professionals with whom I enjoy working and I feel very fortunate to have their support.

First and foremost is my husband, Bob Dees, who said, "You should think about revising your healthy slow cooker book." As usual, he was right. I'd also like to thank Marian Jarkovich, Nina McCreath and Martine Quibell at Robert Rose, for their support of this and all my projects.

The dramatic difference between a manuscript (the typed copy an author works on) and a finished cookbook depends upon the work of designers, photographers and stylists. Thanks to the team at PageWave Graphics, especially Kevin Cockburn, who designed this book. As always, Colin Erricson and Mark Shapiro took fabulous photographs, food stylists Kathryn Robertson and Kate Bush made my recipes look delicious and prop stylist Charlene Erricson provided a perfect setting for their preparations.

I'd also like to thank Doug Cook, RD, MHSC, who was a great help in steering me through the quagmire of nutritional research and helping me sort through some of incomprehensible and often confusing writing in scientific reports.

No matter how diligent I am, the sheer volume of detail ensures that errors will creep in. Thanks to copy editor, Karen Campbell-Sheviak, who catches things the rest of us miss. And last, but certainly not least, my editor, Carol Sherman, whose eagle eye, patient demeanor and great sense of humor always make the editorial process a pleasure.

Nutrient Analysis

The nutrient analyses for all the recipes were prepared by Info Access (1988) Inc, Toronto, Ontario. This also includes the evaluation of recipe servings as sources of nutrients.

The nutrient analyses were based on:

- Imperial measures and weights (except for food typically packaged and used in metric).
- The larger number of servings when there was a range. The smaller amount of ingredients when there was a range.
- The first ingredient listed when there was a choice. The exclusion of "optional" ingredients.
- The exclusion of ingredients with "non-specified" or "to taste" amounts. The analyses were done on the regular recipes, not the "Make Ahead" versions, which might vary slightly in the ingredients used.

The evaluation of recipe servings as sources of vitamins and minerals combined U.S. and Canadian regulations. Bearing in mind that the two countries have different reporting standards, the highest standard was always used. For instance, U.S. regulations allow for a food to be identified as an excellent source of a nutrient if it provides at least 20% of the daily value whereas Canada requires 25%. In such cases, a nutrient providing between 20 and 24% of the DV would be deemed to be only a "good" source in our analysis. To compensate for this and other discrepancies, and to ensure that as many nutrients as possible were captured, the micronutrient analysis includes the category "Source of," which Canadian guidelines recognize as a food supplying between 5 and 14% of the DV of a nutrient.

Introduction

This book is an extensively revised and expanded version of one I published in 2006. When I review the previous version now, I find it difficult to believe that book, which has sold more than 100,000 copies, was on the cutting edge of, as I wrote then, "all the exciting new developments occurring in the field of nutrition." In those days, scientists were just beginning to acknowledge that food has the power to prevent, and possibly even cure, many illnesses, from cardiovascular disease and type-2 diabetes to certain kinds of cancer. In the intervening years, much more research has been done on individual foods and their unique combinations of nutrients, as well as the nutrients themselves, reconfirming and strengthening the idea that a nutritious diet plays a crucial role in health and well-being.

Since then a great deal has changed in what we know about healthy eating. Yet I find it terribly troubling that the fundamental information consumers receive has, for the most part, remained very much the same: keep calories and fat (especially saturated fat) low, and eat an abundance of carbohydrates (at best not refined). Looking back I can see that this key message was being challenged, even then, by heavy hitters such as science writer Gary Taubes and Dr. Walter Willett, who was then Chairman of the Department of Nutrition at the Harvard School of Public Health. However, it gained traction as the institutionally sanctioned strategy for healthy eating and it has obviously been very difficult to get out of the rut.

Today, however, these fundamental concepts are under serious attack. To provide just a few examples, the evidence against saturated fat has been diminishing and the link between blood cholesterol levels and heart disease has been seriously questioned. Books such as *Good Calories, Bad Calories* by Gary Taubes, *Wheat Belly* by cardiologist William Davis and *Grain Brain* by neurologist David Perlmutter make compelling arguments in favor of reducing carbohydrate consumption. It has also become increasingly clear that the relentless focus on counting calories has meant that many people are not consuming adequate nutrients. Although most people are aware of the link between poor diet and the epidemic of so-called "diseases of civilization" such as obesity and type-2 diabetes, so much conflicting information is communicated to consumers on a regular basis that it is difficult to know what to do.

As I see it, when wending your way through this labyrinth, there are three main premises to keep in mind: There is no magic bullet, no single food or specific combination thereof that will produce long-term good health. Secondly, maintaining balance among the intake of macronutrients — healthy fat, protein and carbohydrates — is generally recognized by experts as the most sensible dietary approach (see page 175). And thirdly, long-term health and wellness depends upon consuming adequate amounts and a wide range of micronutrients, including phytonutrients. Although scientists are still in the early stages of understanding phytonutrients, it does seem clear that they, along with micronutrients interact with one another in complex ways, playing an important role in helping the body stay well and defend itself against disease.

In the final analysis, though, the strategy for healthy eating is quite simple: eliminate processed foods from your diet and habitually eat a variety of nutrient-dense whole foods, including an abundance of vegetables, fruits, nuts and seeds. That's the way to ensure that your body is provided with the broad mix of essential nutrients it needs: vitamins, minerals, phytonutrients and dietary fiber.

In other words, it's not difficult to tap into the healing power of food. And once you commit to consuming a diet of nutrient-dense whole foods, improvements may occur in unexpected ways because all the nutrients in foods work together to create synergy in the health benefits they produce (see page 307). Just to provide one example, studies show that the lycopene in red tomatoes and the glucosinolates in green broccoli are far more formidable cancer fighters when combined than is either component on its own. So at mealtime, make sure you see a kaleidoscope of colors on your plate. That signals you are consuming a variety of vitamins, minerals and phytonutrients, all of which team up to keep you healthy.

Making good food choices also means avoiding junk foods and those that are highly refined. These types of foods tend to be high in calories and low in nutrients. Instead, it's important to choose foods that are "nutrient dense," those that deliver optimum nutrition for the calories they provide. These include sustainably caught fish and seafood, pasture-raised meat and poultry, red and orange vegetables, dark leafy greens, pulses, whole grains, nuts, seeds and deeply colored berries, among others. Seasoning your food liberally with spices and herbs is also recommended because recent research has identified many beneficial compounds in these foods.

This means you won't find recipes in this book that focus on being low-fat, low-carb or low-cal. Instead, you'll find recipes that are nutrient-dense. While they tend toward being balanced in terms of the macronutrients (about one-third each), there is no need to be doctrinaire about these relationships. Sunday dinner might provide a higher percentage of fat, meatless Monday might be overloaded with carbs, and your finally-it's-Friday-night meal might be protein-heavy, but so long as you are eating nutrient-dense foods with adequate dietary fiber and varying these ratios throughout the week, you will be on track toward physical well-being.

To heighten your understanding of the healthful benefits of wholesome foods, I have treated every recipe as a focal point for sharing valuable information about nutrition — not only an in-depth nutritional analysis, which includes micronutrient assessments (unfortunately, nutritional analysis has not reached the point where the phytonutrients in foods can be captured for consumer use), but also Mindful Morsels, bits of recipe-relevant information, and Natural Wonders, more in-depth snippets on broader elements of nutrition and healthy eating. These features will help you to make more informed choices about what you eat and to develop a pattern of healthy eating.

As always, in my slow cooker books, I've included a wide range of recipes, from breakfasts and appetizers to hearty soups and elegant desserts. Wherever appropriate, recipes include "Make Ahead" information to help you take full advantage of the convenience provided by a slow cooker. My goal has been to make the results as nutritious as possible without sacrificing one iota of lip-smacking taste. Although this is not a vegetarian cookbook, vegetarian and vegan recipes have been noted.

I hope you will find this book helpful. More importantly, I hope you will use it often to get the most out of the convenience your slow cooker provides by preparing delicious and nutritious meals that help to keep you and yours happy and well.

— *Judith Finlayson*

Using Your Slow Cooker

An Effective Time Manager

In addition to producing great-tasting food, a slow cooker is one of the most effective time management tools any cook can have. Basically, it allows you to be in the kitchen when it suits your schedule. If you prefer, you can do most of the prep work in advance, when it's most convenient for you, and once the appliance is turned on there is little or nothing left for you to do. The slow cooker performs unattended while you carry on with your workaday life. You can be away from the kitchen all day and return to a hot, delicious meal.

Slow Cooker Basics

A Low-Tech Appliance

Slow cookers are amazingly low-tech. The appliance usually consists of a metal casing and a stoneware insert with a tight-fitting lid. For convenience, you should be able to remove the insert from the metal casing. This makes it easier to clean and increases its versatility, not only as a vessel for refrigerating dishes that have been prepared to the Make Ahead stage, but also as a serving dish. The casing contains the heat source, electrical coils that usually surround the stoneware insert. These coils do their work using the energy it takes to power a 100-watt light bulb. Because the slow cooker operates on such a small amount of electricity, you can safely leave it turned on while you are away from home.

Shapes, Sizes and Configurations

Slow cookers are generally round or oval in shape and range in size from 1 to 8.5 quarts. The small round ones are ideal for dips, as well as some soups, main courses and desserts. The smaller oval ones (approximately $1^1/_2$ to 4 quarts) are extremely versatile because they are small enough to work well with smaller quantities but also have enough volume to accommodate some full-batch recipes. The larger sizes (5 to 8.5 quart), usually oval in shape, are necessary to cook big-batch dishes and those that need to be cooked in a dish or pan that can fit into the stoneware.

   I have recommended slow cooker sizes for all my recipes. However, please be aware that so many new models are coming onto the market that I have not been able to test all the configurations myself. Use your common sense. The stoneware should be about one-third to three-quarters full. Dishes that contain an abundance of vegetables and liquid will likely need a model that can accommodate greater volume. Because I use my slow cookers a lot for entertaining, I feel there is a benefit to having at least two: a smaller ($1^1/_2$ to 4 quarts) size which is ideal for preparing dips, roasting nuts or making recipes with smaller yields, and a larger (5 to 6 quart) oval one, which I use most of the time to cook recipes with larger yields as well as those calling for a baking dish or pan set inside the stoneware. Once you begin using your slow cooker, you will get a sense of what suits your needs.

Some manufacturers sell a "slow cooker" which is actually a multi-cooker. These have a heating element at the bottom, and, in my experience they cook faster than traditional slow cookers. Also, since the heat source is at the bottom, the food is likely to scorch unless it is stirred.

Your slow cooker should come with a booklet that explains how to use the appliance. I recommend that you read this carefully and/or visit the manufacturer's website for specific information on the model you purchased. There are now so many models, shapes and sizes of slow cookers on the market that it is impossible to give one-size-fits-all instructions for using them.

Cooking Times

Over the years I've cooked in a wide variety of slow cookers and have found that cooking times can vary substantially from one to another. This is true even among different models sold under the same brand. The quality control on some of the lower-priced models may not be as rigorous as it should be, which accounts for some of the difference. That said, I've also found that some of the newer slow cookers tend to cook much more quickly than those that are a few years old. Please bear these discrepancies in mind if you follow my recipes and find that your food is overcooked. Although it may not seem particularly helpful if you're just starting out, the only firm advice I can give is: *Know your slow cooker.* After trying a few of these recipes, you will get a sense of whether your slow cooker is faster or slower than the ones I use, and you will be able to adjust the cooking times accordingly. Other variables that can affect cooking time are extreme humidity, power fluctuations and high altitude. Be extra vigilant if any of these circumstances affect you.

Cooking Great-Tasting Food

The slow cooker's less-is-better approach is, in many ways, the secret of its success. The appliance does its work by cooking foods very slowly — from about 200°F (90°C) on the Low setting to 300°F (150°C) on High. This slow, moist cooking environment brings the best out of long-cooking whole grains such as wheat berries and barley, as well as legumes for which it is best-known. It also helps to ensure success with delicate puddings and custards, among other dishes. I also love to make cheesecakes in my slow cooker because they emerge from this damp cocoon perfectly cooked every time. They have a beautifully creamy texture and don't dry out or crack, which happens all too easily in the oven.

Some benefits of long, slow cooking:

- it allows the seasoning in complex sauces to intermingle without scorching;
- it makes succulent chilies and stews that don't dry out or stick to the bottom of the pot; and
- it ensures success with delicate dishes such as puddings and custards.

Understanding Your Slow Cooker

Like all appliances, the slow cooker has its unique way of doing things, so you need to understand how it works and adapt your cooking style accordingly. When friends learned I was writing my first slow cooker cookbook, many had the same response: "Oh, you mean that appliance that allows you to throw the ingredients in and return home to a cooked meal!"

"Well, sort of," was my response. Over the years I've learned to think of my slow cooker as an indispensable helpmate and I can hardly imagine living without its assistance. But I also know that it can't work miracles. Off the top of my head, I can't think of any great dish that results when ingredients are merely "thrown together." Success in the slow cooker, like success in the oven or on top of the stove, depends upon using proper cooking techniques. The slow cooker saves you time because it allows you to forget about the food once it is in the stoneware. But you still must pay attention to the advance preparation. Here are a few tips that will help to ensure slow cooker success.

Soften Vegetables

Although it requires an extra pan, I am committed to softening most vegetables before adding them to the slow cooker. In my experience this is not the most time-consuming part of preparing a slow cooker dish — it usually takes longer to peel and chop the vegetables, which you have to do anyway. But it dramatically improves the quality of the dish for two reasons. Not only does browning add color, it also begins the process of caramelization, which breaks down the natural sugars in foods and releases their flavor. It also extracts the fat-soluble components of foods, which further enriches the taste. Moreover, tossing herbs and spices in with the softened vegetables helps to produce a sauce in which the flavors are better integrated than they would be if this step were skipped.

Reduce the Quantity of Liquid

As you use your slow cooker, one of the first things you will notice is that it generates liquid. Because slow cookers cook at a low heat, tightly covered, liquid doesn't evaporate as it does in the oven or on top of the stove. As a result, food made from traditional recipes will be watery. So the second rule of successful slow cooking is to reduce the amount of liquid.

Because I don't want to reduce the flavor, I prefer to cook with broth rather than water.

Cut Root Vegetables into Thin Slices or Small Pieces

Perhaps surprisingly, root vegetables — carrots, parsnips and particularly potatoes — cook very slowly in the slow cooker. Root vegetables should be thinly sliced or cut into small pieces: no larger than 1-inch (2.5 cm) cubes.

Pay Attention to Cooking Temperature

Many desserts such as those containing milk, cream or some leavening agents need to be cooked on High. In these recipes, a Low setting is not suggested as an option. For recipes that aren't dependent upon cooking at a particular temperature, the rule of thumb is that 1 hour of cooking on High equals 2 to $2^{1}/_{2}$ hours on Low.

Don't Overcook

Although slow cooking reduces your chances of overcooking food, it is still not a "one size fits all" solution to meal preparation. Many vegetables such as legumes and root vegetables need a good 8 hour cooking span on Low and may even benefit from a longer cooking time. But most others are cooked in about 6 hours on Low. If you're away from the house all day, it makes sense to have a slow cooker that automatically switches to Warm after the food is cooked. One solution (which is not possible if you are cooking meat because of food safety concerns) is to extend the cooking time by assembling the dish ahead of time, then refrigerating it overnight in the stoneware. Because the mixture and the stoneware are chilled, the vegetables will take longer to cook. (Be sure to use the Low setting and don't preheat the casing before adding the insert. Otherwise, your stoneware might crack.)

Use Ingredients Appropriately

Some ingredients do not respond well to long, slow cooking and should be added during the last 30 minutes after the temperature has been increased to High. These include zucchini, peas, snow peas, leafy greens, milk and cream (which will curdle if cooked too long).

I love to cook with peppers, but I've learned that most become bitter if cooked for too long. The same holds true for cayenne pepper or hot pepper sauces such as Tabasco, and large quantities of spicy curry powder. (Small quantities of mild curry powder seem to fare well, possibly because natural sugars in the vegetables counter any bitterness.) The solution to this problem is to add pepper(s) to a recipe during the last 30 minutes of cooking. All the recipes in this book address these concerns in the instructions.

Many of my recipes contain dairy products. However, I recognize that many people have problems consuming dairy so in some cases, where I am comfortable with the solution, I have suggested non-dairy alternatives. But I have also assumed that if you do not eat dairy, you will be well aware of the alternatives and will have sourced the products that work for you. Try a few of the recipes using non-dairy alternatives, for example olive oil for butter, egg replacement products for eggs, soft tofu or soy yogurt for yogurt, rice, nut or soy milk for milk or cream, the many varieties of soy cheese for those made from milk and ices or soy ice cream for whipped cream or ice cream. You will soon get a feel for those that produce satisfactory results.

Using Dishes and Pans in the Slow Cooker

Some dishes, notably puddings and custards, need to be cooked in an extra dish that is placed in the slow cooker stoneware. Not only will you need a large oval slow cooker for this purpose, finding a dish or pan that fits into the stoneware can be a challenge. I've found that standard 7-inch (18 cm) square, 4-cup (1 L) and 6-cup (1.5 L) ovenproof baking dishes or soufflé dishes are the best all-round pans for this purpose, and I've used them to cook most of the custard-like recipes in this book. A 7-inch (18 cm) springform pan, which fits into a large oval slow cooker, is also a useful item for making cheesecakes.

Before you decide to make a recipe requiring a baking dish, ensure that you have a container that will fit into your stoneware. I've noted the size and dimensions of the containers used in all relevant recipes. Be aware that varying the size and shape of the dish is likely to affect cooking times.

Making Smaller Quantities

Over the years many people have asked me for slow cooker recipes that make smaller quantities, suitable for one or two people. Since most recipes reheat well or can be frozen for future use, making a big-batch recipe can be an efficient strategy for having a delicious, nutritious meal on hand for those nights when there is no time to cook. However, since more and more households comprise single people or couples who want to enjoy the benefits of using a slow cooker, I have noted those recipes that are suitable for being halved. Since slow cookers depend on volume to operate efficiently, it is important to use a small slow cooker (approximately $1\frac{1}{2}$ to $3\frac{1}{2}$ quarts) when cutting a recipe in half.

Making Ahead

If a recipe contains meat, for food safety reasons you cannot brown it ahead of time, nor can uncooked meat be combined with vegetables and held. For small pieces of meat, such as diced bacon, ground meat or sausage meat that are fully cooked with vegetables before being placed in the stoneware, it is important to ensure that the mixture cools quickly to a safe temperature. Therefore I recommend placing these mixtures in a shallow container, then refrigerating them. This ensures that they are out of the danger zone within the preferred 30 minutes.

As a rule of thumb, I recommend refrigerating mixtures in a separate container, then transferring them to the stoneware. However, some vegetarian dishes can be preassembled in the stoneware and refrigerated, in which case be sure not to turn the slow cooker on before dropping the stoneware into the casing — the dramatic temperature change could crack it.

Maximize Slow Cooker Convenience

To get the most out of your slow cooker, consider the following:

- Prepare a recipe up to two days before you intend to cook — when it suits your schedule best.
- Cook a recipe overnight and refrigerate until ready to serve.
- Make a big-batch recipe and freeze a portion for a second or even a third meal.

Food Safety in the Slow Cooker

Because it cooks at a very low temperature for long periods of time, cooking with a slow cooker requires a bit more vigilance about food safety than does cooking at higher temperatures. The slow cooker needs to strike a delicate balance between cooking slowly enough that it doesn't require your attention and fast enough to ensure that food reaches temperatures that are appropriate to inhibit bacterial growth. Bacteria grow rapidly at temperatures higher than 40°F (4°C) and lower than 140°F (60°C). Once the temperature reaches 165°F (74°C), bacteria are killed. That's why it is so important to leave the lid on when you're slow cooking, particularly during the early stages. This helps to ensure that bacteria-killing temperatures are reached in the appropriate amount of time.

Slow cooker manufacturers have designed the appliance to ensure that bacterial growth is not a concern. So long as the lid is left on and the food is cooked for the appropriate length of time, that crucial temperature will be reached quickly enough to ensure food safety.

The following tips will help to ensure that utmost food safety standards are met:

- Keep any foods containing dairy or eggs refrigerated until you are ready to cook. Bacteria multiply quickly at room temperature. Do not allow ingredients to rise to room temperature before cooking.
- Limit the number of times you lift the lid while food is cooking. Each time the lid is removed it takes approximately 20 minutes to recover the lost heat. This increases the time it takes for the food to reach the "safe zone."
- If the power goes out while you are away discard the food if it has not finished cooking. If the food has cooked completely, it should be safe for up to 2 hours.
- Refrigerate leftovers as quickly as possible.
- Do not reheat food in the slow cooker.

Testing for Safety

If you are concerned that your slow cooker isn't cooking quickly enough to ensure food safety, try this simple test. Fill the stoneware insert with 8 cups (2 L) of cold water. Set temperature to Low for 8 hours. Using an accurate thermometer and checking quickly (because the temperature drops when the lid is removed), check to ensure that the temperature is 185°F (85°C). If the slow cooker has not reached that temperature, it's not heating food fast enough to avoid food safety problems. If the temperature is significantly higher than that, the appliance is not cooking slowly enough to be used as a slow cooker.

Leftovers

Many slow cookers have a Warm setting, which holds the food at 165°F (76°C). Programmable models will automatically switch to Warm when the time is up. Cooked food can be kept warm in the slow cooker for up to two hours. At that point it should be transferred to small containers so it cools as rapidly as possible and then be refrigerated or frozen. Because the appliance heats up so slowly, food should never be reheated in a slow cooker.

Creamy Morning Millet
with Apples

Breakfast

Creamy Morning Millet with Apples

If you're tired of the same old breakfast, perk up your taste buds and expand your nutritional range by enjoying millet as a cereal. This recipe provides fiber and is a good way to start your day if you are looking to increase your intake of this nutrient, among others. It is also a good source of vitamin B_{12}, which is difficult to obtain from food if you are a vegan. Don't worry about making more than you need. You can refrigerate leftovers for up to two days and reheat by portions in the microwave.

Makes 4 to 6 servings

Can Be Halved
(see Tips, below)

Tips

If you are halving this recipe, be sure to use a small ($1\frac{1}{2}$ to 2 quart) slow cooker.

For the best flavor, toast millet in a dry skillet over medium heat, until it crackles and releases its aroma, about 5 minutes.

- **Small to medium ($1\frac{1}{2}$ to $3\frac{1}{2}$ quart) slow cooker**
- **Lightly greased slow cooker stoneware**

1 cup	millet (see Tips, left)	250 mL
3 to 4 cups	fortified rice milk or organic soy milk (see Tips, right)	750 mL to 1 L
3	apples, peeled, cored and chopped	3
$\frac{1}{4}$ tsp	sea salt	1 mL
	Chopped pitted dates, fresh berries and toasted nuts, optional	

1. In prepared slow cooker stoneware, combine millet, rice milk, apples and salt. Cover and cook on High for 4 hours or on Low for 8 hours or overnight. Stir well, spoon into bowls and sprinkle with fruit and/or nuts, if using.

Variations

Use half millet and half short-grain brown rice.

If you prefer a non-creamy version, substitute water for the rice milk.

Nutrients Per Serving

Calories	216
Protein	4.4 g
Carbohydrates	44.5 g
Fat (Total)	2.4 g
Saturated Fat	0.2 g
Monounsaturated Fat	0.9 g
Polyunsaturated Fat	0.8 g
Dietary Fiber	3.9 g
Sodium	147 mg
Cholesterol	0 mg

GOOD SOURCE OF vitamin B_{12}, phosphorus and magnesium.
SOURCE OF vitamins A and B_6, calcium, folate, iron and zinc.
CONTAINS a moderate amount of dietary fiber.

Tips

Use plain or vanilla-flavored rice milk. Vary the quantity of rice milk to suit your preference. Three cups (750 mL) produces a firmer result. If you like your cereal to be creamy, use the larger quantity. If using soy milk, be sure to purchase an organic version. Otherwise it is likely to be made from genetically modified soy beans.

Don't pass on sprinkling your cereal with nuts (see Mindful Morsels, right) because you're counting calories. About one-third of the calories in nuts (and seeds) are provided by resistant starch, which means they are not absorbed into your bloodstream.

Mindful Morsels

For maximum health benefits, sprinkle this and other cereals with seeds and/or nuts, which contain healthy fats and other nutrients. Adding fat to your breakfast cereal helps to balance the potential impact of the carbohydrates on your blood sugar. A tablespoon (15 mL) of walnuts, for instance, has 4.5 grams of total fat and is particularly high in desirable omega-3 fats. It will also provide an additional gram of protein, and small amounts of potassium, magnesium and folate, as well as a smattering of other nutrients. An equal quantity of ground flax seeds provides essentially the same calories, less total fat (2.95 grams) and roughly 10 times more omega-3 fatty acids, magnesium, potassium, phosphorus and other nutrients. If you also want to add a dollop of Greek yogurt, which although relatively high in fat adds appealing creamy texture, as well as protein, you are heading in the direction of having a very substantial and extremely nutritious breakfast, well balanced in terms of protein, fat and carbohydrates, and which would sustain you throughout the day. One-third cup (75 mL) of Greek yogurt provides about 55 calories, 4 grams of total fat and almost 6 grams of protein, plus a smattering of other nutrients.

Natural Wonders

Millet

An ancient grain that is still a major form of sustenance in much of the world, including northern China, Africa and India, millet is possibly the world's oldest crop, predating wheat and rice as a cultivated grain. Before corn was grown in Italy, it was the original ingredient used to make polenta. Teff, which is prominent in Ethiopian cuisine and is now grown in the United States, is a variety of millet. It is notable for its very tiny seeds and perhaps best known as the major ingredient in injera, the Ethiopian flatbread.

A nutritious gluten-free whole grain, millet contains a moderate amount of fiber and is relatively high in protein. A half-cup (125 mL) serving of millet is a good source of magnesium, which helps to keep your bones strong and supports your nervous system, among other benefits (see Natural Wonders, page 185). A report in the *Archives of Internal Medicine* found a link between the intake of dietary fiber and magnesium, and a reduced rate of diabetes. People who consumed the most cereal fiber and magnesium had a much lower risk of developing diabetes than those who consumed the least amount of those nutrients. Millet also contains the B-complex vitamins thiamine, niacin, folate and riboflavin, as well as the minerals iron, zinc, manganese, copper and phosphorous. It also contains an assortment of beneficial phytonutrients. To boot, millet is particularly easy to digest.

Breakfast Rice

Simple yet delicious, this tasty combination couldn't be easier to make. This cereal is high in carbs, most of which come from the rice and the rice milk (61 grams in total). To balance any potential rise in blood sugar levels, it would benefit from a generous sprinkling of toasted nuts or fiber-rich seeds such as milled flax or whole chia. These foods add a bit of protein and fat, which helps to control how quickly the carbohydrates are digested and absorbed (see Mindful Morsels, page 21).

Makes 4 servings

Can Be Halved
(see Tips, page 24)

Tips

Made with this quantity of liquid, the rice will be a bit crunchy around the edges, which suits my taste. If you prefer a softer version or will be cooking it longer than 8 hours, add ½ cup (125 mL) of water or rice milk to the recipe.

When using dried fruits such as cranberries, purchase those sweetened with fruit juice rather than sugar.

Nutrients Per Serving

Calories	361
Protein	5.7 g
Carbohydrates	75.7 g
Fat (Total)	4.1 g
Saturated Fat	0.3 g
Monounsaturated Fat	2.2 g
Polyunsaturated Fat	1.0 g
Dietary Fiber	3.5 g
Sodium	116 mg
Cholesterol	0 mg

EXCELLENT SOURCE OF calcium and phosphorus.

GOOD SOURCE OF vitamin A and magnesium.

SOURCE OF vitamins B_6 and B_{12}, iron and zinc.

CONTAINS a moderate amount of dietary fiber.

- **Small to medium (1½ to 3½ quart) slow cooker**
- **Lightly greased slow cooker stoneware**

1 cup	brown rice	250 mL
4 cups	vanilla-flavored fortified rice milk	1 L
½ cup	dried cherries or cranberries (see Tips, left, and Mindful Morsels, below)	125 mL
	Toasted nuts, optional	

1. In prepared slow cooker stoneware, combine rice, rice milk and cherries. Place a clean tea towel folded in half (so you will have two layers) over top of stoneware to absorb moisture. Cover and cook on High for 4 hours or on Low for up to 8 hours or overnight. Stir well and serve garnished with toasted nuts, if desired.

Mindful Morsels

Cherries (along with raspberries, cranberries, blueberries and other red, purple and blue fruits) contain anthocyanins, a flavonoid with anti-inflammatory properties. Since cherries are among the fruits most likely to be contaminated with pesticides, look for those that are organically grown.

Natural Wonders

Sprouting Grains and Legumes

While it is still in the initial stages, there is a growing body of research confirming the health benefits of sprouting whole grains such as quinoa and brown rice, and legumes such as lentils and various types of dried beans. Pulses and grains are among the most common foods that are sprouted. These foods sprout after they have been soaked long enough to germinate. At that point, a small sprout will emerge from the kernel.

In general terms, sprouting, like soaking (see page 31), makes these foods more digestible, neutralizing anti-nutrients such as lectins and phytic acid. It also makes certain nutrients more bioavailable. For instance, in the process of digestion phytic acid devours minerals such as calcium, magnesium, iron and zinc. Once the phytate is defused these nutrients become available to your body. Lectins, which are found in all foods to some degree, but in higher concentrations in dairy products and members of the nightshade family, such as tomatoes and eggplant, as well as in grains and legumes, have been linked with inflammation and intestinal permeability, a situation where partially digested food spills over into the bloodstream, setting the stage for a number of autoimmune diseases. Lectins are also likely to be found in genetically modified foods because they act as natural insecticides.

Sprouting also breaks down complex sugars, such as oligosaccharides. These are the substances in legumes that cause gas. Our bodies can't digest these sugars so they enter the large intestine intact as food for hungry bacteria that make a meal of them, creating gas in the process. In her book *Nourishing Traditions*, Sally Fallon says that sprouting also inactivates aflatoxins, potentially carcinogenic substances found in grains.

An equally beneficial effect of sprouting is that in the process of germination the seed undergoes changes in its nutritional composition. In general terms, sprouted grains and legumes likely have more protein and fiber, B vitamins and amino acids. They may also have more vitamin E and beta-carotene. One group of grain scientists found that sprouting grains produced changes that are similar to those that occur during fermentation. (For more information on sprouted grains visit wholegrainscouncil.org) Although you can easily sprout grains and legumes yourself more and more producers are providing sprouted grains and legumes and flour made from these foods. Look for them at well-stocked natural food stores or Whole Foods.

Steel-Cut Oats

Although rolled oats are very tasty, my favorite oat cereal is steel-cut oats, which are often sold under the name "Irish Oatmeal." They have more flavor than rolled oats and an appealing crunchy texture.

Makes 4 servings

Can Be Halved
(see Tips, below)

Tips

If you are halving this recipe, be sure to use a small (1½ to 2 quart) slow cooker.

If you prefer a creamier version of this cereal make it using half 2% evaporated milk and half water. If using half evaporated milk, or 2 cups (500 mL) in total, the nutrient content increases dramatically. For only an extra 100 calories you get 9.5 g protein, 15 g carb, 371 mg calcium, 35 mg magnesium, 247 mg phosphorus, 425 mg potassium, 1.2 mg of zinc, 504 IU of vitamin A and 100 IU of vitamin D per serving.

- **Small to medium (1½ to 3½ quart) slow cooker**
- **Lightly greased slow cooker stoneware**

1 cup	gluten-free steel-cut oats (see Mindful Morsels, below)	250 mL
½ tsp	sea salt	2 mL
4 cups	water	1 L
	Raisins, chopped bananas or pitted dates, optional	
	Toasted nuts, seeds and milk, optional	

1. In prepared slow cooker, combine oats and salt. Add water. Cover and cook on High for 4 hours or on Low for 8 hours or overnight. Stir well. Stir in fruit to taste, or garnish with nuts, if using, or add milk, if desired.

Mindful Morsels

While oats do not appear to contain gluten, until recently it was thought they were unsuitable for people with celiac disease. Recent research indicates that the problem is not with oats *per se* but rather because the grain is contaminated with gluten from neighboring crops or during processing. Now, organizations including the American Dietetic Association agree that most people with celiac disease may consume small amounts of oats from a source that guarantees it has taken the appropriate steps to eliminate cross-contamination. So if you are sensitive to gluten, look for oats that are certified gluten-free.

However, research done in Italy indicates another potential problem with consuming oats. As a result of cross breeding, some oat cultivars contain a protein that is similar to one in gluten and which may create reactions in some people. Screening for this protein is beyond the scope of most manufacturers. If you are having problems digesting oats be aware that this may be the cause and eliminate them from your diet.

Nutrients Per Serving

Calories	90
Protein	3.6 g
Carbohydrates	15.8 g
Fat (Total)	1.5 g
Saturated Fat	0.4 g
Monounsaturated Fat	0.5 g
Polyunsaturated Fat	0.6 g
Dietary Fiber	2.1 g
Sodium	296 mg
Cholesterol	0 mg

SOURCE OF phosphorus.

CONTAINS a moderate amount of dietary fiber.

Natural Wonders

Fruit, Seeds and Nuts

Although most whole-grain cereals are delicious served with milk or a dairy substitute, and are a good food choice so long as they are consumed in reasonable quantities (most people can happily digest up to $^1/_2$ cup/125 mL), because they are high in carbohydrates, they may increase blood sugar levels in susceptible people. Sprinkling your breakfast cereal with fruit, nuts and/or seeds which add fiber and/or fat will help to mitigate any potential blood sugar effects of consuming a high amount of carbohydrate, while expanding your intake of nutrients (see also Mindful Morsels, page 21).

Fruits, nuts and seeds all contain fiber, one of the allies in balancing blood sugar. Dates are particularly high in this nutrient and provide a dash of other vitamins and minerals, including iron. They are also rich in phytonutrients, including tannins, which are anti-inflammatory, and antioxidant carotenes such as beta-carotene, lutein and zeaxanthin, which are strongly associated with eye health (see Natural Wonders, page 81). Berries and fruits such as dried cranberries and cherries add vitamin C, a small amount of other micronutrients and their own collection of beneficial phytonutrients.

Nuts and seeds are high in essential fatty acids, among other benefits. Sunflower seeds are high in vitamin E and provide a bit of potassium (56 mg per tablespoon/15 mL). Pumpkin seeds are a source of vegetable protein and provide a decent amount of magnesium (7 mg per tablespoon/15 mL), as well as small amounts of iron and zinc. Flax seeds, which are completely free of carbohydrates, provide alpha-linolenic acid, fiber and anti-inflammatory omega-3 fatty acids, as well as cancer-fighting lignans. In fact, the USDA lists 27 anticancer agents in flax. When using flax seeds, buy the milled variety that come in a vacuum-sealed package; once opened, store in the fridge. Or buy whole flax seeds and grind them yourself on an as needed basis. Alpha-linolenic acid is susceptible to oxidation and can go rancid if left exposed to the air. That's why it's best to avoid buying milled flax seed at bulk stores. However, it's important to consume the milled version because whole flax seeds will pass through your system without providing nutritive value.

Maple-Sweetened Congee

If you're having trouble getting your family to eat a healthy breakfast because they are bored with the traditional options, try this. It is absolutely yummy and delightfully different.

Makes 4 servings

Can Be Halved
(see Tips, below)

Tips

If you are halving this recipe, be sure to use a small (1½ to 2 quart) slow cooker.

If you don't have vanilla-flavored rice milk, add 1 tsp (5 mL) vanilla extract to plain rice milk.

Refrigerate any leftovers. This reheats beautifully on the stovetop or in a microwave.

- **Lightly greased slow cooker stoneware**
- **Small to medium (1½ to 3½ quart) slow cooker**

⅓ cup	brown rice, rinsed	75 mL
4 cups	fortified vanilla-flavored rice milk, divided (see Tips, left)	1 L
¼ cup	maple syrup	60 mL
¼ cup	finely chopped soft dates and/or candied ginger	60 mL
¼ cup	toasted almonds or walnuts	60 mL

1. In a small saucepan over medium heat, bring rice and 2 cups (500 mL) of the rice milk to a boil. Boil for 2 minutes. Transfer to slow cooker stoneware. Stir in remaining rice milk and maple syrup.

2. Cover and cook on Low for 8 hours or overnight, or on High for 4 hours. Stir in dates and/or ginger and sprinkle with toasted nuts.

Mindful Morsels

I can purchase ginger that is candied with raw cane sugar (see Natural Wonders, page 313) at my local natural foods store. Ginger is phytonutrient-rich and I enjoy this treat sprinkled on cereal or as a slightly indulgent afternoon nibble.

Nutrients Per Serving

Calories	308
Protein	4.1 g
Carbohydrates	60.0 g
Fat (Total)	6.4 g
Saturated Fat	0.4 g
Monounsaturated Fat	3.9 g
Polyunsaturated Fat	1.5 g
Dietary Fiber	2.4 g
Sodium	110 mg
Cholesterol	0 mg

EXCELLENT SOURCE OF calcium and manganese.

GOOD SOURCE OF vitamin A, phosphorus and magnesium.

SOURCE OF vitamins B_6, B_{12} and E (alpha-tocopherol), riboflavin, potassium, iron, zinc, copper and selenium.

CONTAINS a moderate amount of dietary fiber.

Natural Wonders

It's Better with Breakfast

Recently, two friends questioned the assumption that breakfast is the most important meal of the day. Although there may be snippets of conflicting evidence, in general terms, eating a good breakfast is beneficial. For starters, your body has not been fed for a good while and a good breakfast replenishes your reserves, working to keep you energized and productive throughout the day. Research repeatedly shows that students who eat a nutritious breakfast do better in school by several different measures. For instance, their test scores are likely to be higher, probably because eating complex carbohydrates increases glucose, which helps the body to make acetylcholine, a memory-boosting brain chemical.

Ideally, breakfast should consist of nutrient-dense foods, such as whole-grain cereal, eggs from chickens that roam free or a fresh fruit and/or vegetable smoothie. It's also a good idea to look for balance in the macronutrients provided, ensuring you consume adequate amounts of protein, fat and carbohydrates, which will help to keep your blood sugar levels in check. Balance and variety will work together to keep any cravings at bay and make you far less likely to snack on junk food throughout the day. In addition, eating a good breakfast has been linked with more stable moods and an improved ability to concentrate.

A number of studies have specifically linked a robust breakfast with the ability to maintain a healthy weight, while reaping additional benefits. One study, found that young adults who ate breakfast on a regular basis were less likely to be obese or have high blood pressure, metabolic syndrome or type-2 diabetes. Another 2013 study that looked at two similar groups of women consuming 700 calories at either breakfast or dinner over a period of three months found the big breakfast group lost an average of 17.3 pounds, while the big dinner group shed only an average of 7.3 pounds. The Health Professionals Follow-Up Study concluded that men who skipped breakfast had a 21% higher risk of type-2 diabetes than those who ate breakfast. The reason likely lies in the body's circadian rhythm, which is related to its biological clock. Research indicates that digesting food in the morning burns more calories than at other times of the day.

In the past, endurance athletes were advised to eat nothing up to an hour before exercising to avoid spiking their blood sugar levels. The thought was the consequent drop in blood sugar created a situation known as "rebound hypoglycemia," which it was believed, undermined performance. Current research indicates this isn't the case. In fact, because blood sugar and protein levels are lowest first thing in the morning, it makes more sense to replenish these faded stores. Common symptoms of low blood sugar include a reduced ability to concentrate and less energy. A balanced breakfast, including a good source of carbohydrate, protein and even fat, will help to fuel both brain and brawn by giving muscles the energy they need for a good workout. It doesn't take much food to do this, but the level and type of activity are probably the biggest determinant of what and how much to eat.

Black Sticky Rice Congee with Coconut

I just love black sticky rice in sweet dishes, particularly when it's combined with the flavor of coconut. This is a substantial serving (about 1 cup/250 mL) so it will certainly keep you satisfied throughout the morning. Congee is typically described as "porridge" but it's actually more like soup.

Makes 6 servings

Can Be Halved
(see Tips, page 30)

Tip

Virtually all of the saturated fat in a serving of this congee (11.9 g) comes from the coconut milk, which is healthy fat (see Natural Wonders, page 177). The carbs and fats in this recipe are almost equally balanced (51.4% and 49.6% respectively). That means the fat also balances any potential blood sugar impact of the carbohydrates, provided mainly by the rice, coconut sugar and bananas.

- Small to medium (1½ to 3½ quart) slow cooker
- Lightly greased slow cooker stoneware

3 cups	water	750 mL
⅓ cup	black sticky rice	75 mL
½ cup	coconut sugar	125 mL
1 tsp	almond extract	5 mL
Pinch	sea salt	Pinch
1	can (14 oz/400 mL) coconut milk	1
2	bananas, sliced	2
¼ cup	chopped toasted almonds	60 mL

1. In a small saucepan over high heat, bring water and black sticky rice to a vigorous boil. Boil for 2 minutes. Stir in coconut sugar, almond extract and salt, then transfer to slow cooker stoneware.

2. Cover and cook on Low for 8 hours or overnight, or on High for 4 hours. Stir well, then stir in coconut milk. To serve, ladle into bowls and top with bananas and almonds, dividing equally. Refrigerate any leftovers. This reheats beautifully on the stovetop or in a microwave.

Nutrients Per Serving

Calories	292
Protein	3.5 g
Carbohydrates	37.5 g
Fat (Total)	16.1 g
Saturated Fat	12.2 g
Monounsaturated Fat	2.0 g
Polyunsaturated Fat	0.7 g
Dietary Fiber	1.9 g
Sodium	23 mg
Cholesterol	0 mg

EXCELLENT SOURCE OF manganese.
GOOD SOURCE OF magnesium, potassium and iron.
SOURCE OF vitamins C and B$_6$, folate, phosphorus, zinc and copper.

Mindful Morsels

Black rice gets its rich dark color from the same compounds that give raspberries, blueberries and cherries their vibrant color: anthocyanins. These substances are powerful antioxidants that show promise in fighting a variety of illnesses, including heart disease and cancer. Ounce for ounce, the bran layer of black rice has been shown to contain more anthocyanins than blueberries, which were found to have particularly high antioxidant power.

Natural Wonders

Coconut Sugar

Look for coconut sugar, a very tasty sweetener, in natural foods stores and well-stocked supermarkets. Unlike refined white (or brown) sugar, coconut sugar is a whole food. It is made from the sap of the coconut palm, which is boiled until the liquid evaporates. Although it comes from a different tree, the process by which it is made is very similar to palm sugar, which is derived from the sap of other palm trees, including the date palm.

There is no official (i.e. USDA) data on coconut sugar and as a result its nutritive value is rather controversial. However, according to the Philippine Food and Nutrition Research Institute, coconut sugar provides a smattering of important minerals, such as potassium, magnesium, phosphorus, manganese and zinc, as well as a bit of vitamin C. It also contains the fiber inulin, which has a positive effect on blood glucose response. Their report compared the nutritive value of coconut sugar with other sweeteners, notably refined white sugar, which provides virtually no nutrients. While no sweetener is likely to be nutrient dense, I am inclined to view a whole food sweetener such as coconut sugar within the framework of a study conducted by researchers from Cornell, published in the journal *Nature* in 2000. Studying apples, for instance, they noted that the antioxidant activity of the fruit far exceeded its vitamin C content. They attributed this to the synergy created by consuming whole foods — in other words, all the nutrients, work together as a team to provide your body with the nutrition it needs. Sadly, scientists still don't know very much about how all this works but in the meantime, I'm placing my bets on a diet of whole foods and I'll choose to believe that a whole food sweetener likely has benefits that are yet to be discovered.

Chocolate Atole

Atole is a Mexican beverage made from corn flour and flavored with fruit or chocolate. It makes a delicious breakfast. Incidentally, atole is reputed to be good for curing hangovers.

Makes 4 to 6 servings

Can Be Halved
(see Tips, below)

Tips

If you are halving this recipe, be sure to use a small (1½ to 2 quart) slow cooker.

Refrigerate any leftovers. This reheats beautifully on the stovetop or in a microwave.

Unlike cow's milk, rice milk can cook in the slow cooker for long periods. While not as inherently nutritious as cow's milk, it is lactose free and, if fortified with calcium, and vitamins A and D, it will provide a comparable level of nutrition.

- **Small to medium (2 to 3½ quart) slow cooker**
- **Lightly greased slow cooker stoneware**

⅓ cup	stone-ground cornmeal	75 mL
½ cup	raw cane sugar, such as Turbinado	125 mL
¼ cup	unsweetened cocoa powder	60 mL
1 tsp	ground cinnamon	5 mL
4 cups	fortified rice or soy milk, divided (see Tips, left)	1 L
1 tsp	vanilla extract	5 mL

1. In a saucepan over medium heat, toast cornmeal, stirring, until fragrant, about 4 minutes. Transfer to a mortar and pestle or a clean coffee grinder, and pound or grind as finely as you can. Stir in sugar, cocoa powder and cinnamon.

2. In same saucepan over medium-high heat, bring rice milk to a boil. Gradually add cornmeal mixture in a steady stream, stirring constantly. Return to a boil and transfer to prepared stoneware. Stir in vanilla.

3. Cover and cook on Low for 8 hours or overnight, or on High for 4 hours. Stir well before serving.

Mindful Morsels

Starting the day off with a steaming bowl of whole-grain cereal can turn breakfast into a stress buster. Eating complex carbohydrates appears to replenish the brain chemical serotonin, which helps your body deal with stress.

Nutrients Per Serving

Calories	182
Protein	1.8 g
Carbohydrates	40.4 g
Fat (Total)	2.3 g
Saturated Fat	0.3 g
Monounsaturated Fat	1.1 g
Polyunsaturated Fat	0.3 g
Dietary Fiber	2.4 g
Sodium	77 mg
Cholesterol	0 mg

GOOD SOURCE OF vitamin B_{12} and calcium.
SOURCE OF vitamin A, phosphorus, magnesium, manganese, potassium, iron, zinc and copper.
CONTAINS a moderate amount of dietary fiber.

Natural Wonders

To Soak or Not to Soak Grains

There are differences of opinion on the subject of soaking grains prior to cooking. Many people feel it cuts down on the cooking time and others think it helps the grains to cook more evenly. However, there is a second and perhaps more important reason for giving your grains a good soak before cooking: some people have difficulty digesting grains, even those that do not contain gluten.

Grains contain substances such as tannins, lectins and phytic acid (phytate), which in general terms, are not easily digested and in some cases, interfere with your body's ability to absorb nutrients. Take phytic acid, a so-called anti-nutrient, for instance. While ruminant animals such as cows produce an enzyme called phytase, which breaks down phytic acid, humans are not so lucky. In our stomachs phytate impairs the absorption of important minerals, such as phosphorus, calcium, magnesium, iron and zinc. (On the other hand, it should be noted that while phytates may be hard to digest, they may also have potential health benefits, which scientists are currently exploring.)

In any case, if you have the time, it is a good idea to give your digestive system a boost by soaking grains before you cook them. Studies show that soaking grains in a generous amount of filtered water, covered and at room temperature, for at least 2 hours (and up to 6 hours) will improve digestibility. (Results vary among the grains.) You can improve mineral bioavailability by "souring" your grains. Simply add about 1 tbsp (15 mL) of whey, sauerkraut juice, lemon juice or cider vinegar to the soaking water and set aside at room temperature for 12 hours. Studies show that when grains have been soaked in an acid then cooked, their phytic acid content is significantly reduced.

Spicy Cashews and
Salty Almonds with Thyme

Starters and Snacks

Spicy Cashews

Only slightly nippy with just a hint of cinnamon, these cashews are a tasty and nutritious treat any time of the year.

Makes about 2 cups (500 mL)

Tips

Check your chili powder to make sure it doesn't contain gluten.

For a holiday gift, make up a batch or two and package in pretty jars. If well sealed, the nuts will keep for 10 days.

- Small (maximum 3½ quart) slow cooker

2 cups	raw cashews	500 mL
1 tsp	chili powder (see Tips, left)	5 mL
½ tsp	cayenne pepper	2 mL
¼ tsp	ground cinnamon	1 mL
2 tsp	fine sea salt (see Tip, page 35)	10 mL
1 tbsp	extra virgin olive oil	15 mL

1. In slow cooker stoneware, combine cashews, chili powder, cayenne and cinnamon. Stir to combine thoroughly. Cover and cook on High for 1½ hours, stirring every 30 minutes, until nuts are nicely toasted.

2. In a small bowl, combine sea salt and olive oil. Add to nuts in slow cooker and stir to thoroughly combine. Transfer mixture to a serving bowl and serve hot or let cool.

Mindful Morsels

Like all nuts, cashews are a source of healthy fats. More than half the fat in these tasty tidbits is monounsaturated fat, which has been actively studied as a key component of the Mediterranean diet and has been linked with a wide variety of health benefits such as a reduced risk of heart disease and cancer. Data from the Nurses' Health Study, for instance, suggested that substituting an equal amount of calories from eating nuts for those from carbohydrates, reduced the risk of heart disease by 30%.

Nutrients Per Serving
(about 12 cashews)

Calories	103
Protein	3.1 g
Carbohydrates	5.7 g
Fat (Total)	8.4 g
Saturated Fat	1.5 g
Monounsaturated Fat	4.7 g
Polyunsaturated Fat	1.4 g
Dietary Fiber	0.7 g
Sodium	290 mg
Cholesterol	0 mg

GOOD SOURCE OF magnesium, manganese and copper.

SOURCE OF vitamin K, phosphorus, iron, zinc and selenium.

Salty Almonds with Thyme

I completely agree with Elizabeth David, the late food writer, who wrote: "Nothing yet invented so sets the gastric juices to work as the sight of a plateful of freshly roasted and salted almonds."

Makes about 2 cups (500 mL)

Tip

Sea salt is available in most supermarkets. It is much sweeter than table salt and is essential for these recipes and not only because it is much better for you (see page 37). In these recipes, table salt would impart an unpleasant acrid taste to the nuts.

- **Small (maximum 3½ quart) slow cooker**

2 cups	unblanched almonds	500 mL
½ tsp	freshly ground white pepper	2 mL
1 tbsp	fine sea salt, or more to taste	15 mL
2 tbsp	extra virgin olive oil	30 mL
2 tbsp	fresh thyme leaves	30 mL

1. In slow cooker stoneware, combine almonds and white pepper. Cover and cook on High for 1½ hours, stirring every 30 minutes, until nuts are nicely toasted.
2. In a bowl, combine salt, olive oil and thyme. Add to hot almonds in stoneware and stir thoroughly to combine. Spoon mixture into a small serving bowl and serve hot or let cool.

Mindful Morsels

Imagine — a snack as delicious as these almonds that is also an excellent source of vitamin E, a valuable antioxidant vitamin. Since numerous studies confirm that taking vitamin E in supplements has little benefit and may be harmful in some circumstances, obtaining this nutrient from food makes an enormous amount of sense. Feel free to truly enjoy every satisfying bite.

Nutrients Per Serving (about 12 almonds)

Calories	118
Protein	3.8 g
Carbohydrates	3.6 g
Fat (Total)	10.7 g
Saturated Fat	0.9 g
Monounsaturated Fat	6.9 g
Polyunsaturated Fat	2.3 g
Dietary Fiber	2.2 g
Sodium	432 mg
Cholesterol	0 mg

EXCELLENT SOURCE OF vitamin E (alpha-tocopherol).

GOOD SOURCE OF magnesium and manganese.

SOURCE OF phosphorus, iron, zinc and copper.

CONTAINS a moderate amount of dietary fiber.

Spicy Tamari Almonds

I love eating these tasty tidbits as pre-dinner nibbles with a glass of cold white wine. Tamari is a wheat-free soy sauce, so you can happily serve these as a gluten-free snack.

Makes about 2 cups (500 mL)

Tip

For a holiday gift, make up a batch or two and package in pretty jars. If well sealed, the nuts will keep for 10 days.

- **Small (2 to 3½ quart) slow cooker**

2 cups	whole almonds	500 mL
¼ tsp	cayenne pepper	1 mL
2 tbsp	reduced-sodium tamari sauce or coconut aminos	30 mL
1 tbsp	extra virgin olive oil	15 mL
	Fine sea salt	

1. In slow cooker stoneware, combine almonds and cayenne. Place a clean tea towel folded in half (so you will have 2 layers) over top of stoneware to absorb moisture. Cover and cook on High for 45 minutes.

2. In a small bowl, combine tamari and olive oil. Add to hot almonds and stir thoroughly to combine. Replace tea towel. Cover and cook on High for 1½ hours, until nuts are hot and fragrant, stirring every 30 minutes and replacing towel each time. Sprinkle with salt to taste. Store in an airtight container.

Mindful Morsels

Research has shown that a calorie in an almond may be less fattening than a calorie in some other foods. In one study, substituting almonds for other foods of equal caloric value resulted in greater weight loss, likely because nuts contain resistant starch, most of which your body does not absorb as calories. Moreover, in the digestive process resistant starch produces a substance which helps your body to absorb minerals such as magnesium.

Nutrients Per Serving
(about 12 almonds)

Calories	112
Protein	4.0 g
Carbohydrates	3.6 g
Fat (Total)	9.8 g
Saturated Fat	0.8 g
Monounsaturated Fat	6.3 g
Polyunsaturated Fat	2.2 g
Dietary Fiber	2.1 g
Sodium	88 mg
Cholesterol	0 mg

EXCELLENT SOURCE OF vitamin E (alpha-tocopherol).

GOOD SOURCE OF manganese and magnesium.

SOURCE OF phosphorus, iron, zinc and copper.

CONTAINS a moderate amount of dietary fiber.

Natural Wonders

Salt

Salt, sugar and fat are probably the most demonized ingredients in our food supply and while there are good reasons for this, in my opinion, salt *per se* has been unjustly labeled. There are two basic problems with salt in the modern diet: we eat too much of it, most of which (roughly 85%) comes from processed foods, and the kind of salt we are likely to consume is not real salt. Refined table salt is pure sodium chloride, stripped of any beneficial minerals and chemically treated to improve the color. Worse still, it contains additives to prevent caking, some of which may be harmful to our health.

Our bodies need a certain amount of salt to function. It helps to maintain fluid in our blood cells and carries information to our nerves and muscles. In some respects, salt is like certain essential fatty acids because our bodies can't manufacture it. Although rare, hyponatremia, a condition where the body doesn't get enough sodium (most commonly seen in endurance sports) may have serious consequences. Several years ago a friend's grandmother ended up in hospital after taking her doctor's recommendation to reduce her salt intake so seriously that she virtually eliminated salt from her diet.

Salt also dramatically enhances the flavor of food. I have used a moderate amount of salt in my recipes. I always use *sel gris*, also known as Celtic sea salt, as my everyday cooking salt, or *fleur de sel* and Maldon salt as basic finishing salts. All these "real" salts contain beneficial trace minerals and if consumed in appropriate quantities, as a seasoning for whole foods, should not have negative effects on your health.

Caramelized Onion Dip

This dip is one of life's guilty pleasures. It always disappears to the very last drop. Serve this dip with a nutritious accompaniment such as Oven-Baked Kale Chips (page 58), spears of Belgian endive or even celery sticks, to balance the creamy dairy, and complement the range of nutrients it provides.

Makes about 1½ cups (375 mL)
Makes 8 servings

Tips

Brown rice miso is gluten-free.

Although this dip is not a good source of any individual nutrient, it does provide small amounts of a smattering of nutrients, such as vitamins A and C, B_1, B_2 and folate and minerals including calcium, phosphorus, iron, manganese, magnesium and selenium. While the onions do provide phytonutrients, most notably quercetin (see page 293) it is beyond the scope of conventional nutritional analysis to identify these valuable substances in recipes.

- Small (approx. 2 quart) slow cooker
- Food processor

2	onions, thinly sliced on the vertical	2
4	cloves garlic, chopped	4
1 tbsp	melted butter	15 mL
4 oz	Neufchâtel cheese, cubed and softened	125 g
½ cup	sour cream	125 mL
1 tbsp	brown rice miso (see Tip, left)	15 mL
	Sea salt and freshly ground black pepper	
	Finely snipped chives	

1. In slow cooker stoneware, combine onions, garlic and butter. Toss well to ensure onions are thoroughly coated. Place a clean tea towel folded in half (so you will have two layers) over top of stoneware to absorb moisture. Cover and cook on High for 5 hours, stirring two or three times to ensure onions are browning evenly, replacing towel each time, until onions are nicely caramelized.

2. Transfer mixture to a food processor fitted with a metal blade. Add Neufchâtel cheese, sour cream, miso, and salt and black pepper, to taste. Process until well blended. Transfer to a serving dish and garnish with chives. Serve immediately.

Variation

For a more herbal flavor, add 2 tbsp (30 mL) fresh thyme leaves along with the Neufchâtel cheese.

Mindful Morsels

If you have an identified problem with *Candida albicans* or suffer from recurring yeast infections, try increasing your consumption of vegetables from the allium family such as garlic and onions. These foods help to destroy any fungus growing in the intestinal tract.

Nutrients Per Serving
(about ¼ cup/60 mL)

Calories	91
Protein	3.0 g
Carbohydrates	5.0 g
Fat (Total)	6.8 g
Saturated Fat	4.0 g
Monounsaturated Fat	1.8 g
Polyunsaturated Fat	0.3 g
Dietary Fiber	0.7 g
Sodium	167 mg
Cholesterol	19 mg

SOURCE OF vitamin A.

Natural Wonders

Calcium

The milk and cheese recipes such as Sumptuous Spinach and Artichoke Dip (page 43) and Caramelized Onion Dip (page 38) provide calcium, a mineral that is particularly important for building strong bones and teeth. Dairy products are far and away the best source of calcium and if you are consuming yogurt or cheese, or drinking milk in a reasonable quantity, along with say, a glass of orange juice and a serving of leafy greens on a daily basis, you are probably getting enough of this valuable nutrient. Canned salmon, with the bones, sesame seeds and tofu processed with calcium sulfate are also good sources of calcium.

In 2011, the Institute of Medicine committee on dietary reference intakes for calcium and vitamin D concluded that most people obtain adequate calcium from their diets. Consuming too much calcium is likely not a good idea since higher intakes have been associated with an increased risk of some types of cancer. One study found that men who ingested more than 2,000 mg of calcium a day were almost three times more likely to develop prostate cancer than men whose intake was less than 500 mg a day. Moreover, recent studies have indicated that taking calcium supplements may be at best useless and at worst harmful. When the United States Preventive Services Task Force reviewed more than 135 studies in 2013, they concluded that taking calcium supplements did not prevent fractures in healthy women. Other studies have found that taking calcium supplements increased the risk of having a heart attack by 25% (compared with a control group taking a placebo) and possibly dying as a result of cardiovascular disease.

Calcium works closely with other nutrients, particularly vitamin D, magnesium, vitamin K_2, and protein, to maintain healthy bones and keep osteoporosis at bay. In fact, research shows calcium intake alone does not reduce the risk of fracture. But calcium does support a wide range of important body functions, from assisting your nervous system to helping your muscles, including your heart, to function properly. Calcium deficiency has been linked with hypothyroid disease and an adequate supply of calcium appears to reduce the likelihood of stroke. Research has shown a link between low calcium intake and high blood pressure. In fact, adequate amounts of calcium may help to prevent many ailments, from PMS to inflammatory bowel disease. One study involving more than 45,000 American women found a link between calcium intake and a reduced risk of colon cancer.

Caper-Studded Caponata

I find this version of caponata, which contains a sweet red pepper and capers, particularly delicious. Spread it on your favorite gluten-free crackers or flatbread, such as Yogurt Flatbread (page 62) or over thinly sliced cucumber or spears of Belgian endive, or that old stand-by, celery sticks.

Makes about 2 cups (500 mL)

Tip

Use dry-packed sun-dried tomatoes, soaked in 1½ cups (375 mL) boiling water for 15 minutes. Drain, rinse and chop.

Make Ahead

Complete Step 2. Cover and refrigerate for up to 2 days. When you're ready to cook, complete the recipe.

Nutrients Per Serving (about ¼ cup/60 mL)

Calories	60
Protein	0.9 g
Carbohydrates	7.1 g
Fat (Total)	3.6 g
Saturated Fat	0.5 g
Monounsaturated Fat	2.5 g
Polyunsaturated Fat	0.4 g
Dietary Fiber	1.8 g
Sodium	232 mg
Cholesterol	0 mg

EXCELLENT SOURCE OF vitamin K.

SOURCE OF vitamins C and B$_6$, folate, magnesium and manganese.

- **Small (approx. 2 quart) slow cooker**
- **Large sheet of parchment paper**

1	medium eggplant, peeled, cut into ½-inch (1 cm) cubes and drained of excess moisture (see Tip, page 42)	1
3 tbsp	red wine vinegar	45 mL
1 tsp	coconut sugar	5 mL
2 to 3 tbsp	extra virgin olive oil	30 to 45 mL
4	cloves garlic, minced	4
1 tsp	cracked black peppercorns	5 mL
½ tsp	sea salt	2 mL
¼ cup	reconstituted sun-dried tomatoes (see Tip, left)	60 mL
½	red bell pepper, seeded and diced	½
2 tbsp	drained capers	30 mL
¼ cup	finely chopped parsley leaves	60 mL

1. In a small bowl, combine vinegar and sugar. Stir until sugar dissolves. Set aside.

2. In a skillet, heat 2 tbsp (30 mL) of the oil over medium-high heat. Add eggplant, in batches, if necessary, and cook, stirring and tossing, until it begins to brown, about 3 minutes per batch, adding more oil, if necessary. Transfer to slow cooker stoneware. Add garlic, peppercorns and salt to pan and cook, stirring, for 1 minute. Add sun-dried tomatoes and vinegar mixture and stir to combine. Stir into stoneware.

3. Place a large piece of parchment over the eggplant mixture, pressing it down to brush the food and extending up the sides of the stoneware so it overlaps the rim. Cover and cook on Low for 6 hours or on High for 3 hours, until mixture is hot and bubbly. Lift out parchment and discard, being careful not to spill the accumulated liquid into the mixture. Stir in bell pepper and capers. Cover and cook on High for 15 minutes, until bell pepper is soft and flavors blend. Transfer to a serving bowl and garnish with parsley. Serve warm or at room temperature.

more information on page 42

Tip

To sweat eggplant: Place the cubed eggplant in a colander and sprinkle liberally with salt. Leave for 30 minutes to 1 hour until the moisture comes to the surface. Rinse thoroughly in fresh cold water and, using your hands, squeeze out the excess moisture. If time is short, blanch the pieces for a minute or two in heavily salted water. In either case, rinse thoroughly in fresh cold water and, using your hands, squeeze out the excess moisture. Pat dry with paper towels and it's ready to cook.

Mindful Morsels

Eggplant, the key ingredient in caponata, is a member of the deadly nightshade family, a group of vegetables that has been linked with a disproportionate number of food intolerances. However, if you have no problems consuming eggplant, it is a nutritious choice. It is loaded with a variety of antioxidants, including chlorogenic acid, which appears to boost your immune system. It also rich in a type of soluble fiber called viscous fiber, which is especially effective at keeping cholesterol under control. Moreover, eggplant may even have cancer-fighting abilities.

A serving of this caponata provides numerous vitamins and minerals. Spreading it on a nutritious vegetable, such as a celery stick, will increase the nutrient density and help to create synergy among the nutrients.

Natural Wonders

Celery

Although celery remains one of my favorite vehicles for scooping up a wide variety of dips, such as Caper-Studded Caponata (page 40). I came of age in an era when it was not considered a significant source of nutrition. Certainly, celery is not an excellent source of any nutrient: a medium stalk provides a smattering of vitamins such as A, K and folate, and trace amounts of minerals such as magnesium, calcium and potassium. But topped with a nutrient-dense dip, celery can be the base for a healthful snack by any definition.

However, in recent years researchers have unveiled a hidden side to celery — its phytonutrient content. Turns out that celery is, for starters, a powerful antioxidant, which among other benefits, helps to keep your blood vessels healthy. Celery also has anti-inflammatory punch. It seems that celery is loaded with a range of phenolic compounds that work to keep both your blood vessels and digestive track free from inflammation. Celery seeds are rich in phthalides, a phenolic compound that helps to keep your muscles relaxed and reduces your body's production of some stress hormones. Consumption of celery has been linked with lower blood pressure, thanks to its naturally occurring nitrates. These compounds increase the production of nitric oxide, which helps to relax blood vessels, decreasing the likelihood of hypertension. These substances, along with L-3-N-Butylphthalide also act as diuretic, which helps to explain why celery has long been used in folk medicine as a cure for urinary tract infections. Celery contains coumarin, a natural pesticide, and apigenin, both of which appear to have potential as cancer fighters.

All parts of the celery plant are nutritious — the seeds, stalks and leaves. Don't discard the leaves. Chopped, they make a great garnish for dishes that contain celery. In practical terms, celery is particularly useful because it will keep in your crisper for up to a week.

Sumptuous Spinach and Artichoke Dip

Although spinach and artichoke dip has become a North American classic, its roots lie in Provençal cuisine, where the vegetables are usually baked with cheese and served as a gratin. This chunky dip, simplicity itself, always draws rave reviews and disappears to the last drop. This is great with Oven-Baked Kale Chips (see 58), Homemade Baked Tortilla Chips (see below) or even simple brown rice crackers.

Makes about 3 cups (750 mL)

Tips

If you prefer a smoother dip, place spinach and artichokes in a food processor, in separate batches, and pulse until desired degree of fineness is achieved. Then combine with remaining ingredients in slow cooker stoneware.

If you prefer, use frozen artichokes, thawed, to make this recipe. You will need 6 artichoke hearts.

Nutrients Per Serving (about ¼ cup/60 mL)

Calories	87
Protein	5.2 g
Carbohydrates	4.0 g
Fat (Total)	6.0 g
Saturated Fat	3.6 g
Monounsaturated Fat	1.6 g
Polyunsaturated Fat	0.3 g
Dietary Fiber	1.6 g
Sodium	196 mg
Cholesterol	20 mg

EXCELLENT SOURCE OF vitamins A and K.

GOOD SOURCE OF folate.

SOURCE OF vitamins C and B$_{12}$, calcium, phosphorus, magnesium, manganese, potassium, iron, zinc, copper and selenium.

- **Small to medium (1½ to 3½ quart) slow cooker**

1 cup	shredded mozzarella cheese	250 mL
6 oz	Neufchâtel cheese, cubed	175 g
¼ cup	freshly grated Parmesan cheese	60 mL
1	clove garlic, minced	1
1	can (14 oz/398 mL) artichokes, drained, rinsed and finely chopped (see Tips, left, and Mindful Morsels, page 45)	1
8 oz	trimmed fresh spinach leaves (about 8 cups/2 L)	250 g
¼ tsp	freshly ground black pepper	1 mL

1. In slow cooker stoneware, combine mozzarella, Neufchâtel cheese, Parmesan, garlic, artichokes, spinach and black pepper. Cover and cook on High for 2 hours, until hot and bubbly. Stir well and serve with homemade tortilla chips.

> **Homemade Baked Tortilla Chips**
>
> To make your own healthy tortilla chips, buy fresh corn tortillas from a reliable source. (I get mine hot from a taquería.) Preheat your oven to 350°F (180°C). Brush each tortilla on both sides with extra virgin olive oil. Stack and cut so each individual tortilla produces 8 segments. Transfer to a baking sheet and bake in preheated oven until lightly browned, about 15 minutes. Sprinkle with sea salt.

more information on page 45

Sumptuous Spinach and Artichoke Dip

Natural Wonders

Vitamin D

The cheese in Sumptuous Spinach and Artichoke Dip (page 43) provides calcium, an important mineral for bone health. But the calcium in foods is more readily absorbed if you have an adequate supply of vitamin D. Many people, especially women and seniors, appear to be deficient in this vitamin, which our bodies manufacture from exposure to sun. Low vitamin D status has been linked to a wide variety of diseases, including osteoprosis, breast cancer, heart disease, diabetes and depression, among others.

The best source of vitamin D is not food but sunlight, and some researchers have gone so far as to suggest that the widespread use of sun blocks may be contributing to the vitamin D deficit, which is, obviously, more prevalent in people living in chillier climes. Early humans lived near the equator and spent most of their time outdoors. As we evolved and moved further away from constant sunlight, our vitamin D status likely declined.

For years we have been told to avoid the sun or to use a sun block because overexposure to sunlight increases the risk of skin cancer. However, recent studies indicate that sunlight may actually improve outcomes in people with melanoma. For instance, a study conducted on 500 Connecticut residents diagnosed with melanoma found that the greater their exposure to sun, the less they were likely to die of the disease. Another study of 6,000 Scandinavian residents found the more participants were exposed to sunlight, the lower their risk of non-Hodgkin's lymphoma. A U.S. study of 450 white males found that exposure to sunlight also lowered the risk of prostate cancer. Researchers stress the importance of avoiding sunburn, which does increase the risk of cancer. Moderate sunning, which creates a regular supply of vitamin D, seems to be the key, and increasing vitamin D intake through the use of supplements is widely recommended because there are few food sources of this nutrient. The best food sources of vitamin D are egg yolks, fortified dairy products and oily fish, such as salmon and tuna. Some foods, such as soy and rice beverages and breakfast cereals are also fortified with the vitamin.

Braised Tomato Topping

Fresh field tomatoes, seasoned with fleur de sel and some fresh basil are a luscious summertime pleasure. Some time ago, I came across a recipe from Seattle's Café Lago, which suggested that a braised version of bruschetta could be made using canned tomatoes, so I played with the idea and produced this result. It is simply delicious and a wonderful treat in the midst of winter, when succulent locally grown tomatoes are only a faint memory. I serve it over Polenta Crostini (page 60) for a perfect gluten-free treat.

Makes about 2 cups (500 mL)

Tip

Canned tomatoes should be gluten-free, but manufacturers often change their formulae so check the label.

Make Ahead

Complete the recipe. Cover and refrigerate bruschetta mixture for up to 3 days. Bring to room temperature before serving.

- **Small to medium (1½ to 3½ quart) slow cooker**
- **Large sheet of parchment paper**

¼ cup	extra virgin olive oil, divided	60 mL
1	can (28 oz/796 mL) no-salt-added diced tomatoes, drained (see Tip, left)	1
2	cloves garlic, minced	2
2 tsp	dried oregano	10 mL
1 tsp	coconut sugar	5 mL
½ tsp	sea salt	2 mL
2 tbsp	finely chopped parsley leaves	30 mL
	Freshly ground black pepper	
	Polenta Crostini (page 60)	

1. In slow cooker stoneware, place 2 tbsp (30 mL) of the olive oil and swirl to coat bottom. Add tomatoes and sprinkle with garlic, oregano, sugar and salt. Drizzle with remaining olive oil. Place a large piece of parchment over the tomatoes, pressing it down to brush the food and extending up the sides of the stoneware so it overlaps the rim.

2. Cover and cook on Low for 6 hours or on High for 3 hours, until mixture is hot and bubbly. Lift out parchment and discard, being careful not to spill the accumulated liquid into the tomato mixture. Stir in parsley and season with pepper to taste. Transfer to a serving dish and let cool to room temperature. To serve, spoon onto polenta crostini.

Variation

If you prefer, spread the polenta crostini with a thin layer of soft goat cheese before adding the topping.

Nutrients Per Serving (about ¼ cup/60 mL)

Calories	77
Protein	0.6 g
Carbohydrates	4.2 g
Fat (Total)	6.8 g
Saturated Fat	0.9 g
Monounsaturated Fat	5.0 g
Polyunsaturated Fat	0.7 g
Dietary Fiber	0.7 g
Sodium	108 mg
Cholesterol	0 mg

EXCELLENT SOURCE OF vitamin K.
SOURCE OF vitamins A and C.

Natural Wonders

Frozen or Canned Vegetables

There's no question that freshly picked locally grown vegetables provide optimum nutrition and taste, but sometimes frozen or canned vegetables may be preferable to fresh. During winter, for instance, fresh produce is likely to have traveled several days before it arrives in your city. Then it sits in a store until purchased and once again in your refrigerator until it is used, all the while losing nutrients and flavor. According to researchers at Penn State University, for instance, over the course of a week fresh spinach, even when properly refrigerated, lost about half of its folate content, among other nutrients.

On the other hand, vegetables picked at the peak of ripeness and quickly frozen or canned are likely to have as many nutrients as their "fresh" counterparts. One important thing when buying frozen or canned vegetables is to look for those that are organically grown to avoid consuming pesticide residue. Also make sure that salt or other additives are not included. Always check any canned product to ensure it is gluten-free. A surprising number of products do contain gluten. Moreover, manufacturers are constantly changing their formulae and gluten may suddenly appear in a product that was previously gluten-free. The packaging may also be an issue. For instance, I buy canned tomatoes in glass jars or BPA (bisphenol-A) free cans.

Artichoke and White Bean Spread

The flavor combinations in this spread — onion, garlic, cannellini beans, artichokes, Parmesan and parsley — are simple, elegant and synergistically delicious. I like to serve this to guests on Polenta Crostini (page 60), but gluten-free crackers or crudités also make a good choice.

Makes about 3 cups (750 mL)

Tips

For this quantity of beans, soak, cook and drain 1 cup (250 mL) dried cannellini beans (see Basic Beans, page 284) or drain and rinse 1 can (14 to 19 oz/398 to 540 mL) no-salt added cannellini beans. Cannellini beans are also known as white kidney beans.

If you prefer, use frozen artichokes, thawed, to make this recipe. You will need 6 artichoke hearts.

Nutrients Per Serving (about ¼ cup/60 mL)

Calories	122
Protein	5.7 g
Carbohydrates	13.4 g
Fat (Total)	5.7 g
Saturated Fat	1.2 g
Monounsaturated Fat	3.6 g
Polyunsaturated Fat	0.6 g
Dietary Fiber	4.1 g
Sodium	222 mg
Cholesterol	2 mg

EXCELLENT SOURCE OF vitamin K.
GOOD SOURCE OF folate.
SOURCE OF vitamins C and B$_6$, calcium, phosphorus, iron, magnesium, manganese, potassium, zinc and copper.
CONTAINS a high amount of dietary fiber.

- **Small (approx. 2 quart) slow cooker**
- **Food processor**

½	medium red onion, finely chopped	½
2	cloves garlic, minced	2
¼ cup	extra virgin olive oil, divided	60 mL
2 cups	drained cooked cannellini beans (see Tips, left)	500 mL
1	can (14 oz/398 mL) artichoke hearts, drained and coarsely chopped (see Tips, left, and Mindful Morsels, page 45)	1
½ cup	freshly grated Parmesan cheese or vegan alternative	125 mL
1 tsp	sweet paprika	5 mL
½ tsp	sea salt	2 mL
¼ tsp	freshly ground black pepper	1 mL
½ cup	finely chopped parsley leaves	125 mL

1. In slow cooker stoneware, combine onion, garlic and 2 tbsp (30 mL) of the olive oil. Place a clean tea towel folded in half (so you will have two layers) over top of stoneware to absorb moisture. Cover and cook on High for 30 minutes, until onions are softened.

2. Meanwhile, in a food processor fitted with a metal blade, in batches, if necessary, pulse beans and artichokes until desired consistency is achieved. After onions have softened, add bean mixture to stoneware along with Parmesan, paprika, salt, pepper and remaining olive oil. Replace tea towel. Cover and cook on Low for 4 hours or on High for 2 hours, until hot and bubbly. Add parsley and stir well.

Mindful Morsels

Most of the sodium in a serving of this spread comes from the added salt (96 mg) and the canned artichokes (71 mg). If you are watching your sodium intake, omit the salt and substitute thawed frozen artichoke hearts with no added salt.

Natural Wonders

Potassium

Although bananas get most of the glory, many other foods, including potatoes and the white beans in this spread, are also good sources of potassium. One medium banana provides 422 mg, a medium baked potato provides about 600 mg, and $1/2$ cup (125 mL) of cooked white beans provides about 350 mg. While the recommended daily value for potassium is 4700 mg, which may seem high, a wide variety of foods provide this mineral, including fish, meat and dairy products. Potassium is especially abundant in fruits and vegetables.

Because so many foods provide potassium, we tend to overlook its value as a nutrient. The bad news is that most of us get only about half as much potassium as we need. Potassium works with sodium to help your body maintain a proper fluid balance and it is vulnerable to being depleted from the body. A diet high in refined foods is linked with potassium loss, as is the overconsumption of coffee. Prolonged diarrhea or the use of diuretics can also lead to potassium deficiencies.

Potassium is one of the key nutrients that help your heart to beat in a regular and steady rhythm. Along with magnesium, calcium and sodium, it functions as an electrolyte, working inside your cells to ensure the fluid balance that allows your cells to communicate properly and keep muscles and nerves working effectively. If you are feeling fatigued or experiencing pain or muscle weakness, the problem may be a potassium deficiency.

Among other benefits, research shows that a diet high in potassium and low in sodium has a very beneficial effect on blood pressure (see Natural Wonders, page 69). Higher potassium levels are also linked with a reduced risk of heart disease and stroke. In order to preserve as much potassium as possible, try to keep the water level low when cooking vegetables. Boiling vegetables in large amounts of water causes the potassium to drain off.

Onion-Soused Beans

I've adapted this recipe from one developed by my friend Byron Ayanoglu, who says it is a Greek heirloom treatment for beans. He calls it "Yahni" and serves it as a side with Mediterranean dishes. I like to serve it as a starter. It's great on gluten-free flatbread, such as Yogurt Flatbread (page 62), rice crackers, Oven-Baked Kale Chips (page 58) or even celery sticks.

Makes about 2 cups (500 mL)

Tips

Although fresh tomatoes work well in this recipe, I've successfully made it using the same quantity of drained canned tomatoes, with no-salt added. Use ones that are diced or chop whole ones.

I like the chunky texture that using whole beans provides, but if you prefer, mash or purée the beans before adding them to the recipe.

- Small to medium (1½ to 3½ quart) slow cooker
- Large sheet of parchment paper

2 tbsp	extra virgin olive oil	30 mL
2	onions, thinly sliced on the vertical	2
1	stalk celery, diced	1
6	cloves garlic, minced	6
½ tsp	sea salt	2 mL
½ tsp	cracked black peppercorns	2 mL
2	bay leaves	2
1 tbsp	red wine vinegar	15 mL
1 tsp	coconut sugar	5 mL
½ cup	diced tomatoes (see Tips, left)	125 mL
2 cups	cooked cannellini beans (see Tips, left and right)	500 mL
	Extra virgin olive oil	
¼ cup	diced red or green onion	60 mL
½ cup	finely chopped parsley leaves	125 mL

1. In a skillet, heat oil over medium heat. Add sliced onions and celery and cook, stirring, until softened, about 5 minutes. Add garlic, salt, peppercorns and bay leaves and cook, stirring, for 1 minute. Add vinegar, coconut sugar and tomatoes and cook, stirring, until mixture boils.

2. Transfer to slow cooker stoneware. Stir in beans. Place a large piece of parchment over the beans, pressing it down to brush the food and extending up the sides of the stoneware so it overlaps the rim. Cover and cook on Low for 6 hours or High for 3 hours, until mixture is hot and bubbly. Lift out parchment and discard, being careful not to spill the accumulated liquid into the sauce.

3. Transfer to a serving dish. Drizzle with olive oil and garnish with red onion and parsley. Cover and set aside at room temperature for an hour to develop flavor. Serve at room temperature.

Nutrients Per Serving (¼ cup/60 mL)

Calories	129
Protein	6.0 g
Carbohydrates	18.9 g
Fat (Total)	3.8 g
Saturated Fat	0.5 g
Monounsaturated Fat	2.5 g
Polyunsaturated Fat	0.5 g
Dietary Fiber	4.8 g
Sodium	153 mg
Cholesterol	0 mg

EXCELLENT SOURCE OF vitamin K and folate.

GOOD SOURCE OF potassium and manganese.

SOURCE OF vitamins B_6 and C, phosphorus, magnesium, iron, zinc and copper.

CONTAINS a high amount of dietary fiber.

Tip

For this quantity of beans, soak, cook and drain 1 cup (250 mL) dried cannellini beans (see Basic Beans, page 284) or drain and rinse 1 can (14 to 19 oz/398 to 540 mL) no-salt added cannellini beans. Cannellini beans are also known as white kidney beans.

Make Ahead

Complete Step 1. Cover and refrigerate mixture for up to 2 days. When you're ready to cook, complete the recipe.

Mindful Morsels

Served on a nutritious base, such as celery sticks or kale chips, a dollop of this delicious spread constitutes a very healthy snack. And healthy snacks can be important to overall health. One 2012 study looked at a group of high-risk patients who were 55 or older, suffered from cardiovascular disease or diabetes and were taking drugs for their conditions. When researchers examined participants within the framework of a healthy diet that specifically outlawed "salty snacks" among other foods, they concluded that even with effective drug therapy, the benefits of a healthy diet were significant. Those who ate the healthiest diets lowered their risk of dying from cardiovascular disease by 35%, a heart attack by 14%, and reduced their risk of stroke by 19%. The message is, even if your doctor prescribes a proven drug for your condition, you can improve its effectiveness by eating a healthy diet. Dietitian Doug Cook, who acted as a consultant for this book, says he always tells his clients they cannot medicate to compensate for poor diet or lifestyle choices. As he says, "all medications have maximum doses and side effects. It makes sense to optimize your diet so medications can be more effective when deemed truly appropriate. Often medication dosages can be reduced or sometimes stopped with positive dietary changes."

Natural Wonders

Stress-Busting Spread

Many of the nutrients in spreads and dips made from beans contain complex carbohydrates, vitamin B_6, folate and magnesium, which help your body manage stress. Complex carbohydrates, such as legumes, are a source of B vitamins (see Natural Wonders, page 149), which help your body produce the neurotransmitter or brain chemical, serotonin, known to moderate symptoms of depression and anxiety. Vitamin B_6 (see Natural Wonders, page 139) is also used to make another brain chemical called gamma-aminobutyric acid, or GABA for short. GABA is known as the anti-anxiety neurotransmitter; by helping to calm the nervous system, it helps us to feel relaxed. GABA is also responsible for relaxing our muscles. Some research links folate with antidepressant effects, and among its benefits, magnesium may help your muscles to relax. It is also important to get an adequate amount of vitamin C if you're feeling stressed.

Warm Black Bean Salsa

This dip is a perennial hit. I served it at a birthday party for my daughter a few years ago and guests practically licked the bowl. If you're using sweet peppers rather than poblano and want a zestier result, add an extra jalapeño or chipotle pepper. This is delicious served with Homemade Baked Tortilla Chips (page 43) or a slice of warm gluten-free cornbread.

Makes about 3 cups (750 mL)

Tips

Use 1 can (14 to 19 oz/398 to 540 mL) no-salt added canned beans, drained or cook dried beans yourself (see Basic Beans, page 284).

For convenience, substitute 1 cup (250 mL) drained no-salt added diced canned tomatoes.

To purée garlic use a sharp-toothed grater such as those made by Microplane.

Nutrients Per Serving
(about ¼ cup/60 mL)

Calories	136
Protein	8.6 g
Carbohydrates	11.6 g
Fat (Total)	6.5 g
Saturated Fat	4.0 g
Monounsaturated Fat	1.8 g
Polyunsaturated Fat	0.3 g
Dietary Fiber	3.1 g
Sodium	119 mg
Cholesterol	20 mg

GOOD SOURCE OF vitamins C and K, folate and phosphorus.
SOURCE OF vitamins A, B$_6$ and B$_{12}$, calcium, magnesium, manganese, potassium, iron, zinc, copper and selenium.
CONTAINS a moderate amount of dietary fiber.

- **Small (2 to 3½ quart) slow cooker**

2 cups	cooked black beans, drained, rinsed and mashed (see Tips, left)	500 mL
1 cup	diced (¼ inch/0.5 cm) ripe tomatoes (see Tips, left)	250 mL
4	green onions, finely chopped	4
2	roasted peppers (poblanos or sweet), peeled and diced	2
1	roasted jalapeño, seeded and diced, or 1 chipotle pepper in adobo sauce	1
1 tsp	puréed garlic (see Tips, left)	5 mL
1 tsp	finely grated lime zest	5 mL
2 tbsp	freshly squeezed lime juice	30 mL
2 cups	shredded Cheddar or Monterey Jack cheese	500 mL
2 tbsp	finely chopped cilantro leaves	30 mL
	Finely chopped green onions, optional (see Mindful Morsels, page 54)	

1. In slow cooker stoneware, combine beans, tomatoes, green onions, poblano and jalapeño peppers, garlic, lime zest and juice, and cheese. Stir well. Cover and cook on High for 1½ hours, until mixture is hot and bubbly. Stir in cilantro, sprinkle with green onions, if using, and serve.

Vegan Alternative

Substitute an equal quantity of vegan Cheddar or Monterey Jack cheese.

more information on page 54

Although much milder tasting then some of their allium family relatives, green onions still provide valuable nutrients. This includes the flavonoid quercetin, which is showing promise as an antihistamine, among other benefits (see Natural Wonders, page 293). Although research is in the early stages, this phytonutrient may prevent the release of substances causing allergic reactions such as asthma, hives or hay fever. So if you suffer from allergies you may want to double the quantity of green onions you add to salads or sprinkle over top of stir-fries. You can even sprinkle additional green onion over top of this salsa.

Natural Wonders

B Vitamins for Brain Health

Warm Black Bean Salsa (page 52) is a delicious treat but, more than that, loading up on the B vitamins it provides can help to prevent cognitive decline. Just one serving of this recipe provides the B vitamins folate, B_6 and B_{12}, which along with other B vitamins have been found to slow the rate of cognitive decline in older people, even when taken as supplements. For instance, one 2012 double-blind study published in the *American Journal of Clinical Nutrition*, provided folate and vitamin B_{12} supplements or a placebo to nine hundred people aged 60 to 74 years, who were in elevated psychological distress. After 24 months, the group receiving the vitamins, showed a significant improvement in their cognitive functioning. Other studies of B vitamins in relation to brain health also look very promising. Consider, for instance, the results of a 2010 British study that provided vitamins B_6, B_{12}, and folate to 271 people with fading memories. One of the risks for Alzheimer's disease is a shrinking brain, and brain scans done of 168 of the participants showed that those who took the B vitamins had 90% less brain shrinkage — quite a spectacular result. Some researchers believe that B vitamins work to keep homocysteine levels low (it is speculated that high levels of homocysteine may be linked with Alzheimer's disease), although others have questioned this link.

Taking a broader perspective, epidemiological studies have consistently confirmed a link between a diet high in B vitamins and cognitive health, and the connection seems to be a topic for fairly serious study within the research community.

One word of warning before rushing out to purchase high-dose B-complex vitamins: very high levels of folate have been linked with increased cancer risk. Since it's unlikely that you can consume too much folate from food, once again, enjoying a healthy diet, rich in B vitamins seems to be the safest option for keeping your brain, as well as the rest of your body, in tip-top shape.

Santorini-Style Fava Spread

This spread, which is Greek in origin, is unusual and particularly delicious. Although fava beans do figure in Greek cuisine, for most Greek people fava is synonymous with yellow split peas, one of the major indigenous foods of the island of Santorini. In Santorini, they make many dishes using yellow split peas, including this spread. Serve this with warm gluten-free flatbread, such as Yogurt Flatbread (page 62), plain brown rice crackers or celery sticks and wait for the compliments.

Makes about 2 cups (500 mL)

Tips

Use dry-packed sun-dried tomatoes, soaked in 1 cup (250 mL) boiling water for 15 minutes. You can also use those that have been packed in extra virgin olive oil. In either case, drain before chopping.

I always use Italian flat-leaf parsley because it has much more flavor than the curly leaf variety.

Nutrients Per Serving (about ¼ cup/60 mL)

Calories	223
Protein	6.8 g
Carbohydrates	19.1 g
Fat (Total)	13.9 g
Saturated Fat	1.9 g
Monounsaturated Fat	10.1 g
Polyunsaturated Fat	1.5 g
Dietary Fiber	2.9 g
Sodium	133 mg
Cholesterol	0 mg

EXCELLENT SOURCE OF vitamin K.
GOOD SOURCE OF vitamin E (alpha-tocopherol), thiamine, folate, potassium and manganese.
SOURCE OF vitamins B_6 and C, phosphorus, magnesium, iron, zinc and copper.
CONTAINS a moderate amount of dietary fiber.

- **Small (1½ to 2 quart) slow cooker**
- **Food processor**

½ cup	extra virgin olive oil, divided	125 mL
½ cup	diced shallots (about 2 large)	125 mL
2 tsp	dried oregano	10 mL
½ tsp	sea salt	2 mL
½ tsp	cracked black peppercorns	2 mL
1 cup	yellow split peas	250 mL
4 cups	water	1 L
6	reconstituted sun-dried tomato halves, coarsely chopped (see Tips, left)	6
4	cloves garlic, chopped	4
¼ cup	coarsely chopped Italian flat-leaf parsley (see Tip, left)	60 mL
4	fresh basil leaves, hand-torn	4
3 tbsp	red wine vinegar	45 mL
	Sea salt and freshly ground black pepper	

1. In a skillet, heat 1 tbsp (15 mL) of the oil over medium heat. Add shallots and cook, stirring, until softened, about 3 minutes. Add oregano, salt and peppercorns and cook, stirring, for 1 minute. Add split peas and cook, stirring, until coated. Add water and bring to a boil. Boil for 2 minutes.

2. Transfer to slow cooker stoneware. Cover and cook on Low for 8 hours or on High for 4 hours, until peas have virtually disintegrated. Drain off excess water, if necessary.

3. Transfer solids to a food processor. Add sun-dried tomatoes, garlic, parsley, basil and red wine vinegar. Pulse 7 or 8 times to chop and blend ingredients. With motor running, add remaining olive oil in a steady stream through the feed tube. Season with additional salt and pepper to taste and drizzle with additional olive oil, if desired. Serve warm.

more information on page 57

Santorini-Style Fava Spread

Make Ahead

Complete Step 1. Cover and refrigerate for up to 2 days. When you're ready to serve, heat peas on the stovetop until bubbles form about the edges. Complete the recipe.

Mindful Morsels

Oregano is widely used in both Greek and Turkish cuisine and in Turkey, in particular, there is a strong tradition of using this spice medicinally. Oregano water and tea are regularly consumed for their digestive benefits and oil of oregano is a go-to treatment for aching muscles. One Turkish study found that consuming oregano extract after meals reduced blood levels of both LDL ("bad") cholesterol and C-reactive protein, a marker of inflammation.

Natural Wonders

Dried Peas

All legumes are an excellent source of fiber, but yellow split peas contain more than most. Dried peas, like all legumes, contain both types of fiber: soluble fiber, which may help to keep cholesterol low; and insoluble fiber, which helps to keep you regular and wards off intestinal problems, such as diverticular disease, an inflammation of the intestine. Dried peas are also a source of isoflavones, the phytonutrients that are touted for their apparent ability to act as phytoestrogens, thereby relieving many of the symptoms associated with menopause, among other benefits. Dried peas also contain folate, potassium and iron.

Like all legumes, dried peas are high in carbohydrates. However, their high fiber content balances any tendency to increase blood glucose levels, except perhaps in particularly sensitive individuals. And, like all legumes, they also contain anti-nutrients, such as phytic acid and lectins, which work to prevent your body from absorbing valuable micronutrients and may cause digestive problems.

Lectins are substances in plants that protect them from predators, such as insects. Most plants contain lectins, but some, such as grains and legumes, have levels that are high enough to be potentially problematic. Lectins don't break down easily in the process of digestion. If they stick to the mucosal lining of the intestinal wall that process may set the stage for various problems, ranging in severity from flatulence to the development of autoimmune diseases such as inflammatory bowel disease. Ensuring that your gut has enough healthy bacteria to offset any negative effects associated with consuming lectins is a positive step. You can also set in motion a process for pre-digesting foods that are high in lectins. This involves giving potential offenders such as legumes a good soak in water spiked with a little acid, such as lemon juice or cider vinegar, before cooking (see Natural Wonders, page 253). This initiates the process of fermentation, which at least one study shows is very effective at eliminating lectins from foods. You can also use sprouted legumes, if available, or sprout your own (see Natural Wonders, page 23).

Oven-Baked Kale Chips

In the past few years, kale chips have become very popular, with good reason. They are tasty and nutritious, perfect as a gluten-free dipper or on their own as a satisfying snack. And, if you make your own, you can be sure they don't contain any nasty additives. Increase the quantity to suit your needs.

Makes about 5 chips per stem

Tips

When trimming the kale, remove the tough stem right to the end of the leaf (it has an unpleasantly chewy texture) and discard. Then cut the pieces crosswise into "chips."

I like to use lacinto (also known as black or dinosaur kale) when making chips because its long, relatively solid leaves allow for the creation of a "chip" that has enough heft to support a spread or to be used as a dipper. However, other types of kale also make delicious chips.

● **Preheat oven to 350°F (180°C)**

Per stem of kale:

1	leaf lacinto kale, trimmed and chopped (see Tips, left)	1
1 tsp	extra virgin olive oil	5 mL
	Fine sea salt	
	Sweet or hot paprika, regular or smoked, optional	

1. In a salad spinner, thoroughly dry kale. Place olive oil in a bowl and add kale, in batches, as necessary. Using your hand, toss kale until evenly coated with oil.

2. Place on a baking sheet in a single layer. Bake in preheated oven until leaves crisp up, about 10 minutes. Remove from oven and sprinkle lightly with sea salt and paprika, if using.

Mindful Morsels

Paprika is a spice made from various types of dried ground chile peppers. The peppers vary widely in size and shape, and each type provides a different flavor profile and level of heat. It is a great flavor enhancer for freshly made kale chips and although it isn't used in sufficient quantity to provide significant nutrients, the peppers from which it is made are nutritional powerhouses.

Nutrients Per Serving (5 chips)

Calories	45
Protein	0.4 g
Carbohydrates	1.1 g
Fat (Total)	4.6 g
Saturated Fat	0.6 g
Monounsaturated Fat	3.3 g
Polyunsaturated Fat	0.5 g
Dietary Fiber	0.3 g
Sodium	5 mg
Cholesterol	0 mg

EXCELLENT SOURCE OF vitamin K.
GOOD SOURCE OF vitamin A.
SOURCE OF vitamin C.

Natural Wonders

Kale

Kale chips are very popular these days because they are delicious and very nutritious. This leafy green is probably the biggest box office attraction of the superstar vegetable category. It has so many virtues it is hard to know where to begin. For starters it is nutrient-dense. One cup (250 mL) contains only 34 calories (2% of the DV) and provides a whopping 684% of the DV of vitamin K, 206% of the DV of vitamin A, and 134% of the DV of vitamin C, in addition to providing respectable amounts of vitamin B_6, manganese, calcium, potassium and copper, among other nutrients. In fact, in her book *Eating on the Wild Side*, Jo Robinson says, "Kale is one of the few vegetables that meets or exceeds the nutritional value of some wild greens."

In addition to being a rich source of micronutrients, kale's antioxidant capacity is also legendary. Kale contains more than 45 different flavonoids, including quercetin (see Natural Wonders, page 293) and kaempferol, which are powerful anti-inflammatories, among other benefits.

It is a member of the brassica family and as such its ability to help prevent cancer is well recognized. Kale provides glucosinolates, sulfur-containing compounds that help your body to ward off heart disease in addition to protecting against cancer. Among other benefits, these compounds work with other nutrients such as folate and vitamin C to cleanse your body of free radicals and other toxins. Other substances in kale support its cleansing ability, including sulforaphane, which assists your liver in the process of detoxification. Last but not least, kale is rich in two important phytonutrients: lutein and zeaxanthin, both of which have been shown over and over again to reduce the risk for age-related macular degeneration, the leading cause of blindness in those aged 55 and older (see page 81). By protecting the macula from damaging UV light, specifically light in the blue range frequency, lutein and zeaxanthin act like internal sunglasses for this precious part of the retina.

Kale will keep in the crisper for several days. Its nutritional value is maximized when it is eaten raw, but gentle cooking, such as a brief steaming or sautéing just until it's wilted will maintain most of the nutrients.

Polenta Crostini

Crostini made from polenta can be topped with almost anything you would use to top bread-based crostini, bearing in mind that polenta has a more assertive flavor than white bread. In general terms, you are probably safe with anything that is Italian in flavoring. Using stone-ground cornmeal to make your polenta means you'll be providing your guests with a nutritious whole-grain nibble.

Makes enough for about 36 average-size crostini

Tips

When making the polenta, if you prefer, substitute vegetable or chicken stock for the water.

When cutting polenta crostini use your imagination. Round or fluted cookie cutters make particularly pretty crostini, but simple rectangles, squares or triangles work well, too. You can even cut animal shapes if you're serving crostini at a children's party.

- **15- by 10-inch (38 by 25 cm) jelly roll pan, lined with plastic wrap**
- **Baking sheet, lined with parchment paper**

1	recipe Slow-Cooked Polenta (page 278)	1
	Extra virgin olive oil	

1. Prepare Slow-Cooked Polenta according to recipe.

2. When polenta has finished cooking, transfer to prepared dish or pan. Spread warm polenta evenly over the plastic wrap. Cover completely with another piece of plastic wrap and, using the palm of your hand, flatten to level. (Don't worry if the edges are a bit uneven or if the polenta doesn't completely cover the bottom of the pan. You can trim it when you make the crostini.) Refrigerate, covered, for at least 6 hours or up to 2 days.

3. When you're ready to serve, remove plastic and place polenta sheet on a large cutting board. Cut into desired shapes, using a sharp knife or cookie cutters.

4. *To make crostini:* Preheat oven to 350°F (180°C). Brush top side of the shapes with extra virgin olive oil. Place on prepared baking sheet and bake in preheated oven for 10 minutes. Turn, brush new top side with olive oil, return to oven and bake for 10 minutes. Let cool completely before adding toppings.

Toppings for Polenta Crostini

Polenta crostini provide a great base for many delicious toppings. Here are some of my favorites.

Fontina Cheese Polenta Crostini: Cut cooled polenta into squares, rectangles or triangles. Top with thinly sliced Fontina cheese, to taste. Bake in 350°F (180°C) oven until cheese is nicely melted, about 3 minutes.

Creamy Gorgonzola with Walnut Polenta Crostini: In a small bowl, combine equal parts gorgonzola and mascarpone cheese. Mix well. (Some cheese mongers sell a version of this already mixed; if you have access to it, by all means use it.) Spread on cooled polenta crostini to taste. Sprinkle finely chopped walnuts on top.

Nutrients Per Serving (1 crostini)	
Calories	12
Protein	0.2 g
Carbohydrates	2.6 g
Fat (Total)	0.1 g
Saturated Fat	0 g
Monounsaturated Fat	0 g
Polyunsaturated Fat	0.1 g
Dietary Fiber	0.5 g
Sodium	17 mg
Cholesterol	0 mg

Roasted Garlic Polenta Crostini: Spread cooled polenta crostini with roasted garlic. To roast garlic, separate head into cloves but do not peel. Place in a small ovenproof container and toss with a bit of olive oil (about 2 tsp/10 mL) per head. Roast in 425°F (220°C) oven until softened, about 30 minutes. To serve: squeeze roasted garlic out of skins and spread over crostini. If desired, add a small dollop of Roasted Red Pepper Coulis (page 246).

Tapenade-Topped Crostini: Spread cooled crostini with your favorite tapenade.

Mindful Morsels

If you have trouble digesting cornmeal, look for an artisanal source to make sure it hasn't been genetically modified. Among other concerns, plant lectins, which can be problematic for your digestion, are often spiked on to natural plants in the process of genetic modification. Even if your cornmeal is not genetically modified, it is high in phytic acid so it's a good idea to soak it for at least 8 hours or overnight in warm non-chlorinated water (about 2 parts water to 1 part grain) with a spoonful or so of cider vinegar (preferably with the mother). Drain and rinse before cooking. Not only will the nutrients it contains be more easily absorbed by your body, but your polenta will also be particularly creamy.

Natural Wonders

Whole Grains

Although some people find grains hard to digest (see Natural Wonders, page 31) research has linked eating whole grains, such as stone-ground cornmeal, with a wide range of health benefits. Studies show that regular consumption of whole grains reduces the possibility you will develop type-2 diabetes, makes it less likely you will have a heart attack and helps to keep your blood pressure under control, among other benefits.

And, if that isn't enough, scientists are actively engaged in studying substances contained in whole grains, such as lignans and oligosaccharides, which function as prebiotics. Prebiotics are ingredients that stimulate the growth of healthy bacteria, such as lactobacilli and bifidobacteria (which are known as probiotics). By promoting the growth of beneficial intestinal flora, prebiotics help to keep your gut in tip-top health. In addition, prebiotics appear to have a wide range of other health benefits, from preventing hair loss to reducing menopausal symptoms.

Yogurt Flatbread

Warm from the oven, these little flatbreads are yummy on their own or finished with some fresh herbs (see Variations, below). They also make a good base for spreads and work well as dippers.

Makes about 2½ dozen

Tips

Be sure to use good sea salt, such as *fleur de sel* to finish your bread. Refined table salt has a bitter acrid taste, among other issues (see Natural Wonders, page 37).

Always check the labels of dairy products, such as yogurt, to make sure they are gluten-free.

- Preheat oven to 350°F (180°C)
- 2½-inch (6 cm) round cutter
- Baking sheets, lined with parchment paper

¾ cup	sorghum flour	175 mL
¾ cup	fine brown rice flour	175 mL
½ cup	tapioca flour	125 mL
1 tsp	xanthan gum	5 mL
1 tsp	gluten-free baking powder	5 mL
½ tsp	fine sea salt	2 mL
1 cup	plain yogurt	250 mL
2 tbsp	extra virgin olive oil	30 mL
	Course sea salt	

1. In a bowl, combine sorghum, brown rice and tapioca flours, xanthan gum, baking powder and salt. Add yogurt and, using a wooden spoon, mix as well as you can. Then use your hands to knead until a soft dough forms. Cover and let rest at room temperature for 1 hour.

2. Divide dough into quarters. Working with one piece at a time, on lightly floured board, roll out to a ⅛ inch (3 mm) thickness. Using cutter, cut into rounds and place about 2 inches (5 cm) apart on prepared sheets. Repeat until all the dough has been cut into circles, re-rolling scraps.

3. Bake in preheated oven until nicely puffed, about 15 minutes. Remove from oven and preheat broiler. Place flatbreads under broiler until lightly browned. Brush with olive oil and sprinkle with salt. Serve warm.

Variations

Za'atar-Spiked Flatbread: After the flatbreads have been brushed with olive oil, sprinkle with za'atar (see Tip, right).

Herb-Spiked Flatbread: In a small bowl, combine 1 tbsp (15 mL) minced fresh thyme leaves and 1 tsp (5 mL) finely grated lemon zest. After the flatbreads have been brushed with olive oil, sprinkle with the mixture, then finish with salt to taste.

Nutrients per Serving (1 piece)

Calories	51
Protein	1.0 g
Carbohydrates	8.4 g
Fat (Total)	1.6 g
Saturated Fat	0.5 g
Monounsaturated Fat	0.9 g
Polyunsaturated Fat	0.2 g
Dietary Fiber	0.3 g
Sodium	56 mg
Cholesterol	1 mg

SOURCE OF manganese.

Tip

You can purchase za'atar in specialty spice shops or make your own. In a small bowl, combine 2 tbsp (30 mL) fresh thyme leaves, 1 tbsp (15 mL) toasted sesame seeds and 1 tsp (5 mL) each ground sumac and coarse sea salt. To toast sesame seeds, place in a dry skillet over medium heat and cook, stirring, just until they begin to brown. Immediately transfer to a bowl. Once they start to brown they burn quickly.

Mindful Morsels

Recent studies have linked taking calcium in supplements with an increased risk of heart attack. Although the evidence was not statistically compelling, it did raise interesting questions about nutritional supplements, particularly if they are taken on their own. Other studies indicate that large doses of single nutrients are likely to create imbalances with other nutrients. For instance, too much supplemental zinc can deplete copper from your system, and large doses of vitamin E (in the form of alpha-tocopherol) have been linked with an increased risk of heart failure. Once again, the safest strategy is consuming all the nutrients you need from a diet of nutrient-dense whole foods.

Natural Wonders

Dairy Products

Many people cannot tolerate the lactose in dairy products and some are actually allergic to casein, a protein found in milk. However, if you do not have any problems consuming dairy, fermented milk products such as yogurt and kefir can be a positive addition to your diet. The healthy bacteria they contain are particularly beneficial for those suffering from digestive disorders and/or leaky gut.

When dairy products have been fermented properly, virtually all of the lactose disappears (it is devoured by the fermenting bacteria), which is why it is important to make your own or use only those made by trusted artisanal providers. Not only are the lactic acid bacteria in properly fermented milk products such as yogurt, kefir and sour cream linked with a variety of health benefits, including improved digestion, but recent studies suggest that the acids in fermented milk products may also reduce the impact of certain foods on blood glucose response.

Butter is basically milk fat and it contains virtually no lactose or milk proteins. Even people with a dairy allergy usually don't have problems consuming butter. Clarified butter, which is pure milk fat, is good for cooking on high heat because it has a high smoke point. Ghee is basically clarified butter, but commercially made ghee should be avoided because it often contains additives.

New World Leek and Potato Soup

Soups

New World Leek and Potato Soup

I call this soup "new world" because it's a variation on the classic French leek and potato soup, using sweet potatoes and peppers, two ingredients that Christopher Columbus introduced to Europe during his explorations of the Americas. Serve small quantities as a prelude to a celebratory meal, or add a tossed green salad for a light supper.

Makes 8 servings

Can Be Halved
(see Tips, page 70)

Tips

To clean leeks: Fill a sink full of lukewarm water. Split the leeks in half lengthwise and submerge them in the water, swishing them around to remove all traces of dirt. Transfer to a colander and rinse thoroughly under cold water.

If you prefer, use one red and one green bell pepper.

Nutrients Per Serving

Calories	222
Protein	5.1 g
Carbohydrates	33.5 g
Fat (Total)	8.4 g
Saturated Fat	3.8 g
Monounsaturated Fat	3.2 g
Polyunsaturated Fat	0.8 g
Dietary Fiber	4.2 g
Sodium	44 mg
Cholesterol	34 mg

EXCELLENT SOURCE OF vitamins A, B$_6$ and C.

GOOD SOURCE OF folate, potassium and iron.

CONTAINS a high amount of dietary fiber.

- **Large (approx. 5 quart) slow cooker**
- **Food processor or blender**

1 tbsp	olive oil	15 mL
4	large leeks, white part with just a bit of green, cleaned and thinly sliced (see Tips, left)	4
4	cloves garlic, minced	4
1 tbsp	ground cumin (see Tip, page 81)	15 mL
½ tsp	cracked black peppercorns	2 mL
6 cups	vegetable or chicken stock	1.5 L
2 lbs	sweet potatoes, peeled and cut into 1-inch (2.5 cm) cubes (about 3 potatoes)	1 kg
2	green bell peppers, diced (see Tips, left)	2
1	long red chile pepper, minced, optional	1
	Sea salt, optional	
½ cup	heavy or whipping (35%) cream or non-dairy alternative	125 mL
	Roasted red pepper strips, optional	
	Finely snipped chives	

1. In a skillet, heat oil over medium heat. Add leeks and cook, stirring, until softened, about 5 minutes. Add garlic, cumin and peppercorns and cook, stirring, for 1 minute.

2. Transfer to slow cooker stoneware. Add vegetable stock. Add sweet potatoes. Cover and cook on Low for 6 hours or on High for 3 hours, until potatoes are tender. Add green peppers and chile pepper, if using. Cover and cook on High for 20 to 30 minutes, until peppers are tender. Season to taste with salt, if using.

3. Working in batches, purée soup in a food processor or blender. (You can also do this in the stoneware using an immersion blender.) To serve, ladle soup into bowls, drizzle with cream and garnish with roasted red pepper strips, if using, and chives.

This dish can be partially prepared before it is cooked. Complete Step 1, adding a bit of the vegetable stock to the mixture. Cover and refrigerate overnight or for up to 2 days. When you're ready to cook, complete the recipe.

Mindful Morsels

With the addition of peppers, and the substitution of sweet for white potatoes, this delicious soup is even more nutritious than the traditional version. It contains high amounts of vitamins A, B_6 and C, all of which help your body to fight inflammation, among other benefits.

Natural Wonders

Colorful Food

This colorful soup is more than pretty to look at. The pigments that provide plant foods with their vibrant hues also signal the nutrients they contain and their disease-fighting properties. Sweet potatoes are one of the best sources of beta-carotene, some of which our bodies convert to vitamin A, and a source of vitamin B_6, among other nutrients. Peppers are a great source of vitamin C and are high in bioflavonoids, which are thought to protect against cancer. Leeks contain folate and iron along with kaempferol, an antioxidant that shows promise in protecting against cancer.

To maximize the disease-fighting properties of plant foods, nutritionists tell us to eat at least three different-color vegetables and two different-color fruits every day. Research shows that nutrients in foods have very complex relationships among themselves. Unlike nutrients taken in supplements, they work together synergistically when consumed in different foods, as well as in single foods (see Natural Wonders, page 307). A bowl of this tasty soup goes a long way toward helping you achieve the goal of consuming a wide variety of nutrients by eating colorfully.

Southwestern Turkey Chowder

This soup is so good I can't wait to finish the celebratory turkey and get it started. I think it's the best way to use up leftover turkey. If you're planning to eat lightly following a holiday, it makes a perfect dinner with the addition of salad.

Makes 8 main-course servings

Tips

If you are halving this recipe, be sure to use a small (2 to 3½ quart) slow cooker

Use any combination of long-cooking gluten-free whole grains in this soup, such as Job's tears, hominy, or brown, red or wild rice. All will be delicious.

Nutrients Per Serving

Calories	320
Protein	21.4 g
Carbohydrates	48.0 g
Fat (Total)	6.6 g
Saturated Fat	1.5 g
Monounsaturated Fat	2.6 g
Polyunsaturated Fat	1.8 g
Dietary Fiber	8.3 g
Sodium	107 mg
Cholesterol	51 mg

EXCELLENT SOURCE OF niacin, phosphorus, iron, magnesium, manganese, zinc and selenium.

GOOD SOURCE OF vitamin A, folate, thiamine, riboflavin, pantothenic acid and copper.

SOURCE OF vitamins C and E (alpha-tocopherol) and calcium.

CONTAINS a very high amount of dietary fiber.

- **Large (approx. 5 quart) slow cooker**

10 cups	turkey stock (see recipe, right; and Variations, right)	2.5 L
1 tbsp	olive oil	15 mL
3	onions, diced	3
4	stalks celery, diced	4
1 tbsp	ground cumin (see Tip, page 81)	15 mL
2 tsp	dried oregano	10 mL
4	cloves garlic, minced	4
½ tsp	cracked black peppercorns	2 mL
1½ cups	long-cooking gluten-free whole grains, soaked, rinsed and drained (see Tips, left)	375 mL
1	can (28 oz/796 mL) no-salt-added diced tomatoes including juice (see Tip, right)	1
2 to 3	ancho, guajillo or mild New Mexico dried chiles	2 to 3
2 cups	boiling water	500 mL
1 cup	loosely packed fresh cilantro leaves	250 mL
2 cups	diced cooked turkey	500 mL
2 cups	corn kernels	500 mL

1. In a skillet, heat oil over medium heat. Add onions and celery and cook, stirring, until vegetables are softened, about 5 minutes. Add cumin, oregano, garlic and peppercorns and cook, stirring, for 1 minute. Add whole grains and toss until coated. Add tomatoes with juice and bring to a boil.

2. Transfer to slow cooker stoneware. Add turkey stock and stir well. Cover and cook on Low for 6 to 8 hours or on High for 3 to 4 hours, until grains are tender.

3. In a heatproof bowl, 30 minutes before grains have finished cooking, combine dried chiles and boiling water. Set aside for 30 minutes, weighing chiles down with a cup to ensure they remain submerged. Drain, discarding soaking liquid and stems and chop coarsely. Transfer to a blender. Add cilantro and ½ cup (125 mL) of stock from the chowder. Purée. Add to stoneware along with the turkey and corn. Cover and cook on High until corn is tender and flavors meld, about 20 minutes.

Tip

When using any canned product, such as tomatoes or corn, check the label to make sure ingredients containing gluten have not been added.

Make Ahead

Complete Step 1. Cover and refrigerate overnight or for up to 2 days. When you're ready to cook, complete the recipe.

Variation

Southwestern Chicken Chowder: Substitute chicken stock for the turkey stock and diced cooked chicken for the turkey.

Turkey Stock

To make turkey stock, break the carcass into manageable pieces and place in slow cooker stoneware. Add 2 tbsp (30 mL) apple cider vinegar, 2 each carrots, celery stalks and onions, quartered, plus 8 whole peppercorns. Add 12 cups (3 L) water. Cover and cook on Low for 12 hours or on High for 6 hours. Strain, reserving liquid and discarding solids. You can also make this on the stovetop in a stockpot. Bring to a boil over medium-high heat. Reduce heat to low. Cover and simmer for 3 hours. Strain, reserving liquid and discarding solids.

Mindful Morsels

Oregano, cumin and cilantro, like many herbs, contain flavonoids, along with an abundance of other valuable phytonutrients. Although we consume spices and herbs in minuscule quantities, like all plant-based food, they are rich in a variety of bioactive substances, which Dr. Rui Hai Liu commented in a 2003 article in *The American Journal of Clinical Nutrition*, "may provide desirable health benefits beyond basic nutrition to reduce the risk of chronic diseases."

Natural Wonders

Sodium and Potassium

If you're concerned about your blood pressure, then you're likely watching your intake of sodium because high salt intake has been linked with hypertension. To keep your sodium intake under control, it is crucial to avoid prepared and processed foods, which are loaded with salt. To control hypertension, also keep an eye on the amount of potassium you consume. Potassium is a powerful ally in maintaining healthy blood pressure. Simply reducing sodium intake is only half the equation; simultaneously increasing the amount of potassium you consume will be much more effective in keeping blood pressure under control. You should aim to get about five times as much potassium as sodium to get the most of this blood pressure-friendly mineral. Most fruit, vegetables, meat and fish are high in potassium.

Mixed Mushroom Soup

This delicious soup is loaded with flavorful, earthy mushrooms. Three varieties — porcini, cremini and shiitake, work together to create deep rich flavor. I like to make this with homemade chicken stock, which enhances the meatiness of the mushrooms, but if you are vegetarian, vegetable stock works perfectly well. Add a drizzle of cream if you are craving something resembling old-fashioned cream of mushroom soup, a classic comfort food.

Makes 10 servings

Can Be Halved
(see Tips, below)

Tips

If you are halving this recipe, be sure to use a small (1½ to 3½ quart) slow cooker

If you are not a vegetarian, for maximum flavor make this soup using Homemade Chicken Stock (page 116). If you are using vegetable stock, you might want to substitute about 1 cup (250 mL) Homemade Mushroom Stock (page 119) for part of the vegetable stock to enhance the flavor of the soup.

Nutrients Per Serving

Calories	68
Protein	2.0 g
Carbohydrates	10.2 g
Fat (Total)	2.8 g
Saturated Fat	0.9 g
Monounsaturated Fat	1.3 g
Polyunsaturated Fat	0.2 g
Dietary Fiber	2.0 g
Sodium	18 mg
Cholesterol	3 mg

SOURCE OF vitamins C, B_6 and K, folate, phosphorus, magnesium, potassium, iron and zinc.
CONTAINS a moderate amount of dietary fiber.

- **Medium to large (3½ to 5 quart) slow cooker**
- **Food processor**

2 tbsp	dried porcini mushrooms	30 mL
2 cups	hot water	500 mL
1 tbsp	butter or olive oil	15 mL
8 oz	cremini mushrooms, trimmed and thickly sliced	250 g
8 oz	shiitake mushrooms, stemmed and thickly sliced	250 g
1 tbsp	extra virgin olive oil	15 mL
2	leeks, cleaned and thinly sliced (see Tip, right)	2
1	onion, chopped	1
2	cloves garlic, minced	2
1 tsp	dried thyme	5 mL
1	floury potato, such as russet, peeled and shredded	1
4 cups	vegetable or chicken stock	1 L
2 tbsp	sherry vinegar	30 mL
¼ cup	finely chopped fresh tarragon leaves	60 mL
	Sea salt and freshly ground black pepper	
	Heavy or whipping (35%) cream or soy creamer, optional	

1. In a bowl, combine dried mushrooms and hot water. Let stand for 30 minutes. Drain through a fine sieve, reserving liquid. Pat mushrooms dry with paper towel and chop finely. Set liquid and mushrooms aside.

2. In a large skillet, melt butter over medium-high heat. Add cremini and shiitake mushrooms and cook, stirring, until mushrooms are lightly browned and starting to lose their liquid. Transfer to slow cooker stoneware.

3. Reduce heat to medium and add oil to pan. Add leeks and onion and cook, stirring, until softened, about 5 minutes. Add garlic, thyme and reserved chopped dried mushrooms and cook, stirring, for 1 minute. Stir in potato. Transfer to slow cooker stoneware.

4. Add stock and reserved mushroom liquid. Cover and cook on Low for 6 hours or on High for 3 hours, until mushrooms are very tender. Add vinegar and tarragon and, working in batches, purée soup in a food processor. (You can also do this in the stoneware using an immersion blender.) Season, to taste, with salt and freshly ground pepper. Ladle into bowls and drizzle with cream, if using.

Mindful Morsels

Although a serving (just over 1 cup/250 mL) of this soup provides only 68 calories, it is very hearty and you will find that it fills you up. That's because its main ingredient are meaty mushrooms, which are also very low-cal. This mixture of delectable fungi provides a grand total of 18 calories, just slightly more than the potato (13 calories) or the olive oil (12 calories).

Natural Wonders

Mushrooms and Leeks

This recipe contains an abundance of mushrooms and leeks, two vegetables that have health promoting properties. Traditionally, mushrooms have been used medicinally for their ability to boost the immune system. In Asia, shiitake mushrooms have long been associated with longevity, likely because by stimulating the immune system, they help your body to resist infections. But now researchers are looking at other potential benefits. For instance, recent research suggests they may also defend against cardiovascular disease by protecting blood vessels and helping to keep blood cholesterol low.

Mushrooms provide a variety of nutrients in small quantities, including vitamin D, and iron in a bioavailable form. Some of the nutrients they contain may be of particular value to vegetarians. In addition to providing vitamin B_{12}, cremini mushrooms contain conjugated linolenic acid (CLA) a very beneficial fatty acid, usually found exclusively in animal products. They also provide small amounts of selenium, riboflavin, and zinc, among other nutrients (for more on mushrooms, see Mindful Morsels, page 73).

Because mushrooms soak up the substances they grow in, it is particularly important to buy those that are organically grown.

Leeks belong to the allium family, the same family as onions and garlic, and are rich in sulfur compounds, which may protect against cancer, among other benefits (see Natural Wonders, page 171). They help to keep LDL ("bad") cholesterol and blood pressure under control and provide lutein and zeaxanthin, carotenoids which promote eye health (see Natural Wonders, page 81).

Mushroom Lentil Soup

Lentils and mushrooms are a classic combination for a reason — they blend deliciously because each brings out the best features of the other. This hearty soup, with its deep earthy flavors, makes a great main course in a bowl. Serve it on those evenings when everyone is coming and going at different times. Set out the fixin's for salad and let everyone help themselves.

Makes 8 servings

Can Be Halved
(see Tips, page 80)

Tips

Lentils purchased in bulk may contain bits of dirt or discolored seeds. Before using, it is wise to rinse them thoroughly in a pot of water.

If you prefer, substitute a cup (250 mL) or so of Homemade Mushroom Stock (page 119) for the vegetable or chicken stock. The quantity will depend upon how robustly flavored your mushrooms are. You do not want the mushroom flavor to overpower the soup.

Nutrients Per Serving

Calories	217
Protein	14.2 g
Carbohydrates	37.3 g
Fat (Total)	2.5 g
Saturated Fat	0.4 g
Monounsaturated Fat	1.4 g
Polyunsaturated Fat	0.5 g
Dietary Fiber	7.9 g
Sodium	188 mg
Cholesterol	0 mg

EXCELLENT SOURCE OF vitamins A and K, folate, phosphorus, potassium and iron.

GOOD SOURCE OF vitamins C and B$_6$, magnesium and zinc.

CONTAINS a very high amount of dietary fiber.

- Large (approx. 5 quart) slow cooker

2 cups	hot water	500 mL
2 tbsp	dried wild mushrooms (see Tip, right)	30 mL
1 tbsp	olive oil	15 mL
1	onion, finely chopped	1
4	stalks celery, diced	4
2	carrots, peeled and diced	2
1 tsp	chili powder	5 mL
1	can (28 oz/796) tomatoes, including juice, coarsely chopped	1
4 cups	vegetable or chicken stock (see Tips, left)	1 L
2 cups	brown or green lentils (see Tips, left)	500 mL
2 tbsp	freshly squeezed lemon juice	30 mL
	Freshly ground black pepper	
	Sea salt, optional	
	Plain yogurt, optional	
½ cup	finely chopped parsley leaves or chives	125 mL

1. In a heatproof bowl, combine hot water and dried mushrooms. Let stand for 30 minutes then strain through a fine sieve, reserving liquid. Pat mushrooms dry, chop finely and set aside.

2. In a large skillet, heat oil over medium heat. Add onion, celery and carrots and cook, stirring, until carrots are softened, about 7 minutes. Add chili powder and reserved dried mushrooms and cook, stirring, for 1 minute. Add tomatoes with juice and reserved mushroom liquid and bring to a boil. Transfer to slow cooker stoneware.

3. Add vegetable stock and lentils. Cover and cook on Low for 6 hours or on High for 3 hours, until vegetables are tender. Stir in lemon juice, ground pepper and salt to taste, if using. Ladle into bowls and drizzle with yogurt, if using. Garnish each serving with 1 tbsp (15 mL) parsley.

Tip

If you're using a strongly flavored dried mushroom, such as porcini, to make this soup, 2 tbsp (30 mL) will be sufficient. But if you're using a mixture of mushrooms, some of which may be more mildly flavored, you may need an additional 1 tbsp (15 mL) or so.

Make Ahead

This soup can be assembled before it is cooked. Complete Steps 1 and 2. Cover and refrigerate overnight or for up to 2 days. When you're ready to cook, complete the recipe.

Variation

If you prefer a creamier soup, after the soup has finished cooking, scoop out about 2 cups (500 mL) of the solids, plus a little liquid and purée in a food processor. Return to the stoneware and continue as directed.

Mindful Morsels

Not only are mushrooms very low in calories, they also provide potassium, niacin (vitamin B_3) and zinc (see page 71). To boot, they are virtually sodium-free. Depending on the variety, there is as much potassium in half to one full cup (125 to 250 mL) of chopped raw mushrooms as there is in small to medium sized banana. Why should bananas get all the attention when it comes to potassium?

The other health promoting properties of mushrooms are found in their phytonutrients. These fabulous fungi are packed with a unique antioxidant called l-ergothioneine. Mushrooms contain higher concentrations of l-ergothioneine than either of the two previously recognized best dietary sources — chicken liver and wheat germ. Ounce for ounce, mushrooms provide about forty times as much of this nutrient as wheat germ.

Natural Wonders

Lentils

A serving of Mushroom Lentil Soup is high in complex carbohydrates most of which (28.19 grams) are provided by the lentils. Perhaps not surprisingly, as North Americans become increasingly health conscious, our consumption of legumes such as lentils has been rising. Once dismissed as "peasant food," legumes are now identified as "nutrient dense," and their consumption is linked with a wide range of health benefits. For instance, eating legumes, which are low on the glycemic index, helps to stabilize blood sugar, a great benefit for people with insulin resistance, hypoglycemia or diabetes.

While all legumes are highly nutritious, lentils have some advantages over other varieties. Firstly, unlike dried beans, they don't need to be soaked before cooking (unless you have difficulty digesting starches), which makes them more convenient. And secondly, since there's no time advantage to using canned versions in the slow cooker, you can use raw lentils, which contain almost no sodium. From a nutrient perspective, lentils are high in dietary fiber and an excellent source of iron and protein. If you have trouble digesting legumes, soak lentils, preferably with a bit of cider vinegar (see Natural Wonders, page 253) before cooking, or sprout them. Already-sprouted lentils are available at well-stocked natural foods stores.

Vichyssoise with Celery Root and Watercress

This refreshing soup is delicious, easy to make and can be a prelude to the most sophisticated meal. More nutritious than traditional vichyssoise, its pleasing nutty flavor is enhanced with a garnish of chopped toasted walnuts, which also adds valuable nutrients. In the summer, I aim to have leftovers in the refrigerator and treat myself to a small bowl for a yummy afternoon snack.

Makes 8 servings

Can Be Halved
(see Tips, below)

Tips

If you are halving this recipe, be sure to use a small (approx. 2 quart) slow cooker.

Since celery root oxidizes quickly on contact with air, be sure to use as soon as you have peeled and chopped it, or toss with 1 tbsp (15 mL) lemon juice to prevent discoloration.

To cool the soup more quickly, transfer it to a large bowl before refrigerating.

Nutrients Per Serving

Calories	162
Protein	3.6 g
Carbohydrates	12.6 g
Fat (Total)	12 g
Saturated Fat	4.0 g
Monounsaturated Fat	3.4 g
Polyunsaturated Fat	3.9 g
Dietary Fiber	2.8 g
Sodium	91 mg
Cholesterol	19 mg

EXCELLENT SOURCE OF vitamin K.

GOOD SOURCE OF vitamin A, magnesium and potassium.

SOURCE OF vitamins C and B$_6$, folate, calcium, phosphorus, iron and zinc.

CONTAINS a moderate amount of dietary fiber.

- **Large (approx. 5 quart) slow cooker**
- **Food processor or blender**

1 tbsp	olive oil	15 mL
3	leeks, white and light green parts only, cleaned and coarsely chopped (see Tip, page 71)	3
2	cloves garlic, minced	2
½ tsp	cracked black peppercorns	2 mL
6 cups	chicken or vegetable stock	1.5 L
1	large celery root (about 1 lb/500 g), peeled and sliced	1
2	bunches (each about 4 oz/125 g) watercress, tough parts of the stems removed	2
	Sea salt, optional	
½ cup	heavy or whipping (35%) cream or soy milk	125 mL
½ cup	toasted chopped walnuts	125 mL
	Watercress sprigs, optional	

1. In a skillet, heat oil over medium heat. Add leeks and cook, stirring, until softened, about 5 minutes. Add garlic and peppercorns and cook, stirring, for 1 minute. Add stock and stir well.

2. Transfer to slow cooker stoneware. Stir in celery root. Cover and cook on Low for 6 hours or on High for 3 hours, until celery root is tender. Stir in watercress until wilted.

3. Working in batches, purée mixture in a food processor or blender. (You can also do this in the stoneware using an immersion blender. Season to taste with salt, if using. Stir in cream and refrigerate until thoroughly chilled, about 4 hours (see Tips, left). To serve, ladle into bowls and garnish with toasted walnuts and watercress sprigs, if using.

more information on page 76

Make Ahead

Complete Step 1. Cover and refrigerate overnight or for up to 2 days. When you're ready to cook, continue with Steps 2 and 3.

Mindful Morsels

Most of the saturated fat in a serving of this soup (2.6 grams) comes from the cream. If you are watching your intake of saturated fat, use a dairy-free milk such as fortified rice milk instead. The walnuts, which add both texture and flavor, contain 0.4 grams of saturated fat but they also provide 0.6 grams of desirable omega-3 fats in the form of alpha-linolenic acid (ALA). Experts generally recommend that on a daily basis women obtain 1.1 grams of ALA and men get 1.6 grams, making the walnuts in this soup an excellent source of this nutrient.

Natural Wonders

Watercress

Enhancing a dish with peppery watercress brings more than zip to the table. It also adds a wide range of nutrients to your diet. A dark leafy green, watercress contains important nutrients such as vitamins A, C and K and a variety of B vitamins, as well as the minerals calcium, potassium, magnesium and manganese. It is particularly low in calories and high in vitamins C and K. The watercress in this soup provides 3 calories per serving, one-sixth of the DV of vitamin C and more than half of the DV for vitamin K.

Watercress belongs to the Brassicaceae family and like all leafy greens, it is loaded with phytonutrients. This includes antioxidants such as beta-carotene, which help to slow down the aging process and protect you from disease. The bioflavonoids in watercress appear to work in synergy with vitamin C, enhancing its antioxidant ability. It is also rich in lutein and zeaxanthin, which appear to protect against atherosclerosis and lower the risk of dying from a heart attack, among other benefits (see Natural Wonders, page 81). Other interesting compounds in watercress include isothiocyanates, which researchers are actively studying for their anti-cancer activity. These compounds appear to be particularly potent breast cancer fighters and may also protect against lung cancer.

Caldo Verde

This soup, which is Portuguese in origin, is usually made with white beans and kale. This version, which uses chickpeas and collard greens, is equally delicious and also lends itself to many adaptations. If you can't find collards, use kale.

Tips

When buying any deli meat such as kielbasa, read the label carefully. You don't want additives such as MSG, high fructose corn syrup, synthetic nitrates or gluten.

Shred collard greens as if you were making a chiffonade of basil leaves. Remove the stems, including the thick vein that runs up the bottom of the leaf and thoroughly wash the leaves by swishing them around in warm water. On a cutting board, stack the leaves, 2 or 3 at a time. Roll them into a cigar shape and slice thinly.

Nutrients Per Serving

Calories	190
Protein	7.9 g
Carbohydrates	33.0 g
Fat (Total)	3.7 g
Saturated Fat	0.6 g
Monounsaturated Fat	1.8 g
Polyunsaturated Fat	0.9 g
Dietary Fiber	6.1 g
Sodium	243 mg
Cholesterol	5 mg

SOURCE OF vitamin C, calcium and phosphorus.
CONTAINS a very high amount of dietary fiber.

- **Large (approx. 5 quart) slow cooker**
- **Food processor or blender**

1 tbsp	olive oil	15 mL
2	onions, finely chopped	2
2	carrots, peeled and diced	2
2	cloves garlic, minced	2
1 tsp	ground cumin (see Tip, page 81)	5 mL
½ tsp	cracked black peppercorns	2 mL
6 cups	chicken stock	1.5 L
4 cups	cooked chickpeas or white beans, drained and rinsed (see Mindful Morsels, page 79)	1 L
2	potatoes, peeled and shredded	2
	Sea salt, optional	
2 tsp	paprika, dissolved in 2 tbsp (30 mL) freshly squeezed lemon juice	10 mL
4 cups	shredded collard greens (about one 12 oz/375 g bunch) (see Tips, left)	1 L
4 oz	cooked smoked sausage, such as cured chorizo or turkey kielbasa, sliced and chopped into bite-size pieces, optional (see Tips, left)	125 g
	Red wine vinegar, optional	

1. In a skillet, heat oil over medium heat. Add onions and carrots and cook, stirring, until carrots are softened, about 7 minutes. Add garlic, cumin and peppercorns and cook, stirring, for 1 minute.

2. Transfer to slow cooker stoneware. Add chicken stock and chickpeas and stir well. Add potatoes and stir well. Cover and cook on Low for 6 to 8 hours or on High for 3 to 4 hours, until potatoes are tender. Season to taste with salt, if using. If you prefer a smooth soup, in batches, purée soup. Use a food processor, blender or immersion blender.

3. Stir in paprika mixture. Add collards, in batches, stirring each to submerge before adding the next batch. Add sausage, if using. Cover and cook on High until collards are tender, about 30 minutes. Season to taste with vinegar, if using.

more information on page 79

Caldo Verde

Make Ahead

Complete Step 1, adding a bit of the chicken stock to the mixture. Cover and refrigerate overnight or for up to 2 days. When you're ready to cook, continue with Step 2.

Mindful Morsels

If you are trying to reduce your consumption of sodium, cook dried chickpeas with no added salt. This Caldo Verde recipe was tested using conventional canned chickpeas, which contribute 204 mg of sodium per serving.

Natural Wonders

Garlic

Garlic has a long history in folk medicine. In fact, it has been used medicinally for over five thousand years to treat a wide variety of conditions ranging from coughs and colds to snake bites. Today, as pharmacy professor Heather Boon writes in her book *55 Most Common Medicinal Herbs*, it is the subject of more than 1,300 research papers and "one of the most extensively researched medicinal plants." In general terms, the research recognizes that garlic's medicinal benefits, which include antibacterial, cardioprotective and anti-cancer properties, are rooted in its sulfur-containing elements.

While whole cloves of garlic have relatively little odor, when chopped or crushed, garlic releases its highly pungent aroma. Crushing or chopping breaks the cell walls, connecting the enzyme alliinase with allin, a sulfur-containing compound, and converting it to allicin. Allicin, in turn, rapidly converts to numerous other active sulfur-containing compounds. This succession of chemical reactions produces health-promoting sulfides, which need about 15 minutes of exposure to air to develop. Heating garlic immediately after chopping deactivates a crucial enzyme in this chemical process.

Garlic's heart protective properties are fairly wide-ranging. Numerous studies show that it keeps triglycerides and LDL ("bad") cholesterol low. It also appears to keep blood pressure under control and, even in dietary doses, prevents your blood from clotting. It also works to protect your blood vessels from calcification, slowing down the process of atherosclerosis. Garlic also deserves attention as an antibiotic. Research confirms its use in fighting a range of bacterial infections. It has also demonstrated effectiveness battling some bacteria that have become drug-resistant. Garlic is also well-known as an antifungal and is particularly effective against fungal skin infections, including those caused by *Candida albicans*.

More recently, research indicates that eating garlic may also provide protection from cancer. While this evidence is based mostly on epidemiological studies, such as The Women's Health Study, which found that consuming garlic reduced the risk of colon cancer, preliminary research suggests that garlic intake may also reduce the risk for several other types of cancer, including lung cancer.

And yes, garlic can help to keep colds at bay. Over the course of 12 weeks, 146 subjects in a research study took either a placebo or a supplement containing allicin. Those taking the supplement had significantly fewer colds and recovered more quickly than those taking the placebo.

Cumin-Spiked Lentil Soup with Eggplant and Dill

Although the combination of flavors in this soup is unusual, they work together like a charm. I like to serve this delicious concoction as a main course, followed by salad, for a light weekday dinner, but in smaller portions it's an ideal starter for a Mediterranean-themed dinner.

Makes 6 to 8 servings

Can Be Halved
(see Tips, below)

Tips

If you are halving this recipe, be sure to use a small (2 to 3½ quart) slow cooker.

I have not provided Make Ahead instructions for this soup because the partially cooked eggplant would become soggy if left to sit for any length of time.

Nutrients Per Serving

Calories	154
Protein	7.9 g
Carbohydrates	22.7 g
Fat (Total)	4.4 g
Saturated Fat	0.8 g
Monounsaturated Fat	2.8 g
Polyunsaturated Fat	0.5 g
Dietary Fiber	4.7 g
Sodium	14 mg
Cholesterol	1 mg

EXCELLENT SOURCE OF folate.

GOOD SOURCE of phosphorus, magnesium, potassium and iron.

SOURCE OF vitamins C, B$_6$ and K, calcium and zinc.

CONTAINS a high amount of dietary fiber.

- **Medium to large (3½ to 5 quart) slow cooker**

1	eggplant (about 1 lb/500 g), peeled and cut into 2-inch (5 cm) cubes	1
1 tsp	coarse sea salt	5 mL
2 tbsp	olive oil, divided (approx.)	30 mL
2	onions, finely chopped	2
4	cloves garlic, minced	4
½ tsp	cracked black peppercorns	2 mL
1 tbsp	cumin seeds, toasted and ground (see Tips, right)	15 mL
1 cup	green or brown lentils, picked over and rinsed	250 mL
6 cups	vegetable or chicken stock	1.5 L
1 tbsp	freshly squeezed lemon juice	15 mL
½ cup	finely chopped dill fronds	125 mL
½ cup	plain yogurt or vegan sour cream	125 mL

1. In a colander, combine eggplant and salt. Toss and let stand for 30 minutes. Rinse thoroughly under cold running water. Lay a clean tea towel on a work surface. Working in batches over the sink, squeeze liquid out of the eggplant. Transfer to tea towel. When batches are complete, roll the towel up and press down to remove remaining liquid.

2. In a skillet, heat 1 tbsp (15 mL) of the oil over medium heat. Add eggplant, in batches, and cook until browned, adding more oil as necessary. Transfer to stoneware.

3. Add onions to pan, adding more oil if necessary, and cook, stirring, until softened, about 3 minutes. Add garlic, peppercorns and cumin and cook, stirring, for 1 minute. Add lentils and toss until coated. Add stock and bring to a boil.

4. Transfer to slow cooker stoneware. Cover and cook on Low for 6 hours or on High for 3 hours, until lentils are tender. Stir in lemon juice and dill. Purée using an immersion blender. (You can also do this, in batches, in a food processor or stand blender.) To serve, ladle into bowls and add a dollop of yogurt.

Tip

To toast cumin seeds: Place in a dry skillet over medium heat and cook, stirring, until fragrant, about 3 minutes. Transfer to a spice grinder or mortar and grind finely.

Mindful Morsels

Dill has a long history in herbal medicine and as a natural food preservative. It is also very good for the digestion, preventing the formation of gas in your intestinal tract and inhibiting the growth of harmful bacteria, including those that reside in the urinary tract. So if you are prone to UTI's, consider adding dill to your diet. It's a wonderful accompaniment to fish, among other foods.

Natural Wonders

Age-Related Macular Degeneration

Recent research suggests that deteriorating vision as we age may not be inevitable and that consuming a variety of fruits and vegetables may reduce the risk of macular degeneration, the leading cause of declining vision in people over the age of 55. Various scholarly articles have examined the role of fruit and vegetable consumption in eye health and have concluded that increasing the quantity of two specific phytonutrients, lutein and zeaxanthin, may help to prevent age-related macular degeneration (AMD). The traditional medical approach to treating this illness is that there is no cure.

Lutein and zeaxanthin are carotenoids found in orange and yellow vegetables as well as leafy greens. These nutrients are so important for eye health that the body preferentially concentrates them in the macula, which is located in the back of your eye, a part of the retina. Light is concentrated on the macula, which enables vision. There powerful antioxidants help to prevent excessive damage from sunlight; think of lutein and zeaxanthin as internal sunglasses that protect the macula and help to preserve vision over the years. In some cases, they team up to do their work with a third carotenoid, meso-zeaxanthin, to prevent or slow the progression of AMD. Meso-zeaxanthin is not found in foods, but your body may make it from the lutein you provide.

Research done at Harvard suggests that 6 mg of lutein a day could reduce the risk of AMD by as much as 43%. Another 2011 study of 60 men with early AMD found that 8 mg per day of dietary zeaxanthin over the course of a year, improved night vision and fine detail recognition to the point of being able to read 1.5 lines further down an eye chart. Women are at greater risk for AMD than men because they have approximately 20% less macular pigment in their eyes.

Egg yolks are one of the best food sources of both lutein and zeaxanthin. According to information provided by the American Egg Board, a large egg yolk contains 252 mcg of lutein and zeaxanthin combined. Although this is significantly less than some other foods, studies show that your body absorbs these nutrients from egg yolks better than from other sources. Kale, spinach, Swiss chard and other leafy greens are also good sources, as are yellow vegetables such as corn, zucchini and various kinds of squash. Since leafy greens are high in lutein but low in zeaxanthin, it makes sense to combine these foods with a source that is high in zeaxanthin, such as orange bell pepper.

Creamy Parsnip, Parsley Root and Butterbean Soup

The creaminess in this delicious soup comes from the puréed butterbeans. It's a wonderful winter soup, full of highly nutritious vegetables. This makes a generous serving so it's perfect for a light supper, accompanied by a salad. But it is elegant enough to be served in small portions as the prelude to an important meal.

Makes 6 to 8 servings

Can Be Halved
(see Tips, below)

Tips

If you are halving this recipe, be sure to use a small (approx. 2 quart) slow cooker.

If you prefer, substitute 3 cups (750 mL) frozen lima beans for the dried ones and skip Step 1.

The nutritional analysis on this soup was based on using Basic Vegetable Stock (page 120), which is particularly low in sodium. Be aware that if you use a prepared stock, the sodium content of this recipe will increase.

Nutrients Per Serving

Calories	146
Protein	7.1 g
Carbohydrates	26.2 g
Fat (Total)	2.2 g
Saturated Fat	0.3 g
Monounsaturated Fat	1.3 g
Polyunsaturated Fat	0.4 g
Dietary Fiber	7.8 g
Sodium	160 mg
Cholesterol	0 mg

EXCELLENT SOURCE OF folate and potassium.
GOOD SOURCE OF magnesium and iron.

• **Medium to large (3½ to 5 quart) slow cooker**

1¼ cups	dried butterbeans or lima beans (see Tips, left)	300 mL
1 tbsp	olive oil	15 mL
1	onion, finely chopped	1
2 tbsp	minced shallots (about 2 small)	30 mL
2	stalks celery, diced	2
2 cups	cubed (1 inch/2.5 cm) peeled parsnips (about 3 medium) (see Tips, right)	500 mL
1 cup	cubed (1 inch/2.5 cm) peeled parsley root (4 medium)	250 mL
	Sea salt	
½ tsp	cracked black peppercorns	2 mL
2	bay leaves	2
6 cups	vegetable or chicken stock, divided (see Tips, right)	1.5 L
	Cayenne pepper, optional	
	Finely chopped parsley leaves	
	Heavy or whipping (35%) cream or soy creamer, optional	

1. In a large pot of water, bring beans to a boil over medium heat. Boil rapidly for 3 minutes. Cover, turn off heat and let stand for 1 hour. Drain in a colander placed over a sink and rinse thoroughly under cold running water. Using your hands, pop the beans out of their skins. Discard skins. Set beans aside.

2. In a skillet, heat oil over medium heat. Add onion, shallots, celery, parsnips and parsley root and cook, stirring, until softened, about 5 minutes. Add ½ tsp (2 mL) salt, peppercorns and bay leaves and cook, stirring, for 1 minute. Stir in skinned beans and 2 cups (500 mL) of the stock. Bring to a boil and boil for 1 minute.

Tips

Parsnips and parsley root have a tendency to oxidize if exposed to air. If you are preparing these vegetables ahead of time, place them in an acidulated solution (8 cups/2 L water combined with 3 tbsp/45 mL lemon juice). Drain well before adding to the slow cooker.

Some prepared vegetable broths have very strong flavor, which may overpower the ingredients in this soup. If you are using one of these, I suggest you reduce the quantity to 4 cups (1 L) and add 2 cups (500 mL) water.

Make Ahead

Complete Steps 1 and 2. Cover and refrigerate for up to 2 days. When you're ready to cook, complete the recipe.

3. Transfer to slow cooker stoneware. Add remaining 4 cups (1 L) of stock and stir well. Cover and cook on Low for 6 hours or on High for 3 hours, until vegetables are very tender.

4. Discard bay leaves. Purée using an immersion blender. (You can also do this in batches in a food processor or stand blender.) Add cayenne, to taste, if using, and season with salt, to taste. To serve, ladle into bowls and garnish with parsley. Drizzle with cream, if using.

Mindful Morsels

Shallots have been described as French chefs' secret ingredient. They have a delightful ability to add the flavors of onion and garlic to dishes in a very gentle way. Like their more forceful relatives, shallots are a member of the allium family and have an impressive array of disease-fighting capabilities (see Natural Wonders, page 171).

Natural Wonders

Non-GMO Foods

Agribusiness spends a great deal of money promoting the idea that genetically modified foods are not only safe, but also the key to ending world hunger. However, the evidence on both those points is sparse, and it's basically because the companies that control these crops are actively suppressing research into, and information about, their products on all possible fronts. In 2012, this included their generous funding (to the tune of $45 million dollars), to defeat Proposition 37, the so-called " Right to Know" legislation in California, which sought to require the labeling of genetically modified foods. Basically, genetically modified foods can continue to be used throughout the food chain with consumers having little idea where they might be lurking.

Genetically modified foods were introduced commercially in 1996. Although some scientists questioned the unpredictability of genetic engineering and raised the possibility that genetic modification might produce a cascade of unexpected results, the U.S. government treated the products like traditional foods and allowed them to market without the safety testing required for other ingestibles, such as pharmaceuticals. They also did not demand that these new entities have any special labeling.

Field (yellow dent) corn, soybeans and canola are the major GM crops, but genetically modified versions of sugar beets, alfalfa, Hawaiian papaya, zucchini and yellow crookneck squash are also widely grown and marketed. In 2010, 95% of the sugar beets grown in the U.S. were genetically engineered. While you may like to think that by using your eyes you can avoid eating these foods, consider, for instance, that genetically modified corn ends up in products as diverse as corn oil, cornmeal, breakfast cereals, and snack foods such as tortilla chips and taco shells. And that doesn't include the high-fructose corn syrup that sweetens many processed foods, including soda. Also, genetically engineered foods permeate the food supply as animal feed and may end up in your stomach when you enjoy, for instance, a delicious steak, because that grain-fed steer was fed a diet of GMO corn. Alarmingly, GM food can travel even further than that. Traces of one genetically modified crop, which was restricted to use in animal feed, were found in taco shells taking up real estate on supermarket shelves.

My point is, even if you are super-vigilant you may end up eating GM food whether you want to or not, so the question is, are these foods as safe as we are led to believe? The answer is, we don't really know but the little available evidence suggests they are not. In a 2009 paper published in *Critical Reviews in Food Science and Nutrition*, Greek researchers reviewed the evidence (all animal studies) and found possible links between the consumption of genetically modified foods and negative effects on a wide variety of bodily functions, ranging from the liver and kidneys to the gastrointestinal tract and increased allergic responses. Another Canadian study found that the DNA of bacteria dwelling in soil where GMO crops were grown appeared to be altered. The only human study, "Assessing the survival of transgenic plant DNA in the human gastrointestinal tract," published in *Nature Biotechnology* in 2004, found genetic contamination extending into the human gut.

This is not good news. I, like many intelligent well-informed people I know, am becoming increasingly convinced that the proliferation of genetically modified foods may be contributing to the so called "epidemic" of autoimmune diseases (among others) that have been linked to imbalanced gut flora and damaged intestinal walls.

The good news, agritech companies tell us, is that GMO seed allows farmers to produce more food under more unpredictable conditions, thereby feeding more people and reducing world hunger. However, the Union of Concerned Scientists commissioned a report, published in 2009, that found genetically engineered corn and soybeans did not increase yield over conventional seeds. Agritech companies also claim that GMO seeds reduce the use of herbicides and pesticides, thereby reducing the environmental impact of agriculture. Not so, say the few studies that have actually been conducted. The well-regarded 2012 Benbrook study found that between 1996 and 2008, genetically engineered crops actually increased the use of herbicides. This may be having unintended effects on biodiversity. A November 2013 article in *The New York Times* on the dramatic decline in insect populations raised the issue of the herbicide Roundup, which was developed for use on genetically modified crops and kills virtually all conventional plants it comes in contact with. This has resulted in a massive loss of native vegetation, which was a crucial food source for insects such as bees and Monarch butterflies.

However, studies on GMO seeds have been few and far between. In 2009, *Scientific American* took the agritech companies to task for this situation. As they wrote in an editorial "it is impossible to verify that genetically modified crops perform as advertised." The reason, the editors said, is that these companies have used the intellectual property laws to prevent researchers from publishing any information on their products. Their user agreements "have explicitly forbidden the use of their seeds for any independent research."

Not only can scientists not do independent research into genetically modified crops, since food labeling laws have never been passed in the United States, it's impossible to track the proliferation of GM foods throughout the food supply. However, some groups, such as Whole Foods and the Non-GMO Shopping Guide are committed to doing just that. Whole Foods has made a commitment to labeling genetically engineered products by 2018. Moreover, some 150 brands are enrolled in the Non-GMO project and their site also includes shopping tips on avoiding genetically modified foods. Visit them at: www.nongmoshoppingguide.com

Curried Parsnip Soup with Green Peas

Flavorful and elegant, this soup makes a great introduction to a more substantial meal or a satisfying lunch.

Makes 8 servings

Can Be Halved
(see Tips, page 82)

Tips

The nutritional analysis on this soup was based on using Basic Vegetable Stock (page 120), which is particularly low in sodium. If you use a prepared stock, the sodium content of this recipe will increase.

To enhance the Asian flavors and expand the range of nutrients, substitute extra virgin coconut oil for the olive oil. Its flavors blend very well with the others in this recipe.

Nutrients Per Serving

Calories	176
Protein	4 g
Carbohydrates	24.1 g
Fat (Total)	8.4 g
Saturated Fat	5.6 g
Monounsaturated Fat	1.8 g
Polyunsaturated Fat	0.4 g
Dietary Fiber	5.4 g
Sodium	38 mg
Cholesterol	0 mg

EXCELLENT SOURCE OF folate.
GOOD SOURCE OF magnesium, potassium and iron.
SOURCE OF vitamins A, B$_6$, C and K, calcium, phosphorus and zinc.
CONTAINS a very high amount of dietary fiber.

- **Large (approx. 5 quart) slow cooker**
- **Food processor or blender**

1 tbsp	olive oil or extra virgin coconut oil	15 mL
2	onions, finely chopped	2
4	cloves garlic, minced	4
2 tsp	ground cumin (see Tip, page 81)	10 mL
2 tsp	ground coriander	10 mL
½ tsp	cracked black peppercorns	2 mL
1	piece (1 inch/2.5 cm) cinnamon stick	1
1	bay leaf	1
6 cups	vegetable or chicken stock (see Tips, left)	1.5 L
6 cups	sliced peeled parsnips (about 1½ lbs/750 g) (see Tip, right)	1.5 L
1 cup	coconut milk	250 mL
2 tsp	curry powder	10 mL
2 cups	sweet green peas, thawed if frozen	500 mL

1. In a skillet, heat oil over medium heat. Add onions and cook, stirring, until softened, about 3 minutes. Add garlic, cumin, coriander, peppercorns, cinnamon stick and bay leaf and cook, stirring, for 1 minute.

2. Transfer to slow cooker stoneware. Add vegetable stock and parsnips and stir well. Cover and cook on Low for 6 hours or on High for 3 hours, until parsnips are tender. Discard cinnamon stick and bay leaf.

3. Working in batches, purée soup in a food processor or blender. (You can also do this in the stoneware using an immersion blender.)

4. In a small bowl, combine ¼ cup (60 mL) of the coconut milk and curry powder. Mix well. Add to slow cooker stoneware along with the remaining coconut milk and peas. Cover and cook on High for 20 minutes, until peas are tender and flavors meld.

Tip

If you are using large parsnips in this recipe, cut away the woody core and discard.

Make Ahead

This dish can be partially prepared before it is cooked. Complete Step 1, adding a bit of the vegetable stock to the mixture. Cover and refrigerate overnight or for up to 2 days. When you're ready to cook, complete the recipe.

Natural Wonders

Parsnips

When thinking about vegetables, parsnips are usually a bit of an afterthought, which is unfortunate. I love their sweet, nutty flavor, and they make a refreshing change from more common root vegetables, such as turnips and carrots, particularly during the winter, when they are widely available and at their sweetest. In fact, the best parsnips are harvested after the first frost, just when the supply of other fresh local vegetables begins to taper off.

Their positive nutritional profile is another reason for consuming this vegetable, which belongs to the family (Umbelliferous) that includes carrots, celery, coriander and parsley. The parsnips in one serving of this soup (approximately 100 g) provide 71 calories (4% of the DV) and about 22% of the DV for vitamin C, 14% for folate, 15% for manganese and 10% for potassium, among other vitamins and minerals. They also provide 2.8 grams of fiber, more than half the amount in one serving of this soup.

And like all fruits and vegetables, parsnips contain a variety of phytonutrients. Scientists are studying their phenolic acids for their anticarcinogenic properties and British studies suggest that the polyacetylene compounds in parsnips may be anti-fungal and anti-inflammatory, as well as anticarcinogenic.

Pepper Pot Soup

This delicious vegetable soup is a meal in itself and it's so good, you'll want seconds — assuming you have room because this is a very generous serving (about 2 cups/500 mL). I particularly like the way the sweetness of the coconut sugar and the coconut milk combines with the heat of the chile.

Makes 8 servings

Can Be Halved
(see Tips, page 90)

Tip

Although any chile pepper will provide heat, only Scotch bonnet or habanero peppers, truly capture the flavor of the Caribbean, where this recipe originated. Short, squat and slightly wrinkled and ranging in color from yellow to red to green, these superhot chiles have, depending on the variety, unique smoky and/ or fruity flavors in addition to powerful heat. Be particularly cautious when handling them, as they are among the world's hottest peppers.

Nutrients Per Serving

Calories	248
Protein	7.2 g
Carbohydrates	31.4 g
Fat (Total)	12.5 g
Saturated Fat	9.3 g
Monounsaturated Fat	1.8 g
Polyunsaturated Fat	0.6 g
Dietary Fiber	7.3 g
Sodium	161 mg
Cholesterol	0 mg

EXCELLENT SOURCE OF folate, potassium and iron.

GOOD SOURCE OF vitamins A, B_6, C and K, magnesium and phosphorus.

SOURCE OF calcium and zinc.

CONTAINS a very high amount of dietary fiber.

• **Medium (approx. 4 quart) slow cooker**

1 tbsp	olive or extra virgin coconut oil	15 mL
2	onions, finely chopped	2
4	stalks celery, peeled and thinly sliced	4
4	cloves garlic, minced	4
1 tbsp	minced gingerroot	15 mL
1 tsp	ground coriander (see Step 1, page 170)	5 mL
1 tsp	cracked black peppercorns	5 mL
½ tsp	sea salt	2 mL
1 tbsp	coconut sugar	15 mL
4 cups	acorn or butternut squash, peeled and cut into ½-inch (1 cm) cubes, or 4 cups (1 L) carrots, peeled and thinly sliced	1 L
2 cups	cooked red kidney beans (see Tips, page 180)	500 mL
1	can (28 oz/796 mL) no-salt added tomatoes, including juice, chopped	1
4 cups	vegetable or chicken stock (see Tips, page 86)	1 L
1	can (14 oz/400 mL) coconut milk	1
2 tbsp	chili powder (see Tip, right)	30 mL
1	green bell pepper, diced	1
½ to 1	Scotch bonnet or habanero chile pepper, finely chopped (see Tip, left)	½ to 1
½ cup	finely chopped cilantro or parsley	125 mL

1. In a skillet, heat oil over medium heat. Add onions and celery and cook, stirring, until softened, about 5 minutes. Add garlic, ginger, coriander, peppercorns and salt and cook, stirring, for 1 minute. Add sugar and stir to combine. Add squash, kidney beans and tomatoes with juice.

2. Transfer to slow cooker stoneware. Stir in stock. Cover and cook on Low for 6 hours or on High for 3 hours, until vegetables are tender.

3. In a small bowl, combine ¼ cup (60 mL) of the coconut milk and the chili powder. Mix well. Add to slow cooker stoneware along with the remaining coconut milk, bell pepper and chile pepper. Cover and cook on High for another 15 to 20 minutes, until heated through. Garnish with cilantro.

Tip

Check your chili powder to make sure it is gluten-free.

Make Ahead

Complete Step 1. Cover and refrigerate mixture for up to 2 days. When you're ready to cook, complete the recipe.

Mindful Morsels

A serving of this soup provides 87 mcg of folate and is an excellent source of that B vitamin (see Natural Wonders, page 269). Folate has a role in many bodily functions, including keeping the DNA in your cells working well. Most of the folate in this recipe (57 mcg) comes from the red kidney beans, but the squash, onions, celery and coconut milk all provide small amounts, as well.

Natural Wonders

Chile Peppers

From mild and fruity to smoky and just plain fiery, chiles add depth as well as heat to any dish. They also add nutrition and medicinal value. Ounce for ounce, chile peppers are one of the best food sources of vitamin C. One chile pepper, which provides 18 calories (1% of the DV), delivers a whopping 108% of the DV for this important antioxidant, in addition to other valuable nutrients. With their ability to clear congestion, chiles have long been used as a natural remedy for the common cold. And as a source of the antioxidants vitamin C and beta-carotene, they also support your immune system.

In general terms, the hotter the chile, the more health benefits it is likely to have. That's because heat levels are related to the amount of capsaicin the chile contains. Capsaicin is concentrated in the veins of the pepper. It's the substance that gives chiles their burn and also provides many of their health benefits. Basically, capsaicin triggers a neurotransmitter response that is a proven pain reliever. Used in topical creams, capsaicin has been found to reduce the pain associated with osteoarthritis. Capsaicin is also a metabolism booster. Several studies suggest it increases the rate at which your body burns calories and reduces your appetite. So if you are trying to lose weight, you might be smart to eat more chiles.

Epidemiological studies indicate that countries where large quantities of chile peppers are consumed have lower rates of cardiovascular disease. A number of factors may be relevant. Research indicates, for instance, that capsaicin has anticoagulant properties. Animal studies show it reduces LDL ("bad") cholesterol and also that it may prevent dangerous heart arrhythmias. And, if you think it was those chiles you had with dinner that upset your tummy, you may need to think again. Research done in India indicates that eating chiles may actually help to prevent and heal ulcers.

Another study, published in the *New England Journal of Medicine* found that people who consumed 2.5 g of red chile powder a day, reduced their symptoms of dyspepsia, a digestive disorder.

Today, scientists are exploring the ability of chile peppers to fight heart attacks and strokes, as well as cancer and chronic conditions such as psoriasis and type-2 diabetes. As the research continues we'll discover more and more health benefits to consuming these fiery little foods. In the meantime, think about turning up the heat when you eat.

Thai-Style Pumpkin Soup

This soup is both versatile and delicious. It has an exotic combination of flavors and works well as a prelude to a meal. If you prefer a more substantial soup, top each serving with cooked shrimp or scallops, or add some brown rice (see Variation, right).

Makes 8 servings

Can Be Halved
(see Tips, below)

Tips

If you are halving this recipe, be sure to use a small (2 to 3½ quart) slow cooker.

For best results, toast and grind cumin seeds yourself. Place in a dry skillet over medium heat and cook, stirring, until fragrant, about 3 minutes. Immediately transfer to a spice grinder or mortar and grind finely.

Check the label to make sure your curry paste does not contain gluten.

Nutrients Per Serving

Calories	130
Protein	2.5 g
Carbohydrates	14.3 g
Fat (Total)	8.4 g
Saturated Fat	5.7 g
Monounsaturated Fat	1.8 g
Polyunsaturated Fat	0.4 g
Fiber	2.4 g
Sodium	9 mg
Cholesterol	0 mg

GOOD SOURCE OF vitamin A, magnesium, potassium and iron.

SOURCE OF vitamin C and phosphorus.

CONTAINS a moderate amount of dietary fiber.

- **Large (approx. 5 quart) slow cooker**
- **Food processor or blender**

1 tbsp	olive oil or extra virgin coconut oil	15 mL
2	onions, finely chopped	2
4	cloves garlic, minced	4
2 tbsp	minced gingerroot	30 mL
1 tsp	cracked black peppercorns	5 mL
2	stalks lemongrass, trimmed, smashed and cut in half crosswise	2
1 tbsp	ground cumin (see Tips, left)	15 mL
6 cups	vegetable or chicken stock, divided (see Tips, right)	1.5 L
8 cups	cubed, peeled pumpkin or other orange squash (2-inch/5 cm cubes)	2 L
1 cup	coconut milk	250 mL
1 tsp	Thai red curry paste (see Tips, left)	5 mL
	Finely grated zest and juice of 1 lime	
¼ cup	toasted pumpkin seeds, optional	60 mL
	Cherry tomatoes, halved, optional	
	Finely chopped cilantro	

1. In a skillet, heat oil over medium heat. Add onions and cook, stirring, until softened, about 3 minutes. Add garlic, ginger, peppercorns, lemongrass and cumin and cook, stirring, for 1 minute. Add 1 cup (250 mL) of the stock and stir well.

2. Transfer to slow cooker stoneware. Add pumpkin and remaining stock. Cover and cook on Low for 6 hours or on High for 3 hours, until pumpkin is tender. Skim off 1 tbsp (15 mL) of the coconut milk. In a small bowl, combine with curry paste and blend well. Add to slow cooker along with remaining coconut milk and lime zest and juice. Cover and cook on High until heated through, about 20 minutes. Discard lemongrass.

3. Working in batches, purée soup in a food processor or blender. (You can also do this in the stoneware using an immersion blender.) Ladle into bowls, and garnish with pumpkin seeds and tomatoes, if using, and cilantro.

Tip

The nutritional analysis on this soup was based on using Basic Vegetable Stock (page 120), which is particularly low in sodium. Be aware that if you use a prepared stock, the sodium content of this recipe will increase.

Make Ahead

This soup can be partially prepared before it is cooked. Complete Step 1. Cover and refrigerate overnight or for up to 2 days. When you're ready to cook, complete the recipe.

Variation

For a more substantial soup, add 1 cup (250 mL) brown rice, rinsed, along with the pumpkin. You can also finish the soup with a topping of cooked salad shrimp or scallops (about 1 lb/500 g). If using scallops, pat them dry, cut into quarters and dust with 1 tsp (5 mL) of your favorite chili powder. Sauté in 1 tbsp (15 mL) olive or coconut oil, in 2 batches, for about $1\frac{1}{2}$ minutes per side.

Mindful Morsels

I like to garnish this soup with toasted pumpkin seeds because they add pleasing texture and flavor as well as nutrients. Pumpkin seeds provide linoleic fatty acids, vitamin E, magnesium, niacin (vitamin B_3), vegetable protein and iron, among other nutrients.

Natural Wonders

Coconut Oil

Almost all of the saturated fat in this recipe comes from the coconut milk. For decades, coconut oil, the fat in coconut milk, has been derided as a health hazard because it contains a significant amount of saturated fat. Now, not only has our thinking about saturated fat changed, but researchers are also piecing together a case urging the inclusion of coconut oil in our diets and many believe it to be a superfood. Coconut oil is very high in antioxidants and lauric acid, a component of breast milk, which appears to be an excellent immune-system booster. It is a "medium chain triglyceride" fat, which means it is easily metabolized and quickly burned by the body for energy, so it doesn't collect around your middle. One Brazilian study specifically linked the consumption of coconut oil with reduced abdominal fat. It also concluded that consumption of coconut oil did not increase LDL ("bad") cholesterol, while raising levels of HDL (heart healthy cholesterol).

Two-Bean Soup with Pistou

I love the flavors in this classic French country soup: the hint of licorice in the fennel and the nip of paprika is nicely balanced by the pleasing blandness of the potatoes and beans.

Makes 8 servings

Can Be Halved
(see Tips, page 100)

Tips

Adding the green beans while they are still frozen ensures that they will not be mushy when the soup has finished cooking. If you prefer to use fresh green beans, cut them into 2-inch (5 cm) lengths and cook them in a pot of boiling salted water for 4 minutes, until tender crisp. Add them to the slow cooker after stirring in the paprika.

To toast fennel seeds: Place in a dry skillet over medium heat and cook, stirring, until seeds are fragrant, about 3 minutes. Transfer to a mortar or a spice grinder and grind.

Nutrients Per Serving

Calories	270
Protein	10.4 g
Carbohydrates	35.2 g
Fat (Total)	11.1 g
Saturated Fat	2.4 g
Monounsaturated Fat	6.8 g
Polyunsaturated Fat	1.1 g
Fiber	10.0 g
Sodium	549 mg
Cholesterol	5 mg

EXCELLENT SOURCE OF vitamins A and K and potassium.

GOOD SOURCE OF vitamins C and B_6, folate, magnesium, calcium, phosphorus and iron.

CONTAINS a very high amount of dietary fiber.

• **Large (approx. 5 quart) slow cooker**

1 tbsp	olive oil	15 mL
3	onions, finely chopped	3
2	carrots, peeled and diced	2
1	bulb fennel, trimmed and sliced (see page 294)	1
1 tsp	fennel seeds, toasted (see Tips, left)	5 mL
1	can (28 oz/796 mL) diced tomatoes, including juice	1
6 cups	vegetable or chicken stock	1.5 L
2	potatoes, peeled and shredded	2
4 cups	cooked white beans (see Mindful Morsels, page 94 and Tips, page 126)	1 L
2 cups	frozen sliced green beans	500 mL
2 tsp	paprika dissolved in 1 tbsp (15 mL) water	10 mL
	Sea salt, optional	
	Freshly ground black pepper	

Pistou

1 cup	packed fresh basil leaves	250 mL
4	cloves garlic, minced	4
½ cup	finely grated Parmesan cheese	125 mL
¼ cup	extra virgin olive oil	60 mL

1. In a skillet, heat oil over medium heat. Add onions, carrots and fennel bulb and cook, stirring, until vegetables are softened, about 7 minutes. Add toasted fennel seeds and cook, stirring, for 1 minute. Add tomatoes with juice and bring to a boil. Transfer to slow cooker stoneware.

2. Add stock, potatoes, white beans and green beans. Cover and cook on Low for 6 hours or on High for 3 hours, until vegetables are tender. Stir in paprika solution and season to taste with salt, if using, and pepper. Cover and cook on High for 20 minutes.

3. *Pistou:* In a food processor fitted with a metal blade, combine basil, garlic and Parmesan. Process until smooth. Slowly add olive oil down the feeder tube until integrated. Ladle soup into bowls and top each serving with a dollop of pistou.

more information on page 94

Make Ahead

You can partially prepare this soup ahead of time. Complete Step 1. Cover and refrigerate overnight or for up to 2 days. When you're ready to cook, continue with Steps 2 and 3.

Mindful Morsels

We tested Two-Bean Soup with Pistou using regular canned beans, which are high in sodium. The beans in this recipe contribute 251 mg of sodium per serving. To reduce sodium, cook your own or use canned tomatoes with no added salt.

Natural Wonders

What About Fiber?

There are two kinds of fiber — insoluble and soluble. The substance we traditionally associate with fiber is insoluble fiber, which doesn't dissolve in water. Insoluble fiber absorbs water in your digestive track and moves waste through your system, preventing constipation. The other kind of fiber, soluble fiber, does dissolve in water, forming a gel-like substance. This type has been linked with many health benefits. For instance, it helps to control blood sugar levels by slowing down the rate at which food breaks down in your digestive track, thereby reducing the likelihood that your blood sugar will spike. A third type of fiber is a carbohydrate known as resistant starch, which passes to the large intestine undigested, where it ferments and seeds the growth of beneficial bacteria.

Most people in North America do not consume enough fiber. Adult women should consume 21 to 25 grams a day, while men should eat 30 to 38 grams a day. Some health professionals recommend that children should consume, on a daily basis, an amount equal to or greater than their age plus 5 grams. Despite its many benefits, now well supported by research, no daily value has been established for soluble fiber intake. However, nutritionists generally recommend that 20 to 30% of your total daily intake of fiber be the soluble type. A diet high in whole grains, legumes and high-fiber fruits and vegetables such as bananas and okra will help you to meet these goals.

Although the connection between increased intake of soluble fiber and lower blood cholesterol levels has been long established, more recent research indicates that fiber may have even more health-promoting properties than we thought. Consider, for instance, a 2012 study published in the *Journal of Nutrition* that linked dietary fiber with improvements to gut flora. Researchers found not only that the consumption of any type of fiber increased positive bacteria in general, but also that specific types of fiber promoted the growth of different types of bacteria. For instance, the consumption of soluble corn fiber increased production of lactobacillus, a common ingredient in over-the-counter probiotics.

Gut flora has become a hot button topic in medical circles, and researchers have associated unbalanced flora with a vast array of diseases ranging from weakened immune systems to autoimmune disorders such as rheumatoid arthritis. In fact, some researchers have gone so far as to link specific species of microbes with particular disorders. It has been suggested that we may be able to look forward to the day when physicians will be able to prevent the onset of a serious illness by prescribing specific probiotics that would deter its development. In the meantime, consuming appropriate amounts of fiber, from as wide a variety of foods as possible, also looks like a positive preventive strategy.

Beet Soup with Lemongrass and Lime

This Thai-inspired soup, which is served cold, is elegant and refreshing. Its jewel-like appearance and intriguing flavors make it a perfect prelude to any meal. I especially like to serve it at summer dinners in the garden.

Makes 8 servings

Can Be Halved
(see Tips, below)

Tips

If you are halving this recipe, be sure to use a small (1½ to 3½ quart) slow cooker.

I often use coconut oil when making this soup because its pleasantly nutty taste complements the Thai flavors in this soup. Moreover, in recent years significant health benefits have been identified in this food (see Natural Wonders, page 91).

Nutrients Per Serving

Calories	85
Protein	2.4 g
Carbohydrates	16.3 g
Fat (Total)	2.0 g
Saturated Fat	0.3 g
Monounsaturated Fat	1.3 g
Polyunsaturated Fat	0.3 g
Dietary Fiber	2.9 g
Sodium	85 mg
Cholesterol	0 mg

EXCELLENT SOURCE OF vitamin C and folate.

GOOD SOURCE OF potassium.

SOURCE OF vitamin A.

CONTAINS a moderate amount of dietary fiber.

- **Medium to large (3½ to 5 quart) slow cooker**

1 tbsp	olive oil or extra virgin coconut oil (see Tips, left)	15 mL
1	onion, chopped	1
4	cloves garlic, minced	4
2 tbsp	minced gingerroot	30 mL
2	stalks lemongrass, trimmed, smashed and cut in half crosswise	2
2 tsp	cracked black peppercorns	10 mL
6	medium beets, peeled and chopped (about 2½ lbs/1.25 kg)	6
6 cups	vegetable stock	1.5 L
1	red bell pepper, seeded and diced	1
1	long red chile pepper, seeded and diced, optional	1
	Zest and juice of 1 lime	
	Sea salt, optional	
	Coconut cream, optional	
	Finely chopped cilantro	

1. In a skillet, heat oil over medium heat. Add onion and cook, stirring, until softened, about 3 minutes. Add garlic, ginger, lemongrass and peppercorns and cook, stirring, for 1 minute. Transfer to slow cooker stoneware.

2. Add beets and stock. Cover and cook on Low for 6 to 8 hours or on High for 3 to 4 hours, until beets are tender. Add red pepper and chile pepper, if using. Cover and cook on High for 30 minutes, until peppers are tender. Remove lemongrass and discard.

3. Working in batches, purée soup in a food processor or blender. (You can also do this in the stoneware using an immersion blender.) Transfer to a large bowl. Stir in lime zest and juice. Season to taste with salt, if using. Chill thoroughly, preferably overnight.

4. When ready to serve, spoon into individual bowls, drizzle with coconut cream, if using, and garnish with cilantro.

more information on page 97

Beet Soup with Lemongrass and Lime

Make Ahead

Ideally, make this soup the day before you intend to serve it so it can chill overnight in the refrigerator.

Mindful Morsels

The peppers in this recipe provide capsaicin, which has many health benefits (see Natural Wonders, page 89).

Natural Wonders

Beets

Over half of the carbohydrates in one serving of this soup (10.7 grams) come from the beets, which are extremely nutritious. The consumption of beets, especially in the form of freshly squeezed beet juice, has long been a folk medicine tonic, where it is thought to be an excellent liver cleanser and detoxifier. Current research appears to confirm that assumption. The consumption of beetroot juice has also been linked with lower blood pressure and a consequent reduction in the risk of cardiovascular disease. Recent evidence indicates that eating beets may also help your body defend itself against cancer and other diseases.

Beets contain anthocyanins, a group of phytonutrients that researchers are studying for their ability to fight cancer and their anti-inflammatory powers, among other benefits. Betaine, the compound that gives beets their deep red color, is a powerful antioxidant and anti-inflammatory. Studies indicate that people who consume the most betaine from food are the least likely to have blood markers for inflammation such as C-reactive protein. Betaine has also been linked with lower levels of homocysteine. In alternative medicine, high levels of homocysteine are associated with an increased risk of heart disease and stroke.

High in natural sugar yet low in calories, beets are also an excellent source of folate, an important B vitamin that can be challenging to obtain through dietary sources. Beets also provide potassium, which helps your muscles and metabolism to function (see Natural Wonders, page 49). They also contain phytonutrients that appear to bind cholesterol in the digestive tract, protecting the body against heart disease. And beets are a vegetable that buys into the concept of nose-to-tail eating, associated with meat. Beet greens, as well as the root, are extremely nutritious. They are particularly rich in the carotenoids beta-carotene and lutein. In culinary terms they resemble Swiss chard. Toss small leaves into salads, steam or sauté larger ones or add them to soup, as you would any leafy green.

One word of caution: Because beets — especially the greens — contain oxalic acid people with kidney or gallbladder problems may want to be cautious about eating them. And don't panic if you see red in your urine or stool after eating beets. It's not blood, but beeturia, a harmless condition resulting from the consumption of betaine.

Gingery Carrot Soup with Orange and Parsley

In my books, carrots and ginger always make a superlative combination. Here, they are enhanced with zesty orange and a hit of earthy parsley to produce a delicious and versatile soup. Serve this with a tossed green salad for a light but nourishing supper or as a first course to a more substantial meal. If you prefer a creamy soup and a hint of exotic coconut flavor, add a drizzle of coconut milk and use coconut oil to soften the onions.

Makes 8 servings

Can Be Halved
(see Tips, page 95)

Tips

If you find ginger a bit assertive, use the smaller amount. If you like its flavor go for the larger quantity.

Because you are using the skin of the fruit to add flavor to this soup, I recommend buying organically grown oranges for use in this recipe.

Use flat-leaf rather than curly parsley because it has more flavor.

Nutrients Per Serving

Calories	88
Protein	1.8 g
Carbohydrates	16.8 g
Fat (Total)	2.1 g
Saturated Fat	0.3 g
Monounsaturated Fat	1.3 g
Polyunsaturated Fat	0.3 g
Dietary Fiber	3.0 g
Sodium	58 mg
Cholesterol	0 mg

EXCELLENT SOURCE OF vitamins A, C and K.

GOOD SOURCE OF potassium.

SOURCE OF vitamin B$_6$.

CONTAINS a moderate amount of dietary fiber.

- **Medium to large (3½ to 5 quart) slow cooker**
- **Food processor or blender**

1 tbsp	olive oil or extra virgin coconut oil	15 mL
2	onions, chopped	2
2 to 3 tbsp	minced gingerroot (see Tips, left)	30 to 45 mL
1 tbsp	finely grated orange zest (see Tips, left)	15 mL
1 tsp	cracked black peppercorns	5 mL
2	bay leaves	2
6 cups	thinly sliced peeled carrots (about 6 large carrots)	1.5 L
4 cups	vegetable or chicken stock	1 L
1½ cups	freshly squeezed orange juice	375 mL
1 cup	packed parsley leaves (see Tips, left)	250 mL
	Sea salt, optional	
	Coconut milk, optional	

1. In a skillet, heat oil over medium heat. Add onions and cook, stirring, until softened, about 3 minutes. Add ginger, orange zest, peppercorns and bay leaves and cook, stirring, for 1 minute. Transfer to slow cooker stoneware. Add carrots and vegetable stock and stir well.

2. Cover and cook on Low for 6 hours or on High for 3 hours, until carrots are tender. Add orange juice and parsley. Cover and cook on High for 20 minutes, until heated through. Discard bay leaves.

3. Working in batches, purée soup in a food processor or blender. (You can also do this in the stoneware using an immersion blender.) Season to taste with salt, if using. Ladle into serving bowls and drizzle with coconut milk, if using. Serve hot.

Make Ahead

This soup can be partially prepared before cooking. Complete Step 1, cover and refrigerate overnight or for up to 2 days. When you're ready to cook, continue with Steps 2 and 3.

Natural Wonders

Carotenoids

Although it contains a range of nutrients, this soup is particularly rich in carotenoids. They are pigments that give plants their vibrant colors and there are more than 600 of these substances that we know of. Carotenoids act as powerful antioxidants, fighting off free radicals and preventing damage to your DNA. Carotenoids are the building blocks of vitamin A. They protect your body from numerous diseases, such as age-related macular degeneration (see Natural Wonders, page 81), heart disease and certain cancers. Studies show, for instance, that foods rich in the carotenoids lutein, zeaxanthin, lycopene, beta-carotene and alpha-carotene, may reduce the risk of breast cancer.

Beta-carotene, which is found in carrots, among other sources, is, perhaps, the best known of these phytonutrients. Among its potential benefits, beta-carotene is thought to boost the immune system. A 2003 study published in the *Asia Pacific Journal of Clinical Nutrition* found a link between dietary intake of beta-carotene and increased bone density in older women. Research indicates that food is the best source of this valuable nutrient, since recent studies testing the benefits of supplements have produced inconsistent results.

Another carotenoid, beta-cryptoxanthin, which is found in oranges, helps to keep your respiratory track healthy and may lower your risk of developing rheumatoid arthritis. It may also protect against esophageal, lung and colon cancers. One study indicated that a diet high in beta-cryptoxanthin might reduce the risk of lung cancer by as much as 30%.

Nettle and Asparagus Soup

This is a great soup to make in spring when nettles and asparagus are in season — at least in my part of the world. The delightful combination of earthy nettles and elegant asparagus speaks well to the locavore dictum that foods that grow together taste good when combined.

Makes 6 servings

Can Be Halved
(see Tips, below)

Tips

If you are halving this recipe, be sure to use a small (approx. 2 quart) slow cooker.

Nettle leaves can sting so be very careful not to touch them when they are raw. Blanching removes their nasty bite. Use tongs to remove them from their packaging and plunge them directly into the boiling water without touching them. Once blanched they are fine to touch.

Nutrients Per Serving

Calories	142
Protein	4.7 g
Carbohydrates	15.5 g
Fat (Total)	7.8 g
Saturated Fat	4.7 g
Monounsaturated Fat	2.1 g
Polyunsaturated Fat	0.4 g
Dietary Fiber	6.7 g
Sodium	316 mg
Cholesterol	23 mg

EXCELLENT SOURCE OF vitamins A and K, folate and calcium.

GOOD SOURCE OF magnesium and potassium.

SOURCE OF vitamins C and B$_6$, phosphorus, iron and zinc.

CONTAINS a very high amount of dietary fiber.

- **Medium to large (4 to 5 quart) slow cooker**

24	asparagus stalks (1½ bunches or 1½ lbs/750 g)	24
2 tbsp	butter or extra virgin olive oil	30 mL
2	onions, chopped	2
2	cloves garlic, minced	2
2 tbsp	brown rice, rinsed (see Tip, right)	30 mL
½ tsp	sea salt	2 mL
4 cups	vegetable or chicken stock (see Mindful Morsels, right)	1 L
4 cups	packed nettles, leaves and tender stems (see Tips, left)	1 L
¼ tsp	cayenne pepper	1 mL
2 tbsp	freshly squeezed lemon juice	30 mL
½ cup	finely snipped chives	125 mL
	Sea salt and freshly ground black pepper	
¼ cup	heavy or whipping (35%) cream or soy creamer	60 mL

1. Cut off asparagus tips and set aside. Peel stocks and chop into pieces (about 1 inch/2.5 cm). Set aside.

2. In a skillet, melt butter over medium heat. Add asparagus stalks, onions and garlic and cook, stirring, until onion is softened, about 3 minutes. Stir in rice and salt.

3. Transfer to slow cooker stoneware. Stir in stock. Cover and cook on Low for 6 hours or on High for 3 hours, until asparagus is tender.

4. Meanwhile, in a large pot of boiling salted water, blanch nettle leaves for 2 minutes. Drain and rinse under cold running water. Pluck leaves from stems and chop finely.

5. Dissolve cayenne in lemon juice and add to stoneware. Working in batches, purée soup in a food processor or blender. (You can also do this in the stoneware using an immersion blender.) Return to stoneware, if necessary. Add chives and reserved asparagus tips. Cover and cook on High for 15 minutes until asparagus tips are tender. Season to taste with salt and freshly ground pepper. Transfer to serving bowls. Drizzle with cream.

Tip

If you prefer, substitute 1 potato, shredded, for the brown rice.

Natural Wonders

Stinging Nettle

Stinging nettle has a long history in folk medicine. Nettle leaves are thought to be highly nutritious and have traditionally been used to promote milk production in nursing mothers. Certainly, they provide nutrients such as vitamins A and K and a range of B vitamins including folate. They also provide minerals such as calcium, magnesium and potassium.

In herbal medicine, nettle leaves have traditionally been used to treat joint pain, including that associated with osteoarthritis and gout (they have a diuretic effect, which may assist with eliminating toxins such as uric acid), and for inflammatory skin conditions such as eczema. Laboratory tests suggest that nettle leaves may also have a role in lowering blood pressure and preventing blood clots from forming. In at least one clinical trial nettle leaf was found to reduce the symptoms of hay fever, if taken at the onset of symptoms. In Europe, researchers have commonly used nettle root to treat benign prostatic hyperplasia (BPH), an enlarged prostate gland.

The leaves and stems of the stinging nettle plant are covered in fine hairs that release irritating chemicals when touched. Blanching them before using eliminates this potentially harmful effect.

Creamy Sunchoke Soup

If you live in northern regions where they grow wild, sunchokes, which are also known as Jerusalem artichokes, start coming into farmers' markets in the fall. This relative of the sunflower has a lovely crispy texture and a mild nutty flavor and makes a beautifully creamy soup with a uniquely delicate taste.

Makes 4 to 6 servings

Can Be Halved
(see Tips, page 112)

Tips

Jerusalem artichokes oxidize quickly. To prevent browning, place them in a large bowl of acidulated water (6 cups/1.5 L water combined with 2 tbsp/30 mL lemon juice). Drain well before adding to the slow cooker.

All the cholesterol in this soup is provided by the butter. If you have a problem with the cholesterol in foods, substitute olive oil, which contains no cholesterol.

Nutrients Per Serving

Calories	139
Protein	3.0 g
Carbohydrates	24.2 g
Fat (Total)	4.0 g
Saturated Fat	2.5 g
Monounsaturated Fat	1.0 g
Polyunsaturated Fat	0.2 g
Dietary Fiber	2.9 g
Sodium	190 mg
Cholesterol	10 mg

EXCELLENT SOURCE OF vitamin K and iron.

GOOD SOURCE OF potassium.

SOURCE OF vitamins A, C and B$_6$, folate, calcium, phosphorus and magnesium.

CONTAINS a moderate amount of dietary fiber.

- **Medium to large (3½ to 5 quart) slow cooker**

2 tbsp	butter or olive oil	30 mL
2	leeks, white part only with just a bit of green, cleaned and sliced (see Tip, page 105)	2
4	stalks celery, diced	4
2	cloves garlic, minced	2
½ tsp	sea salt	2 mL
½ tsp	cracked black peppercorns	2 mL
½ tsp	dried thyme	2 mL
1	bay leaf	1
4 cups	vegetable or chicken stock (see Tip, page 91)	1 L
3 cups	peeled, sliced (1 inch/2.5 cm) Jerusalem artichokes (see Tips, left)	750 mL
1	floury potato, peeled and shredded	1
¼ cup	finely chopped parsley leaves or snipped chives	60 mL
	Heavy or whipping (35%) cream or soy creamer, optional	

1. In a skillet, melt butter over medium heat. Add leeks and celery and cook, stirring, until softened, about 5 minutes. Add garlic, salt, peppercorns, thyme and bay leaf and cook, stirring, for 1 minute. Add stock and bring to a boil. Transfer to slow cooker stoneware.

2. Add Jerusalem artichokes and potato. Cover and cook on Low for 6 hours or on High for 3 hours, until chokes and potatoes are tender. Discard bay leaf. Purée using an immersion blender. (You can also do this in batches in a food processor or stand blender.) To serve, ladle into bowls, garnish liberally with parsley, and drizzle with cream, if using.

Make Ahead

Complete Step 1. Cover and refrigerate for up to 2 days. When you're ready to cook, complete the recipe.

Natural Wonders

Potatoes

I have used a floury potato to thicken this soup because floury potatoes are a great thickener. They are loaded with nutrients, which makes them preferable to ingredients such as refined flour or cornstarch. They also add flavor and creamy texture to dishes, which means they can be used in place of cream, thereby avoiding dairy.

However, potatoes are often dismissed as being unhealthy and are somewhat controversial in the nutrition world because they are thought to be starchy high-carbohydrate foods that can cause blood sugar to spike. While potatoes may not be right for people who have difficulty processing carbohydrates, or for those with autoimmune problems that may be affected by some of the compounds they contain, there is little doubt they are nutritious. Potatoes provide a wide range of nutrients. For instance, they are one of the best food sources of potassium. One medium potato, plus skin provides 620 milligrams (18% DV) of this valuable nutrient. It is also very high in vitamin C (45% DV) and a good source of manganese (about 22% DV) and provides a wide range of other nutrients, including the B vitamins B_6, niacin and folate, as well as magnesium, copper and zinc. One baked potato will provide about 12% of the DV of fiber, among other nutrients and it does all this while providing a relatively modest 161 calories or 8% of the DV.

On the weight-control front, potatoes are a complex carb, which means they are digested slowly and keep you full longer, reducing the risk of binge eating, among other benefits. As for that blood sugar problem, when combined with vegetables that are high in fiber or healthy fat, their glycemic response is mitigated. That means that you don't need to feel guilty about adding a pat of butter to your mash. It's a good strategy for managing your blood sugar.

Potatoes are also phytonutrient rich. They contain compounds called kukoamines, which may help to keep blood pressure under control. Also, the skins are rich in phytonutrients, particularly flavonoids, which help to keep LDL ("bad") cholesterol under control, among other benefits.

Chilled Sorrel Soup

This classic French preparation is deliciously tart and, when thoroughly chilled, especially refreshing on a hot summer day. It is often thickened with egg yolks but, if you're so inclined, a drizzle of cream is much simpler and just as delicious. It is traditionally made with chicken stock, but if you are cooking for vegetarians, by all means use vegetable stock.

Makes 4 to 6 servings

Can Be Halved
(see Tips, page 112)

Tips

If you are in a hurry, you can soften the leek and garlic on the stovetop in a saucepan. It will take about 5 minutes. Then transfer to the stoneware.

The potato is used to thicken the soup and add flavor. If you prefer, substitute 2 tbsp (30 mL) short-grain brown rice, rinsed.

Russets are the most common variety of floury potato.

Nutrients Per Serving

Calories	107
Protein	6.3 g
Carbohydrates	14.5 g
Fat (Total)	4.0 g
Saturated Fat	1.4 g
Monounsaturated Fat	0.8 g
Polyunsaturated Fat	0.3 g
Dietary Fiber	6.0 g
Sodium	126 mg
Cholesterol	18 mg

EXCELLENT SOURCE OF vitamins A, C and B$_6$, magnesium, potassium and iron.
GOOD SOURCE OF phosphorus.
SOURCE OF vitamins B$_{12}$ and K, folate, calcium and zinc.
CONTAINS a very high amount of dietary fiber.

- **Medium (approx. 4 quart) slow cooker**
- **Food processor or blender**

1 tbsp	butter or extra virgin olive oil	15 mL
2	leeks, white part with a bit of green, cleaned and thinly sliced (see Tip, right)	2
2	cloves garlic, minced	2
4 cups	chicken or vegetable stock	1 L
1	floury potato, peeled and shredded (see Tips, left)	1
8 cups	loosely packed, coarsely chopped trimmed sorrel leaves	2 L
	Sea salt and freshly ground white pepper	
2 tbsp	finely chopped fresh tarragon leaves	30 mL
	Heavy or whipping (35%) cream, optional	

1. In slow cooker stoneware, combine butter, leek and garlic. Toss well to coat. Cover and cook on High for 1 hour, until softened (see Tips, left). Add stock and potato. Cover and cook on High for 3 hours or on Low for 6 hours, until potato is falling apart. Add sorrel, in batches, stirring each to submerge before adding the next batch. Cover and cook on High until sorrel is tender, about 20 minutes.

2. Working in batches, purée soup in a food processor or blender. (You can also do this in the stoneware using an immersion blender.) Transfer to a large bowl and chill thoroughly. Season to taste with salt and freshly ground white pepper.

3. When you're ready to serve, ladle into individual bowls, garnish with tarragon and drizzle with cream, if using.

Mindful Morsels

Looking at the nutrients in this soup that are provided by the sorrel alone substantiates the traditional wisdom that the darker the leafy green, the more nutritious it is. The sorrel in one serving of this soup provides 5.1 g of fiber, 60 mg of vitamin C (two-thirds of the DV for men), 691 mg of potassium, 78 mg of calcium and 4.3 mg of iron, among other nutrients. To highlight just one example of a specific benefit, the combination of vitamins A and K and calcium and magnesium contained in sorrel work together to promote bone health.

Natural Wonders

Sorrel

Sorrel is a leafy green that looks a lot like spinach but has a very bitter bite. It has a totally different taste from spinach and the two cannot be used interchangeably. However, for a refreshing change, try adding a handful or two of sorrel to your favorite spinach soup. Look for it in farmers' markets where, in season, it is abundant and economical. Sorrel is a hardy perennial, so if you have space, grow your own.

Sorrel is very low in calories (1 cup/250 mL of chopped sorrel leaves provides a mere 29 calories) but rich in minerals such as magnesium and potassium, while providing abundant amounts of vitamins C and A, and a smattering of B vitamins. In fact, sorrel is such a rich source of vitamin C that it has been used, like citrus fruits, to prevent scurvy. It has also been used in folk medicine for its diuretic and blood cleaning ability, a capacity which current research is confirming. Research also indicates that sorrel has strong antibacterial properties, inhibiting *E. coli* bacteria in laboratory situations.

Because it contains high amounts of oxalic acid (like spinach), sorrel should not be consumed by people who are prone to forming kidney stones. Don't confuse French-type sorrel, which is the leafy green used to make this soup, with red sorrel, which is a member of the hibiscus family and is used extensively in the Caribbean to make refreshing drinks.

Leafy Greens Soup

This delicious country-style soup is French in origin and based on the classic combination of leeks and potatoes, with the addition of healthful leafy greens. Sorrel, which has an intriguing but bitter taste, adds delightful depth to the flavor (see page 105). Sorrel is available from specialty greengrocers or at farmers' markets during the summer, but if you're unsuccessful in locating it, arugula or parsley also work well in this recipe.

Makes 8 servings

Can Be Halved
(see Tips, below)

Tips

If you are halving this recipe, be sure to use a small (2 to 3½ quart) slow cooker

The nutritional analysis on this soup was based on using Basic Vegetable Stock (page 120), which is particularly low in sodium. Be aware that if you use a prepared stock, the sodium content of this recipe will increase.

Nutrients Per Serving

Calories	122
Protein	3.6 g
Carbohydrates	21.8 g
Fat (Total)	3.5 g
Saturated Fat	1.2 g
Monounsaturated Fat	1.7 g
Polyunsaturated Fat	0.4 g
Dietary Fiber	5.1 g
Sodium	475 mg
Cholesterol	5 mg

EXCELLENT SOURCE OF vitamins A, C and K, magnesium, potassium and iron.
GOOD SOURCE OF vitamin B_6 and folate.
SOURCE OF calcium.
CONTAINS a high amount of dietary fiber.

- **Large (approx. 5 quart) slow cooker**
- **Food processor or blender**

1 tbsp	butter or olive oil	15 mL
1 tbsp	olive oil	15 mL
6	small leeks, white and light green parts only, cleaned and thinly sliced (see Tip, page 105)	6
4	cloves garlic, minced	4
1 tsp	sea salt	5 mL
1 tsp	dried tarragon	5 mL
½ tsp	cracked black peppercorns	2 mL
6 cups	vegetable or chicken stock (see Tips, left)	1.5 L
3	medium potatoes, peeled and cut into ½-inch (1 cm) cubes	3
4 cups	packed torn Swiss chard leaves (about 1 bunch)	1 L
1 cup	packed torn sorrel, arugula or parsley leaves	250 mL
	Heavy or whipping (35%) cream or non-dairy alternative, optional	

1. In a large skillet over medium heat, melt butter and olive oil. Add leeks and cook, stirring, until softened, about 5 minutes. Add garlic, salt, tarragon and peppercorns and cook, stirring, for 1 minute. Add stock and bring to a boil.

2. Transfer to slow cooker stoneware. Stir in potatoes. Cover and cook on Low for 6 to 8 hours or on High for 3 to 4 hours, until potatoes are tender. Add Swiss chard and sorrel, in batches, stirring after each to submerge the leaves in the liquid. Cover and cook on High for 20 minutes, until greens are tender.

3. Working in batches, purée soup in a food processor or blender. (You can also do this in the stoneware using an immersion blender.) Spoon into individual serving bowls and drizzle with cream, if using.

more information on page 108

Make Ahead

Complete Step 1, cover and refrigerate overnight or for up to 2 days. When you're ready to cook, continue with Steps 2 and 3.

Natural Wonders

Swiss Chard

I've added Swiss chard to this traditional leek and potato soup because along with kale, collards and other dark leafy greens, it is a nutritional superstar. A relative of the beet family, Swiss chard is a good source of numerous vitamins and minerals, including vitamins K, A and C, as well as magnesium and potassium. In fact, a half-cup (125 mL) serving of Swiss chard contains more than 150% of the recommended daily value of vitamin K.

Like all leafy greens Swiss chard is loaded with antioxidants. It contains vitamin E, a free radical fighter, and beta-carotene, which helps to keep your eyes healthy. It is a rich source of the powerful antioxidants lutein and zeaxanthin. These compounds are one reason why Swiss chard and other dark leafy greens have been shown to reduce the risk for cataracts and macular degeneration, the leading cause of blindness in people over the age of 55 (see page 81). Some researchers also think the anthocyanins in Swiss chard may prevent cancers of the digestive tract. Other research indicates that consumption of chard may be linked with reduced rates of colon cancer. And, with just 35 calories a cup (250 mL) adding chard to your meal plan makes great sense as part of any weight control program.

Vegetable Gumbo

This tasty soup reminds me of a delicious version of one of my favorite canned soups when I was a kid. Served with salad, it makes an excellent lunch.

Makes 6 servings

Can Be Halved
(see Tips, see page 112)

Tips

You can reduce the amount of sodium by using canned tomatoes with no salt added.

This quantity of rice, combined with the okra, produces a dense soup, which condenses even more when refrigerated. If you prefer a more soup-like consistency, add an additional cup (250 mL) of stock.

Okra is a great thickener for broths but be sure not to overcook it because it will become unpleasantly sticky. Gently scrub the pods, cut off the top and tail and slice.

Nutrients Per Serving

Calories	148
Protein	4.5 g
Carbohydrates	28.0 g
Fat (Total)	3.2 g
Saturated Fat	0.5 g
Monounsaturated Fat	1.9 g
Polyunsaturated Fat	0.6 g
Dietary Fiber	4.7 g
Sodium	238 mg
Cholesterol	0 mg

EXCELLENT SOURCE OF vitamins C and K and potassium.

GOOD SOURCE OF vitamins A and B$_6$, magnesium, folate and iron.

SOURCE OF calcium and phosphorus.

CONTAINS a high amount of dietary fiber.

• **Large (approx. 5 quart) slow cooker**

1 tbsp	olive oil	15 mL
2	onions, finely chopped	2
6	stalks celery, diced	6
4	cloves garlic, minced	4
2 tsp	dried thyme	10 mL
½ tsp	cracked black peppercorns	2 mL
1	bay leaf	1
1	can (28 oz/796 mL) diced tomatoes, including juice	1
½ cup	brown rice (see Tips, left)	125 mL
4 cups	vegetable or chicken stock (see Tips, page 106)	1 L
2 tsp	paprika, dissolved in 4 tsp (20 mL) freshly squeezed lemon juice	10 mL
	Sea salt	
2 cups	sliced okra (¼-inch/0.5 cm slices) (see Tips, left)	500 mL
1	green bell pepper, diced	1

1. In a skillet, heat oil over medium heat. Add onions and celery and cook, stirring, until celery is softened, about 5 minutes. Add garlic, thyme, peppercorns and bay leaf and cook, stirring, for 1 minute. Add tomatoes with juice and bring to a boil.

2. Transfer to slow cooker stoneware. Add brown rice and stock. Cover and cook on Low for 6 hours or on High for 3 hours, until rice is tender. Discard bay leaf. Add paprika solution and stir well. Season to taste with salt, if using. Stir in okra and green pepper. Cover and cook on High for 20 minutes, until pepper is tender.

more information on page 111

Vegetable Gumbo

Make Ahead

Complete Step 1. Cover and refrigerate overnight or for up to 2 days. When you're ready to cook, complete the recipe.

Natural Wonders

Okra

Okra is a traditional ingredient in gumbo, where it is often used as a thickener in place of filé powder. But okra adds much more to this soup than a thick consistency. This low-cal vegetable is also a source of many nutrients, including vitamins C and B_6, folate, thiamine and magnesium.

The pectin in okra, which enables it to thicken this soup, is a source of soluble fiber. It helps to keep blood cholesterol levels under control and, at the same time, balances blood sugar levels by slowing down how quickly carbohydrates are absorbed. Okra also contains glutathione, a cancer-fighting antioxidant (see Natural Wonders, page 291). One study found that people who consumed high amounts of glutathione were half as likely to develop cancers of the throat and mouth than those with low levels of this compound.

Summer Borscht

I call this Summer Borscht because it's the name my friend Margret Hovanec bestowed on beet borscht made with the addition of the nutrient-dense beet greens. Presumably, it is traditionally made in summer when fresh young beets, with their luscious greens attached, are widely available. It is one of those refreshing cold soups I love to have on hand in the fridge for an energizing snack on hot humid days.

Makes 10 servings

Can Be Halved
(see Tips, below)

Tips

If you are halving this recipe, be sure to use a small (approx. 2 quart) slow cooker.

Unless you're cooking for vegetarians, to maximize health benefits use homemade beef broth when making this soup. Not only is it more flavorful, among other benefits it is rich in real gelatin, an extremely nutritious substance (see Natural Wonders, page 115).

Nutrients Per Serving

Calories	107
Protein	3.2 g
Carbohydrates	14.5 g
Fat (Total)	4.5 g
Saturated Fat	2.5 g
Monounsaturated Fat	1.1 g
Polyunsaturated Fat	0.2 g
Dietary Fiber	2.2 g
Sodium	149 mg
Cholesterol	10 mg

EXCELLENT SOURCE OF vitamin K.
GOOD SOURCE OF vitamin A, folate and potassium.
SOURCE OF vitamins B_6 and C, calcium, phosphorus, magnesium and iron.
CONTAINS a moderate amount of dietary fiber.

- **Medium to large (4 to 5 quart) slow cooker**
- **Food processor or blender**

2 tbsp	butter or extra virgin olive oil	30 mL
2	onions, finely chopped	2
4	stalks celery, chopped	4
4	cloves garlic, minced	4
¼ tsp	crushed black peppercorns	1 mL
1 tbsp	coconut sugar	15 mL
1	can (14 ounces/398 mL) no-salt added tomatoes including juice	1
4	medium beets, peeled and cut into ½-inch (1 cm) cubes (about 1½ lbs/750 g)	4
	Leaves from the beets, washed, coarsely chopped and set aside in the refrigerator (about 4 cups/1 L loosely packed)	
1	potato, peeled and shredded	1
4 cups	beef or vegetable stock	1 L
2 tbsp	red wine vinegar	30 mL
½ cup	sour cream, crème fraîche or vegan sour cream	125 mL
½ cup	finely chopped dill fronds	125 mL
	Sea salt	

1. In a skillet, melt butter over medium heat. Add onions and celery and cook, stirring, until softened, about 5 minutes. Add garlic and peppercorns and cook, stirring, for 1 minute. Add coconut sugar and tomatoes with juice and bring to a boil.

2. Transfer to slow cooker stoneware. Add beets, potato and stock. Cover and cook on Low for 6 hours or on High for 3 hours, until beets are tender.

3. Add vinegar, and beet greens, in batches, stirring each to submerge before adding the next batch. Cover and cook on High for 20 minutes until greens are nicely wilted.

Make Ahead

Complete Step 1. Cover and refrigerate overnight or for up to 2 days. When you're ready to cook, complete the recipe.

4. Working in batches, purée soup in a food processor or blender. (You can also do this in the stoneware using an immersion blender.) Transfer to a large bowl as completed. Cover and refrigerate until thoroughly chilled or for up to 4 days. To serve, transfer to individual bowls and garnish each with a dollop of sour cream and a sprinkling of dill. Taste and add salt, if needed.

Mindful Morsels

If you routinely throw away beet greens, you are wasting valuable nutrients. In one serving of this soup, those often-discarded tops provide virtually all of the vitamin K, and a smattering of other nutrients, including vitamins A and C, folate, potassium, magnesium and calcium. A number of these nutrients (calcium, magnesium and vitamins A and K) work together to keep your bones healthy.

Natural Wonders

Keeping Blood Pressure Under Control

Among other benefits, eating nutrient-rich plant foods, which usually provide potassium and magnesium, will help to keep your blood pressure under control. Studies show that people who have low intakes of these important minerals are more likely to have high blood pressure.

If do you have high blood pressure, try tweaking your lifestyle before taking medication. Experts tell us that making two or more dietary-lifestyle changes may control blood pressure as well as drug therapy, which is usually effective but may initiate negative side effects. Maintaining a healthy weight and being active are an excellent start, as is limiting your sodium intake. Experts now recommend 1,500 mg of sodium a day for those who have been diagnosed with high blood pressure.

If you are trying to reduce your sodium intake, don't focus on the salt shaker — most of the salt we consume is invisible, lurking in processed foods such as canned soups and snacks, as well as fast foods. Eliminating these foods from your diet and replacing them with healthy whole foods will go a long way toward keeping your blood pressure under control. Use homemade rather than prepared stocks when making soups and stews (see pages 114 through 120) and look for canned legumes with no salt added in natural foods stores, or cook your own, which is very easy to do using a slow cooker (see Basic Beans, page 284).

Hearty Beef Stock

Nurturing "bone broth" is a hearty gelatin-rich beef stock. Among other benefits, by binding with water, the gelatin in a homemade beef stock supports digestion. Traditionally, bone broth has also been used as an elixir — good for whatever ails you.

Makes about 12 cups (3 L)

Tip

Demi-glace is intensely flavored stock that has been concentrated. It is useful for adding a burst of flavor to dishes. I always like to have some in my freezer. After making stock, transfer about 2 cups (500 mL) to a saucepan. Bring to boil, then reduce heat and simmer for about 1½ hours until syrupy (you should have about ½ cup/125 mL). Let cool then transfer to a shallow dish and refrigerate. After it has solidified, lift it out in 1 piece, place on a cutting board, then cut it into squares (each containing about 1 tbsp/15 mL). (You should get about 8 pieces.) Wrap individually in plastic and freeze. When frozen, place in resealable bags and label.

- **Large (approx. 6 quart) slow cooker**
- **Preheat oven to 375°F (190°C)**
- **Sieve, lined with a double layer of cheesecloth**

3	each onions, quartered and carrots, cut into chunks	3
3	stalks celery	3
6	cloves garlic	6
2 tbsp	extra virgin olive oil or melted butter	30 mL
3 lbs	beef bones	1.5 kg
4	sprigs parsley	4
3	sprigs fresh thyme	3
10	black peppercorns	10
¼ cup	dried alfalfa leaves, optional (page 121)	60 mL
3 tbsp	red wine vinegar	45 mL
12 cups	filtered water	3 L

1. Place onions, carrots, celery and garlic in a roasting pan and toss well with oil. Add bones and toss again. Arrange in a single layer (as much as possible) in pan and roast in preheated oven until ingredients are browning nicely, about 1 hour. Transfer to stoneware, along with juices.

2. Add parsley, thyme, peppercorns, alfalfa leaves, if using, vinegar and water. Cover and cook on Low for 12 hours or on High for 6 hours, until stock is brown and flavorful. Strain through prepared sieve and discard solids. Cool slightly. Refrigerate for up to 5 days or freeze in portions in airtight containers.

Nutrients Per Serving (1 cup/250 mL)

Calories	15
Protein	1.0
Carbohydrates	0
Fat (Total)	1.1 g
Saturated Fat	0
Monounsaturated Fat	0
Polyunsaturated Fat	0
Dietary Fiber	0
Sodium	125 mg
Cholesterol	0 mg

Mindful Morsels

Although none of the nutrients in this broth are present in quantities large enough to qualify as a "source," the process of extracting minerals from bone in broth does capture a range of beneficial minerals in small quantities. All of these nutrients, including many such as glycine and proline, which conventional nutritional analysis is unable to capture, work together to create this nutritious broth. As with chicken stock (see page 116) sodium is extracted from bone in the process of making broth.

Natural Wonders

Bone Broth

For centuries, across many cultures, broth made from meat, bones and vegetables has provided essential nourishment. Its medicinal value has also been recognized and recipes such as homemade chicken soup have justifiably (according to current research) earned monikers along the lines of "Jewish penicillin." Broth made from bones (and collagen-rich cartilage, the material attached to the ends of bones) provides a smattering of important minerals, such as calcium, magnesium, manganese, potassium and phosphorus as well as beneficial compounds such as hyaluronic acid and chondroitin sulfate, which is well known as a treatment for osteoarthritis.

While all these nutrients are valuable tools in promoting good health, the miracle ingredient in well-made broth is gelatin. In traditional Chinese medicine, for instance, e jiao (the gelatin component in broth) is a herbal tonic. In the late 19th and early 20th centuries, American scientists actively studied gelatin, identifying it as an excellent digestive, among other benefits. In those days, researchers recommended adding gelatin to infant feeding formulas to improve the digestibility of cow's milk and help babies absorb its nutrients. As nutritionist Dr. Kaayla Daniel points out, "infants fed gelatin-enriched formulas showed reduced allergic symptoms, vomiting, colic diarrhea, constipation and respiratory ailments than those on straight cow's milk." Other studies identified gelatin's positive effect on the digestibility of beans and the bioavailability of certain nutrients in grains, particularly those containing gluten. However, as Dr. Daniel notes, the health benefits of gelatin got lost in the shuffle sometime after the 1930s.

Now contemporary researchers are taking a second look at gelatin and the results are very positive. Consider, for instance, that gelatin is rich in the nutrients glycine and proline. These are non-essential amino acids, which means the body can, in theory, manufacture them. However, new research suggests that our bodies usually can't make enough of these substances. Adequate glycine intake, for instance, has been associated with a greatly reduced risk of asthma, better digestion and faster wound healing, in addition to being an important support for the liver and an excellent detoxifier.

An article published in 2005, in *The Townsend Letter*, an alternative medicine publication, listed 73 conditions that benefit from the consumption of bone broth, ranging from arthritis and inflammatory bowel disease to osteoporosis. However, they stressed that the quality of the broth (and the gelatin) is important to its efficacy. Today, most commercial gelatin is made from animal skin, which means it lacks some of the nutrients contained in bone broth. It also contains small amounts of MSG. Moreover, since we don't know exactly how commercially prepared broths are made, it's possible that crucial steps are skipped, such as adding an acid (vinegar) to extract minerals from the bones. It's also possible that manufacturers may not be using bones to make their broth, both of which would strip their products of nutrients.

In any case, your great-grandmother knew what she was doing when she made soup for people who weren't feeling well. Homemade bone broth is extremely restorative — mouthwatering medicine in a bowl.

Homemade Chicken Stock

There's nothing quite like the flavor of homemade chicken stock, which is very easy to make and, as a classic bone broth, wonderfully nourishing (see page 115).

Makes about 12 cups (3 L)

Tips

The more economical parts of the chicken, such as necks, backs and wings, make the best stock.

The acid in the vinegar helps to draw nutrients from the bones and intensifies the flavor of the stock.

● **Large (approx. 5 quart) slow cooker**

4 lbs	bone-in skin-on chicken parts (see Tips, left)	2 kg
3	onions, coarsely chopped	3
4	carrots, scrubbed and coarsely chopped	4
4	stalks celery, coarsely chopped	4
6	sprigs parsley	6
3	bay leaves	3
10	black peppercorns	10
1 tsp	dried thyme	5 mL
¼ cup	dried alfalfa leaves, optional	60 mL
3 tbsp	apple cider vinegar	45 mL
12 cups	water	3 L

1. In slow cooker stoneware, combine ingredients. Cover and cook on High for 8 hours. Strain into a large bowl, discarding solids. Cover and refrigerate for up to 5 days.

Mindful Morsels

One cup (250 mL) of this stock, with no salt added, contains 150 mg of sodium. The same quantity of a typical prepared stock likely contains more than 500 mg of sodium. While there are prepared stocks on the market with no salt added, which contain less than 70 mg of sodium per cup (250 mL), they do not have the health benefits of homemade bone broth. I feel strongly that natural sodium in foods is not likely to have negative health effects. For instance, 1 cup (250 mL) of 1% milk contains 107 mg of sodium and the idea that you give up drinking milk because it contains sodium is ludicrous.

As you can see, no salt has been added when making this stock. All the sodium comes from the bones and it is extracted along with the other minerals. I have made chicken stock without adding an acid to facilitate mineral extraction and the same quantity of stock provides only 21 mg of sodium. However, it does not provide as high a level of nutrients, especially minerals, as this version does.

Nutrients Per Serving (1 cup/250 mL)

Calories	22
Protein	2.6 g
Carbohydrates	0.4 g
Fat (Total)	1.1 g
Saturated Fat	0.3 g
Monounsaturated Fat	0.4 g
Polyunsaturated Fat	0.2 g
Dietary Fiber	0.1 g
Sodium	150 mg
Cholesterol	20 mg

SOURCE OF vitamins B_6 and B_{12} and phosphorous.

Natural Wonders

Common Medicinal Herbs

One of the major shortcomings of North American society is, in my opinion, the lack of information regarding the health benefits of herbs. This includes common culinary herbs such as parsley and oregano and less common herbs, such as burdock, which are usually used for medicinal purposes. In most parts of Europe, herbal pharmacies are common and herbs are actively researched by scientists. People are more likely to visit a herbalist or herbal pharmacy than a physician for minor ailments.

However, even on this side of the pond, the dried leaves and/or roots of many herbs are commonly available in well-stocked natural foods stores. Adding a handful to the pot when making stock may be beneficial to your health. Just make sure to use those that are mild in flavor such as alfalfa (see page 121), astragalus or plantain leaves, so they don't overpower your stock. It is impossible to quantify the nutritional benefit of adding these herbs to your diet because nutritional data is unavailable for consumer purposes and they have only been studied medicinally. However, herbalism has a long history and there is a great deal of empirical evidence to support the use of herbs as dietary supplements.

Take astragalus, for instance. It is well known as a tonic. In traditional Chinese medicine (it has been extensively studied in Asia) it is believed to boost *qi*, the body's fundamental energy, and is recommended in situations of chronic illness or general weakness. Taken post surgery, astragalus helps your body with the healing process. Research suggests that astragalus may also stimulate the immune system, so perhaps not surprisingly it is often used as a treatment for the common cold. Researchers are also looking into its potential benefit for people undergoing cancer treatment. Animal studies indicate that astragalus significantly increased cancer-fighting substances and improved the cure rates of mice treated with the herb solution, compared to those receiving saline. Along with other herbs, astragalus has long been used as a cancer fighter in traditional Chinese medicine.

Dried plantain leaves (do not confuse the herb with the starchy fruit related to bananas) have a long history as herbal medicine in Europe, where the plants grow wild. It is strongly anti-inflammatory and is widely used in topical treatments, such as salves, to treat skin ailments such as burns, or insect bites and stings. It also has antibiotic properties and may be useful in fighting throat or respiratory tract infections. Although not yet justified by research, plantain contains substances that may be useful in removing uric acid from the body, indicating its potential benefit as a treatment for gout.

I often see burdock root in the vegetable section of my neighborhood natural food store. According to pharmacist Heather Boone, burdock is well known as a treatment for various skin conditions, such as eczema. As she writes in her book *55 Most Common Medicinal Herbs*, it has been used both in Western and Chinese herbal medicine as a detoxifying agent and to treat chronic inflammation associated with illnesses such as rheumatism and gout, as well as for skin conditions such as "acne, boils, abscesses and eczema." I like to use burdock root in place of potatoes to thicken soups. Just scrub it well, slice and add a small quantity to your recipe. After cooking, it will purée nicely.

Flavorful Fish Stock

Homemade fish stock is a great base for luscious fish soups and stews.

Tips

Be sure not to use oily fish such as salmon, mackerel or tuna or your stock may be unpleasantly pungent.

The acid in the wine helps to draw nutrients from the bones and intensifies the flavor of the stock. If you prefer, substitute 2 tbsp (30 mL) white wine vinegar and add an additional ½ cup (125 mL) of water.

I do not recommend making fish stock on High because for best results the liquid should never boil.

- **Large (approx. 5 quart) slow cooker**
- **Sieve, lined with a double layer of cheesecloth**

3 lbs	fish trimmings, including heads (see Tips, left)	1.5 kg
2	onions or well-washed green parts of 3 large leeks, coarsely chopped	2
1	carrot, coarsely chopped	1
1	stalk celery, coarsely chopped	1
4	sprigs parsley	4
2	sprigs fresh thyme	1
2	bay leaves	2
2 tsp	fennel seeds	10 mL
2 tbsp	dried alfalfa leaves, optional	30 mL
1 cup	dry white wine (see Tips, left)	250 mL
12 cups	filtered water	3 L

1. In slow cooker stoneware, combine fish trimmings, onions, carrot, celery, parsley, thyme, bay leaves, fennel seeds, alfalfa leaves, wine, and water. Cover and cook on Low for 8 hours (see Tips, left). Strain through prepared sieve and discard solids. Refrigerate for up to 5 days or freeze in portions in airtight containers.

Mindful Morsels

When making bone broths of any sort (for instance, beef and chicken as well as fish) make sure you add an acid such as vinegar or lemon juice to the water. The nutrients in the bones will not be as efficiently extracted if acid is omitted.

Nutrients Per Serving (1 cup/250 mL)

Calories	18
Protein	1.2 g
Carbohydrates	0.2 g
Fat (Total)	0 g
Saturated Fat	0 g
Monounsaturated Fat	0 g
Polyunsaturated Fat	0 g
Dietary Fiber	0 g
Sodium	124 mg
Cholesterol	0 mg

SOURCE OF phosphorus.

Homemade Mushroom Stock

There are many advantages to making your own mushroom stock. You know exactly what is in it, and it is more economical than buying a prepared version. This makes a mildly flavored version, which I prefer. If a stronger mushroom flavor appeals to you, double the quantity of dried portobello mushrooms.

Makes about 12 cups (3 L)

Can Be Halved
(see Tips, below)

Tips

If you are halving this recipe, be sure to use a small (approx. 2 quart) slow cooker.

If you have mushroom stems left over from another recipe, add them to the stoneware. However, make sure they are in good condition. When making stock of any kind you should never use vegetables that are passed their peak.

You can substitute the green part of leeks or scallions for all or part of the onions in this recipe. Use about 2 cups (500 mL) coarsely chopped and packed for each onion.

Nutrients Per Serving (1 cup/250 mL)

Calories	10
Protein	0 g
Carbohydrates	0 g
Fat (Total)	1.1 g
Saturated Fat	0.2 g
Monounsaturated Fat	0.8 g
Polyunsaturated Fat	0.1 g
Dietary Fiber	0 g
Sodium	64 mg
Cholesterol	0 mg

- **Large (approx. 5 quart) slow cooker**
- **Sieve, lined with a double layer of cheesecloth**

1	package (½ oz/14 g) dried portobello mushrooms, crumbled	1
1 cup	hot water	250 mL
1 tbsp	extra virgin olive oil or butter	15 mL
2	onions, coarsely chopped	2
4	stalks celery, peeled and coarsely chopped	4
4	cloves garlic, coarsely chopped	4
1 tsp	dried thyme	5 mL
1 tsp	cracked black peppercorns	5 mL
½ tsp	sea salt	2 mL
8	sprigs parsley	8
12 cups	water	3 L

1. In a bowl, combine dried mushrooms and hot water. Stir well and let stand for 30 minutes. Drain liquid into stoneware. Set solids aside.

2. Meanwhile, in a skillet, heat oil over medium heat. Add onions and celery and cook, stirring, until softened, about 5 minutes. Add garlic, thyme, peppercorns, salt, parsley and reserved reconstituted mushrooms and cook, stirring, for 1 minute.

3. Transfer to slow cooker stoneware. Add water. Cover and cook on High for 6 hours. Strain through a prepared sieve and discard solids. Refrigerate for up to 5 days or freeze in portions in airtight containers.

Basic Vegetable Stock

All the stock recipes in this book (Hearty Beef Stock, Homemade Chicken Stock, Flavorful Fish Stock, Homemade Mushroom Stock and Basic Vegetable Stock) make enough for two average soup recipes. They can be made ahead and frozen. For convenience, cook them overnight in the slow cooker. If your slow cooker is not large enough to make a full batch, you can halve the recipes.

Makes about 12 cups (3 L)

Tips

To freeze this stock and all others, transfer to airtight containers in small, measured portions (2 cups/500 mL or 4 cups/ 1 L are handy), leaving at least 1-inch (2.5 cm) headspace for expansion. Refrigerate until chilled, cover and freeze for up to 3 months. Thaw in refrigerator before using.

We have not included a nutrient analysis for Basic Vegetable Stock because it contains such a minute quantity of nutrients. One serving (approximately 1 cup/250 mL provides just one calorie and about 2% of the DV for both folate and potassium). However, it is more flavorful than using water as a base for soup and it doesn't contain nearly as much sodium as commercially prepared stocks. One cup (250 mL) of this stock with no salt added, contains 0 mg of sodium. The same quantity of a typical prepared stock likely contains more than 500 mg of sodium.

- **Large (approx. 5 quart) slow cooker**

8	carrots, scrubbed and coarsely chopped	8
6	stalks celery, coarsely chopped	6
3	onions, coarsely chopped	3
3	cloves garlic, coarsely chopped	3
6	sprigs parsley	6
3	bay leaves	3
10	black peppercorns	10
¼ cup	dried alfalfa leaves, optional (see Natural Wonders, right)	60 mL
1 tsp	dried thyme	5 mL
	Sea salt, optional	
12 cups	water	3 L

1. In slow cooker stoneware, combine carrots, celery, onions, garlic, parsley, bay leaves, peppercorns, alfalfa leaves, if using, thyme, salt to taste, if using, and water. Cover and cook on Low for 8 hours or on High for 4 hours. Strain and discard solids. Cover and refrigerate for up to 5 days or freeze in an airtight container.

Variation

Enhanced Vegetable Stock: To enhance 8 cups (2 L) Basic Vegetable or prepared stock, combine in a large saucepan over medium heat with 2 carrots, peeled and coarsely chopped, 1 tbsp (15 mL) tomato paste, 1 tsp (5 mL) celery seeds, 1 tsp (5 mL) cracked black peppercorns, $1/2$ tsp (2 mL) dried thyme leaves, 4 parsley sprigs, 1 bay leaf and 1 cup (250 mL) white wine. Bring to a boil. Reduce heat to low and simmer, covered, for 30 minutes, then strain and discard solids.

Natural Wonders

Alfalfa

If you can easily find dried alfalfa leaves, I recommend adding a handful or so to the pot when making stock (see page 117, as well). This herb has a very mild flavor and it is loaded with phytonutrients, which, unfortunately, it is not possible to quantify at the consumer level. (This is the work scientists are currently doing in laboratories and even they are finding identifying and quantifying the phytonutrients in foods to be a gargantuan task.)

However, alfalfa has an impressive history as a "functional food." Centuries ago, the Arabs bestowed the name alfalfa, which means "the father of all foods" on this perennial legume because they recognized its superior nutritional qualities. In fact, they fed it to their legendary horses, in addition to using it as a medicinal herb. Alfalfa is commonly used in Ayurvedic and Traditional Chinese Medicine to treat digestive disorders or to promote joint health, but in the western world today, alfalfa is mostly used as animal feed.

This is unfortunate for humans because the herb is a robust functional food that, among other benefits, has significant value as a general tonic. Alfalfa provides vitamins A, B_1, B_6, B_{12}, C, E and K in addition to a smattering of minerals such as potassium and zinc. It is also rich in phytonutrients, such as the isoflavone flavonoids genistein, daidzein and formononetin. Several studies suggest that it helps to keep cholesterol levels low and prevents atherosclerosis, among other cardiovascular benefits. Although there is no scientific evidence to support its use in women's health, alfalfa has traditionally been used to manage the symptoms of menopause and to relieve menstrual discomfort.

Herbalists suggest brewing a tea of dried alfalfa leaves. Because it has a very mild flavor, another easy way to add valuable nutrients to your diet is to include a few spoonfuls when making stocks. Dried alfalfa leaves are available at well-stocked natural foods stores or from online vendors. Just check to make sure you are purchasing organically grown alfalfa as a genetically modified version is widely available. And when adding alfalfa to liquids make sure to use the dried leaves, not alfalfa sprouts, which have an entirely different nutritional profile and have not been linked with any medicinal properties.

Chili with Black Beans and Grilled Chicken

Poultry

Chili with Black Beans and Grilled Chicken

The addition of grilled chicken adds a flavorful and festive note to this simple chili. I like to use leftover chicken alla diavola (marinated in extra virgin olive oil, lemon juice and chile peppers), which we often make on the barbecue. It adds pleasant hints of citrus and hot pepper to the mix, but if you're opting for convenience, use a store-bought rotisserie chicken instead. You won't be disappointed.

Makes 6 servings

Can Be Halved
(see Tips, below)

Tips

If you are halving this recipe, be sure to use a small (1½ to 3 quart) slow cooker.

Use a single ground mild chile powder, such as ancho or Anaheim, or a combination thereof.

Nutrients Per Serving

Calories	262
Protein	22.2 g
Carbohydrates	29.7 g
Fat (Total)	7.1 g
Saturated Fat	1.5 g
Monounsaturated Fat	3.3 g
Polyunsaturated Fat	1.5 g
Dietary Fiber	7.7 g
Sodium	476 mg
Cholesterol	48 mg

EXCELLENT SOURCE OF vitamins C and B$_6$, folate, phosphorus, magnesium, potassium and iron.

GOOD SOURCE OF vitamin K and zinc.

SOURCE OF vitamins A and B$_{12}$ and calcium.

CONTAINS a very high amount of dietary fiber.

- **Medium to large (3½ to 5 quart) slow cooker**

1 tbsp	oil	15 mL
2	onions, finely chopped	2
4	stalks celery, diced	4
4	cloves garlic, chopped	4
1 tbsp	ground cumin (see Tip, right)	15 mL
2 tsp	dried oregano leaves	10 mL
1 tsp	sea salt	5 mL
1 tsp	cracked black peppercorns	5 mL
2 tbsp	tomato paste	30 mL
1	can (14 oz/ 398 mL) no-salt added crushed tomatoes	1
2 cups	chicken stock	500 mL
2 cups	cooked black beans	500 mL
2 tsp	pure chile powder (see Tips, left)	10 mL
½ tsp	cayenne pepper, optional	2 mL
2 cups	cubed (1 inch/2.5 cm) grilled chicken	500 mL
1	green bell or poblano pepper, seeded and diced	1
1	can (4½ oz/127 mL) chopped mild green chiles	1
	Avocado Topping (see page 148) or shredded	
	Cheddar or Jack cheese or sour cream	
	Finely chopped red or green onion	

1. In a skillet, heat oil over medium heat. Add onions and celery and cook, stirring, until softened, about 5 minutes. Add garlic, cumin, oregano, salt and peppercorns and cook, stirring, for 1 minute. Add tomato paste and tomatoes and bring to a boil.

2. Transfer to slow cooker stoneware. Add stock and beans and stir well. Cover and cook on Low for 6 hours or on High for 3 hours.

Tip

For the best results, toast and grind the cumin yourself. Place seeds in a dry skillet over medium heat and cook, stirring, until fragrant, about 3 minutes. Using a mortar and pestle or a spice grinder, pound or grind as finely as you can.

Make Ahead

Complete Step 1. Cover and refrigerate mixture for up to 2 days. When you're ready to cook, complete the recipe.

3. Stir in chile powder and cayenne, if using. Add chicken, bell pepper and green chiles and stir well. Cover and cook on High for 20 minutes, until bell pepper is tender and chicken is heated through. Serve with topping(s) of your choice.

Mindful Morsels

Always use pasture-raised organic poultry. Turkeys and chickens that are allowed to range free, eating insects and grass, and that receive organically grown non-GMO feed mixes to supplement will be more nutrient-dense because of their superior diet. For starters, they will be higher in healthy omega-3 fatty acids, (which our modern diet lacks) than their "conventional" counterparts.

Natural Wonders

Canned Tomatoes

Although I usually avoid processed foods, there are many excellent "canned" tomato products on the market and because most people use a slow cooker for convenience, I have used them in some recipes in this book. In fact, in at least one respect, canned tomatoes are more nutritious than fresh ones. Tomatoes contain lycopene, a phytonutrient that appears to be protective against heart disease and some kinds of cancer. Cooking or canning (which uses heat) tomatoes makes their lycopene more bioavailable.

To make the best tomato choices, look for those that are organically grown, with no salt added, and come in glass jars or BPA-(bisphenol-A) free cans. Although it is still legal for manufacturers to use BPA, studies have linked it to health conditions such as diabetes, heart disease and even infertility. When using canned tomatoes (or any canned product) check to make sure they are gluten-free. A surprising number do contain gluten. Moreover, manufacturers are constantly changing their formulae and gluten may suddenly appear in a product that was previously gluten-free.

Chicken Cassoulet

This hearty one-dish meal is always a hit — I particularly like the dill finish, which adds an intriguing hint of flavor. A salad of shredded carrots makes a nice accompaniment.

Makes 8 servings

Can Be Halved
(see Tips, page 128)

Tips

For this quantity of beans, cook 2 cups (500 mL) dried beans (see Basic Beans, page 284) or use 2 cans (each 14 to 19 oz/398 to 540 mL) of beans.

If you're using small cremini mushrooms, just trim and use them whole. Cut larger ones in half or quarters, depending on the size. If using portobello mushrooms, remove the stems and gills and cut each into 6 equal wedges.

Nutrients Per Serving

Calories	281
Protein	24.4 g
Carbohydrates	32.7 g
Fat (Total)	6.8 g
Saturated Fat	1.4 g
Monounsaturated Fat	2.6 g
Polyunsaturated Fat	1.5 g
Dietary Fiber	10.3 g
Sodium	948 mg
Cholesterol	69 mg

EXCELLENT SOURCE OF vitamins A, B₆ and K, magnesium, potassium, iron and zinc.

GOOD SOURCE OF vitamin C, folate, calcium and phosphorus.

CONTAINS a very high amount of dietary fiber.

- **Large (approx. 5 quart) slow cooker**

1 tbsp	olive oil	15 mL
2	onions, finely chopped	2
8	carrots, peeled and sliced	8
4	stalks celery, sliced	4
4	cloves garlic, minced	4
2 tsp	herbes de Provence	10 mL
1 tsp	sea salt	5 mL
1 tsp	cracked black peppercorns	5 mL
1	can (28 oz/796 mL) tomatoes, including juice, coarsely chopped	1
1 cup	chicken or vegetable stock	250 mL
4 cups	cooked white beans, drained and rinsed (see Tips, left and Mindful Morsels, right)	1 L
2	bay leaves	2
2 lbs	skinless bone-in chicken thighs (about 8 thighs)	1 kg
1 lb	cremini or portobello mushrooms (see Tips, left)	500 g
½ cup	finely chopped dill fronds	125 mL

1. In a large skillet, heat oil over medium heat. Add onions, carrots and celery and cook, stirring, until carrots are softened, about 7 minutes. Add garlic, herbes de Provence, salt and peppercorns and cook, stirring, for 1 minute. Add tomatoes with juice, chicken stock, beans and bay leaves and bring to a boil. Remove from heat.

2. Spoon half of the bean mixture into slow cooker stoneware. Lay chicken evenly over top. Arrange mushrooms evenly over chicken. Spoon remainder of sauce over mushrooms.

3. Cover and cook on Low for 6 hours or on High for 3 hours, until juices run clear when chicken is pierced with a fork. Remove bay leaves. Stir in dill. Cover and cook on High for 15 minutes, until flavors meld.

Make Ahead

Complete Step 1. Cover and refrigerate bean mixture for up to 2 days. When you're ready to cook, complete the recipe.

Mindful Morsels

This recipe is relatively high in sodium because the nutritional analysis was done using regular prepared chicken stock and canned beans. For a more acceptable nutritional profile, use Homemade Chicken Stock (page 116) and cook dried white beans from scratch (page 284) or use a canned variety with no salt added.

Natural Wonders

Fiber-Rich Legumes

Chicken Cassoulet, like some other recipes in this book, is an excellent source of fiber, more than half of which (5.4 grams) comes from the beans. You can nurture your heart and help to keep your weight under control by regularly adding fiber-rich legumes, such as beans, to your diet. A number of studies link a higher intake of fiber with a lower risk of heart disease. For instance, legumes provide both soluble and insoluble fiber as well as resistant starch (see Natural Wonders, page 94). Depending on the variety, expect legumes to provide 7 grams of total fiber and 2 grams of soluble fiber per $1/2$ cup (125 mL) serving.

   One long-term study, which followed approximately 10,000 subjects for a 19-year period, found that participants who consumed 21 grams of fiber a day had a 12% reduction in coronary heart disease and an 11% reduction in cardiovascular disease, compared with those who consumed only 5 grams a day. Studies also show that a high intake of fiber-rich foods protects against obesity. Because legumes are nutrient dense, they combine the ability to quickly satiate with a nutritional wallop. In other words, you don't need to consume a lot of calories to feel satisfied, while meeting nutritional objectives.

Easy "Paella"

Although this lazy person's adaptation of the classic Spanish dish lacks the complexity of a full-fledged version, it is very easy to make and captures enough of the traditional flavors to satisfy all but sticklers for authenticity. The chorizo provides Spanish resonance, but in a pinch Italian sausage will do. This is a very generous serving because it is intended to be a one-dish meal. By adding say, a salad, you can easily stretch this to serve more people.

Makes 4 servings

Can Be Halved
(see Tips, below)

Tips

If you are halving this recipe, be sure to use a small (2 to 3 quart) slow cooker.

Check to make sure your sausage does not contain gluten.

If you prefer, substitute ½ cup (125 mL) chicken stock mixed with 1 tsp (5 mL) lemon juice for the wine. Add along with the remaining chicken stock.

Nutrients Per Serving

Calories	583
Protein	51.4 g
Carbohydrates	52.8 g
Fat (Total)	18.4 g
Saturated Fat	4.4 g
Monounsaturated Fat	6.2 g
Polyunsaturated Fat	3.6 g
Dietary Fiber	6.4 g
Sodium	816 mg
Cholesterol	193 mg

EXCELLENT SOURCE OF vitamins A, C, B_6 and K, phosphorus, magnesium, potassium, iron and zinc.

GOOD SOURCE OF folate.

SOURCE OF vitamin B_{12} and calcium.

CONTAINS a very high amount of dietary fiber.

• **Large (approx. 5 quart) slow cooker**

2 lbs	skinless bone-in chicken thighs (about 8 thighs)	1 kg
1 tbsp	olive oil	15 mL
4 oz	fresh chorizo or Italian sausage, removed from casings (see Tips, left)	125 g
1	onion, finely chopped	1
2	stalks celery, diced	2
4	cloves garlic, minced	4
1 tsp	dried oregano	5 mL
½ tsp	cracked black peppercorns	2 mL
¼ tsp	saffron threads, crumbled	1 mL
1 cup	long-grain brown rice	250 mL
½ cup	dry white wine (see Tips, left)	125 mL
1	can (14 oz/398 mL) no-salt added diced tomatoes including juice	1
1½ cups	chicken stock	375 mL
2 tsp	sweet paprika (see Tip, right)	10 mL
1 cup	frozen green peas	250 mL
1	red bell pepper, seeded and diced	1
¼ cup	finely chopped parsley leaves	60 mL
	Hot pepper sauce, optional	

1. Arrange chicken evenly over bottom of stoneware.

2. In a skillet, heat oil over medium heat. Add chorizo, onion and celery and cook, stirring, breaking sausage up with a spoon, until meat is cooked through, about 6 minutes. Add garlic, oregano, peppercorns and saffron and cook, stirring, for 1 minute. Add rice and toss until evenly coated with mixture. Add wine, bring to a boil and boil for 2 minutes. Add tomatoes with juice and stock and bring to a boil.

3. Transfer to slow cooker stoneware. Place a clean tea towel folded in half (so you will have 2 layers) over top of stoneware to absorb moisture.

4. Cover and cook on Low for 5 hours or on High for $2\frac{1}{2}$ hours. Sprinkle paprika evenly over top of rice, then stir in peas and bell pepper. Cover and cook on High for 20 minutes, until peas are tender. Garnish liberally with parsley. Pass hot pepper sauce at the table, if using.

Mindful Morsels

A serving of this recipe is very high in sodium because the nutritional analysis was done using standard chorizo, which provides 526 mg of sodium. To reduce the amount of sodium, use homemade chorizo (or chorizo from a butcher, made on-premises) that does not contain added salt.

Natural Wonders

Hidden Gluten

If you have celiac disease, gluten sensitivity, or are not eating gluten for any number of reasons, you need to be constantly on the lookout for its presence. Many grains, in addition to wheat, contain gluten: barley and rye are the most common, but various varieties/ relatives of wheat, such as spelt, also contain this troublesome protein. Grains that are gluten-free include, amaranth, buckwheat, corn, millet, oats (see Mindful Morsels, page 24), quinoa, rice, sorghum, teff and wild rice.

While avoiding grains that contain gluten can be a bit tricky, the real challenge comes with identifying hidden gluten. Not the least of the problems is that wheat as an additive is, to borrow from Michael Pollan, often identified in language your grandmother wouldn't understand. Ingredients such as hydrogenated vegetable protein, hydrolyzed plant protein, textured vegetable protein, monosodium glutamate, malt and modified food starch may signal the presence of gluten. The important thing is to be aware that gluten appears in a wide variety of prepared foods, from canned broth to deli meats, sausages and spice blends, which means that you need to train yourself to read labels very carefully. When in doubt, contact the manufacturer.

Gluten also makes regular appearances in skin care products, cosmetics, shampoos, and so on. I have heard people who should know better dismiss this as a concern; in their opinion, gluten in products that are used topically is not problematic because it's not ingested. However, I speak from experience when I say that in sensitive individuals it can evoke a distressing eczema-like response.

Because manufacturers are constantly changing their formulae, gluten may suddenly appear in a familiar product that was previously gluten-free. Cross contamination may also be an issue. Although a product may not contain gluten, it may have been processed in a facility where foods containing gluten are prepared. As a result it may come in contact with or attract gluten and may pose problems for people with sensitivities. In my experience, gluten turns up in the most surprising places, so you need to be constantly vigilant.

Moroccan-Style Chicken with Prunes and Quinoa

A variation on a traditional Moroccan tagine, this delicious dish makes the most of the bittersweet combination of prunes, honey and lemon. Traditionally, this dish is served with couscous, but I've used quinoa, which is every bit as tasty, more nutritious and gluten-free.

Makes 8 servings

Can Be Halved
(see Tips, below)

Tips

If you are halving this recipe, be sure to use a small (1½ to 3½ quart) slow cooker

If you are marinating the chicken overnight, refrigerate the prune mixture separately.

- Medium to large (3½ to 5 quart) slow cooker

1½ cups	chopped pitted prunes	375 mL
1½ cups	water	375 mL
1 tbsp	liquid honey	15 mL
1 tsp	grated lemon zest	5 mL
4	cloves garlic, minced	4
1 tbsp	dried oregano, crumbled	15 mL
1 tbsp	grated lemon zest	15 mL
½ tsp	sea salt	2 mL
½ tsp	cracked black peppercorns	2 mL
2 lbs	skinless bone-in chicken thighs (about 8 thighs)	1 kg
2 cups	chicken stock	500 mL
¼ cup	freshly squeezed lemon juice	60 mL
3 cups	water	750 mL
1½ cups	quinoa, rinsed (see Tip, right)	375 mL

1. In a bowl, combine prunes, water, honey and lemon zest. Cover and set aside (see Tips, left).

2. In a bowl, combine garlic, oregano, lemon zest, salt and peppercorns. Add chicken and toss until evenly coated. Cover and refrigerate for at least 1 hour or overnight.

3. Transfer reserved chicken mixture to stoneware. Add chicken stock and lemon juice and stir well. Cover and cook on Low for 5 hours or on High for 2½ hours, until juices run clear when chicken is pierced with a fork. Add prunes with liquid. Cover and cook on High for 30 minutes to meld flavors.

4. Meanwhile, in a pot over high heat, bring 3 cups (750 mL) of the water to a boil. Reduce heat to medium. Add quinoa in a steady stream, stirring to prevent lumps from forming and return to a boil. Cover, reduce heat to low and simmer until tender and liquid is absorbed, about 15 minutes. Set aside.

5. To serve, spoon quinoa onto a plate and top with chicken mixture.

Nutrients Per Serving

Calories	283
Protein	17.7 g
Carbohydrates	42.5 g
Fat (Total)	5.3 g
Saturated Fat	1.0 g
Monounsaturated Fat	1.6 g
Polyunsaturated Fat	1.6 g
Dietary Fiber	5.5 g
Sodium	440 mg
Cholesterol	53 mg

EXCELLENT SOURCE OF magnesium and iron.

GOOD SOURCE OF vitamins B_6 and K, potassium and zinc.

SOURCE OF vitamin C and phosphorus.

CONTAINS a high amount of dietary fiber.

Tip

Some quinoa has a resinous coating called saponin, which needs to be rinsed off. To ensure your quinoa is saponin-free, before cooking fill a bowl with warm water and swish the kernels around, then transfer to a sieve and rinse thoroughly under cold running water.

Make Ahead

Complete Steps 1 and 2. Cover and refrigerate. When you're ready to cook, complete the recipe.

Mindful Morsels

I've used nutrient-dense quinoa in this recipe, because it is gluten-free. However, couscous, which is made from wheat, is a more conventional accompaniment for this classic dish.

If you have difficulty digesting grains, you may want to soak your quinoa overnight in plenty of water, preferably with a tbsp (15 mL) of apple cider vinegar. Drain and rinse thoroughly before using. You can also use sprouted quinoa, which is available in natural foods stores and some well-stocked supermarkets.

Natural Wonders

Prunes

Dietary guidelines suggest that people consuming 2,000 calories a day eat 2 cups (500 mL) of fruit a day. Adding prunes to your diet as an enhancement to the main course can help you achieve that goal.

Simply stated, prunes are highly nutritious. They contain antioxidant phenols and beta-carotene. They are also a source of potassium, which helps to keep blood pressure under control and may promote healthy bones by decreasing calcium excretion, among other benefits (see page 49). But prunes are best known as an excellent source of fiber. Just ¼ cup (60 mL) of prunes contains 3 grams of dietary fiber, which is associated with a wide range of healthful benefits, in addition to keeping you regular (see page 94). Prunes are also low on the glycemic index, which is good news for people with diabetes.

Be aware, however, that because they contain sugar there is a lot of conflicting information about the nutritional benefits of eating any fruit. I've even come across the odd dietitian who advises people not to eat fruit because it will spike a blood glucose response. In fact, most knowledgeable experts agree that for healthy individuals who do not suffer from diabetes or insulin resistance, eating fruit is beneficial (see page 331). The caveat is you need to consume whole fruit, which contains fiber. The fiber in the whole food slows down the rate at which your body absorbs the fructose, which is the glucose-spiking culprit.

Tagine of Chicken with Apricots

I love the juxtaposition of hot and sweet flavors in this dish. Apricots and chicken make a surprisingly tasty combination, and the harissa adds a nice hit of heat that is softened by the honey. Nutrient-dense brown rice or quinoa makes a great accompaniment. For an impressive presentation, arrange the cooked grain in a ring around the edge of a deep platter and fill the center with the chicken mixture. Then garnish with the pine nuts and cilantro. This makes a generous serving, so you won't need anything else.

Makes 8 servings

Can Be Halved
(see Tips, page 128)

Tip

Harissa is a North African condiment made from hot peppers. Look for it in specialty food stores. You can easily make your own (see Tip, page 133).

Make Ahead

Complete Step 2. Cover and refrigerate mixture for up to 2 days. When you're ready to cook, complete the recipe.

Nutrients Per Serving

Calories	390
Protein	31.5 g
Carbohydrates	25.7 g
Fat (Total)	19.0 g
Saturated Fat	3.3 g
Monounsaturated Fat	8.9 g
Polyunsaturated Fat	4.5 g
Dietary Fiber	4.9 g
Sodium	499 mg
Cholesterol	125 mg

EXCELLENT SOURCE OF vitamins A and B$_6$, phosphorus, potassium, iron and zinc.

GOOD SOURCE OF magnesium.

SOURCE OF vitamins C, B$_{12}$ and K, folate and calcium.

CONTAINS a high amount of dietary fiber.

• **Medium to large (3½ to 5 quart) slow cooker**

3 lbs	skinless bone-in chicken thighs (about 12 thighs)	1.5 kg
1 tbsp	olive oil	15 mL
2	onions, thinly sliced on the vertical	2
4	cloves garlic, minced	4
1 tbsp	minced gingerroot	15 mL
½ tsp	sea salt	2 mL
½ tsp	cracked black peppercorns	2 mL
2	bay leaves	2
1	piece (2 inches/5 cm) cinnamon stick	1
2 cups	chicken stock	500 mL
24	dried apricots	24
2 tbsp	harissa (see Tip, left and right)	30 mL
1 tbsp	liquid honey	15 mL
¼ cup	finely chopped cilantro leaves	60 mL
¼ cup	toasted pine nuts	60 mL

1. Arrange chicken evenly over bottom of stoneware.
2. In a skillet, heat oil over medium heat. Add onions and cook, stirring, until softened, about 3 minutes. Add garlic, ginger, salt, peppercorns, bay leaves and cinnamon stick and cook, stirring, for 1 minute. Stir in stock.
3. Transfer to slow cooker stoneware. Stir in apricots. Cover and cook on Low for 5 hours or on High for 2½ hours, until juices run clear when chicken is pierced with a fork. Remove and discard bay leaves.
4. In a small bowl, combine harissa and honey. Mix well. Add to slow cooker and stir well. Cover and cook on High for 10 minutes to blend flavors. Garnish with cilantro and pine nuts and serve.

Mindful Morsels

When buying dried apricots be sure to source them at a natural food store to ensure they have not been treated with sulfates. Brown in color rather than an appealing shade of orange, they may not look as pretty, but it's unlikely they will produce an allergic reaction.

Apricots contain vitamins A and C and fiber, as well as the phytonutrients beta-carotene and lycopene. They also provide goodly amounts of potassium. One serving of this dish is an excellent source of potassium, most of which comes from the apricots, along with the harissa; the chicken broth, onions and pine nuts contribute small amounts. We tend to take this mineral for granted, possibly because it is contained in a wide variety of foods. However, most people in North America don't get enough of this valuable nutrient, likely because we don't consume adequate amounts of fruits and vegetables, where it is usually plentiful. Potassium plays very important roles in the body, such as ensuring that your heart beats in a regular fashion (see Natural Wonders, page 49).

Natural Wonders

Food Combining

Although the idea that certain foods shouldn't be eaten together has gained a lot of traction, I've never found the arguments entirely convincing and neither has my respected nutritional consultant, Doug Cook. As he says, "the digestive tract is huge, with a surface area estimated to be the size of a tennis court. Given the structure of the small intestine, which is some 18 feet long (5.5 m), convoluted with villi and microvilli and assisted by a variety of enzymes and processes, the burden of proof is on those who support this theory. Where's the research?"

People have suggested that eating fruit (some even go so far as to include any carbohydrate-containing foods) with protein-rich foods will interfere with proper digestion. However, this is highly unlikely. The digestive tract is highly sophisticated. It is designed to ensure that your body makes the most of the nutrients you feed it and uses digestive enzymes, stomach acid, and even bile to do its work, which starts in the mouth, progresses to the stomach and continues on throughout the small intestine. Under most circumstances, barring any health issues that might involve the digestive tract, the body is more than capable of absorbing all that it needs from mixed-meals — a variety of foods containing protein, fats and carbohydrates.

French Basil Chicken

I call this French Basil Chicken to distinguish it from the well-known dish Thai basil chicken. I like to serve this with fluffy rice garnished with plenty of toasted pine nuts.

Makes 6 to 8 servings

Can Be Halved (see Tips, page 137)

Tips

If you prefer, substitute an equal amount of chicken stock for the wine.

To reduce sodium, use a reduced-sodium stock or make your own with no salt added (see page 116).

Make Ahead

Complete Step 1. Cover and refrigerate for up to 2 days. When you're ready to cook, complete the recipe.

Nutrients Per Serving

Calories	227
Protein	26.3 g
Carbohydrates	12.1 g
Fat (Total)	8.2 g
Saturated Fat	1.9 g
Monounsaturated Fat	3.2 g
Polyunsaturated Fat	1.8 g
Dietary Fiber	3.4 g
Sodium	437 mg
Cholesterol	103 mg

EXCELLENT SOURCE OF vitamins C and B$_6$.

GOOD SOURCE OF vitamins A and K, phosphorus, potassium, magnesium, iron and zinc.

SOURCE OF vitamin B$_{12}$, folate and calcium.

CONTAINS a moderate amount of dietary fiber.

- **Medium to large (3½ to 5 quart) slow cooker**

1 tbsp	extra virgin olive oil	15 mL
2	onions, finely chopped	2
4	cloves garlic, minced	4
1 tsp	herbes de Provence	5 mL
½ tsp	sea salt, or to taste	2 mL
½ tsp	cracked black peppercorns	2 mL
½ cup	dry white wine (see Tips, left)	125 mL
1 cup	chicken stock (see Tips, left)	250 mL
1	can (14 oz/398 mL) diced no-salt-added tomatoes including juice	1
1	can (14 oz/398 mL) artichoke hearts, drained, rinsed and quartered	1
3 lbs	skinless bone-in chicken thighs (about 12 thighs)	1.5 kg
2 cups	diced red bell pepper	500 mL
½ cup	finely chopped fresh basil leaves	125 mL

1. In a skillet, heat oil over medium heat. Add onions and cook, stirring, until softened, about 3 minutes. Add garlic, herbes de Provence, salt and peppercorns and cook, stirring, for 1 minute. Add wine and cook, stirring, for 1 minute. Add chicken stock and tomatoes with juice and bring to a boil. Stir in artichoke hearts and remove from heat.

2. Arrange chicken pieces evenly over the bottom of slow cooker stoneware and cover with tomato mixture. Cover and cook on Low for 6 hours or on High for 3 hours, until juices run clear when chicken is pierced with a fork. Stir in red pepper and basil. Cover and cook on High for 30 minutes, or until pepper is tender.

Mindful Morsels

Onions are the base for so many soups, stews and sauces that we take them for granted. But onions contain many nutrients, including quercetin, a flavonoid that may stop the growth of colon cancer, among other benefits (see Natural Wonder, page 293).

more information on page 136

Natural Wonders

Culinary Herbs

Culinary herbs do more than add color and flavor to a dish: they also have significant health benefits. For instance, USDA researchers have found that many culinary herbs such as parsley, sage, dill, thyme, rosemary and oregano are loaded with antioxidants. It's also worth knowing that more than half of the vitamin K in a serving of French Basil Chicken (page 134) comes from the basil.

Fragrant and pungent, basil also contains flavonoids, a group of phytonutrients that may protect cells and chromosomes from free radical damage. Along with isoflavones and ellagic acid, flavonoids belong to the polyphenol family of phytonutrients, which appear to have the ability to fight viruses and cancer. Moreover, a study published in the *American Journal of Clinical Nutrition* in 2002 linked a high intake of flavonoids with a lower incidence of heart disease and stroke. Research focused on basil's volatile oils has shown promising results in another area. Because these compounds restrict bacterial growth, researchers are exploring their potential value in treating antibiotic-resistant bacteria. Basil also contains eugenol, which inhibits activity of an enzyme causing inflammatory conditions such as arthritis.

One of the reasons plants develop phytonutrients is to protect themselves from predators, such as insects. It is now interesting to see how these compounds apparently protect humans from a wide variety of diseases, as well as how they can be used to heal the body when illness strikes. Phytonutrients are found in all plants, and there are so many of them even in individual plants such as basil, that we simply don't have the ability to identify how they all work in a laboratory, let alone the human body. This branch of nutritional science is, relatively speaking, in the early stages, but it shows great promise for the future.

Peppery Turkey Casserole

With five different kinds of peppers, this dish is a testament to the depth and variety of this useful ingredient. I've added quinoa because it's a nutritious complete protein. Here, I've stirred it in after the dish has finished cooking to make a casserole, but if you prefer, serve it on the side.

Makes 8 servings

Can Be Halved
(see Tips, below)

Tips

If you are halving this recipe, be sure to use a small (1½ to 3½ quart) slow cooker.

For convenience use bottled roasted red peppers or if you prefer, roast your own.

Some quinoa has a resinous coating called saponin, which needs to be rinsed off. To ensure your quinoa is saponin-free, before cooking fill a bowl with warm water and swish the kernels around, then transfer to a sieve and rinse thoroughly under cold running water.

Nutrients Per Serving

Calories	256
Protein	22.2 g
Carbohydrates	30.5 g
Fat (Total)	5.2 g
Saturated Fat	0.9 g
Monounsaturated Fat	2.3 g
Polyunsaturated Fat	1.3 g
Dietary Fiber	3.5 g
Sodium	385 mg
Cholesterol	37 mg

EXCELLENT SOURCE OF vitamins C and B$_6$, phosphorus, magnesium, potassium and iron.

GOOD SOURCE OF zinc.

SOURCE OF vitamin A.

CONTAINS a moderate amount of dietary fiber.

- **Medium to large (3½ to 5 quart) slow cooker**

1 tbsp	olive oil	15 mL
2	onions, finely chopped	2
4	cloves garlic, minced	4
2 tsp	dried oregano, crumbled	10 mL
½ tsp	cracked black peppercorns	2 mL
1 cup	dry white wine	250 mL
1	can (14 oz/398 mL) diced tomatoes, including juice (see Tip, page 46)	1
2 cups	chicken or turkey stock	500 mL
	Sea salt, optional	
1½ lbs	bone-in turkey breast, skin removed, cut into ½-inch (1 cm) cubes (about 2½ cups/625 mL)	750 g
2 tsp	sweet paprika, dissolved in 2 tbsp (30 mL) water	10 mL
1	jalapeño pepper, finely chopped	1
2	green bell peppers, diced	2
1	roasted red bell pepper, diced	1
3 cups	water	750 mL
1½ cups	quinoa, rinsed (see Tips, left)	375 mL

1. In a skillet, heat oil over medium heat. Add onions and cook, stirring, until softened, about 3 minutes. Add garlic, oregano and peppercorns and cook, stirring, for 1 minute. Add white wine and tomatoes with juice and bring to a boil.

2. Transfer to slow cooker stoneware. Add chicken stock and stir well. Season to taste with salt, if using. Add turkey and stir well. Cover and cook on Low for 6 hours or on High for 3 hours, until turkey is tender.

3. Add paprika solution, jalapeño pepper, bell peppers and roasted red pepper to slow cooker stoneware and stir well. Cover and cook on High for 30 minutes, until peppers are tender.

4. Meanwhile, in a pot, bring water to a boil. Add quinoa in a steady stream, stirring to prevent lumps from forming, and return to a boil. Cover, reduce heat to low and simmer until tender and liquid is absorbed, about 15 minutes. Set aside.

recipe continued on page 139

Peppery Turkey Casserole

Tip

If you have difficulty digesting grains, soak your quinoa overnight in plenty of water, preferably with a tbsp (15 mL) of apple cider vinegar. Drain and rinse thoroughly before using. You can also use sprouted quinoa, which is available in natural foods stores.

Make Ahead

Complete Step 1. Cover and refrigerate overnight or for up to 2 days. When you're ready to cook, continue with Steps 2 through 5.

5. When peppers are tender, add cooked quinoa to slow cooker stoneware and stir well. Serve immediately.

Variation

Peppery Turkey Stew: Omit the quinoa. Serve the stew over hot rice or mashed potatoes.

Mindful Morsels

Although many culinary herbs act as antioxidants, of those they have studied, USDA researchers have found oregano to have the most powerful antioxidant activity. Although the evidence isn't definitive, it also appears that oil of oregano may have value as an antifungal. Some laboratory research indicates that it can destroy fungi, including *Candida albicans*.

Natural Wonders

Vitamin B_6

A serving of Peppery Turkey Casserole (page 137) provides about 30% of the daily value of vitamin B_6. The bell peppers and the turkey are a source of this vitamin, which is best known for keeping skin healthy. B_6 is one of eight vitamins, often delivered in a B-complex vitamin supplement, which work together to perform a number of bodily functions (see page 149). Although vitamin B_6 is readily available in foods such as meat, poultry and fish and some fruits and vegetables, for various reasons some people, particularly those who are elderly, have difficultly getting enough of this nutrient (along with its relatives B_{12} and folate) in their diet.

The main jobs of vitamin B_6 are to break down protein and make red blood cells, which produce infection-fighting antibodies. But (along with vitamin B_{12} and folate) it also plays a role in keeping your mind sharp (see page 54). Perhaps that explains why energy drinks such as Red Bull contain high amounts of this vitamin. Vitamin B_6 also appears to boost serotonin, which helps to keep depression at bay and to alleviate morning sickness in pregnant women. According to a study reported in the *Journal of the National Cancer Institute*, vitamin B_6 may also lower the risk of colon cancer, one of the most common cancers in North America. A deficiency of this vitamin can lead to depression and certain skin conditions.

Once again, however, studies testing the efficacy of B vitamins taken in supplements have been extremely disappointing to say the least. In fact, research has shown that taking more than the DV of vitamin B_6 on a daily basis can lead to nerve damage. So, as always with nutrients, it makes sense to obtain this vitamin by consuming it in food.

Indian-Style Chicken with Puréed Spinach

This mouthwatering dish is an adaptation of one of my favorite recipes from Suneeta Vaswani's terrific book Easy Indian Cooking. *I usually serve it as the centerpiece of a meal, accompanied by rice.*

Makes 8 servings

Can Be Halved
(see Tips, page 142)

Tips

The nutrient analysis on this recipe was done using 1 tsp (5 mL) of salt. If you're concerned about your sodium intake, use less.

One chile produces a medium-hot result. Add a second chile only if you're a true heat seeker.

If using fresh spinach, be sure to remove the stems, and if it has not been pre-washed, rinse it thoroughly in a basin of lukewarm water.

Nutrients Per Serving

Calories	290
Protein	34.9 g
Carbohydrates	9.7 g
Fat (Total)	12.4 g
Saturated Fat	2.7 g
Monounsaturated Fat	5.3 g
Polyunsaturated Fat	2.5 g
Dietary Fiber	2.9 g
Sodium	665 mg
Cholesterol	138 mg

EXCELLENT SOURCE OF vitamins A, B₆ and K, folate, magnesium, potassium, iron and zinc.

GOOD SOURCE OF vitamin C.

SOURCE OF calcium.

CONTAINS a moderate amount of dietary fiber.

- **Large (approx. 5 quart) oval slow cooker**
- **Food processor or blender**

4 lbs	skinless bone-in chicken thighs (about 16 thighs)	2 kg
¼ cup	freshly squeezed lemon juice	60 mL
2 tbsp	olive oil	30 mL
2	onions, thinly sliced on the vertical	2
1 tbsp	minced gingerroot	15 mL
1 tbsp	minced garlic	15 mL
1 tbsp	ground cumin (see Tip, page 125)	15 mL
2 tsp	ground coriander	10 mL
1 tsp	cracked black peppercorns	5 mL
1 tsp	sea salt, or to taste (see Tips, left)	5 mL
1	can (14 oz/398 mL) diced tomatoes including juice	1
1 tsp	ground turmeric	5 mL
	Juice of 1 lime or lemon	
2	packages (each 10 oz/300 g) fresh or frozen spinach (see Tips, left)	2
1 to 2	long red or green chiles, chopped (see Tips, left)	1 to 2
1 cup	chicken stock	250 mL

1. Rinse chicken under cold running water and pat dry. In a bowl, combine chicken and lemon juice. Toss well and set aside for 20 to 30 minutes.

2. In a skillet, heat oil over medium-high heat. Add onions and cook, stirring, until they begin to color, about 5 minutes. Reduce heat to medium and cook, stirring, until golden, about 12 minutes. Add ginger, garlic, cumin, coriander, peppercorns and salt and cook, stirring, for 1 minute. Stir in tomatoes with juice and bring to a boil. Remove from heat.

3. Arrange marinated chicken evenly over the bottom of slow cooker stoneware. Pour tomato mixture over top. Cover and cook on Low for 6 hours or on High for 3 hours, until juices run clear when chicken is pierced with a fork.

4. In a small bowl, combine turmeric and lime juice. Set aside.

Make Ahead

This dish can be partially prepared before it is cooked. Complete Step 1. Cover and refrigerate chicken. Complete Step 2. Cover and refrigerate separately from chicken. The next day, continue with Steps 3, 4 and 5.

5. In a food processor or blender, combine spinach, chile(s) and chicken stock. Pulse until spinach is puréed. Add to chicken along with turmeric mixture and stir well. Cover and cook on High for 20 minutes, until mixture is bubbly.

Mindful Morsels

One serving of this dish provides almost 400% of the daily value of vitamin K, virtually all of which comes from the spinach.

Natural Wonders

Cumin

Cumin, a spice with a unique peppery yet earthy flavor, is used liberally in many cuisines, perhaps most notably in Indian and Mexican cooking, where it is an essential ingredient in curry and chili powders, respectively. But there's more to this versatile spice than aromatics: like most spices, cumin, which contains the essential minerals calcium, iron, potassium and manganese, as well as vitamins A and C and powerful phytonutrients, such as phytoestrogens, has nutrient value. Traditional wisdom is that cumin improves digestion, and new research explains why it has this effect. Cumin stimulates the pancreas, producing enzymes that help the body digest food and assimilate nutrients. Researchers are also exploring its cancer-preventing properties. In India, it has been found to inhibit bacteria that cause food poisoning. In a separate study, also completed in India, researchers found that cumin was very effective in protecting against bone loss and preventing osteoporosis.

When using cumin, I like to use the whole seeds, which I toast and grind (see Tip, page 125). Not only does toasting bring out the spice's pleasant nuttiness, but it also makes the kitchen deliciously fragrant. Also, whole seeds maintain their freshness much longer than ground powder. Stored in an airtight container in a cool dry place, away from light, cumin seeds will keep for as long as three years, whereas ground cumin keeps only for a year.

Spicy Peanut Chicken

This is a lively dish, chock-full of many flavors, all of which work together to create the "yum" factor. I like to serve this over brown basmati rice to add fiber and complete the meal.

Makes 6 to 8 servings

Can Be Halved
(see Tips, below)

Tips

If you are halving this recipe, be sure to use a small (1½ to 3½ quart) slow cooker.

Always check the labels of prepared products, such as curry paste, to ensure they don't contain unwanted additives, such as gluten.

Make Ahead

Complete Step 1. Cover and refrigerate for up to 2 days. When you're ready to cook, complete the recipe.

• **Medium to large (3½ to 5 quart) slow cooker**

1 tbsp	olive or extra virgin coconut oil	15 mL
2	onions, finely chopped	2
2	carrots, peeled and diced	2
4	stalks celery, diced	4
4	cloves garlic, minced	4
1 tbsp	minced gingerroot	15 mL
½ tsp	cracked black peppercorns	2 mL
1 cup	chicken stock	250 mL
3 lbs	skinless bone-in chicken thighs (about 12 thighs)	1.5 kg
3 tbsp	smooth natural peanut butter	45 mL
2 tbsp	freshly squeezed lemon juice	30 mL
2 tbsp	reduced-sodium gluten-free soy sauce	30 mL
2 tsp	Thai red curry paste (see Tips, left)	10 mL
½ cup	coconut milk	125 mL
2 cups	sweet green peas, thawed if frozen	500 mL
1	red bell pepper, diced	1
¼ cup	chopped roasted peanuts	60 mL
½ cup	finely chopped cilantro leaves	125 mL

1. In a skillet, heat oil over medium heat. Add onions, carrots and celery and cook, stirring, until carrots are softened, about 7 minutes. Add garlic, ginger and peppercorns and cook, stirring, for 1 minute. Add chicken stock and bring to a boil.

2. Arrange chicken over bottom of slow cooker stoneware and add vegetable mixture. Cover and cook on Low for 5 hours or on High for 2½ hours, until juices run clear when chicken is pierced with a fork.

3. In a bowl, combine peanut butter, lemon juice, soy sauce and red curry paste. Mix well. Add to slow cooker stoneware and stir well. Add coconut milk, peas and red pepper and stir well. Cover and cook on High for 20 minutes, until pepper is tender and mixture is hot. Garnish with peanuts and cilantro and serve.

Natural Wonders

Peanuts

Although they have many of the healthful features of nuts, despite their name, peanuts are not a nut but a legume. They are rich in monounsaturated fats, the same kind found in olive oil. A source of vitamin E, niacin, folate and magnesium, peanuts also contain an array of healthful antioxidants. These include resveratrol, which is found in red wine and thought to be linked to lower rates of cardiovascular disease, and polyphenols, which appear to have antiviral and anticarcinogenic properties. Peanuts also contain arginine, an amino acid, which boosts nitric oxide, thereby fostering healthy blood vessels. Eating peanuts can also help to prevent gallstones. The Nurses' Health Study found that women who ate at least 1 ounce (30 g) of nuts, peanuts or peanut butter a week, lowered their risk of developing gallstones by 25%.

The one problem with peanuts is that many people are highly allergic to them, so make sure you are not serving a dish containing peanuts to anyone who might have a peanut allergy. Peanut allergies can be quite challenging because all foods and food products that contain peanuts, peanut-derived ingredients or are made in a facility that handles peanuts need to be avoided. The scope of this can be huge. Steer clear of any products with an ingredient list that states the product "may contain," or "may contain traces of," or is "made in a facility that handles" peanuts.

To be a savvy shopper, always check the ingredient list and be aware that nomenclature can be confusing. In some jurisdictions, new labeling laws have been introduced to help consumers sort through this maze. In Canada, for instance, if the product contains any peanuts the word must appear on the package. Products that should be avoided include:

- Arachis oil
- Beer nuts
- Goober nuts, goober peas
- Ground nuts
- Kernels
- Mandelonas, Nu-Nuts™
- Nut meats
- Valencias

There are many theories as to way peanut allergies are on the rise, but at the time of this writing, none are conclusive.

Miso Mushroom Chicken with Chinese Cabbage

I love the combination of flavors in this luscious stew. Serve it over hot brown rice for a delicious meal.

Makes 8 servings

Can Be Halved
(see Tips, below)

Tips

If you are halving this recipe, be sure to use a small (2 to 3 quart) slow cooker.

Brown rice miso, unlike other kinds of miso, is gluten-free.

Nutrients Per Serving

Calories	229
Protein	22.4 g
Carbohydrates	19.0 g
Fat (Total)	7.2 g
Saturated Fat	1.6 g
Monounsaturated Fat	2.9 g
Polyunsaturated Fat	1.5 g
Dietary Fiber	2.4 g
Sodium	890 mg
Cholesterol	85 mg

EXCELLENT SOURCE OF vitamins B_6 and K.

GOOD SOURCE OF folate, phosphorus, magnesium, potassium and zinc.

SOURCE OF vitamins B_{12} and C, calcium and iron.

CONTAINS a moderate amount of dietary fiber.

- **Large (approx. 5 quart) slow cooker**

1	package (½ oz/14 g) dried wood ear mushrooms	1
1 cup	hot water	250 mL
1 tbsp	oil	15 mL
2	onions, finely chopped	2
4	stalks celery, diced	4
6	cloves garlic, minced	6
1 tbsp	minced gingerroot	15 mL
1 tsp	cracked black peppercorns	5 mL
½ tsp	sea salt	2 mL
8 oz	shiitake mushrooms, stems discarded, sliced	250 g
½ cup	mirin	125 mL
¼ cup	reduced-sodium gluten-free soy sauce or coconut aminos	60 mL
2 cups	chicken stock	500 mL
2 lbs	skinless bone-in chicken thighs (about 8)	1 kg
2 tbsp	brown rice miso (see Tips, left)	30 mL
6 cups	packed shredded napa cabbage	1.5 L

1. In a bowl, combine dried mushrooms and hot water. Let stand for 30 minutes. Drain through a fine sieve, discarding soaking liquid. Pat mushrooms dry with paper towel, chop finely and set aside.

2. In a skillet, heat oil over medium heat. Add onions and celery and cook, stirring, until softened, about 5 minutes. Add garlic, ginger, peppercorns, salt and reserved dried mushrooms and cook, stirring, for 1 minute. Add shiitake mushrooms and toss until coated. Add mirin and bring to a boil. Boil for 1 minute. Stir in soy sauce and stock.

3. Arrange chicken evenly over bottom of stoneware and pour mushroom mixture over top. Cover and cook on Low for 6 hours or on High for 3 hours, until chicken is falling off the bone. Stir in miso. Add cabbage, in batches, stirring until each batch is submerged. Cover and cook on High for 15 minutes, until cabbage is wilted and flavors meld.

Mindful Morsels

A serving of this chicken is relatively high in sodium, most of which comes from the soy sauce and miso (350 mg and 295 mg, respectively). Both these ingredients add significant flavor and depth to the dish. The mirin provides 100 mg of sodium and the added salt 97 mg. To reduce the sodium in this recipe, I recommend omitting the added salt and reducing the quantity of mirin by half; that would reduce the amount of sodium per serving to 743 mg. This is quite a large serving, so you don't need to add anything other than some brown rice. A half cup (125 mL) serving of brown rice would add only 5 mg of sodium to the meal, along with valuable nutrients such as manganese, selenium, copper, thiamine and niacin, as well as additional phosphorus, magnesium and zinc.

Natural Wonders

Cabbage

Cabbage, like all members of the crucifer family, which also includes arugula, broccoli, kale, cauliflower, cabbage, turnip, collard greens, bok choy, Brussels sprouts, rutabaga, collard greens, rapini, turnip and watercress, among others, is such a healthful vegetable that it is known as a "functional food." This means it has been identified as a food that offers health benefits beyond basic nutrition. The National Cancer Institute, for instance, has identified cabbage as a food with high cancer-fighting power. Cabbage contains two particularly potent cancer-fighting phytonutrients: indoles, which protect against breast cancer by helping to metabolize estrogen; and isothiocyanates, which help the body to detoxify carcinogens. Research shows that people who consume significant quantities of cabbage have particularly low rates of colon cancer.

Low in calories, cabbage provides vitamin C, folate, potassium and dietary fiber. One caveat: if you have thyroid problems you might want to limit your consumption of this vegetable because cabbage contains substances that may interfere with thyroid functioning.

Two-Bean Turkey Chili

This delicious chili, which has just a hint of heat, is perfect for family get-togethers. Add a tossed green salad, sprinkled with shredded carrots.

Makes 8 servings

Can Be Halved
(see Tips, below)

Tips

If you are halving this recipe, be sure to use a small (1½ to 3½ quart) slow cooker.

You can also make this chili using leftover turkey. Use 3 cups (750 mL) of shredded cooked turkey and add along with the bell peppers.

Add the jalapeño pepper if you're a heat seeker, or the chipotle in adobo sauce, if you like a hint of smoke, as well.

Nutrients Per Serving

Calories	277
Protein	29.6 g
Carbohydrates	30.7 g
Fat (Total)	4.5 g
Saturated Fat	1.0 g
Monounsaturated Fat	2.3 g
Polyunsaturated Fat	0.9 g
Dietary Fiber	7.7 g
Sodium	764 mg
Cholesterol	51 mg

EXCELLENT SOURCE OF vitamins C, B$_6$ and K, phosphorus, magnesium, potassium and iron.
GOOD SOURCE OF vitamin A, folate and zinc.
SOURCE OF calcium.
CONTAINS a very high amount of dietary fiber.

- **Medium to large (3½ to 5 quart) slow cooker**

1 tbsp	olive oil	15 mL
2	onions, finely chopped	2
4	stalks celery, diced	4
6	cloves garlic, minced	6
2 tsp	dried oregano, crumbled	10 mL
½ tsp	cracked black peppercorns	2 mL
	Zest of 1 lime	
1 tbsp	ground cumin (see Tip, page 125)	15 mL
2 tbsp	fine stone-ground cornmeal	30 mL
1 cup	chicken or turkey stock	250 mL
1	can (28 oz/796 mL) tomatoes, including juice, coarsely chopped	1
2 lbs	bone-in turkey breast, skin removed, cut into ½-inch (1 cm) cubes (about 3 cups/750 mL)	1 kg
4 cups	cooked pinto beans	1 L
2 cups	frozen sliced green beans	500 mL
1 tbsp	New Mexico or ancho chili powder, dissolved in 2 tbsp (30 mL) freshly squeezed lime juice	15 mL
1	each green and red bell pepper, diced	1
1	can (4.5 oz/127 mL) diced mild green chiles	1
1	jalapeño pepper or chipotle pepper in adobo sauce, diced, optional (see Tips, left)	1

1. In a skillet, heat oil over medium heat. Add onions and celery and cook, stirring, until celery is softened, about 5 minutes. Add garlic and cook, stirring, for 1 minute. Add oregano, peppercorns, lime zest and cumin and cook, stirring, for 1 minute. Add cornmeal and toss to coat. Add chicken stock and cook, stirring, until mixture boils, about 1 minute. Add tomatoes with juice and return to a boil.

2. Transfer to slow cooker stoneware. Add turkey, pinto beans and green beans and stir well. Cover and cook on Low for 8 hours or on High for 4 hours, until turkey is tender and mixture is bubbly.

Make Ahead

Complete Step 1. Cover and refrigerate overnight or for up to 2 days. When you're ready to cook complete the recipe.

3. Add chili powder solution, green and red bell peppers, mild green chiles, and jalapeno, if using. Cover and cook on High for 30 minutes, until bell peppers are tender.

Mindful Morsels

The nutrient analysis on this recipe was done using regular canned pinto beans. To reduce the amount of sodium, use dried beans (see Basic Beans, page 284) or canned organic pinto beans with no salt added. The brand I use, which is very tasty, is seasoned with kombu seaweed and contains only 17 mg of sodium per ½ cup (125 mL) serving.

Natural Wonders

Turkey

Turkey is one of the best sources of complete protein because once the skin is removed it is a very lean meat. In addition to being rich in protein, turkey is also a good source of important B vitamins — niacin, B_6 and B_{12} — as well as zinc, an immune system protector that can be challenging to obtain from dietary sources. The body can utilize the zinc in turkey and other meats more readily than that from non-meat sources. Turkey is also a good source of the trace mineral selenium, an antioxidant that supports a number of bodily functions, such as regulating thyroid function and keeping the immune system on track. Recent research indicates that selenium may reduce the risk of coronary artery

disease and protect the body from prostate, colorectal and lung cancers. Some researchers suggest taking selenium before spending time in the sun because it may reduce the occurrence of skin cancer.

Turkey Chili with Black-Eyed Peas

This delicious chili is lighter than those made with red meat and it's a favorite with my family. This is a generous serving, so you don't need much, if anything, to complete the meal. I like to serve this (and almost any chili) with an Avocado Topping (see below), which adds healthy fats and additional nutrients as well as lip-smacking flavor. If you prefer, finish the chili with more traditional toppings, such as shredded Monterey Jack cheese, finely chopped red onion or cilantro and/or sour cream.

Makes 6 to 8 servings

Can Be Halved
(see Tips, page 146)

Tip

For this quantity of beans, use 1½ cans (14 to 19 oz/398 to 540 mL) drained and rinsed black-eyed peas with no salt added, or soak and cook 1½ cups (375 mL) dried black-eyed peas (see Basic Beans, page 284).

Nutrients Per Serving

Calories	273
Protein	34.1 g
Carbohydrates	25.1 g
Fat (Total)	4.2 g
Saturated Fat	1.0 g
Monounsaturated Fat	2.0 g
Polyunsaturated Fat	1.0 g
Dietary Fiber	7.0 g
Sodium	95 mg
Cholesterol	70 mg

EXCELLENT SOURCE OF vitamins C and B_6, niacin, folate, phosphorus, potassium, iron and manganese.
GOOD SOURCE OF vitamins B_{12} and K, thiamine, pantothenic acid, magnesium, selenium and zinc.
SOURCE OF vitamin A, riboflavin, calcium and copper.
CONTAINS a very high amount of dietary fiber.

- **Medium to large (3½ to 5 quart) slow cooker**

1 tbsp	olive oil	15 mL
2	onions, finely chopped	2
3	cloves garlic, minced	3
2 tsp	dried oregano	10 mL
2 tsp	ground coriander (see Step 1, page 170)	10 mL
2 tsp	ground cumin	10 mL
1 tsp	cracked black peppercorns	5 mL
	Sea salt	
1	can (28 oz/796 mL) no-salt added diced tomatoes, including juice	1
2 cups	chicken stock	500 mL
2 lbs	skinless boneless turkey breast or thighs, cut into 1-inch (2.5 cm) cubes	1 kg
3 cups	cooked black-eyed peas (see Tip, left)	750 mL
2	green bell peppers, seeded and cut into thin strips	2
2	jalapeño peppers, finely chopped	2
2 tbsp	chili powder	30 mL

Avocado Topping (Optional)

1	avocado, cubed (½ inch/1 cm)	1
2 tbsp	finely chopped red onion	30 mL
2 tbsp	finely chopped cilantro leaves	30 mL
1 tbsp	freshly squeezed lime juice	15 mL
	Sea salt and freshly ground black pepper	

1. In a skillet, heat oil over medium heat. Add onions and garlic and cook, stirring, until softened, about 3 minutes. Add oregano, coriander, cumin, peppercorns, and salt to taste, and cook, stirring, for 1 minute. Add tomatoes with juice and chicken stock and bring to a boil.

2. Transfer to stoneware. Add turkey and peas and stir to combine. Cover and cook on Low for 6 to 8 hours or on High for 3 to 4 hours, until turkey is no longer pink inside.

Make Ahead

Slice bell peppers, cover and refrigerate. Complete Step 1. Cover and refrigerate mixture for up to 2 days. When you're ready to cook, complete the recipe.

3. Stir in bell peppers, jalapeño peppers and chili powder. Cover and cook for 20 to 25 minutes, until peppers are tender. Spoon into individual bowls and top each with a healthy dollop of Avocado Topping, if using, and/or additional garnishes, as desired.

4. *Avocado Topping, optional:* In a bowl, combine avocado, red onion, cilantro and lime juice. Mix well. Season to taste with salt and freshly ground black pepper.

Mindful Morsels

Eating a healthy diet should be a lifelong commitment, not just something you do to solve a short-term problem. Consider, for instance, one Chinese study that looked at the consumption of garlic and the antioxidants vitamins C and E, and selenium (all of which are provided in a serving of this chili, with added avocado topping), in relation to the incidence of gastric or esophageal cancer. When researchers examined results over a period of 7.3 years they found no benefit. However, when the time frame was extended to 14.7 years, there was a significant reduction in both diseases.

Natural Wonders

B Vitamins

A serving of Turkey Chili with Black-Eyed Peas provides a panoply of B vitamins — B_6, folate, riboflavin, niacin, thiamine and pantothenic acid (vitamin B_5). As a group, B vitamins are involved in a variety of biological functions, many of which overlap. In this sense, B vitamins, like all nutrients, wear many different hats when it comes to keeping you healthy.

As a group, the B vitamins (there are eight in all) work together to support brain function (see page 54) and help to promote healthy balanced moods; all eight are involved in neurotransmitter production and function. They also help you to cope with stress by increasing serotonin production and counteracting fatigue. If you are feeling chronically tired, irritable and anxious, you may be suffering from a deficiency of B vitamins.

B vitamins are essential for the growth and development of all blood cells, especially red blood cells, which transport oxygen throughout the body. They are needed for the metabolism of protein, fat and carbohydrate and ensure that your body has an adequate supply of energy. But the good news doesn't stop there. They also help to keep your skin healthy by maintaining skin integrity, and are also crucial for a robust immune system. Your body cannot make the hundreds of hormones needed for everyday health, such as testosterone, estrogen, calcitriol (from vitamin D), or retinoic acid (from vitamin A) without a steady supply of B vitamins.

Thai-Style Coconut Fish Curry

Fish and Seafood

Thai-Style Coconut Fish Curry

This luscious dish has everything going for it: a centerpiece of succulent fish, a sauce of creamy coconut accented with zesty Asian flavors and an abundance of tasty vegetables to complement the mix. Serve this over brown basmati rice to add nutrients and fiber and complete the meal.

Makes 8 servings

Can Be Halved
(see Tips, below)

Tips

If you are halving this recipe, be sure to use a small (1½ to 3½ quart) slow cooker

Check the label to make sure your curry paste does not contain unwanted additives, such as gluten.

Nutrients Per Serving

Calories	243
Protein	24.0 g
Carbohydrates	12.1 g
Fat (Total)	11.5 g
Saturated Fat	6.1 g
Monounsaturated Fat	2.9 g
Polyunsaturated Fat	1.5 g
Dietary Fiber	3.1 g
Sodium	516 mg
Cholesterol	52 mg

EXCELLENT SOURCE OF vitamins C, B_6 and B_{12} and phosphorus.
GOOD SOURCE OF vitamins A and K, magnesium, potassium, folate and zinc.
SOURCE OF iron.
CONTAINS a moderate amount of dietary fiber.

- **Medium to large (3½ to 5 quart) slow cooker**

1 tbsp	olive or extra virgin coconut oil	15 mL
2	onions, finely chopped	2
4	cloves garlic, minced	4
1 tbsp	minced gingerroot	15 mL
1 tsp	finely grated lime zest	5 mL
1 cup	vegetable stock	250 mL
½ cup	fish stock	125 mL
2 tbsp	freshly squeezed lime juice	30 mL
2 tsp	Thai green curry paste (see Tips, left)	10 mL
1 cup	coconut milk	250 mL
2 tbsp	gluten-free fish sauce	30 mL
2 lbs	firm white fish, such as snapper, skin removed, cut into bite-size pieces, if desired	1 kg
2 cups	drained rinsed canned bamboo shoot strips	500 mL
2 cups	sweet green peas, thawed if frozen	500 mL
1	red bell pepper, diced	1
½ cup	finely chopped cilantro leaves	125 mL
	Toasted sesame seeds, optional	

1. In a skillet, heat oil over medium heat. Add onions and cook, stirring, until softened, about 3 minutes. Add garlic, ginger and lime zest and cook, stirring, for 1 minute. Add vegetable and fish stock and stir well. Transfer to slow cooker stoneware. Cover and cook on Low for 6 hours or on High for 3 hours.

2. In a bowl, combine lime juice and curry paste. Add to slow cooker stoneware and stir well. Stir in coconut milk, fish sauce, fish, bamboo shoots, green peas and red pepper. Cover and cook on High for 20 to 30 minutes, until fish flakes easily when pierced with a fork and mixture is hot. Garnish with cilantro and toasted sesame seeds, if using.

Variation

Substitute 12 oz (375 g) peeled cooked shrimp for half of the fish.

Make Ahead

This dish can be partially prepared ahead of time. Complete Step 1. Cover and refrigerate for up to 2 days. When you're ready to cook, complete Step 2.

Natural Wonders

Omega-3 Fatty Acids

Fish, particularly oily fish, such as salmon and tuna, provides omega-3 fatty acids, which are in short supply in the food North Americans regularly eat. Omega-3s were discovered by Danish scientists in the 1970s, who observed that Eskimos in Greenland, who consumed a diet high in fish fat, were remarkably free from heart disease. Since then, research has confirmed the value of these essential fats in helping to reduce the risk of a wide range of illnesses, from arthritis to depression. Unfortunately, the predominance of industrialized agriculture has decreased the amount of omega-3 fats in many foods, from leafy greens to eggs, fish and meats.

Even though our bodies can't manufacture these fatty acids, they are essential to good health. Without them the membranes of our cells are weakened, which may make us vulnerable to a wide range of health problems, from dry skin and brittle nails to depression and joint pain, not to mention more serious diseases. Studies show that an adequate supply of omega-3 fatty acids can reduce the risk of coronary artery disease, slightly lower blood pressure and strengthen the immune system. Researchers are also studying the possibility that consumption of omega-3 fatty acids may protect against some forms of cancer and help reduce the symptoms of autoimmune diseases such as multiple sclerosis, psoriasis, lupus and rheumatoid arthritis.

It is worth noting that the benefits of omega-3 fatty acids begin while babies are still in the womb. Studies show that pregnant women who consume adequate supplies of omega-3s give birth to babies with healthier birth weights and higher IQs. They were also less likely to have allergies as infants. And there are also benefits to new mothers themselves, such as being less likely to suffer from postpartum depression.

Although the U.S. does not have a recommended daily value for this nutrient, the 2002 Report of Recommendations for Healthy Eating from the National Academies' Institute of Medicine recommends that men get 1.6 grams of omega-3s and women 1.1 grams every day, and the World Health Organization suggests 300 to 500 mg/day of EPA and DHA combined and 800 mg to 1.1 g/day of alpha-linolenic acid (ALA). The average American gets about 100 to 200 mg/day of EPA and DHA and about 1.4 g/day of ALA.

Cioppino

This zesty stew originated on the San Francisco pier, where it was prepared using whatever was bountiful in the catch that day. The rouille adds flavor and richness, and unless you are rigorously counting calories you don't need to worry about adding a small dollop per serving if your mayonnaise is made with extra virgin olive oil, which is extremely nutritious. Serve this with a green salad.

Makes 8 servings

Can Be Halved
(see Tips, below)

Tips

If you are halving this recipe, be sure to use a small (2 to 3½ quart) slow cooker.

When making cioppino, I like to use Italian San Marzano tomatoes, which are thick and flavorful. If you have access to this product, you can omit the tomato paste.

Nutrients Per Serving

Calories	199
Protein	28.8 g
Carbohydrates	11.0 g
Fat (Total)	4.4 g
Saturated Fat	0.8 g
Monounsaturated Fat	1.8 g
Polyunsaturated Fat	0.9 g
Dietary Fiber	2.3 g
Sodium	558 mg
Cholesterol	100 mg

EXCELLENT SOURCE OF vitamin B$_{12}$, phosphorus, magnesium and potassium.
GOOD SOURCE OF vitamins C and B$_6$, folate and zinc.
SOURCE OF vitamin A and calcium.
CONTAINS a moderate amount of dietary fiber.

- **Large (approx. 5 quart) slow cooker**

1 tbsp	olive oil	15 mL
2	onions, finely chopped	2
1	bulb fennel, cored and chopped	1
6	cloves garlic, minced	6
4	anchovy fillets, finely chopped	4
1 tsp	cracked black peppercorns	5 mL
½ tsp	fennel seeds, toasted and ground (see Tip, right)	2 mL
1 tbsp	tomato paste (see Tips, left)	15 mL
1	can (28 oz/796 mL) tomatoes, including juice, coarsely chopped	1
1 cup	dry white wine	250 mL
4 cups	fish stock	1 L
1 lb	skinless firm white fish, such as snapper, cut into bite-size pieces	500 g
8 oz	cooked peeled, deveined shrimp, thawed if frozen	250 g
8 oz	cooked crabmeat	250 g
1	red bell pepper, diced	1
1	long red chile pepper, diced, optional	1
	Sea salt, optional	

Easy Rouille (optional)

⅓ cup	mayonnaise	75 mL
2	cloves garlic, puréed	2
1 tbsp	extra virgin olive oil	15 mL
1 tsp	freshly squeezed lemon juice	5 mL
¼ tsp	hot or regular paprika	1 mL

1. In a skillet, heat oil over medium heat. Add onions and fennel and cook, stirring, until softened, about 3 minutes. Add garlic, anchovies, peppercorns and toasted fennel seeds and cook, stirring, for 1 minute. Stir in tomato paste. Add tomatoes with juice and white wine and bring to a boil.

Tip

To toast fennel seeds: Place in a dry skillet over medium heat and cook, stirring, until seeds are fragrant, about 3 minutes. Immediately transfer to a mortar or a spice grinder and grind.

Make Ahead

This dish can be partially prepared before it is cooked. Complete Step 1. Cover and refrigerate overnight or for up to 2 days. When you're ready to cook, continue with Steps 2 through 4.

2. Transfer to slow cooker stoneware. Add fish stock and stir well. Cover and cook on Low for 6 to 8 hours or on High for 3 to 4 hours. Add fish, shrimp, crabmeat, red pepper, and chile pepper, if using, and stir well. Cover and cook on High for 20 minutes, until fish flakes easily when pierced with a fork and seafood is heated through. Season with salt to taste.

3. *Easy Rouille (optional):* In a small bowl, combine mayonnaise, garlic, olive oil, lemon juice and paprika. Mix until thoroughly blended.

4. To serve, ladle cioppino into warm bowls, garnish each serving with a dollop of rouille, if using.

Mindful Morsels

Oysters, clams and mussels contain sterols. These mollusks were once thought to be high in cholesterol, which, it was believed, had a negative impact on blood cholesterol levels. Not only do we now understand that the cholesterol in food isn't likely to be problematic, we also now realize that the cholesterol in mollusks consists of plant sterols, which actually work to keep blood cholesterol low.

Natural Wonders

Fennel Seed

Fennel is a particularly interesting plant because its various parts have different roles, both in culinary and medicinal terms (see page 295). While fennel seed is often used to add flavor to dishes (as it is used here) and is often added to spice blends such as Chinese five-spice powder, it also has a distinguished place in herbal medicine. Fennel seed has traditionally been used to treat digestive problems and is particularly valued for its ability to combat bloating and flatulence. More recently, researchers in Bulgaria found it relieved "diarrhea syndrome" in people suffering from inflammatory bowel disease. Fennel water has a long history in herbal medicine as an ingredient in "gripe water," which is used to treat infant colic. Recent studies confirm the efficacy of this treatment.

Fennel seed is the most concentrated form of the disease-fighting phytonutrient anethole, which scientists are currently studying for its anti-inflammatory and cancer-preventing properties. Studies have found the phytonutrients in fennel seeds to be helpful in relieving a variety of symptoms, ranging from menstrual pain to arthritis. For instance, fennel has been shown to reduce the swelling and pain associated with arthritis, to prevent blood from clotting and to help keep blood pressure under control, among other benefits.

Bistro Fish Soup

Although it is described as soupe de poisson *in France, where it is a mainstay of bistro culture, this ambrosial concoction is more closely related to a stew. It makes a satisfying main course accompanied by a green salad.*

Makes 8 to 10 servings

Tips

If you don't have a mini-chopper, you can chop the roasted red pepper very finely and grate the garlic or put it through a press. Combine in a bowl with the mayonnaise and hot pepper sauce.

To make crostini: Brush 8 to 10 gluten-free baguette slices with olive oil on both sides. Toast under preheated broiler, turning once, until golden, about 2 minutes per side.

Nutrients Per Serving

Calories	220
Protein	7.8 g
Carbohydrates	26.4 g
Fat (Total)	9.7 g
Saturated Fat	1.2 g
Monounsaturated Fat	5.8 g
Polyunsaturated Fat	2.2 g
Dietary Fiber	3.5 g
Sodium	990 mg
Cholesterol	13 mg

EXCELLENT SOURCE OF vitamins C and K.

GOOD SOURCE OF vitamin B$_6$, potassium, folate and magnesium.

SOURCE OF vitamin A, phosphorus and iron.

CONTAINS a moderate amount of dietary fiber.

- **Large (minimum 5 quart) slow cooker**

2 tbsp	olive oil	30 mL
3	large leeks, white part with a bit of green, cleaned and thinly sliced	3
1	onion, diced	1
1	bulb fennel, trimmed, cored and chopped, or 6 stalks celery, chopped	1
4	sprigs parsley or chervil	4
4	cloves garlic, minced	4
1 tsp	fennel seeds, crushed	5 mL
½ tsp	sea salt	2 mL
½ tsp	cracked black peppercorns	2 mL
1	can (28 oz/796 mL) tomatoes, including juice, coarsely chopped	1
6 cups	vegetable stock (see Mindful Morsels, right)	1.5 L
2 lbs	fish bones and pieces	1 kg
2	potatoes (about 1 lb/500 g), diced	2
1 tbsp	Pernod, optional	15 mL
½ cup	parsley leaves, finely chopped	125 mL
	Gluten-Free Crostini (see Tips, left)	

Rouille

¼ cup	mayonnaise	60 mL
1	roasted red pepper, peeled and chopped	1
2	cloves garlic, minced	2
	Hot pepper sauce	
	Finely chopped parsley	

1. In a skillet, heat oil over medium heat. Add leeks, onion and fennel and cook, stirring, until fennel is softened, about 6 minutes. Add parsley, garlic, fennel seeds, salt and peppercorns and cook, stirring, for 1 minute. Add tomatoes with juice and bring to a boil. Transfer to slow cooker stoneware.

Make Ahead

This recipe can be partially prepared before it is cooked. Complete Step 1. Cover and refrigerate overnight or for up to 2 days. When you're ready to cook, continue with Steps 2 and 3.

2. Add vegetable stock, fish trimmings and potatoes and stir well. Cover and cook on Low for 8 hours, until vegetables are very tender. Place a sieve over a large bowl or saucepan. Working in batches, ladle the soup into the sieve, removing and discarding any visible bones. Using a wooden spoon, push the solids through the sieve. Add Pernod, if using, to the strained soup. Add parsley and stir well.

3. *Rouille:* In a mini-chopper, combine mayonnaise, red pepper, garlic and hot pepper sauce to taste. Process until smooth. To serve, ladle hot soup into individual bowls and float a crostini on top of each serving. Garnish with parsley and top with a dollop of rouille.

Mindful Morsels

The nutrient analysis on this recipe was done using prepared vegetable stock, which is high in sodium. If you are concerned about the sodium, make Basic Vegetable Stock (page 120), which will reduce the amount of sodium to 403 mg.

Natural Wonders

Extra Virgin Olive Oil

Extra virgin olive oil is one of the few fats that has been linked with good health for a relatively long time. In 1958, Dr. Ancel Keys began a study that revealed a link between lower rates of heart disease and a diet rich in fruits, vegetables, fish, poultry, nuts, pasta and olive oil. Surprisingly, more than 35% of the calories in this "Mediterranean" diet came from fat, on par with the North American diet. However, the North American diet was linked with a high rate of heart disease.

For many years, it was thought that the saturated fat in the North American diet was to blame. Now, the picture is changing and it looks like the refined vegetable and seed oils, which dominate supermarket shelves and contain too many omega-6 fatty acids (among other problems), have played a role by encouraging inflammatory processes in your body. Cold-pressed olive oil, on the other hand, is rich in nutrient-and-energy-dense monounsaturated fats. At its most basic, these fats, reduce LDL ("bad") cholesterol and increase HDL ("good") cholesterol, which may help to reduce your risk of heart attack. Extra virgin olive oil contains powerful antioxidants, which, for instance, prevent LDL cholesterol from oxidizing, thereby reducing the possibility that you will develop atherosclerosis. Olive oil has also been shown to be protective against several types of cancer. It also reduces the possibility that you will have a stroke because it helps to keep your blood from clotting.

Mediterranean-Style Mahi-Mahi

I love the in-your-face flavors of the gremolata used to finish this dish. This recipe is great for entertaining because you can assemble it just before your guests arrive and turn the slow cooker on when they come through the door. By the time everyone is enjoying drinks and nibblies, the conversation is flowing and you're thinking about moving to the table, the fish will be cooked. I like to serve this with a big platter of sautéed spinach or Swiss chard.

Makes 4 servings

Can Be Halved
(see Tips, below)

Tips

If you are halving this recipe, be sure to use a small (1½ to 3 quart) slow cooker.

It is difficult to be specific about the timing because of the configuration of the fish, but you should begin checking for doneness after 1 hour. Be aware it may take up to 1½ hours.

Nutrients Per Serving

Calories	370
Protein	44.6 g
Carbohydrates	13.7 g
Fat (Total)	15.4 g
Saturated Fat	2.3 g
Monounsaturated Fat	10.3 g
Polyunsaturated Fat	1.8 g
Dietary Fiber	3.5 g
Sodium	820 mg
Cholesterol	166 mg

EXCELLENT SOURCE OF vitamins A, C, B$_6$, B$_{12}$ and K, niacin, phosphorus, magnesium, potassium and iron.
GOOD SOURCE OF vitamin E (alpha-tocopherol), pantothenic acid and calcium.
SOURCE OF folate, riboflavin, manganese, zinc and copper.
CONTAINS a moderate amount of dietary fiber.

• **Medium to large (3½ to 5 quart) oval slow cooker**

2 lbs	mahi-mahi steaks	1 kg
1 tsp	dried oregano	5 mL
1	lemon, thinly sliced	1
1	can (28 oz/796 mL) no-salt added tomatoes, including juice, coarsely chopped	1
½ cup	dry white wine	125 mL
¼ cup	extra virgin olive oil, divided	60 mL
½ tsp	sea salt (see Tip, right)	2 mL
	Freshly ground black pepper	

Gremolata

½ cup	finely chopped parsley leaves	125 mL
3 tbsp	drained capers, minced	45 mL
2	whole anchovies, rinsed and finely chopped	2
	Freshly ground black pepper	
	Chopped black olives	

1. Place fish in slow cooker stoneware. Sprinkle with oregano and lay lemon slices evenly over top. In a bowl, combine tomatoes with juice, wine, 2 tbsp (30 mL) of the olive oil, salt, and pepper to taste. Pour over fish. Cover and cook on High for 1 hour (see Tips, left), until fish flakes easily when pierced with a knife.

2. *Gremolata:* Meanwhile, in a bowl, combine parsley, capers, anchovies, remaining 2 tbsp (30 mL) of the olive oil and pepper to taste. Mix well and set aside in refrigerator until fish is cooked.

3. To serve, transfer fish and tomato sauce to a warm platter. Spoon gremolata evenly over top and garnish with olives.

If you are concerned about the sodium in this recipe, you can easily reduce it by eliminating the added salt, which adds 387 mg per serving.

Mindful Morsels

Eating fish may reduce your risk of stroke. One study found that women who ate fish two to four times a week were 27% less likely to have a stroke than women who ate fish once a month. Another 2006 meta-analysis, which concluded that people who ate 1 to 2 servings of fish per week reduced their risk of coronary death by 36%, although researchers have speculated that people who regularly consume fish may also have a healthier lifestyle, which affects results.

Natural Wonders

Sustainably Caught Fish

There are many reasons for making sure the fish you eat is sustainably caught. For starters, if suppliers continue to ignore the environmental impact of current practices, we may not have any wild fish left. At least one study has predicted that virtually all species of commercially caught fish will disappear by 2030. Overfishing by large industrialized operations has severely diminished fish stocks. (In North America the Newfoundland cod fishery, which was virtually destroyed, is just one case in point.) Harmful practices such as bottom trawling severely damage existing ecosystems, contributing to further depletion in fish stocks. In 2003, an article published in the science journal *Nature* estimated that at that point as much as 90% of ocean fish may already have been destroyed.

And fish farms are likely not the answer. Although farmed fish is generally less expensive than wild-caught fish, it is probably not as nutritious. Studies have shown that popular farmed fish such as catfish, tilapia and salmon contain significantly less (two to three times fewer) omega-3 fatty acids than wild fish. Farmed fish is also much more likely to contain harmful contaminants, including pesticides and antibiotic residue. Moreover, the lower cost of farmed fish may, in general terms, be contributing to declining stock in natural fisheries. By putting pressure on the price of wild-caught fish, aquaculture is making fishing less lucrative as an occupation, thereby driving people out of the business.

There are several ways to ensure that you are buying sustainably caught fish. Firstly, check to make sure it is not on the endangered list. Several years ago, I downloaded the Monterey Bay Aquarium's Seafood Watch Program (www.montereybayaquarium.org) onto my iPhone. If I'm in a restaurant or at a fishmonger that doesn't label its sources, I can check the offerings against their lists and be confident I am making a sustainable choice. Once you have determined that the offerings are sustainable, choose fish that has been harvested in small boats, and when purchasing larger fish, check to see that it has been line-caught or harpooned. And learn to enjoy less-popular fish, for instance mackerel, which encourages balance in the fragile ecosystem.

Poached Halibut with Dill Hollandaise

This is an elegant dish, perfect for entertaining. I like to serve it with parsleyed potatoes and a green vegetable. Don't be intimidated by the hollandaise. As long as you keep the heat low your eggs won't curdle, and even if they do, the problem is easy to fix (see Tips, right).

Makes 6 to 8 servings

Can Be Halved
(see Tips, below)

Tips

If you are halving this recipe, be sure to use a small (2 to 3½ quart) slow cooker.

The cooking time depends upon the configuration of your fish. The thicker it is, the longer it will take. Start checking for doneness after 1 hour. I've made this using a thick chunk of halibut and it took close to 1½ hours.

Nutrients Per Serving

Calories	241
Protein	24.4 g
Carbohydrates	0.3 g
Fat (Total)	15.4 g
Saturated Fat	8.1 g
Monounsaturated Fat	4.4 g
Polyunsaturated Fat	1.5 g
Dietary Fiber	0 g
Sodium	400 mg
Cholesterol	115 mg

EXCELLENT SOURCE OF vitamin B12, niacin, phosphorus, magnesium and selenium.

GOOD SOURCE OF vitamins A, B6 and E (alpha-tocopherol) and potassium.

SOURCE OF folate, calcium, iron and zinc.

- Medium to large (3½ to 5 quart) slow cooker

Poaching Liquid

1	onion, chopped	1
2	stalks celery, including leaves, chopped	2
4	sprigs parsley	4
8	peppercorns	8
1 tsp	coarse sea salt	5 mL
2	bay leaves	2
6 cups	water	1.5 L
½ cup	white wine or lemon juice	125 mL
1	halibut fillet (about 2 lbs/1 kg)	1

Dill Hollandaise

2	egg yolks	2
1 tbsp	cold water	15 mL
½ cup	butter, cubed	125 mL
1 tbsp	freshly squeezed lemon juice	15 mL
1 tsp	sea salt (approx.) (see Tips, right)	5 mL
Pinch	cayenne pepper	Pinch
¼ cup	finely chopped dill fronds	60 mL

1. *Poaching Liquid:* In a saucepan, combine onion, celery, parsley, peppercorns, salt, bay leaves, water and wine. Bring to a boil, reduce heat and simmer for 30 minutes. Strain and discard solids.

2. Preheat slow cooker on High for 15 minutes and add hot poaching liquid. Add halibut. Cover and cook on High, about 1 hour and 15 minutes, until fish flakes easily when pierced with a knife (see Tips, left). Using a slotted spoon, transfer fish to a warm platter and keep warm. Remove and discard bay leaves.

3. *Dill Hollandaise:* Meanwhile, in a heavy saucepan over low heat (or in the top of a double boiler), whisk egg yolks and water. Add butter, one piece at a time, whisking until each piece melts before adding the next one.

Tips

When making Hollandaise, if the mixture begins to scramble, remove from heat and whisk in 1 tbsp (15 mL) cold water.

I use unsalted butter. If you are using butter that is salted, taste before adding salt and adjust the quantity accordingly. Also, if you are watching your sodium intake, feel free to reduce the amount called for, which adds 193 mg of sodium per serving. I like a lemony hollandaise and always add more lemon juice so I call for extra salt to balance that acidity.

4. When all the butter has been added, continue to whisk until mixture thickens. Whisk in lemon juice, salt and cayenne. Stir in dill. Serve immediately over fish or keep warm over hot water until ready to serve.

Variation

Poached Salmon with Dill Hollandaise: Substitute an equal quantity of salmon fillet for the halibut.

Mindful Morsels

If you've been drinking skim milk because you think it is healthier than its full-fat relative, think again. One 2012 study published in *The American Journal of Clinical Nutrition* linked the conjugated linoleic acid (CLA) in milk from grass-fed cows with a 49% reduction in heart attack risk. CLA is a component of dairy fat, and pasture grazing significantly increases the amount that milk contains.

Natural Wonders

Butter

If you are phobic about butterfat, as you likely have been told you should be, you will be horrified by the recipe for Dill Hollandaise. Don't be. Not only is it delicious enough to qualify as an "occasional indulgence," I am firmly of the opinion that butter, eaten in moderation (like all foods), is a nutritious dietary choice.

For starters, butter is, according to nutritionist Sally Fallon and lipid scientist Mary Enig, "America's best and most easily absorbed source of vitamin A." This nutrient helps our bodies to fight illnesses such as heart disease, cancer and osteoporosis, keeps your thyroid functioning well, boosts your immune system, and promotes healthy growth in children, among other benefits. Butter also provides tiny bits of vitamin D (9 IU per tbsp/15 mL from feedlot-raised animals), which is important for building strong bones, and small amounts of antioxidants such as vitamin E and selenium, all of which vary depending upon what the cows are fed and, if they are pastured, the quality of the soil. (The milk of grass-fed cows is higher in both vitamin A and vitamin E.) Butter is also one of the few sources of conjugated linoleic acid (CLA), a well-known cancer fighter, which may also protect against heart disease (see Mindful Morsels, above). As for butter being fattening, in their article *Why Butter is Better* (available online), Ms. Fallon and Dr. Enig point out that your body uses the short- and medium-chain fatty acids in butter for immediate energy, rather than storing them around your middle. As with milk, butter should be organic, made from the milk of cows that are grass-fed.

Shrimp 'n' Grits

I first tasted this delectable combination many years ago in Charleston, South Carolina, and I haven't been able to get enough of it since. Serve this to guests for a special lunch with a crisp green salad or fresh asparagus (which provides folate, among other nutrients; see Mindful Morsels, page 164) in season. Or just it enjoy it with your family, as I often do.

Makes 4 servings

Tip

Make sure to buy stone-ground grits made from heirloom corn, which is not genetically modified. Whole-grain stone-ground grits (the tastiest and most nutritious kind) take a long time to cook. Preparing them on the stovetop requires about 2 hours of attention and frequent stirring. If, like me, you're a grits lover, having a slow cooker is very advantageous.

- **Small (approx. 3½ quart) slow cooker**
- **Lightly greased slow cooker stoneware**

Grits

4 cups	water	1 L
1 tbsp	olive oil	15 mL
½ tsp	freshly ground black pepper	2 mL
1 cup	coarse, stone-ground grits (see Tip, left)	250 mL
1 tbsp	olive oil	15 mL
2	cloves garlic, minced	2
1 lb	medium shrimp, peeled and deveined	500 g
¼ tsp	cayenne pepper	1 mL
1 tbsp	freshly squeezed lemon juice	15 mL
2 cups	Basic Tomato Sauce (page 296)	500 mL

1. *Grits:* In a saucepan over medium heat, bring water, olive oil and pepper to boil. Gradually add grits, stirring constantly until smooth and blended. Continue cooking and stirring until grits are slightly thickened, about 4 minutes. Transfer to prepared stoneware. Cover and cook on High for 4 hours or on Low for 8 hours, until set.

2. In a skillet, heat oil over medium heat. Add garlic and cook, stirring, for 1 minute. Add shrimp and cook, stirring, until shrimp firm up and turn pink, about 3 minutes. Sprinkle with cayenne and toss. Add lemon juice and toss. Add tomato sauce and bring to a boil.

3. To serve, spoon grits onto a warm platter and top with shrimp sauce.

more information on page 164

Nutrients Per Serving

Calories	351
Protein	22.5 g
Carbohydrates	43.9 g
Fat (Total)	11.1 g
Saturated Fat	1.3 g
Monounsaturated Fat	5.8 g
Polyunsaturated Fat	1.4 g
Dietary Fiber	4.5 g
Sodium	170 mg
Cholesterol	129 mg

EXCELLENT SOURCE OF vitamin A and iron.

GOOD SOURCE OF vitamin B_{12}, magnesium and phosphorus.

SOURCE OF vitamins B_6, C and K, folate, calcium, potassium and zinc.

CONTAINS a high amount of dietary fiber.

Natural Wonders

A Healthy Diet

As Dr. Walter Willet, of the Department of Nutrition at the Harvard School of Public Health, says in his excellent book *Eat, Drink and Be Healthy*, "No single food will make or break good health." Research confirms it is the overall quality of your diet that matters. A pattern of healthy eating includes plenty of high-fiber plant-based foods such as fruits, vegetables and whole grains. Current evidence suggests that consumption of red meat and processed meats should be limited. Not only has heavy consumption of red meat and processed meats been linked with an increased risk of colon cancer, a Tufts University study found that people who consumed a "meat and potatoes" diet were six times more likely to gain weight as they aged, compared with those who ate more fruits, vegetables and whole grains.

However, eating a healthy diet requires vigilance and planning. For starters, most people constantly feel pressed for time and fast food is always available. Taking the time to pack a healthy lunch is often sacrificed to the expediency of a burger and fries.

Also, over the past fifty years the quality of our food supply has declined thanks to unsustainable agricultural practices, such as the use of chemical fertilizers and various pesticides and herbicides. Whether these substances are harmful to human health in the quantities consumed is beside the point. They definitely diminish the nutrients in our food. One study showed a 30 to 70% reduction in the nutrient content of certain "conventionally" grown vegetables between 1963 and 2000. Finding a source for organically grown fruits and vegetables (which studies confirm are higher in phytonutrient content) and consuming the required number of servings is a positive step in the right direction. Over the long term, keeping your weight under control and following a healthy diet appears to lower the risk of cancer and other chronic diseases, among other benefits.

Sweet Potato Coconut Curry with Shrimp

I love the combination of sweet and spicy flavors in this luscious dish. Serve this over brown basmati rice and add a platter of steamed spinach sprinkled with toasted sesame seeds to complete the meal.

Tips

Check the label to make sure your curry paste does not contain gluten.

If you are adding the almond garnish, try to find slivered almonds with the skin on. They add color and nutrients to the dish.

Make Ahead

Complete Step 1. Cover and refrigerate overnight or for up to 2 days. When you're ready, complete the recipe.

Nutrients Per Serving

Calories	348
Protein	27.0 g
Carbohydrates	32.7 g
Fat (Total)	12.3 g
Saturated Fat	6.3 g
Monounsaturated Fat	3.8 g
Polyunsaturated Fat	1.4 g
Dietary Fiber	2.9 g
Sodium	587 mg
Cholesterol	221 mg

EXCELLENT SOURCE OF vitamins A, B$_6$ and B$_{12}$ and iron.
GOOD SOURCE OF vitamin C, phosphorus, magnesium, potassium and zinc.
CONTAINS a moderate amount of dietary fiber.

- **Medium to large (3½ to 5 quart) slow cooker**

1 tbsp	olive or extra virgin coconut oil	15 mL
2	onions, finely chopped	2
4	cloves garlic, minced	4
1 tbsp	minced gingerroot	15 mL
1 cup	vegetable stock	250 mL
2	sweet potatoes, peeled and cut into 1-inch (2.5 cm) cubes	2
2 tsp	Thai green curry paste (see Tips, left)	10 mL
1 tbsp	freshly squeezed lime juice	15 mL
½ cup	coconut milk	125 mL
1 lb	cooked peeled shrimp, thawed if frozen	500 g
¼ cup	toasted slivered almonds, optional	60 mL
¼ cup	finely chopped cilantro leaves	60 mL

1. In a skillet, heat oil over medium heat. Add onions and cook, stirring, until softened, about 3 minutes. Add garlic and ginger and cook, stirring, for 1 minute. Add vegetable stock. Transfer to slow cooker stoneware.

2. Add sweet potatoes and stir well. Cover and cook on Low for 6 hours or on High for 3 hours, until sweet potatoes are tender.

3. In a small bowl, combine curry paste and lime juice. Add to slow cooker stoneware and stir well. Stir in coconut milk and shrimp. Cover and cook on High for 20 minutes, until shrimp are hot. Transfer to a serving dish. Garnish with almonds, if using, and cilantro and serve.

Mindful Morsels

Almonds are a source of vitamin E and contain a trace of the mineral selenium, among other nutrients.

more information on page 167

Sweet Potato Coconut Curry with Shrimp

Natural Wonders

Shrimp

Like all shellfish, shrimp contain B vitamins such as B_6, B_{12} and niacin, as well as the essential minerals magnesium and zinc. Shrimp are also a source of low-fat, high-quality protein. Four ounces (125 g) of shrimp contain only 124 calories and less than half a gram of saturated fat, while supplying 26 grams of high-quality protein.

Many people avoid shrimp because they contain quite a bit of sodium and are high in cholesterol. For starters, I simply don't believe that the natural sodium in foods is in any way problematic. Also, the cholesterol in food is not as much of a problem as previously thought (see page 197). In one study, in which participants ate 300 grams of shrimp a day, researchers found that while their LDL ("bad") cholesterol increased by 7%, their HDL ("good") cholesterol went up by 12%, producing a net benefit. The shrimp diet also lowered triglycerides by 13%. (High triglyceride levels have been linked with coronary artery disease.)

Poached Salmon with Sorrel Sauce

Although I love salmon cooked almost any way, poaching produces the moistest result. Serve poached salmon, warm or cold, as the focus of an elegant buffet or dinner, attractively garnished with sliced lemon and sprigs of parsley or dill and accompany with your favorite sauce, such as this tart sorrel sauce, which is one of my favorites.

Makes 6 to 8 servings as a main course or 12 to as a buffet dish

Tips

Make sure that the salmon is completely covered with the poaching liquid. If you do not have sufficient liquid, add water to cover.

When using sorrel, remove the stems and wash it carefully, rinsing it thoroughly in a basin of lukewarm water.

- **Large (minimum 5 quart) oval slow cooker**
- **Food processor**

Poaching Liquid

6 cups	water	1.5 L
1	onion, chopped	1
2	stalks celery, chopped or ½ tsp (2 mL) celery seed	2
4	sprigs parsley	4
½ cup	white wine or lemon juice	125 mL
8	peppercorns	8
1	bay leaf	1

Salmon

1	salmon fillet (about 3 lbs/1.5 kg)	1
	Lemon slices	
	Sprigs fresh parsley or dill	

Sorrel Sauce

1 lb	sorrel leaves, washed thoroughly and stems removed (see Tips, left)	500 g
¼ cup	water	60 mL
½ tsp	dried tarragon	2 mL
1 tsp	Dijon mustard	5 mL
¼ cup	heavy or whipping (35%) cream	60 mL
	Sea salt and freshly ground black pepper	

1. *Poaching Liquid:* In a saucepan, combine ingredients. Bring to a boil and simmer for 30 minutes. Strain. Discard solids.

2. *Salmon:* Preheat slow cooker on High for 15 minutes. Fold a 2-foot (60 cm) piece of foil in half lengthwise. Place on bottom and up sides of stoneware. Lay salmon over foil strip. Return poaching liquid to a boil and pour over salmon.

3. Cover and cook on High for 1 hour. Remove stoneware from slow cooker. Allow salmon to cool in stoneware for 20 minutes. If serving cold, place stoneware in refrigerator and chill salmon in liquid. When cold, lift out and transfer to a platter. If serving hot, transfer to a platter. Garnish and serve.

Nutrients Per Serving

Calories	388
Protein	35.7 g
Carbohydrates	1.6 g
Fat (Total)	25.7 g
Saturated Fat	6.8 g
Monounsaturated Fat	7.2 g
Polyunsaturated Fat	6.7 g
Dietary Fiber	1.2 g
Sodium	113 mg
Cholesterol	103 mg

EXCELLENT SOURCE OF vitamin E (alpha-tocopherol), pantothenic acid, phosphorus, magnesium, potassium and selenium.

GOOD SOURCE OF vitamin A.

SOURCE OF vitamin C, niacin, iron, manganese, zinc and copper.

Tips

When the salmon is cooked, it should feel firm to the touch and the skin should peel off easily.

If you prefer, omit the sorrel sauce and serve the salmon with your favorite accompaniment.

Make Ahead

Make the poaching liquid the day before you intend to cook. Cover and refrigerate until you are ready to use.

4. *Sorrel Sauce:* In a heavy saucepan with a tight-fitting lid, combine sorrel, water and tarragon. Cover and cook over low heat until sorrel is wilted. Transfer sorrel and cooking liquid to a food processor. Add Dijon mustard and whipping cream and process until smooth. Season with salt and freshly ground black pepper to taste. Spoon over salmon, or pass separately in a sauceboat.

Mindful Morsels

A serving of this dish is relatively high in fat, virtually all of which comes from the salmon. (The cream provides 2.5 grams of fat, 1.6 grams of which is saturated.) This analysis was based on using farmed Atlantic salmon. If wild salmon had been used, some of the saturated fat would have been replaced by beneficial omega-3 fatty acids. Fat content or not, fish is still a healthy choice.

Natural Wonders

The Importance of Balance

It makes sense to regularly consume a high-quality protein that is low in saturated fat, such as fish. But it's also sensible to balance a serving of fish with a helping of vegetables. Not only does it extend the range of nutrients you consume, it also improves the ratio of carbohydrates to protein in your diet, which may help your body to maintain calcium. While too little protein is a known risk factor for fractures, too much protein may also have the same effect. The Nurses' Health Study found that women who consumed more than 95 grams of protein a day over a 12-year period were 20% more likely to have broken their wrist than those whose consumption averaged less than 68 grams a day. Comparing women who ate red meat more than five times a week with those who ate red meat less than once a week produced a similar conclusion. Although the explanations for these findings appear to be complex, a simple solution is to make sure your diet reflects balance among the macronutrients.

Onion-Braised Shrimp

This is a great dish for a buffet, an Indian-style meal with numerous small plates, or a light dinner. The substantial quantity of onions, which are cooked until they begin to caramelize and release their sugars, produces a dish that is pleasantly sweet. I like to serve this over brown basmati rice.

Makes 4 servings

Can Be Halved
(see Tips, page 172)

Tip

The quantity of pepper in the recipe produces a mildly spicy result. Heat seekers can add an extra half of a fresh chile, finely chopped or more cayenne pepper. You can add up to ½ tsp (2 mL) cayenne pepper in addition to the fresh red chile or, if you don't have a fresh chile, substitute that amount of cayenne instead. Just be sure to dissolve the powdered pepper in the lemon juice before adding to the slow cooker.

Nutrients Per Serving

Calories	247
Protein	26.9 g
Carbohydrates	20.7 g
Fat (Total)	6.5 g
Saturated Fat	1.5 g
Monounsaturated Fat	3.1 g
Polyunsaturated Fat	1.2 g
Dietary Fiber	3.2 g
Sodium	402 mg
Cholesterol	175 mg

EXCELLENT SOURCE OF vitamin B$_{12}$, phosphorus, potassium and iron.
GOOD SOURCE OF vitamins A, C and B$_6$, calcium, magnesium and zinc.
SOURCE OF folate and vitamin K.
CONTAINS a moderate amount of dietary fiber.

- **Medium to large (3½ to 5 quart) slow cooker**

1 tsp	coriander seeds	5 mL
1 tbsp	olive oil	15 mL
4	onions, finely chopped	4
2	cloves garlic, minced	2
1 tbsp	minced gingerroot	15 mL
1 tsp	ground turmeric	5 mL
½ tsp	sea salt, or to taste	2 mL
½ tsp	cracked black peppercorns	2 mL
1	can (14 oz/398 mL) no-salt added diced tomatoes, including juice	1
1	long red chile pepper, seeded and finely chopped (see Tip, left)	1
1 tbsp	freshly squeezed lemon juice	15 mL
1 lb	peeled cooked shrimp, thawed if frozen	500 g
½ cup	plain yogurt	125 mL
2 tbsp	finely chopped cilantro leaves	30 mL

1. In a dry skillet over medium heat, toast coriander seeds, stirring, until fragrant, about 3 minutes. Immediately transfer to a mortar or a spice grinder and grind. Set aside.

2. In same skillet, heat oil over medium heat. Add onions and cook, stirring, until they turn golden and just begin to brown, about 7 minutes. Add garlic, ginger, turmeric, salt, peppercorns and reserved coriander and cook, stirring, for 1 minute. Add tomatoes with juice and stir well.

3. Transfer to slow cooker stoneware. Cover and cook on Low for 6 hours or on High for 3 hours, until mixture is hot and bubbly. Stir in chile pepper and lemon juice. Add shrimp and stir well. Cover and cook on High for 20 minutes, until shrimp are heated through. Stir in yogurt. Garnish with cilantro and serve.

Make Ahead

Complete Steps 1 and 2. Cover and refrigerate overnight or for up to 2 days. When you're ready to cook, continue with Step 3.

Natural Wonders

Onions

Along with garlic and leeks, onions belong to the allium family. They are loaded with compounds containing sulfur, the substance that makes your eyes water. But these compounds are also responsible for many of the vegetable's health benefits. These sulfur-rich compounds, along with the quercetin, which is also found in onions, are active cancer fighters. Sulfur is also used to make glutathione (see Natural Wonders, page 291), one of the key antioxidant enzymes in the liver that helps that organ in its detoxifying role. (One rule of thumb suggests that the more pungent the onion, the more beneficial it is; in laboratory studies, timid onions, such as Vidalias and Texas 1015s, showed dramatically less cancer fighting ability than their more assertive relatives.)

Recent research also indicates that eating onions on a regular basis raises levels of beneficial high-density lipoproteins (HDL) and lowers harmful triglycerides. Other studies show onion consumption helps to prevent high blood pressure, thereby reducing the risk of heart attack or stroke. In fact, recent analysis identifies onions as one of a select few vegetables and fruits that you should eat to significantly reduce your risk of heart disease.

One word of caution: some people have difficulty digesting onions and other alliums. If, for instance, you suffer from irritable bowel syndrome (IBS) you may need to watch your consumption of onions. People following a low FODMAP diet for this condition may be told to restrict their intake of onions because they contain insoluble fibers with potential to irritate the gastrointestinal tract.

Caribbean Fish Stew

I love the combination of flavors in this tasty stew. The allspice and the Scotch bonnet peppers add a distinctly island tang. For a distinctive and delicious finish, be sure to include the dill. Serve this with crusty gluten-free rolls to soak up the sauce, a fresh green salad and some crisp white wine.

Makes 8 servings

**Can Be Halved
(see Tips, below)**

Tips

If you are halving this recipe, be sure to use a small (2 to 3½ quart) slow cooker.

One Scotch bonnet pepper is probably enough for most people, but if you're a heat seeker, use two. You can also use habanero peppers instead.

Make Ahead

Complete Steps 1 and 2. Cover and refrigerate overnight or for up to 2 days. When you're ready to cook, continue with Step 3.

Nutrients Per Serving

Calories	164
Protein	22.9 g
Carbohydrates	10.2 g
Fat (Total)	3.2 g
Saturated Fat	0.5 g
Monounsaturated Fat	1.6 g
Polyunsaturated Fat	0.6 g
Dietary Fiber	2.2 g
Sodium	128 mg
Cholesterol	64 mg

EXCELLENT SOURCE OF potassium.
GOOD SOURCE OF vitamins C, B₆, B₁₂ and K, magnesium, phosphorus and iron.
SOURCE OF vitamin A, folate, calcium and zinc.
CONTAINS a moderate amount of dietary fiber.

• **Large (approx. 5 quart) slow cooker**

2 tsp	cumin seeds	10 mL
6	whole allspice	6
1 tbsp	olive oil	15 mL
2	onions, finely chopped	2
4	cloves garlic, minced	4
2 tsp	dried thyme, crumbled	10 mL
1 tsp	ground turmeric	5 mL
1 tbsp	grated orange or lime zest	15 mL
½ tsp	cracked black peppercorns	2 mL
1	can (28 oz/796 mL) no-salt added tomatoes, including juice, coarsely chopped	1
2 cups	fish stock	500 mL
	Sea salt	
1 to 2	Scotch bonnet peppers, minced	1 to 2
2 cups	sliced okra (¼ inch/0.5 cm)	500 mL
1½ lbs	skinless grouper fillets, cut into bite-size pieces	750 g
8 oz	shrimp, cooked, peeled and deveined	250 g
½ cup	finely chopped dill fronds	125 mL

1. In a large dry skillet over medium heat, toast cumin seeds and allspice, stirring, until fragrant and cumin seeds just begin to brown, about 3 minutes. Immediately transfer to a mortar or a spice grinder and grind. Set aside.

2. In same skillet, heat oil over medium heat. Add onions and cook, stirring, until softened, about 3 minutes. Add garlic, thyme, turmeric, orange zest, peppercorns and reserved cumin and allspice and cook, stirring, for 1 minute. Add tomatoes with juice and fish stock and bring to a boil. Season with salt to taste.

3. Transfer to slow cooker stoneware. Cover and cook on Low for 6 hours or on High for 3 hours. Add chile peppers to taste, okra, fish fillets and shrimp. Cover and cook on High for 20 minutes, until fish flakes easily with a fork and okra is tender. Stir in dill.

Natural Wonders

Fish

In terms of cancer prevention, it makes sense to pass on the red meat and eat fish instead. A study conducted by French researchers who tracked the diets of half a million people aged 35 to 70, who were cancer-free for an average of five years when the study began, found that as fish consumption rose, rates of colon cancer appeared to drop. Those who ate the most fish (an average of 3 ounces/90 g per day), including canned and smoked fish, lowered their risk of this form of cancer by almost one-third.

Other studies confirm that eating fish regularly can help protect against certain types of cancer. A Canadian study of more than 7,000 participants found that those who got most of their fat calories from fish were 28% less likely to have leukemia, 36% less likely to have multiple myeloma and 29% less likely to have non-Hodgkin's lymphoma. A Spanish study found that people who ate fish had fewer incidences of three other types of cancer: ovarian, pancreatic, and cancers of all parts of the digestive tract.

From a nutritional standpoint, coldwater fish, such as wild salmon is one of the best food sources of omega-3 fatty acids (see Natural Wonders, page 153). Not only do omega-3 fats help to reduce your risk of cancer, they also work to keep your blood pressure low and lower harmful triglycerides. They also reduce your risk of having a stroke. Fish is an excellent source of protein and one of the few dietary sources of vitamin D. Depending on the type, fish provides varying degrees of minerals, such as magnesium and calcium (shellfish and the bones from canned salmon are a particularly good source of this nutrient). However, fish also contains methylmercury, which may be toxic, particularly for a developing fetus. In general terms, the largest fish, such as albacore tuna, shark or swordfish are the most contaminated with this substance. Bear this in mind when purchasing fish and balance eating larger fish with smaller ones such as lake trout, sardines, mackerel or skipjack tuna. One bit of good news is that recent studies indicate that the selenium provided by fish may protect your body against the potentially negative effects of this toxin.

Creamy Coconut Grouper

The sweet potato in this tasty stew lends an appealing hint of sweetness that is nicely balanced by the spicy cayenne. If you like heat, add a fresh chile along with the coconut milk. Serve this over plain brown rice. You won't be disappointed.

Makes 8 servings

Can Be Halved
(see Tip, below)

Tip

If you are halving this recipe, be sure to use a small (2 to 3½ quart) slow cooker.

Make Ahead

Complete Steps 1 and 2. Cover and refrigerate fish and vegetable mixtures separately overnight. When you're ready to cook, continue with the recipe.

Nutrients Per Serving

Calories	289
Protein	25.0 g
Carbohydrates	18.9 g
Fat (Total)	13.1 g
Saturated Fat	9.5 g
Monounsaturated Fat	1.9 g
Polyunsaturated Fat	0.7 g
Dietary Fiber	3.1 g
Sodium	198 mg
Cholesterol	42 mg

EXCELLENT SOURCE OF vitamins A and B$_6$, manganese, potassium and iron.
GOOD SOURCE OF vitamins K and B$_{12}$, magnesium and phosphorous.
SOURCE OF vitamin C, folate, niacin, calcium, zinc and copper.
CONTAINS a moderate amount of dietary fiber.

- **Medium to large (3½ to 5 quart) slow cooker**

1 cup	finely chopped cilantro leaves	250 mL
2 tbsp	freshly squeezed lime juice	30 mL
¼ tsp	cayenne pepper	1 mL
2 lbs	skinless grouper fillets, cut into 1-inch (2.5 cm) cubes	1 kg
1 tbsp	olive or coconut oil	15 mL
2	onions, finely chopped	2
2	stalks celery, diced	2
4	cloves garlic, minced	4
1 tsp	cracked black peppercorns	5 mL
1 tsp	dried oregano	5 mL
½ tsp	sea salt	2 mL
1	can (28 oz/796 mL) no-salt added diced tomatoes including juice	1
1	floury potato, peeled and shredded (see Tip, right)	1
1	sweet potato, peeled and cubed	1
1 cup	fish or vegetable stock or water	250 mL
1	can (14 oz/400 mL) coconut milk	1
1	long red chile pepper, seeded and minced, optional	1

1. In a bowl, combine cilantro, lime juice, cayenne and grouper. Mix well. Cover and refrigerate until ready to use.

2. In a skillet, heat oil over medium heat. Add onions and celery and cook, stirring, until softened, about 5 minutes. Add garlic, peppercorns, oregano and salt and cook, stirring, for 1 minute. Add tomatoes with juice and bring to a boil.

3. Transfer to slow cooker stoneware. Add potato, sweet potato and fish stock. Cover and cook on Low for 6 hours or on High for 3 hours, until sweet potato is tender. Add grouper mixture, coconut milk and chile, if using. Cover and cook on High about 10 minutes, until fish flakes easily when pierced with a knife and mixture is hot and bubbly.

Tip

The shredded white potato is used to thicken the soup and add flavor. If you prefer, substitute 2 tbsp (30 mL) short-grain brown rice, rinsed.

Mindful Morsels

In *The Truth About Vitamins and Minerals: Choosing the Nutrients You Need to Stay Healthy*, published by the Department of Nutrition of the Harvard School of Public Health, there is a rule of thumb for assessing the quality of carbohydrates: When reading nutrient data look for at least a 10 to 1 ratio of carbohydrate to dietary fiber. Any food that passes muster would contain at least 10 grams of carbohydrate for every gram of fiber provided.

Based on that analysis, the carbohydrate quality in this recipe is high, which is true for the vast majority of recipes in this book. Some of the desserts didn't quite make the cut because they are sweetened with natural sugars, nor did some of the breakfast cereals, largely because they use ingredients such as rice milk, which add carbohydrates without adding fiber. In the case of breakfast recipes, the ratio is easily amended with the addition of high-fiber garnishes, such as seeds and nuts (see page 25).

Natural Wonders

A Balanced Diet

Low Carb? High Protein? Low Fat? These days there are so many trendy diets it's hard to know what to eat. One approach, taken by the National Academies' Institute of Medicine is to recognize that protein, carbohydrate and fat (the macronutrients) substitute for one another to meet the body's energy needs. In a report sponsored by U.S. and Canadian government agencies, with the assistance of corporate partners, scientists recommended flexible ranges rather than fixed daily values for the macronutrients. Noting that extremely low-fat diets can decrease levels of HDL ("good") cholesterol and that high-fat diets may lead to obesity, researchers advised that fats (mainly unsaturated) should provide from 20 to 35% of calories. They also suggested that protein provide from 10 to 35% and carbohydrates from 45 to 65% of the calories regularly consumed. The report recommended that children as well as adults consume at least 130 grams of carbohydrates daily, while limiting the amount of added sugars (those found in prepared foods such as candy bars and soft drinks) to less than 25% of total calories consumed. A serving of a nutrient-rich dish such as Creamy Coconut Grouper, accompanied by brown rice or mashed potatoes, works toward achieving the kind of balance the report recommends.

In practical terms, these targets can be achieved simply by following some basic tenets: eat a variety of wholesome foods that are minimally processed and avoid extremes such as cutting out (and/or over-consuming) whole categories of foods. The recipes in this book adhere to these principles. Usually, all you need to add is a nutrient-dense accompaniment — salad, a whole grain or a vegetable — to enjoy an extremely nutritious meal.

Caribbean Pepper Pot

There are two dishes known as pepper pot — one that apparently originated during the American revolutionary war and a Caribbean version. Although both are traditionally based on ingredients the cook has on hand, the results are very different. The original version of Philadelphia pepper pot included tripe and black peppercorns, but in the islands the dish contains a hodgepodge of local ingredients, including incendiary Scotch bonnet peppers and leafy green callaloo. It is often finished with coconut milk, producing a nicely spicy and lusciously creamy stew. This makes a very large serving (more than 2 cups/500 mL) so it's all you need for a delicious and nutritious meal.

Makes 6 servings

Can Be Halved
(see Tips, below)

Tips

If you are halving this recipe, be sure to use a small (2 to 3½ quart) slow cooker.

Callaloo, also known as pigweed or amaranth leaves, is becoming increasingly available in greengrocers. Also look for it in farmers' markets.

Nutrients Per Serving

Calories	435
Protein	36.2 g
Carbohydrates	39.2 g
Fat (Total)	16.8 g
Saturated Fat	8.8 g
Monounsaturated Fat	3.6 g
Polyunsaturated Fat	2.1 g
Dietary Fiber	6.1 g
Sodium	398 mg
Cholesterol	184 mg

EXCELLENT SOURCE OF
vitamins A, C, B$_6$ and K, niacin, phosphorous, iron, magnesium, manganese, potassium, zinc, copper and selenium.

GOOD SOURCE OF vitamins B$_{12}$ and E (alpha-tocopherol), folate, thiamine, riboflavin, pantothenic acid and calcium.

CONTAINS a very high amount of dietary fiber.

- **Large (approx. 5 quart) slow cooker**

1 tbsp	olive oil	15 mL
3	onions, thinly sliced on the vertical	3
4	cloves garlic, minced	4
2 tbsp	minced gingerroot	30 mL
1 tsp	cracked black peppercorns	5 mL
1 tsp	ground allspice	5 mL
½ tsp	sea salt	2 mL
½ tsp	dried thyme	2 mL
2	bay leaves	2
½ cup	short-grain brown rice	125 mL
1	can (14 oz/398 mL) no-salt added diced tomatoes including juice	1
2 cups	chicken stock	500 mL
4 cups	cubed (1 inch/2.5 cm) butternut squash (about 1)	1 L
1 lb	skinless boneless chicken thighs, cut into 1-inch (2.5 cm) cubes	500 g
4 cups	chopped kale or callaloo (see Tips, left)	1 L
1 lb	cooked, peeled deveined shrimp (see Tips, right)	500 g
1 to 2	minced habanero or Scotch bonnet chile peppers (see Tips, right)	1 to 2
1 cup	coconut milk	250 mL

1. In a skillet, heat oil over medium heat. Add onions and cook, stirring, until softened, about 3 minutes. Add garlic, ginger, peppercorns, allspice, salt, thyme and bay leaves and cook, stirring, for 1 minute. Add rice and toss until well coated with mixture. Stir in tomatoes with juice and stock and bring to a boil. Boil for 1 minute.

If you are using large shrimp, chop them into bite-size pieces before adding to the stew.

Only use a second habanero pepper if you are a true heat seeker.

Make Ahead

Complete Step 1. Cover and refrigerate for up to 2 days. When you're ready to cook, continue with the recipe.

2. Transfer to slow cooker stoneware. Stir in squash and chicken. Cover and cook on Low for 6 hours or on High for 3 hours, until chicken is no longer pink. Working in batches, stir in kale. Add shrimp, chile peppers to taste and coconut milk. Cover and cook on High about 20 minutes, until kale is wilted and flavors meld. Remove and discard bay leaves.

Mindful Morsels

Virtually all of the saturated fat in a serving of this recipe (7.1 g) comes from the coconut milk. It is now thought to be a beneficial fat (see below).

Natural Wonders

Coconut Milk

The coconut milk in this recipe is a source of saturated fat. For decades, coconut products have been demonized for their fat content. However, once researchers started to take a close look at coconut, a different story emerged. For instance, one study of a group of people on Pacific Islands who ate a high-fat coconut-based diet found the populace to be remarkably lean and free of illnesses traditionally associated with saturated fat intake, such as atherosclerosis and heart disease.

Coconut milk, which is the liquid expressed from grated coconut meat combined with water, is extremely nutritious. One cup (250 mL) of coconut milk contains a smattering of B vitamins and an impressive collection of valuable minerals such as iron, magnesium, potassium and phosphorous, providing more than 20% of the daily value of each. Not only is it a good source of important electrolytes, which help to keep your body hydrated and properly functioning, it also provides more than 100% of the daily value of manganese and almost one-quarter of the daily value for the antioxidant selenium. Because coconut milk is high in fat, it also helps your body make good use of the fat-soluble vitamins A, D, E and K.

It is also worth noting that coconut milk shares a common ingredient with mother's milk — lauric acid, an immune system booster that helps your body to fight infections and viruses. Moreover, because the fats in coconut milk are medium-chain triglycerides, they are used for energy, not stored as fat around your middle. These fats also may be anticarcinogenic and boost your immune system.

If you can't consume dairy, coconut milk makes a nice addition to coffee or tea because it is higher in fat than other non-dairy milks. You can easily make your own by combining unsweetened dried shredded coconut and filtered water in a blender and straining through a nut bag.

When purchasing coconut milk look for an organic version in a BPA-free can.

Butternut Chili

Beef and Veal

Butternut Chili

I love this chili. The combination of beef, butternut squash, ancho chiles and cilantro is a real winner in terms of taste, as well as nutrients. Don't be afraid to make extra — it's great reheated.

Makes 6 servings

Can Be Halved
(see Tips, page 186)

Tips

Use 1 cup (250 mL) dried kidney beans, soaked, cooked and drained (see Basic Beans, page 284), or 1 can no-salt added (14 to 19 oz/ 398 to 540 mL) canned beans, drained and rinsed.

If you prefer, soak and purée the chiles while the chili cooks; refrigerate until you're ready to use.

Most of the sodium in a serving of this recipe comes from the added salt (382 mg). If you are watching your sodium intake, omit the salt or reduce the quantity.

Nutrients Per Serving

Calories	376
Protein	25.0 g
Carbohydrates	40.8 g
Fat (Total)	13.9 g
Saturated Fat	4.6 g
Monounsaturated Fat	6.5 g
Polyunsaturated Fat	1.1 g
Dietary Fiber	9.8 g
Sodium	463 mg
Cholesterol	45 mg

EXCELLENT SOURCE OF
vitamins A, B_6 and B_{12}, folate, phosphorus, magnesium, potassium, iron and zinc.
GOOD SOURCE OF vitamins C and K and calcium.
CONTAINS a very high amount of dietary fiber.

- **Medium to large (3½ to 5 quart) slow cooker**
- **Blender**

2 cups	cooked kidney beans (see Tips, left)	500 mL
1 tbsp	olive oil	15 mL
1 lb	lean ground beef	500 g
2	onions, finely chopped	2
4	cloves garlic, minced	4
1	piece (2 inches/5 cm) cinnamon stick	1
1 tbsp	ground cumin (see Tips, page 202)	15 mL
2 tsp	dried oregano	10 mL
1 tsp	sea salt (see Tips, left)	5 mL
½ tsp	cracked black peppercorns	2 mL
1	can (28 oz/796 mL) no-salt added diced tomatoes including juice	1
3 cups	cubed (1 inch/2.5 cm) butternut squash	750 mL
2	dried New Mexico, ancho or guajillo chiles	2
2 cups	boiling water	500 mL
½ cup	coarsely chopped fresh cilantro leaves	125 mL

1. In a skillet, heat oil over medium-high heat. Add beef and onions and cook, stirring and breaking meat up with a spoon, until beef is no longer pink, about 10 minutes. Add garlic, cinnamon stick, cumin, oregano, salt and peppercorns and cook, stirring, for 1 minute. Add tomatoes with juice and bring to a boil.

2. Transfer to slow cooker stoneware. Add squash and beans and stir well. Cover and cook on Low for 6 hours or on High for 3 hours, until squash is tender.

3. About an hour before recipe has finished cooking, in a heatproof bowl, soak dried chiles in boiling water for 30 minutes, weighing down chiles with a cup to ensure they remain submerged. Drain, reserving ½ cup (125 mL) of the soaking liquid. Discard stems and coarsely chop chiles. Transfer to a blender and add cilantro and reserved soaking liquid. Purée.

4. Add chile mixture to stoneware and stir well. Cover and cook on High for 30 minutes, until mixture is hot and bubbly and flavors meld. Discard cinnamon stick.

Make Ahead

Complete Steps 1 and 3. Cover and refrigerate tomato and chile mixtures separately overnight. The next morning, continue with the recipe.

Mindful Morsels

The next time you find yourself weeping while chopping onions, think kindly thoughts: that the sulfur compound that make your eyes water may also help to keep your blood pressure low and, if you suffer from diabetes, your blood sugar under control.

Natural Wonders

Vitamin A

The squash in recipes such as Butternut Chili is an excellent source of beta-carotene, the plant form of vitamin A. (For more on carotenoids, see Natural Wonders, page 99.) Beta-carotene is not, technically speaking, vitamin A; along with some other carotenoids it is known as a pro-vitamin A carotenoid. Your body converts these substances to vitamin A.

Vitamin A is justifiably famous for keeping your eyes healthy and contributing to your night-vision capabilities, (how often did your mother tell you to eat your carrots because they were good for your eyes?) but it has other important functions in your body, as well. For instance, it supports bone growth and keeps your cells functioning well. It also helps your body to fight infections. Recent research suggests it may also have anticarcinogenic properties.

Vitamin A is a fat-soluble vitamin, which means your body will not effectively absorb and utilize the vitamin A in foods unless you have an adequate intake of dietary fat. However, your body stores fat-soluble vitamins, which means taking a high dose supplement isn't a good idea. Any excess will remain in your body, where it has the potential to become toxic.

Obtaining vitamin A from foods such as orange vegetables and fruits is the best strategy for good health, and not only to avoid possible excess intake from supplements. Emerging evidence indicates that obtaining vitamin A in a pro-vitamin form is preferable to consuming what is known as the pre-formed version. Pre-formed vitamin A is provided by animal-based foods such as milk and eggs and fortified cereals. Studies show that consuming too much pre-formed vitamin A (which is easy to do in the typical North American diet) actually increases your risk of osteoporosis. On the other hand, there is no such risk with consuming beta-carotene.

Taking beta-carotene in supplements is not the answer either. When researchers gave beta-carotene supplements to smokers they found it increased their risk of developing lung cancer. One study that provided subjects with 30 mg of beta-carotene plus 25,000 IU of vitamin A in supplements raised their risk of dying from lung cancer by 46% over people taking a placebo. However, long term epidemiological studies showed that people who obtain these nutrients from their diets were less likely to develop numerous types of cancer. The best food sources of beta-carotene in addition to squash, are carrots, spinach, kale and apricots.

Onion-Braised Brisket

Impress your friends with this easy-to-make yet absolutely delicious brisket. My next-door neighbor, who was invited in for a tasting, described it as "ambrosial." When it's served alongside steaming garlic-mashed potatoes, he's not far wrong.

Makes 8 servings

Can Be Halved
(see Tips, below)

Tips

If you are halving this recipe, be sure to use a small (2½ to 3½ quart) slow cooker. Reduce cooking time to about 6 hours on Low or 3 hours on High.

These cooking times are estimates. Cooking times vary substantially among slow cookers (see Cooking Times, page 12) and people have different preferences with regard to how well they like their meat done. If you prefer fork-tender results, start checking after the food has cooked for 6 hours on Low.

Nutrients Per Serving

Calories	366
Protein	40.8 g
Carbohydrates	10.1 g
Fat (Total)	17.1 g
Saturated Fat	5.3 g
Monounsaturated Fat	8.7 g
Polyunsaturated Fat	0.8 g
Dietary Fiber	1.6 g
Sodium	247 mg
Cholesterol	123 mg

EXCELLENT SOURCE OF vitamins B$_6$, B$_{12}$ and K, phosphorous, iron and zinc.
GOOD SOURCE OF potassium and magnesium.
SOURCE OF vitamin C and folate.

• **Large (approx. 5 quart) slow cooker**

2 tbsp	olive oil, divided	30 mL
4 to 5 lbs	double beef brisket, trimmed (see Tip, page 185)	2 to 2.5 kg
4	onions, thinly sliced on the vertical	4
6	cloves garlic, minced	6
1 tsp	dried thyme	5 mL
½ tsp	sea salt	2 mL
½ tsp	cracked black peppercorns	2 mL
2 tbsp	red wine vinegar	30 mL
1 tbsp	Dijon mustard	15 mL
1 cup	dry red wine	250 mL
¼ cup	tomato paste	60 mL
1 cup	beef stock	250 mL
2 tbsp	cornstarch dissolved in ¼ cup (60 mL) beef stock	30 mL
½ cup	finely chopped parsley leaves	125 mL

1. In a skillet, heat 1 tbsp (15 mL) of oil over medium-high heat. Add brisket and brown well on both sides, about 6 minutes. Transfer to slow cooker stoneware.

2. Add remaining tbsp (15 mL) of oil to stoneware. Add onions and cook, stirring, until they begin to turn golden, about 5 minutes. Add garlic, thyme, salt and peppercorns and cook, stirring, for 1 minute. Add vinegar, mustard and wine and bring to a boil. Cook, stirring and scraping up brown bits from bottom of pan, for 2 minutes. Stir in tomato paste and stock.

3. Transfer to slow cooker stoneware. Cover and cook on Low for 8 to 10 hours or on High for 4 to 5 hours, until brisket is very tender (see Tips, left).

4. Transfer meat to a deep platter, slice and keep warm. Transfer sauce to a saucepan and bring to a boil. Reduce heat and simmer for 5 minutes to slightly reduce. Remove from heat and add cornstarch solution, stirring until sauce thickens. Pour over meat and garnish with parsley.

Complete Step 2. Cover and
refrigerate for up to 2 days.
When you're ready to cook,
complete the recipe.

Mindful Morsels

This recipe is an excellent source of zinc, a mineral that
boosts your immune system and, as a result, is often
studied as a potential treatment for the common cold. So
far studies assessing the value that zinc lozenges as a cold
fighter have not produced definitive results. Moreover,
consuming too many can upset your digestive system.

Natural Wonders

Pasture-Raised Meat

After reading Michael Pollan's book *The Omnivore's Dilemma* in 2006, I stopped buying
meat from the supermarket. I was appalled at the horrible and unhealthy conditions (for us,
as well as for the animals) that cattle were raised in. I now buy only pasture-raised meat
from a butcher who is completely committed to this model. Not only is it more humane, but
since 2006 the evidence has been mounting that from a dietary perspective pasture-raised
meat is also a more nutritious and healthier option.

In a 2010 article published in *Nutrition Journal* and based on an overview of the existing
studies, principal author Dr. Cynthia Daley writes that the meat from beef fed on grass
has a significantly better fatty acid profile and higher antioxidant content than meat from
grain-fed cattle. She points out that red meat, regardless of how it is fed, is nutrient-dense. It
provides important nutrients such as essential amino acids, minerals, including iron, zinc
and selenium, and vitamins A, B_6, B_{12}, D and E. Meat is also a source of fat, which among
other benefits helps your body to utilize the fat-soluble vitamins.

However, it is the differences in the fatty-acid profiles of grass- vs grain-fed beef that
are particularly compelling. While pasture-raised beef is lower in total fat, it is higher in
certain beneficial fats, such as omega-3s. Perhaps most significantly, it has a much more
favorable ratio of omega-3 to omega-6 fats than grain-fed beef. Although estimates vary,
Dr. Daley states that a healthy diet should consist of approximately one to four times
omega-3 to omega-6 fats. The ratio in a typical North American diet is 11 to 30 times
more omega-6 fats. The preponderance of omega-6 fats in our diets sets the stage for
inflammatory conditions and a series of diseases.

In addition to this healthy ratio, another significant benefit of grass-fed beef is that it is
higher in conjugated linoleic acid (CLA), which among other benefits is a powerful cancer
fighter. One Finnish study linked CLA levels with as much as a 60% reduction in breast
cancer risk. CLA has also been found to be a powerful anti-inflammatory. Consumption
of this fatty acid has also been linked with a reduced risk of obesity, diabetes, and various
autoimmune disorders, such as Crohn's disease.

Studies also show that the vitamin E content of grass-fed beef is significantly higher than
grain-fed beef (2.1 to 7.73 ug/g compared to 0.75 to 2.92 ug/g). Vitamin E has been linked
with various health benefits, including a lower risk of heart disease and cancer.

David's Dream Cholent

Thanks to our friend David Saffir, who passed along his family's treasured cholent recipes. From them I pieced together this version of a traditional Sabbath dish. My version uses whole-grain rice rather than barley, which although more traditional, contains gluten. This is a substantial serving of a hearty dish and condiments are all you will need to add.

Makes 12 servings

Can Be Halved
(see Tips, below)

Tips

If you are halving this recipe, be sure to use a small (2½ to 3½ quart) slow cooker.

Celery root, also known as celeriac, is actually a type of celery with crispy white flesh and a pleasing peppery flavor. Since it oxidizes quickly on contact with air, be sure to use it as soon as it is shredded or toss with 1 tbsp (15 mL) lemon juice and water to prevent discoloration.

Nutrients Per Serving

Calories	586
Protein	35.9 g
Carbohydrates	33.2 g
Fat (Total)	33.9 g
Saturated Fat	13.0 g
Monounsaturated Fat	15.1 g
Polyunsaturated Fat	1.5 g
Dietary Fiber	5.5 g
Sodium	325 mg
Cholesterol	109 mg

EXCELLENT SOURCE OF vitamins A, B$_6$, B$_{12}$ and folate, phosphorus, magnesium, potassium, iron and zinc.

SOURCE OF vitamins C and K and calcium.

CONTAINS a high amount of dietary fiber.

• **Large (minimum 5 quart) slow cooker**

½ cup	each dried red kidney and dried white navy or kidney beans, soaked and drained	125 mL
1 tbsp	olive oil	15 mL
4 to 5 lbs	double beef brisket, trimmed (see Tip, right) and patted dry	2 to 2.5 kg
2	bone-in English-style short ribs (about 8 oz/250 g), patted dry	2
2	large potatoes, peeled and cut into ½-inch (1 cm) cubes	2
3	onions, finely chopped	3
4	carrots, peeled and diced	4
6	cloves garlic, minced	6
2 tsp	dried thyme	10 mL
1 tsp	each sea salt and cracked black peppercorns	5 mL
2 cups	shredded peeled celery root (see Tips, left)	500 mL
½ cup	long-grain brown or red rice	125 mL
4 cups	beef stock, divided	1 L
	Horseradish, dill pickles, Dijon or grainy mustard	

1. In a large skillet, heat oil over medium-high heat. Add brisket, fat side down, and brown, turning once, about 6 minutes. Transfer to stoneware. Add short ribs and cook, turning, until well browned, about 6 minutes. Transfer to stoneware. Add potatoes to skillet, in batches, and cook, stirring, until lightly browned, about 4 minutes. Transfer to stoneware as completed. Drain off all but 2 tbsp (30 mL) of fat.

2. Reduce heat to medium. Add onions and carrots and cook, stirring, until softened, about 7 minutes. Add garlic, thyme, salt and peppercorns and cook, stirring and scraping up brown bits from bottom of pan, for 1 minute. Add celery root and rice and toss to coat. Add beans and 2 cups (500 mL) of the stock and bring to a boil. Boil for 1 minute.

Tip

If the whole piece of brisket won't fit in your slow cooker, cut it in half and lay the two pieces on top of each other.

Make Ahead

Complete Step 2, adding 1 tbsp (15 mL) oil to pan before softening vegetables. Cover and refrigerate mixture for up to 2 days. When you're ready to cook, complete the recipe.

3. Transfer to stoneware. Add remaining stock and water barely to cover. Cover and cook on Low for 8 to 10 hours or on High for 4 to 5 hours, until meat and beans are very tender. Serve with horseradish, pickles and mustard.

Mindful Morsels

This recipe is very high in fat, most of which comes from the brisket (11.4 grams of saturated fat, 12.9 grams of monounsaturated fat and 1 gram of polyunsaturated fat). The nutrient analysis for this recipe was done using grain-fed beef. If using grass-fed beef, it would be lower in total fat and higher in beneficial fats such as conjugated linoleic acid (CLA). If you are concerned about fat intake, trim as much of the visible fat from the meat as possible. About half the calories in untrimmed beef come from the fat. Meat, both grass- and grain-fed, is one of the best food sources of vitamin B_{12} (see Natural Wonders, page 235).

Natural Wonders

Magnesium

This recipe is an excellent source of magnesium, a mineral that supports every major bodily system and which, experts say, is under-represented in typical diets. Among its functions, magnesium helps to keep bones strong; an insufficient intake may increase the risk of osteoporosis. It also supports the nervous system, working with calcium to keep nerves relaxed. Without an adequate supply of magnesium, muscles may react, triggering cramps and spasms. If you are pregnant and experiencing leg cramps (about 50% of women do), taking about 300 mg of magnesium daily may reduce their frequency and severity. Muscle tension, anxiety and various heart ailments, including potentially dangerous arrhythmias, have also been linked with a magnesium deficiency.

In addition, magnesium helps to regulate blood sugar, and higher intakes have been shown to reduce the risk of insulin resistance. Research links higher intakes of magnesium with lower rates of diabetes as well as lower rates of high blood pressure, stroke and migraines. A diet high in magnesium may also reduce your risk of developing colon cancer.

Magnesium also helps to regulate a brain receptor, and research indicates that it may keep memory functioning as we age. A magnesium deficiency may be triggered by over-consumption of alcohol, which increases its secretion in the urine, so watch your intake of this mineral if you're inclined to over-imbibe. If you live in an area with "soft" tap water, you should also be aware that it contains less magnesium than hard water.

Mediterranean Beef Ragoût

Succulent peppers, sweet or hot, are so much a part of Mediterranean cooking that it's interesting to recall they are indigenous to North America and didn't cross the Atlantic until Columbus brought them to Spain. Here they combine with cumin, olives and tomatoes to transform humble stewing beef into an Epicurean delight.

Makes 8 servings

Can Be Halved
(see Tips, below)

Tips

If you are halving this recipe, be sure to use a small (1½ to 3½ quart) slow cooker.

Substitute an equal quantity of lemon thyme for the thyme, if you prefer.

This amount produces a robust cumin flavor. If you don't like the taste of cumin, reduce the quantity to about 1 tbsp (15 mL).

Nutrients Per Serving

Calories	279
Protein	24.2 g
Carbohydrates	8.3 g
Fat (Total)	16.5 g
Saturated Fat	5.4 g
Monounsaturated Fat	9.3 g
Polyunsaturated Fat	1.0 g
Dietary Fiber	1.7 g
Sodium	601 mg
Cholesterol	67 mg

EXCELLENT SOURCE OF vitamins C, B$_{12}$ and K, iron and zinc.
GOOD SOURCE OF vitamin B$_6$, potassium, phosphorus and magnesium.
SOURCE OF vitamin A, folate and calcium.

• **Medium to large (3½ to 5 quart) slow cooker**

2 lbs	trimmed stewing beef, cut into 1-inch (2.5 cm) cubes and patted dry	1 kg
2 tbsp	olive oil, divided	30 mL
2	onions, chopped	2
4	cloves garlic, minced	4
2 tbsp	ground cumin (see Tips, page 202)	30 mL
1 tsp	dried thyme	5 mL
1 tsp	grated lemon zest, optional	5 mL
½ tsp	salt	2 mL
½ tsp	cracked black peppercorns	2 mL
1 cup	beef stock	250 mL
½ cup	dry red wine	125 mL
1	can (14 oz/398 mL) no-salt added diced tomatoes, including juice	1
2	bay leaves	2
2	roasted red bell peppers, thinly sliced, then cut into 1-inch (2.5 cm) pieces	2
½ cup	sliced pitted green olives	125 mL
½ cup	finely chopped parsley leaves	125 mL

1. In a skillet, heat 1 tbsp (15 mL) of the oil over medium-high heat. Add beef, in batches, and cook, stirring, adding more oil as necessary, until browned, about 4 minutes per batch. Transfer to slow cooker stoneware as completed.

2. Reduce heat to medium. Add onions and garlic to pan and cook, stirring, until onions are softened, about 3 minutes. Add cumin, thyme, lemon zest, if using, salt and peppercorns and cook, stirring, for 1 minute. Add beef stock, wine, tomatoes with juice and bay leaves and bring to a boil. Add to slow cooker and stir well.

3. Cover and cook on Low for 6 hours or on High for 3 hours, until mixture is bubbly and beef is tender. Stir in roasted peppers, olives and parsley. Cover and cook on High for 15 minutes, until peppers are heated through. Discard bay leaves.

more information on page 188

Make Ahead

This dish can be partially prepared before it is cooked. Heat oil and complete Step 2. Refrigerate overnight or for up to 2 days. When you're ready to cook, complete Steps 1 and 3.

Natural Wonders

Olives

Although they are high in sodium, in addition to beneficial nutrients, olives add a burst of flavor to this tasty stew. Olives are a good source of healthy monounsaturated fats and polyphenols, which protect cells from damage and inflammation. Polyphenols are powerful antioxidants that appear to protect against cardiovascular disease and may also play a role in preventing cancer. One study found that women who regularly consumed olive oil lowered their risk of breast cancer by 25%. A recent study published in the journal *Nature* identified an anti-inflammatory agent in olive oil, a natural painkiller, which acts like ibuprofen. The anti-inflammatory components of olives may reduce the severity of osteoarthritis and rheumatoid arthritis, among other conditions.

Zesty Braised Beef with New Potatoes

It's hard to believe that this simple combination of ingredients can taste so luscious. I like to serve this with a big platter of roasted carrots. Save leftovers and enjoy in a bowl like a hearty soup.

Makes 8 servings

Can Be Halved
(see Tips, below)

Tips

If you are halving this recipe, be sure to use a small (2 to 3½ quart) slow cooker.

Because it's important to bring the potatoes to a boil in order to ensure they cook in the slow cooker, I do not recommend making part of this dish ahead of time.

Nutrients Per Serving

Calories	352
Protein	26.9 g
Carbohydrates	22.5 g
Fat (Total)	16.9 g
Saturated Fat	5.8 g
Monounsaturated Fat	8.9 g
Polyunsaturated Fat	1.0 g
Dietary Fiber	2.2 g
Sodium	313 mg
Cholesterol	78 mg

EXCELLENT SOURCE OF vitamins B_6, B_{12} and K, potassium, iron and zinc.
GOOD SOURCE OF phosphorous and magnesium.
SOURCE OF vitamin C and folate.
CONTAINS a moderate amount of dietary fiber.

- **Medium to large (3½ to 5 quart) slow cooker**

2 tbsp	olive oil, divided	30 mL
2 oz	chunk pancetta, preferably hot pancetta, diced	60 g
2 lbs	trimmed stewing beef, cut into 1-inch (2.5 cm) cubes and patted dry	1 kg
2	onions, finely chopped	2
4	cloves garlic, minced	4
1 tsp	dried thyme	5 mL
½ tsp	sea salt	2 mL
½ tsp	cracked black peppercorns	2 mL
½ cup	dry white wine (see Tips, page 128)	125 mL
2 cups	chicken stock	500 mL
2 lbs	small new potatoes, scrubbed and thinly sliced (about 30 tiny ones)	1 kg
¼ tsp	cayenne pepper, dissolved in 1 tbsp (15 mL) freshly squeezed lemon juice	1 mL
¼ cup	finely chopped parsley leaves	60 mL

1. In a skillet, heat 1 tbsp (15 mL) of the oil over medium-high heat. Add pancetta and cook, stirring, until nicely browned, about 3 minutes. Transfer to slow cooker stoneware.

2. Add beef to skillet, in batches, and cook, stirring, until browned, about 4 minutes per batch. Transfer to stoneware as completed.

3. Reduce heat to medium. Add remaining tbsp (15 mL) of oil to pan. Add onions and cook, stirring, until softened, about 3 minutes. Add garlic, thyme, salt and peppercorns and cook, stirring, for 1 minute. Add wine, bring to a boil and boil, stirring and scraping up brown bits from bottom of pan, for 2 minutes. Add stock and potatoes and bring to a boil. Simmer for 2 minutes.

4. Transfer to stoneware. Cover and cook on Low for 8 hours or on High for 4 hours, until potatoes are tender. Stir in cayenne solution. Cover and cook on High for 10 minutes. Transfer to a serving dish and garnish with parsley.

more information on page 191

Zesty Braised Beef with New Potatoes

Mindful Morsels

The meat in this recipe provides high quality protein. On a daily basis we need to consume about 9 grams of protein for every 20 pounds of weight (1 gram per kilogram).

Natural Wonders

Fatty Acids

At first glance, many of the recipes in this chapter seem high in fat. But most is unsaturated fatty acids, both monounsaturated (MUFA) and polyunsaturated (PUFA), which experts traditionally associated with healthful benefits. Also, recent research indicates that saturated fatty acids (SFA) are not nearly as bad as we once thought they were. Consider, for instance, that one serving of Zesty Braised Beef with New Potatoes provides 5.8 grams of SFA, 8.9 grams of MUFA and 1 gram of PUFA, which isn't untypical of the breakdown in beef recipes.

In the past, when we were told to reduce our intake of SFA as a way to reduce LDL ("bad") cholesterol, replacing SFA with MUFA was emphasized as a way to maintain healthful levels of HDL ("good") cholesterol. Having higher levels of HDL and lower levels of LDL helps to prevent plaque formation in your arteries. The less plaque you have, the less your risk for cardiovascular disease.

For many years, major health organizations urged us to keep fat intake to 30% or less of the total calories we consumed; they linked the consumption of fat with increased incidence of cardiovascular disease and overall death or mortality. We were also advised to reduce our total fat intake and to replace that fat with fat-free carbohydrates. The unintended consequence of this strategy was a drop in HDL cholesterol and a rise in triglycerides (another type of blood fat that increases the risk for heart disease).

Today, we know better. As we understand more about the various kinds of fat, these recommendations have become less stringent. Two large long-term studies conducted by Harvard researchers found no link between the overall percentage of calories from fat and any significant health outcome, including weight gain. The important factor was the kind of fat. Quality matters. As mentioned elsewhere in this book, we need to tweak our intake of PUFA's. Omega-6 fats, found predominately in grain and seed oils, such as soy, corn, grapeseed, sunflower and safflower need to be reduced. At the same time, we need to consume more omega-3 fats, found primarily in fish, seafood, pasture-raised meats, and truly free-range poultry (due to lax regulations, some growers are allowed to describe poultry that does not really qualify as "free range") and their eggs.

Undisputedly, trans fats are by far the worst offenders when it comes to fat. These partially hydrogenated oils are found mainly in commercially prepared and processed foods such as margarines containing partially hydrogenated oils, baked goods, such as muffins, doughnuts, scones, cookies, crackers and cereal bars, and deep-fried foods.

Greek-Style Beef with Eggplant

This ambrosial stew reminds me of moussaka without the topping, and it is far less work. Made with red wine and lycopene-rich tomato paste, it develops a deep and intriguing flavor. Serve this over hot quinoa and accompany with steamed broccoli and a tossed green salad for a delicious and nutrient-rich meal.

Makes 6 to 8 servings

Can Be Halved
(see Tips, below)

Tip

If you are halving this recipe, be sure to use a small (1½ to 3½ quart) slow cooker.

Nutrients Per Serving

Calories	225
Protein	13.9 g
Carbohydrates	17.8 g
Fat (Total)	11.7 g
Saturated Fat	3.7 g
Monounsaturated Fat	6.0 g
Polyunsaturated Fat	0.7 g
Dietary Fiber	4.8 g
Sodium	204 mg
Cholesterol	34 mg

EXCELLENT SOURCE OF vitamin K, potassium and zinc.

GOOD SOURCE OF vitamins C, B₁₂ and B₆, folate, phosphorus, magnesium and iron.

SOURCE OF vitamin A.

CONTAINS a high amount of dietary fiber.

- **Medium to large (3½ to 5 quart) slow cooker**
- **Large rimmed baking sheet**

2	medium eggplant (each about 1 lb/500 g) peeled, halved and each half cut into quarters	2
2 tbsp	coarse sea or kosher salt	30 mL
2 tbsp	olive oil, divided	30 mL
1 lb	lean ground beef	500 g
4	onions, thinly sliced on the vertical	4
4	cloves garlic, minced	4
2 tsp	dried oregano, crumbled	10 mL
1 tsp	ground cinnamon	5 mL
½ tsp	sea salt	2 mL
½ tsp	cracked black peppercorns	2 mL
1	can (5½ oz/156 mL) tomato paste	1
1 cup	dry red wine	250 mL
1 cup	packed parsley leaves, finely chopped	250 mL
	Freshly grated Parmesan cheese	

1. In a colander over a sink, combine eggplant and coarse salt. Toss and let stand for 30 minutes. Rinse thoroughly under cold running water. Lay a clean tea towel on a work surface. Working in batches over the sink and using your hands, squeeze liquid out of the eggplant. Transfer to the tea towel. When batches are complete, roll the towel up and press down to remove remaining liquid. Meanwhile, preheat oven to 400°F (200°C). Brush eggplant all over with 1 tbsp (15 mL) of the oil. Place on baking sheet and bake until soft and fragrant, about 20 minutes. Transfer to slow cooker stoneware.

2. In a skillet, heat remaining 1 tbsp (15 mL) of oil over medium heat. Add ground beef and onions and cook, stirring and breaking up with a spoon, until beef is no longer pink, about 10 minutes. Add garlic, oregano, cinnamon, salt and peppercorns and cook, stirring for 1 minute. Add tomato paste and red wine and stir well.

Make Ahead

Complete Steps 1 and 2, placing eggplant and meat mixtures in separate containers. Cover and refrigerate overnight or for up to 2 days. When you're ready to cook, combine mixtures in stoneware and complete Step 3.

3. Transfer to slow cooker stoneware. Stir well. Cover and cook on Low for 6 hours or on High for 3 hours, until mixture is bubbly and eggplant is tender. Stir in parsley and serve. Pass Parmesan at the table.

Mindful Morsels

Although we tend to think that fresh is always best, one study found that tomato paste has more than six times as much available lycopene, a carotenoid, than fresh tomatoes. Cooking tomatoes increases the bioavailability of this valuable nutrient. Eating a cooked tomato product, or any other carotenoid-rich vegetable, with a little fat, further increases bioavailability.

Natural Wonders

Vitamin K

I often use a fair bit of parsley in my recipes for two reasons: it's very tasty and it's loaded with nutrients. If you've ever thought about using parsley for more than a garnish, this recipe is a case in point. Each serving contains 48.8 mcg of vitamin K, 40.5 mcg of which comes from parsley. That's over half the recommended daily value of this important nutrient, which is found mainly in leafy greens, some fruits and certain oils such as olive oil. In fact, the more we learn about vitamin K, the more significant it becomes.

Long recognized as an important blood-clotting agent, researchers have linked vitamin K intake with reduced rates of osteoporosis in older women and now think it plays an important role in bone health. Vitamin K helps to keep your bones strong by stimulating production of a bone protein that draws calcium into your bones. Interestingly, leafy greens, such as parsley, are also one of the best and most easily absorbed sources of calcium, the mineral we most commonly associate with bone health. Parsley also provides magnesium, which along with vitamin D, helps your body absorb calcium. Vitamin K also helps with the process of regulating calcium excretion in your urine. All these nutrients likely work together to ensure strong healthy bones.

Other research suggests that vitamin K is a powerful antioxidant. Adequate consumption of this vitamin protects against cardiovascular disease by preventing calcium from reaching the linings of your arteries, which causes them to stiffen.

Persian-Style Beef and Split Pea Stew

If you're looking for something unusual to serve to guests, try this luscious combination of highly seasoned meat and split peas. The substantial hit of saffron coupled with tomato and the unique tang of dried limes is a deliciously exotic flavor. According to Persian food authority Margaret Shaida, this dish is often garnished with fried potatoes, so I have included an oven-baked alternative as an option.

Makes 6 to 8 servings

Can Be Halved
(see Tips, below)

Tips

If you are halving this recipe, use 2 limes and a small (2 to 3½ quart) slow cooker.

Dried limes are available in Middle Eastern markets. They do contain sodium, which we couldn't account for when doing the nutritional analysis because data was not available.

Nutrients Per Serving

Calories	301
Protein	27.2 g
Carbohydrates	13.0 g
Fat (Total)	15.4 g
Saturated Fat	5.3 g
Monounsaturated Fat	8.3 g
Polyunsaturated Fat	1.0 g
Dietary Fiber	2.1 g
Sodium	289 mg
Cholesterol	74 mg

EXCELLENT SOURCE OF vitamin B$_{12}$, phosphorus and zinc.

GOOD SOURCE OF vitamin B$_6$, folate, potassium, magnesium and iron.

SOURCE OF vitamins C and K.

CONTAINS a moderate amount of dietary fiber.

- **Medium to large (3½ to 5 quart) slow cooker**

2 tbsp	olive oil, divided	30 mL
2 lbs	trimmed stewing beef, cut into 1-inch (2.5 cm) cubes, and patted dry	1 kg
3	dried limes, pierced with a sharp knife (see Tips, left)	3
2	onions, chopped	2
1 tsp	ground turmeric	5 mL
½ tsp	saffron threads, crumbled	2 mL
½ tsp	sea salt	2 mL
½ tsp	cracked black peppercorns	2 mL
¼ cup	tomato paste	60 mL
½ cup	yellow split peas, rinsed	125 mL
3 cups	chicken or vegetable stock or water	750 mL
¼ cup	freshly squeezed lemon juice	60 mL
	Oven-Fried Potato Wedges, optional (see Tip, right)	

1. In a skillet, heat 1 tbsp (15 mL) of the oil over medium-high heat. Add beef, in batches, and cook, stirring, until lightly browned on all sides, about 4 minutes per batch. Transfer to slow cooker stoneware as completed. Bury dried limes in meat to keep them submerged.

2. Reduce heat to medium. Add remaining tbsp (15 mL) of oil to pan. Add onions and cook, stirring frequently, until golden, about 10 minutes. Stir in turmeric, saffron, salt and peppercorns and cook for 1 minute. Stir in tomato paste and split peas. Add stock. Bring to a boil and cook, stirring and scraping up brown bits, for 2 minutes.

3. Transfer to slow cooker stoneware. Cover and cook on Low for 8 hours or on High for 4 hours, until beef and peas are tender. Discard dried limes. Stir in lemon juice. Taste and adjust seasoning. To serve, transfer to a deep platter or shallow serving bowl and arrange potato wedges, if using, on top.

Tip

Oven-Baked Potato Wedges: Preheat oven to 400°F (200°C). Thoroughly scrub 4 baking potatoes. Microwave on High for 5 minutes and let stand for 2 minutes. On a cutting board, cut each potato in half, then cut each half into quarters. Brush liberally with olive oil and roast in preheated oven until nicely browned, about 20 minutes.

Make Ahead

Complete Step 2. Cover and refrigerate for up to 2 days. When you're ready to cook, complete the recipe.

Variation

Substitute 2 lbs (1 kg) cubed lamb shoulder for the beef.

Mindful Morsels

Tomato paste is, basically, a highly concentrated tomato purée. It is an excellent flavor enhancer in many dishes, because a little goes a long way. When purchasing tomato paste (as with all canned products), read the label carefully. It should not contain, to paraphrase Michael Pollan, any ingredients your great grandmother wouldn't recognize. Commercially prepared tomato paste may contain a panoply of dreadful ingredients, from high fructose corn syrup to hidden gluten and even MSG. I buy mine at a natural foods store. It contains only organic tomatoes and salt.

Natural Wonders

Protein

Meat is one of the best sources of high-quality protein. Protein plays a number of vital roles in bodily functions, from building and maintaining bones, muscles and skin to creating antibodies to fight against infection. High energy levels are also dependent upon having adequate supplies of this nutrient. While the jury is still out on the risks and benefits of a high-protein diet, the Nurses' Health Study found that women who consumed about 110 grams of protein a day were 25% less likely to have suffered a heart attack or to have died from heart disease than those who consumed less protein, about 68 grams a day.

New research suggests we may need more protein than was previously thought. Recommendations on healthy eating suggest that adults should get between 10 and 35% of their calories from protein. However, a study reported in the *Journal of Bone and Mineral Research* linked low levels of protein with bone loss and suggested that dieting, exercise and aging all place more demands on the body for protein. These researchers recommended that at least 20% of calories be derived from protein.

Indian-Spiced Beef with Eggplant

Because it uses ground beef, this dish is very easy to make, yet the results seem exotic. The eggplant adds luscious texture and the mild Indian spicing produces intriguing flavor. I serve this over brown rice and add a simple green salad to complete the meal.

Makes 6 servings

Can Be Halved
(see Tips, below)

Tips

If you are halving this recipe, be sure to use a small (2 to 3½ quart) slow cooker.

This recipe is relatively high in fat, most of which (17.9 g) comes from the beef. If you are trying to reduce your consumption of fat, substitute extra-lean ground beef for the lean version called for. The saturated fat (8.3 grams) would be lower if pasture-raised beef was used.

Nutrients Per Serving

Calories	508
Protein	34.3 g
Carbohydrates	24.5 g
Fat (Total)	30.6 g
Saturated Fat	10.8 g
Monounsaturated Fat	15.1 g
Polyunsaturated Fat	1.5 g
Dietary Fiber	4.9 g
Sodium	286 mg
Cholesterol	98 mg

EXCELLENT SOURCE OF vitamins C and B$_{12}$, phosphorus, potassium, iron and zinc.

GOOD SOURCE OF vitamin B$_6$, folate, calcium and magnesium.

SOURCE OF vitamins A and K.

CONTAINS a high amount of dietary fiber.

• **Medium to large (3½ to 5 quart) slow cooker**

1	large eggplant (about 1½ lbs/750 g), peeled and cut into 2-inch (5 cm) cubes	1
2 tsp	coarse sea or kosher salt	10 mL
3 tbsp	olive oil (approx.)	45 mL
2 lbs	lean ground beef	1 kg
2	onions, finely chopped	2
4	cloves garlic, minced	4
1 tbsp	minced gingerroot	15 mL
2 tsp	ground cumin	10 mL
1 tsp	ground coriander	5 mL
½ tsp	sea salt	2 mL
½ tsp	cracked black peppercorns	2 mL
1	can (28 oz/796 mL) no-salt added diced tomatoes including juice	1
½ cup	beef stock	125 mL
1 cup	full-fat plain yogurt	250 mL
1 tbsp	garam masala	15 mL
1	green bell pepper, seeded and diced	1
1	long red chile pepper, seeded and minced	1

1. In a colander over a sink, combine eggplant and coarse salt. Toss and let stand for 30 minutes. Rinse thoroughly under cold running water. Lay a clean tea towel on a work surface. Working in batches over the sink and using your hands, squeeze liquid out of the eggplant. Transfer to the tea towel. When batches are complete, roll the towel up and press down to remove remaining liquid.

2. In a nonstick skillet, heat 1 tbsp (15 mL) of the oil over medium-high heat. Add sweated eggplant, in batches, and cook until browned, adding more oil as necessary. Transfer to slow cooker stoneware.

3. Add remaining oil to pan. Add beef and onions and cook, stirring, until meat is no longer pink, about 7 minutes. Add garlic, ginger, cumin, coriander, salt and peppercorns and cook, stirring, for 1 minute. Add tomatoes with juice and stock and bring to a boil.

Make Ahead

Complete Steps 1, 2 and 3. Cover mixture, ensuring it cools promptly (see Making Ahead, page 16), and refrigerate for up to 2 days. When you're ready to cook, complete the recipe.

4. Transfer to slow cooker stoneware. Cover and cook on Low for 6 to 8 hours or on High for 3 to 4 hours, until hot and bubbly.

5. In a small bowl, combine yogurt and garam masala. Add to stoneware along with bell pepper and chile pepper. Stir well, cover and cook on High until pepper is tender, about 15 minutes.

Mindful Morsels

Eggplant is low in calories and contains small amounts of a wide variety of nutrients. However, it has a high antioxidant capacity and is exceptionally rich in viscous fiber. Viscous is the "sticky" type of soluble fiber that helps to balance blood sugar and blood lipids, such as cholesterol and triglycerides. Foods rich in viscous fiber, such as okra, flax, whole grains such as oats, as well as dried beans and lentils, may help to keep you feeling full longer, which some research has shown helps you to lose weight and keep it off.

Natural Wonders

Food and Cholesterol

Like all animal foods, meat is a source of dietary cholesterol. (For instance, the beef in one serving of Indian Spiced Beef with Eggplant provides 90 g of cholesterol; the yogurt provides 7 g and the various vegetables and spices provide none.) Not only has research raised serious questions about blood cholesterol levels as a risk factor for cardiovascular disease (see page 247), the relationship between the cholesterol you consume in food and the cholesterol in your blood is not clear. Although dietary cholesterol has long been thought to be a major factor in raising the levels of LDL ("bad") cholesterol in blood, research indicates this likely isn't the case and that the real culprits are trans fats. Traditionally, saturated fats have been implicated as well, but emerging research suggests they aren't the problem either.

Blood cholesterol levels are affected by factors such as family history, diabetes, body weight and shape and physical activity level. Research also shows that some people (those that are hypercholesterolemic) react more to the cholesterol in food than others. While it's worth keeping an eye on your blood cholesterol levels to ensure you aren't at risk, if you have no family history of cardiovascular disease and are not diabetic, keep your weight within a healthy range, exercise regularly and eat a balanced diet containing cholesterol-lowering nutrients, particularly soluble fiber, you probably don't need to be overly vigilant about the amount of dietary cholesterol you consume. You may want to consider that the American Heart Association, which takes a conservative position on this issue, recommends that healthy adults consume less than 300 milligrams of dietary cholesterol a day.

Texas-Style Chili con Carne

Although I call this Texas-Style Chili — because it is made with chunks of beef rather than ground meat — it's not the real thing since it contains beans. I like to serve this garnished with shredded Cheddar or Monterey Jack cheese, sour cream and finely chopped green onions. Yum!

Makes 8 servings

Can Be Halved
(see Tips, below)

Tips

If you are halving this recipe, be sure to use a small (2½ to 3½ quart) slow cooker.

For this quantity of beans, cook 1 cup (250 mL) dried beans (page 284) or use 1 can (14 to 19 oz/398 to 540 mL) kidney beans, drained and rinsed.

Nutrients Per Serving

Calories	318
Protein	29 g
Carbohydrates	21.5 g
Fat (Total)	13.1 g
Saturated Fat	5.0 g
Monounsaturated Fat	6.0 g
Polyunsaturated Fat	0.9 g
Dietary Fiber	5.5 g
Sodium	251 mg
Cholesterol	69 mg

EXCELLENT SOURCE OF vitamins B$_6$ and B$_{12}$, folate, phosphorus, potassium, iron and zinc.

GOOD SOURCE OF vitamin A and magnesium.

SOURCE OF vitamins C and K and calcium.

CONTAINS a high amount of dietary fiber.

- **Large (approx. 5 quart) slow cooker**
- **Blender**

2 cups	cooked drained red kidney beans (see Tips, left)	500 mL
2	slices bacon, finely chopped	2
2 lbs	stewing beef, cut into 1-inch (2.5 cm) cubes, and patted dry	1 kg
2	onions, thinly sliced on the vertical	2
4	cloves garlic, minced	4
1 tbsp	ground cumin (see Tips, page 202)	15 mL
1 tbsp	dried oregano	15 mL
½ tsp	sea salt	2 mL
½ tsp	cracked black peppercorns	2 mL
1	can (28 oz/796 mL) no-salt added tomatoes, including juice, coarsely chopped	1
1 cup	beef stock	250 mL
1 cup	dry red wine	250 mL
2	dried ancho, New Mexico or guajillo chile peppers	2
1 cup	boiling water	250 mL
1 to 2	jalapeño peppers, quartered	1 to 2
¼ cup	finely chopped cilantro leaves	60 mL

1. In a skillet over medium-high heat, cook bacon until crisp. Using a slotted spoon, transfer to paper towels to drain. Cover and refrigerate until ready to use.

2. Add beef to pan, in batches, and cook, stirring, until browned, about 4 minutes per batch. Transfer to slow cooker stoneware.

3. Add onions to pan and cook, stirring, until softened, about 3 minutes. Add garlic, cumin, oregano, salt and peppercorns and cook, stirring, for 1 minute. Stir in tomatoes with juice, stock and wine and bring to a boil.

4. Transfer to stoneware. Stir in beans. Cover and cook on Low for 6 to 8 hours or on High for 3 to 4 hours, until beef is very tender.

Make Ahead

Complete Steps 1 and 3. Cover and refrigerate bacon and tomato mixtures separately for up to 2 days. When you're ready to cook, brown the beef in 1 tbsp (15 mL) oil and complete the recipe.

5. About an hour before recipe has finished cooking, in a heatproof bowl, soak dried chiles in boiling water for 30 minutes, weighing down with a cup to ensure they are submerged. Drain and discard liquid. Remove stems, pat dry and coarsely chop chiles. In a blender, combine rehydrated chile and jalapeño pepper to taste with $1/2$ cup (125 mL) of liquid from the chili. Purée. Add to stoneware along with reserved bacon. Cover and cook on High for 20 minutes, until flavors meld. Garnish with cilantro and serve.

Mindful Morsels

Ounce for ounce, nippy jalapeño peppers contain more nutrients than bell peppers, their sweet-tasting relatives.

Natural Wonders

Zinc

Like all meat, beef is a good source of zinc. Among its functions, zinc stimulates enzyme activity, helps wounds heal, boosts the immune system and supports growth during key periods of development. For instance, zinc improves pregnancy outcomes and helps children develop reasoning skills and eye-hand coordination. Adolescents, particularly girls, who are more inclined to be vegetarians, may not be getting enough of this important mineral.

The best food sources of zinc are oysters and red meat. Poultry, fish, whole grains, legumes, nuts and seeds, particularly pumpkin seeds, also contain varying amounts of zinc. It is important to obtain zinc from food sources as some studies show that intakes just slightly higher than 15 mg (an amount you would be likely to get from a supplement) can trigger negative effects.

Chunky Black Bean Chili

Here is a great-tasting, stick-to-the-ribs chili that is perfect for a family dinner or casual evening with friends. The combination of milder New Mexico and ancho chile peppers gives the mix unique flavoring, and the zestier fresh chile peppers add heat. To expand the range of nutrients, serve with a big green salad and if friends are coming, open a bottle of robust red wine.

Makes 8 servings

Can Be Halved
(see Tips, page 206)

Tip

For this quantity of beans, use 1½ cups (375 mL) dried beans, soaked, cooked and drained (see Basic Beans, page 284), or 1½ cans (each 14 to 19 oz/398 to 540 mL) beans, drained and rinsed.

Make Ahead

Complete Steps 2 (adding 1 tbsp/15 mL) oil to pan in Step 4. Cover and refrigerate onion and chili mixtures separately. When you're ready to cook, complete the recipe.

Nutrients Per Serving

Calories	453
Protein	35.0 g
Carbohydrates	43.0 g
Fat (Total)	16.5 g
Saturated Fat	5.4 g
Monounsaturated Fat	8.3 g
Polyunsaturated Fat	1.5 g
Dietary Fiber	13.7 g
Sodium	227 mg
Cholesterol	67 mg

EXCELLENT SOURCE OF vitamins A, B_6 and B_{12}, folate, phosphorus, magnesium, potassium, iron and zinc.
SOURCE OF vitamins C, K and calcium.
CONTAINS a very high amount of dietary fiber.

- **Medium to large (3½ to 5 quart) slow cooker**
- **Blender**

3 cups	cooked black beans (see Tip, left)	750 mL
2 tbsp	olive oil	30 mL
2 lbs	stewing beef, cut into 1-inch (2.5 cm) cubes and patted dry	1 kg
2	onions, finely chopped	2
4	cloves garlic, minced	4
1 tbsp	ground cumin (see Tips, page 202)	15 mL
1 tsp	cracked black peppercorns	5 mL
½ tsp	sea salt	2 mL
1	can (28 oz/796 mL) no-salt-added tomatoes with juice	1
1½ cups	beef stock	375 mL
3	dried ancho chile peppers	3
2	dried New Mexico chile peppers	2
4 cups	boiling water	1 L
1 to 2	fresh chile peppers, quartered (see Tips, page 202)	1 to 2
	Sour cream, optional	
	Finely chopped red or green onion, optional	
	Shredded Monterey Jack cheese, optional	
	Salsa, optional	
	Avocado Topping, optional (see page 148)	

1. In a skillet, heat oil over medium-high heat. Add beef, in batches, and brown, about 4 minutes per batch. Using a slotted spoon, transfer to slow cooker stoneware. Reduce heat to medium.

2. Add onions and cook, stirring, until softened, about 3 minutes. Add garlic, cumin, peppercorns and salt and cook, stirring, for 1 minute. Add tomatoes with juice and cook, breaking up with the back of a spoon, until desired consistency is achieved. Bring to a boil.

recipe continued on page 202

Tips

For the best flavor, toast and grind cumin seeds yourself. Place seeds in a dry skillet over medium heat and cook stirring, until fragrant, about 3 minutes. Immediately transfer to a spice grinder or mortar and grind.

Almost any kind of fresh chile pepper will work in this recipe. Use habanero, jalapeño or long red or green chile peppers, depending upon your preference, and being aware that habanero are significantly hotter than most others.

3. Transfer to slow cooker stoneware. Add stock and beans and stir well. Cover and cook on Low for 8 hours or on High for 4 hours, until beef is very tender.

4. About an hour before the beef has finished cooking, in a heatproof bowl, soak dried chiles in boiling water for 30 minutes. Drain and discard liquid. Remove stems, pat dry and coarsely chop chiles. In a blender, combine rehydrated chiles and fresh chile to taste with $1/2$ cup (125 mL) cooking liquid from the chili. Purée.

5. Add chili mixture to stoneware. Cover and cook on High for 20 minutes to meld flavors. To serve, ladle into bowls and top with your favorite garnishes.

Mindful Morsels

Garlic is more than a flavor enhancer for many dishes. It may also help to keep LDL ("bad") cholesterol under control and protect against certain types of cancer (see page 79).

Natural Wonders

Avocados

I like to finish this and other chilies with a healthy dollop of avocado topping (see page 148) because although they are high in calories, ounce for ounce, avocados are extremely nutritious. They are a great source of vitamin K and folate and are high in potassium and fiber. They also contain carotenoids and vitamin E, which, among other benefits, appear

to work together to battle prostate cancer cells. Recent studies also show that avocados help your body make better use of antioxidants. Adding avocado to a salad containing baby spinach, lettuce and carrots dramatically enhanced absorption of the carotenoids alpha-carotene, beta-carotene and lutein. Similarly, when avocado was added to tomato salsa, lycopene absorption was increased by 4.4 times and beta-carotene absorption was 2.6 times higher than without the avocado.

Beef and Chickpea Curry with Spinach

This combination of beef and chickpeas in an Indian-inspired sauce is particularly delicious. I like to serve this with brown basmati rice, not only because I like its pleasant nutty flavor but also for its nutritional value. This is a generous serving (almost 2 cups/500 mL) so there will be more than enough to fill you up.

Makes 4 servings

Can Be Halved
(see Tips, below)

Tips

If you are halving this recipe, be sure to use a small (1½ to 3½ quart) slow cooker.

If using fresh spinach, be sure to remove the stems, and if it has not been pre-washed, rinse it thoroughly in a basin of lukewarm water.

Nutrients Per Serving

Calories	438
Protein	36.2 g
Carbohydrates	37.6 g
Fat (Total)	16.6 g
Saturated Fat	5.7 g
Monounsaturated Fat	8.6 g
Polyunsaturated Fat	1.3 g
Dietary Fiber	10.5 g
Sodium	456 mg
Cholesterol	67 mg

EXCELLENT SOURCE OF
vitamins A, B₆ and K, folate, phosphorus, magnesium, potassium, iron and zinc.
GOOD SOURCE OF calcium.
SOURCE OF vitamin C.
CONTAINS a very high amount of dietary fiber.

• **Medium to large (3½ to 5 quart) slow cooker**

1 tbsp	olive oil	15 mL
1 lb	trimmed stewing beef, cut into ½-inch (1 cm) cubes	500 g
2	onions, finely chopped	2
4	cloves garlic, minced	4
1 tbsp	minced gingerroot	15 mL
½ tsp	cracked black peppercorns	2 mL
1	piece (1 inch/2.5 cm) cinnamon stick	1
1	bay leaf	1
1 cup	beef stock	250 mL
2 cups	cooked chickpeas, drained	500 mL
1 tsp	curry powder, dissolved in 2 tsp (10 mL) freshly squeezed lemon juice	5 mL
1 lb	fresh spinach, stems removed, or 1 package (10 oz/300 g) spinach leaves, thawed if frozen (see Tips, left)	500 g
	Plain yogurt, optional	

1. In a skillet, heat oil over medium-high heat. Add beef, in batches, and cook, stirring, adding additional oil if necessary, until browned, about 4 minutes per batch. Transfer to slow cooker stoneware.

2. Reduce heat to medium. Add onions to pan and cook, stirring, until softened, about 3 minutes. Add garlic, ginger, peppercorns, cinnamon stick and bay leaf and cook, stirring, for 1 minute. Add beef stock and bring to a boil.

3. Transfer to slow cooker stoneware. Add chickpeas and stir well. Cover and cook on Low for 8 hours or on High for 4 hours, until beef is tender. Add curry powder solution and stir well. Add spinach, in batches, stirring until each batch is submerged in the curry. Cover and cook on High for 20 minutes, until spinach is wilted. Discard cinnamon stick and bay leaf. Ladle into bowls and drizzle with yogurt, if using.

more information on page 205

Beef and Chickpea Curry with Spinach

Make Ahead

Heat 1 tbsp (15 mL) of the oil and complete Step 2. Cover and refrigerate overnight or for up to 2 days. When you're ready to cook, either brown the beef as outlined in Step 1 or add it to the stoneware without browning. Stir well and continue with Step 3.

Mindful Morsels

Although North Americans tend to associate cinnamon with sweet dishes, in many parts of the world, including India, it is often used in savory dishes, as it was used here. Including cinnamon in your diet as often as possible makes sense because its medicinal uses have been studied quite extensively and it has many positive benefits. Cinnamon may help to prevent or treat a wide variety of diseases, ranging from metabolic syndrome to heart disease and cancer (see page 315).

Natural Wonders

Glycine

High protein foods, such as meat, are the best food sources of glycine, one of the most important amino acids, which, taken together, are involved in every metabolic process in your body. Because your body can manufacture glycine it has not been deemed an "essential" amino acid. However, nutritionist Kaayla Daniel makes the point that new research is moving away from that position. As she sees it, evidence is mounting that for various reasons, most people can't create adequate supplies of this nutrient and that it should be considered a "conditionally essential" amino acid.

Glycine plays major roles in many physical processes. Along with GABA (gamma-aminobutyric acid) glycine is the body's most important neurotransmitter and is actively involved in how well your central nervous system works. It is also a significant player in the digestive system, where, among other functions, it enhances gastric acid secretions improving digestion and facilitating nutrient absorption. It is one of three amino acids (glutamine and cysteine are the other two) that supports your body's ability to produce glutathione (see Natural Wonders, page 291).

Glycine is a potent detoxifier that can help to rid your body of harmful chemicals. As a result, it is an important nutrient in various strategies for liver detoxification. It also helps build strong cartilage and bones as well as healthy skin. In fact, glycine has significant antiaging benefits. Approximately one-third of the skin's collagen (which keeps it resilient; studies show that collagen is a key component of youthful-looking skin) is composed of glycine. So perhaps not surprisingly, glycine also plays a vital role in your body's ability to heal wounds.

The poor quality of the typical "westernized" diet has been cited as a reason why we may be losing our ability to produce adequate supplies of glycine, but keeping a careful watch on your diet should be enough to ensure adequate reserves. Glycine is a key nutrient in gelatin (see Natural Wonders, page 115). The best food sources of this nutrient, in addition to meat, are other high-protein foods such as fish and dairy. Vegetarian sources include organic soybeans, leafy greens and bananas.

Mexican Meatballs

These simple meatballs are revved up with the addition of zesty chipotle chiles. I find that two chiles provide a nice level of punch. If you're a heat seeker, use three; if you are heat-averse, stick with one. These are great served over plain brown rice, beans or hot corn tortillas. This recipe makes generous servings, so you won't need anything else, except perhaps a small green salad.

Makes 8 servings

Can Be Halved
(see Tips, below)

Tips

If you are halving this recipe, be sure to use a small (2 to 3½ quart) slow cooker.

I like to use buckwheat in meatballs because it is a nutritious whole grain, with many healthful properties (see Mindful Morsels, right, and Natural Wonders, page 209).

Nutrients Per Serving

Calories	408
Protein	24.8 g
Carbohydrates	18.2 g
Fat (Total)	26.4 g
Saturated Fat	8.8 g
Monounsaturated Fat	12.5 g
Polyunsaturated Fat	3.2 g
Dietary Fiber	3.4 g
Sodium	385 mg
Cholesterol	99 mg

EXCELLENT SOURCE OF vitamin B$_{12}$, potassium and zinc.
GOOD SOURCE OF vitamins B$_6$ and K, phosphorus, magnesium and iron.
SOURCE OF vitamins A and C, folate and calcium.
CONTAINS a moderate amount of dietary fiber.

• **Medium to large (3½ to 5 quart) slow cooker**

Meatballs

½ cup	buckwheat groats (see Tips, left)	125 mL
1 cup	boiling water	250 mL
1 lb	lean ground beef	500 g
1 lb	ground pork	500 g
1	onion, finely chopped	1
2 tbsp	almond flour	30 mL
2 tsp	dried oregano	10 mL
1 tsp	ground cumin (see Tips, page 202)	5 mL
½ tsp	sea salt	2 mL
	Freshly ground black pepper	
1	egg, beaten	1
2 tbsp	olive oil, divided	30 mL
¼ cup	minced onion	60 mL
4	stalks celery, diced	4
4	cloves garlic, minced	4
1 tsp	dried oregano	5 mL
½ tsp	sea salt	2 mL
½ tsp	cracked black peppercorns	2 mL
¼ cup	tomato paste	60 mL
1	can (28 oz/796 mL) no-salt added tomatoes, including juice, coarsely chopped	1
½ cup	chicken, beef or vegetable stock	125 mL
1 to 2	chipotle chile in adobo sauce, minced	1 to 2
¼ cup	finely chopped cilantro leaves	60 mL

1. *Meatballs:* In a saucepan, combine buckwheat groats and boiling water. Cover and cook over low heat until all the water has been absorbed, about 10 minutes. Remove from heat and set aside.

2. In a bowl, combine beef, pork, onion, almond flour, oregano, cumin, cooked buckwheat, and salt and pepper to taste. Mix well. Add egg, and using your hands, mix until well combined. Shape mixture into 16 equal balls.

Make Ahead

Complete Step 4. Cover and refrigerate mixture for up to 2 days. When you're ready to cook, complete the recipe.

3. In a skillet, heat 1 tbsp (15 mL) of the oil over medium-high heat. Add meatballs, in batches, and cook, turning, until lightly browned on all sides, about 3 minutes per batch. Transfer to slow cooker stoneware. Reduce heat to medium.

4. Add remaining tbsp (15 mL) of oil to pan. Add minced onion and celery and cook, stirring and scraping up brown bits from bottom of pan, until softened, about 5 minutes. Add garlic, oregano, salt and peppercorns and cook, stirring, for 1 minute. Stir in tomato paste. Add tomatoes with juice and stock and cook, stirring, until mixture comes to a boil.

5. Transfer to slow cooker stoneware. Cover and cook on Low for 6 hours or on High for 3 hours, until hot and bubbly and meatballs are cooked through. Stir in chipotle chile to taste. Cover and cook on High for 15 minutes, until flavors blend. Garnish with cilantro.

Mindful Morsels

Buckwheat, a gluten-free whole grain, has shown great promise in managing diabetes, among other benefits. In one study, Canadian researchers found that buckwheat extracts lowered the glucose levels of rats from 12 to 19%. Researchers believe that the compound d-chiro-inositol, which is found in relatively high amounts in buckwheat but not commonly found in other foods, may be responsible for this positive effect. Further research is underway.

Natural Wonders

Cilantro

Cilantro, the fragrant leaves of the coriander plant, is a culinary herb that is widely used in Indian, South-East Asian and Latin American cooking. Although the health benefits of coriander seeds (and the oil that is extracted from them) have been well documented, cilantro has not been as closely studied.

Cilantro belongs to the same horticultural family as parsley. It provides a smattering of vitamins and minerals, but its real value seems to lie in its antioxidant power. Cilantro contains the substance dodecenal, a powerful antibacterial agent, which has been shown to be effective at killing salmonella in a laboratory study. Perhaps folk wisdom helps to explain cilantro's popularity in tropical climates — it's a natural antidote to potential food pathogens. Laboratory studies suggest that cilantro may also be helpful in the management of diabetes. And it is reputed to be useful at removing toxic metals from the body.

Buckwheat Meatballs in Tomato Sauce

More like a saucy meatloaf than traditional meatballs swimming in sauce, this tasty dish is at home over hot brown rice or fluffy mashed potatoes I like to serve this with a platter of steamed bitter greens, such as rapini, drizzled with extra virgin olive oil and freshly squeezed lemon juice, but steamed broccoli also makes a nice accompaniment.

Makes 8 servings

Can Be Halved
(see Tips, below)

Tips

If you are halving this recipe, be sure to use a small (1½ to 3½ quart) slow cooker

When toasted, buckwheat groats are known as kasha. Toasting intensifies the flavor. If you prefer, use kasha in this recipe.

Nutrients Per Serving

Calories	235
Protein	14.7 g
Carbohydrates	17.9 g
Fat (Total)	12.1 g
Saturated Fat	3.8 g
Monounsaturated Fat	6.3 g
Polyunsaturated Fat	0.7 g
Dietary Fiber	2.9 g
Sodium	354 mg
Cholesterol	57 mg

EXCELLENT SOURCE OF vitamin K and zinc.
GOOD SOURCE OF vitamin B$_{12}$, potassium, magnesium and iron.
SOURCE OF vitamins A, C and B$_6$, folate, calcium and phosphorus.
CONTAINS a moderate amount of dietary fiber.

- **Medium to large (3½ to 5 quart) slow cooker**

Meatballs

½ cup	buckwheat groats (see Tips, left)	125 mL
1 cup	boiling water	250 mL
1	onion, finely chopped	1
½ cup	finely chopped parsley	125 mL
½ tsp	salt	2 mL
¼ tsp	freshly ground black pepper	1 mL
¼ tsp	ground cinnamon	1 mL
1 lb	lean ground beef	500 g
1	egg, beaten	1
2 tbsp	olive oil, divided (approx.)	30 mL

Tomato Sauce

2	onions, finely chopped	2
4	cloves garlic, minced	4
1 tsp	dried oregano, crumbled	5 mL
½ tsp	sea salt	2 mL
½ tsp	cracked black peppercorns	2 mL
1	can (28 oz/796 mL) no-salt added tomatoes, including juice, coarsely chopped	1
1 cup	dry red wine	250 mL

1. *Meatballs:* In a saucepan, combine buckwheat groats and boiling water. Cover and cook over low heat until all the water has been absorbed, about 10 minutes. Remove from heat and set aside.

2. In a bowl, mix together onion, parsley, salt, pepper and cinnamon. Add ground beef and egg, and using your hands, mix until well combined. Using a wooden spoon (it will still be hot), mix in cooked buckwheat. Form into 24 meatballs, each about 1½ inches (4 cm) in diameter.

Tip

Do all your preparation for the sauce as well as the meatballs while the buckwheat cooks, so you'll be ready to start cooking as soon as it is completed.

Make Ahead

Complete Step 4. Cover and refrigerate mixture for up to 2 days. When you're ready to cook, complete the recipe.

3. In a skillet, heat 1 tbsp (15 mL) of the oil over medium-high heat. Add meatballs, in batches, and brown well, about 5 minutes per batch. Transfer to slow cooker stoneware.

4. *Tomato Sauce:* Reduce heat to medium and add additional oil to pan if necessary. Add onions to pan and cook, stirring, until softened, about 3 minutes. Add garlic, oregano, salt and peppercorns and cook, stirring, for 1 minute. Add tomatoes with juice and wine and bring to a boil.

5. Pour over meatballs. Cover and cook on Low for 6 hours or on High for 3 hours, until hot and bubbly.

Mindful Morsels

The nutritional analysis in this recipe, as well as all the other meat recipes in this book was based on using grain-fed (feedlot) beef because the necessary in-depth nutrient analysis for pasture-raised meat was unavailable. However, available research indicates that eating pasture-raised meat is a healthy strategy. Grass-fed beef contains more omega-3 fatty acids and may have as much as five times the amount of beneficial conjugated linoleic acid (CLA) as grain-fed beef (see Natural Wonders, page 183).

Natural Wonders

Buckwheat

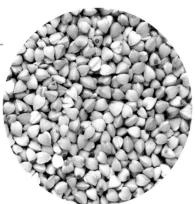

Despite its name, buckwheat is not a form of wheat and does not contain gluten. In fact, buckwheat is technically a fruit, one that contains many essential amino acids. Research suggests that a diet high in buckwheat may be beneficial in managing diabetes (see Mindful Morsels, page 207), as well as being particularly effective in lowering cholesterol and keeping blood pressure under control. Buckwheat is high in flavonoids, particularly rutin, and the mineral magnesium.

An easy way to add buckwheat to your diet is by serving soba noodles with meals. Traditionally a Japanese delicacy, these tasty noodles are often added to soups and stir-fries and are particularly delicious served cold and tossed with a simple oil and vinegar dressing. However, read the label carefully. Many soba noodles contain wheat along with buckwheat. I buy mine at a Japanese grocery store, where they have a wide selection of 100% buckwheat noodles.

Veal Goulash

This version of goulash, a luscious Hungarian stew seasoned with paprika, is lighter than the traditional one made with beef. It is usually served over hot noodles, but fluffy mashed potatoes make a particularly sybaritic finish. Not only do the red bell peppers enhance the flavor, they also add valuable nutrients to the dish.

Makes 8 servings

Can Be Halved
(see Tips, page 212)

Tips

I like to use small whole cremini mushrooms in this stew, but if you can't find them, white mushrooms or larger cremini mushrooms, quartered or sliced, depending upon their size, work well, too.

There is a real hit of caraway in this recipe. If you prefer a milder flavor, decrease the quantity of caraway to as little as 1 tsp (5 mL). To grind the seeds, pound in a mortar or use a spice grinder.

Nutrients Per Serving

Calories	203
Protein	25.5 g
Carbohydrates	10.4 g
Fat (Total)	6.7 g
Saturated Fat	1.4 g
Monounsaturated Fat	3.5 g
Polyunsaturated Fat	0.9 g
Dietary Fiber	2.8 g
Sodium	221 mg
Cholesterol	95 mg

EXCELLENT SOURCE OF vitamins C, B_6 and B_{12}, phosphorus, potassium and zinc.

GOOD SOURCE OF vitamin A, magnesium and iron.

SOURCE OF vitamin K, folate and calcium.

CONTAINS a moderate amount of dietary fiber.

- **Medium to large (3½ to 5 quart) slow cooker**

2 tbsp	olive oil, divided (approx.)	30 mL
2 lbs	trimmed stewing veal, cut into 1-inch (2.5 cm) pieces	1 kg
1 lb	mushrooms, trimmed (see Tips, left)	500 g
2	onions, finely chopped	2
4	cloves garlic, minced	4
1 tbsp	caraway seeds, coarsely ground (see Tips, left)	15 mL
½ tsp	cracked black peppercorns	2 mL
1	can (14 oz/398 mL) no salt added diced tomatoes, including juice	1
1 cup	chicken stock (see Mindful Morsels, page 127)	250 mL
1 tbsp	sweet Hungarian paprika, dissolved in 2 tbsp (30 mL) water or chicken stock	15 mL
2	red bell peppers, diced	2
½ cup	finely chopped dill fronds	125 mL
	Sour cream, optional	

1. In a skillet, heat 1 tbsp (15 mL) of oil over medium-high heat. Add veal, in batches, and cook, stirring, adding more oil as necessary, until browned, about 5 minutes per batch. Using a slotted spoon, transfer to slow cooker stoneware.

2. Add remaining oil to pan. Add mushrooms and stir-fry until they begin to brown, about 5 minutes. Using a slotted spoon, transfer to stoneware. Reduce heat to medium. Add onions to pan and cook, stirring, until softened, about 3 minutes. Add garlic, caraway seeds and peppercorns and cook, stirring, for 1 minute. Add tomatoes with juice and chicken stock and bring to a boil. Transfer to slow cooker stoneware. Stir well.

3. Cover and cook on Low for 8 hours or on High for 4 hours, until veal is tender.

Make Ahead

This dish can be partially prepared before it is cooked. Heat 1 tbsp (15 mL) of the oil and complete Step 2. Cover and refrigerate overnight or for up to 1 day. When you're ready to cook, either brown the veal as outlined in Step 1 or add it to the stoneware without browning. Stir well and continue with Steps 3 and 4.

4. Add paprika solution to slow cooker stoneware and stir well. Add red peppers and stir well. Cover and cook on High for 30 minutes, until peppers are tender. To serve, ladle into bowls and top each serving with 1 tbsp (15 mL) of the dill and a dollop of sour cream, if using.

Mindful Morsels

The red bell peppers in this recipe (which are also known as sweet red peppers), are low in calories (about 32 calories in one medium pepper) and are extremely nutritious. These tasty and versatile vegetables are rich in powerful antioxidants, such as beta-carotene and vitamin C, which help to keep your immune system healthy, among other benefits. In fact, ounce for ounce, red peppers contain more vitamin C than oranges!

Natural Wonders

Caraway

Earthy and pungent, caraway is an ancient herb that has been used for medicinal and culinary purposes throughout history. It features prominently in Eastern European cooking, where it is often used to season cabbage, including sauerkraut, as well as various kinds of goulash. It even makes an appearance in some sweet dishes, particularly those containing apples. Long recognized as a digestive aid, caraway had its fifteen minutes of fame when Dr. Oz recommended it as a dietary supplement to battle bloating. Caraway has carminative properties, which means it either prevents gas from forming in your intestinal tract or facilitates its expulsion. Caraway helps to prevent bloating by discouraging the growth of bad bacteria in your gut.

Caraway seed, which is actually the fruit of the caraway plant, provides a smattering of nutrients such as vitamin C and various B vitamins, as well as the minerals calcium, iron, magnesium, manganese and zinc. It also provides antioxidant flavonoids. In recent years caraway seeds have been identified as a source of limonene, a powerful phytochemical that may help to protect against breast cancer, among other benefits.

Braised Veal with Pearl Onions and Sweet Peas

Here veal is braised in white wine and chicken stock to produce a richly satisfying yet surprisingly light stew. I serve this with a simple risotto for a delicious meal.

Makes 8 servings

Can Be Halved
(see Tips, below)

Tips

If you are halving this recipe, be sure to use a small (approx. 1½ to 3 quart) slow cooker.

The pancetta in this recipe adds 123 mg of sodium, but it also packs a very flavorful punch. If you are watching your sodium intake, omit the added salt, which provides 129 mg.

Nutrients Per Serving

Calories	296
Protein	36.3 g
Carbohydrates	11.3 g
Fat (Total)	11.1 g
Saturated Fat	2.6 g
Monounsaturated Fat	5.6 g
Polyunsaturated Fat	1.2 g
Dietary Fiber	3.2 g
Sodium	486 mg
Cholesterol	142 mg

EXCELLENT SOURCE OF vitamins A, B$_6$, B$_{12}$ and K, phosphorus, potassium and zinc.
GOOD SOURCE OF folate, magnesium and iron.
SOURCE OF vitamin C and calcium.
CONTAINS a moderate amount of dietary fiber.

• Medium to large (3½ to 5 quart) slow cooker

2 tbsp	olive oil (approx.), divided	30 mL
2 oz	pancetta, diced	60 g
2 lbs	trimmed stewing veal, cut into 1-inch (2.5 cm) cubes	1 kg
2	carrots, peeled and diced	2
2	stalks celery, diced	2
2	cloves garlic, minced	2
1 tsp	dried thyme	5 mL
½ tsp	sea salt	2 mL
½ tsp	cracked black peppercorns	2 mL
2	bay leaves	2
1 cup	dry white wine	250 mL
2 cups	chicken or veal stock	500 mL
24	pearl onions, peeled (see Tip, right)	24
2 cups	sweet green peas, thawed if frozen	500 mL
	Freshly ground black pepper	
	Heavy or whipping (35%) cream, optional	

1. In a skillet, heat 1 tbsp (15 mL) of the oil over medium heat. Add pancetta and cook, stirring, until browned, about 3 minutes. Using a slotted spoon, transfer to stoneware. Increase heat to medium-high. Add veal, in batches, and brown, adding more oil if necessary. Transfer to stoneware as completed.

2. Reduce heat to medium. Add remaining oil to pan. Add carrots and celery and cook, stirring, until softened, about 7 minutes. Add garlic, thyme, salt, peppercorns and bay leaves and cook, stirring, for 1 minute. Add wine and bring to a boil, stirring and scraping up brown bits from the bottom of the pan. Add stock.

3. Transfer to stoneware. Stir in onions. Cover and cook on Low for 8 hours or on High for 4 hours, until veal is very tender. Add peas and cook on High about 10 minutes, until tender. Season with pepper to taste. If desired, add a drizzle of cream. Serve immediately.

Tip

To peel pearl onions, cut an "x" in the root end and drop them into a pot of rapidly boiling water for about 30 seconds. Drain in a colander and run under cold running water. The skins should lift off quite easily with a little prodding from you and a sharp paring knife.

Make Ahead

Complete Step 2. Cover and refrigerate for up to 2 days. When you're ready to cook, complete the recipe.

Mindful Morsels

Although eating a nutrient-dense diet is a very significant component of good health, if you are not careful about cleanliness when preparing food, you may undermine your efforts by succumbing to a food-borne illness. Be especially careful about washing your hands and cleaning utensils and cutting boards in plenty of hot soapy water, particularly if you are cooking meat, poultry or fish, which are the most common sources of potential pathogens. If you have any concerns about your food supply, rinse your cutting boards in a mild bleach solution.

Natural Wonders

Sweet Green Peas

In terms of perception their nutritional value, sweet green peas seem to be the forgotten relative of their superstar cousins, legumes. While legumes are definitely nutritional powerhouses, their less-recognized family member has more than enough star quality of its own. For starters, they are nutrient dense. One cup (250 mL) of raw green peas delivers just 7% of the calories an average person requires for the day, yet provides 52% of the vitamin K; 36% of the vitamin C; 28% of the thiamine; 26% of the vitamin A; 25% of the folate and 42% of the mineral manganese. They also provide 35% of the DV of dietary fiber and 17% of the protein, as well as goodly amounts of vitamin B_6, niacin, riboflavin and the minerals phosphorus, magnesium, iron, copper and zinc.

While their micronutrient content is certainly impressive, it may well be that green peas excel most in the phytonutrients they provide. They are loaded with compounds that have a wide variety of antioxidant and anti-inflammatory properties. These include flavonoids, carotenes, phenolic acids, and a particularly intriguing polyphenol, coumestrol, which is being studied for its ability to protect against stomach cancer. Researchers also believe that the unusual combination of phytonutrients in green peas may lower the risk of type-2 diabetes. Although some people dismiss peas because they are thought to be high in starch, 1 cup (250 mL) of green peas has about 21 g of total carbohydrate. If you factor in the 7 to 8 grams of fiber it also provides, the available carbohydrates work out to about 12 g per cup (250 mL) about the same as a medium-size apple.

If you have difficulty consuming legumes, be aware that green peas are not likely to be a problem. Although they are classified as legumes in the botanical sense, they do not qualify as dietary legumes because they are not dried — they are a vegetable that can be eaten raw or just lightly cooked. Yes, they are sweet and starchy, but they are also a good source of protein, as well as fiber, so they are not likely to raise blood glucose levels.

Ribs with Hominy and Kale

Pork and Lamb

Ribs with Hominy and Kale

This hearty stew is perfect for an early spring day when there is still a chill in the air but fresh radishes are appearing in the markets. A steaming bowl of pozole (as it is known in Mexico), garnished with fresh radishes, blends winter comfort food with the promise of spring.

Makes 8 servings

Can Be Halved
(see Tips, page 218)

Tips

Prepared hominy is available in well-stocked supermarkets. It is likely to be high in sodium so rinse it well or cook your own hominy from scratch. Although not traditional, chickpeas make an acceptable substitute in this recipe.

If you are using small Hass avocados, use two in this recipe. Don't prepare avocados until you are ready to use them. Otherwise they will discolor.

Nutrients Per Serving	
Calories	252
Protein	22.7 g
Carbohydrates	19.8 g
Fat (Total)	9.6 g
Saturated Fat	1.0 g
Monounsaturated Fat	2.1 g
Polyunsaturated Fat	1.2 g
Dietary Fiber	4.2 g
Sodium	427 mg
Cholesterol	65 mg

EXCELLENT SOURCE OF vitamins A, C, B$_6$ and K, folate, potassium and zinc.
GOOD SOURCE OF vitamin B$_{12}$, magnesium and phosphorus, iron.
SOURCE OF calcium.
CONTAINS a high amount of dietary fiber.

- **Large (approx. 5 quart) slow cooker**

1 tbsp	olive oil	15 mL
2½ lbs	sliced country-style or side pork ribs, trimmed of fat	1.25 kg
2	onions, finely chopped	2
6	cloves garlic, minced	6
2 tsp	dried oregano	10 mL
½ tsp	cracked black peppercorns	2 mL
1 tbsp	ground cumin (see Tips, page 202)	15 mL
2 cups	chicken or vegetable stock	500 mL
2 tbsp	tomato paste	30 mL
4 cups	cooked hominy (approx.)	1 L
1 tbsp	ancho chili powder, dissolved in 2 tbsp (30 mL) lime juice	15 mL
1	jalapeño pepper or chipotle pepper in adobo sauce, minced	1
8 cups	chopped, stemmed kale (about 1 large bunch)	2 L
½ cup	finely chopped red or green onion	125 mL
½ cup	finely chopped cilantro leaves	125 mL
1	avocado, peeled and diced, optional (see Tips, left)	1
	Sliced radishes, optional	
	Lime wedges	

1. In a skillet, heat oil over medium-high heat. Add ribs, in batches, and brown on both sides, about 5 minutes per batch. Transfer to slow cooker stoneware.

2. In same skillet, reduce heat to medium and add onions to pan and cook, stirring, until softened, about 5 minutes. Add garlic, oregano, peppercorns and cumin and cook, stirring, for 1 minute. Add chicken stock and tomato paste and bring to a boil. Transfer to slow cooker stoneware.

3. Add hominy and stir well. Cover and cook on Low for 8 hours or on High for 4 hours, until ribs are tender and falling off the bone.

Make Ahead

This dish can be partially prepared before it is cooked. Heat 1 tbsp (15 mL) of the oil and complete Step 2. Cover and refrigerate overnight or for up to 2 days. When you're ready to cook, brown the ribs as outlined in Step 1 and add to stoneware. Stir well and continue with Steps 3 and 4.

4. Add chili powder solution and jalapeño pepper and stir well. Add kale, in batches, completely submerging each batch in the liquid before adding another. Cover and cook on High for 20 to 30 minutes, until kale is tender. To serve, ladle into bowls and garnish with onion, cilantro and avocado and/or radishes, if using. Pass lime wedges at the table.

Mindful Morsels

Kale is an excellent source of vitamin K. One serving of this dish provides almost 700% of the daily value of this vitamin. (For more about vitamin K, see page 193.)

Natural Wonders

Hominy

Hominy (also known as pozole) is whole dried kernels of corn that have been soaked in a solution of lye or slaked lime. It is a whole grain, made from starchy field corn and is different from sweet corn, which is a vegetable. Whole grain corn is nutrient-dense. It is particularly high in antioxidants and is rich in phytonutrients such as carotenoids as well as certain minerals. The only problem is most of the field corn grown in North America has been genetically modified, which means it is worth making an effort to find heirloom varieties. Despite the consistent reassurances of agribusiness, scientific studies are finding problems with genetically modified foods (see page 84). For instance, one 2009 study published in the *International Journal of Biological Sciences* found that rats fed genetically modified corn displayed signs of liver and kidney damage.

In any case, to make hominy, corn kernels are washed with lye or slaked lime to loosen the hull, which is discarded. This process, which has an alkalizing effect on the grain, making it particularly digestible, is known as nixtamalization. When hominy is partially ground, the result is hominy grits. Hominy flour is used to make masa harina, the basis for Mexican tortillas. Do not confuse hominy flour or corn flour made from stone-ground cornmeal (both of which are whole-grain products) with cornstarch, which is the highly refined starch ground from the kernel's endosperm. It has no food value, although if you are gluten-free, it's a useful ingredient to have in the kitchen because it aids in browning.

Hominy is widely available already cooked and canned. It can be found in its dried form in Latin American food stores.

Pork with Pot Likker

This recipe is a riff on collard greens with pot likker, the flavorful broth that comes from the long slow cooking of these nutritious greens, often with a smoked pork hock. Here, a piece of pork shoulder butt, spiked with a bit of bacon, provides the meat component, and a good dollop of paprika, finished with tart cider vinegar, adds zest to the delicious broth.

Makes 8 servings

Can Be Halved
(see Tips, below)

Tips

If you are halving this recipe, be sure to use a small (2 to 3½ quart) slow cooker.

Many butchers sell cut-up pork stewing meat, which is fine to use in this recipe.

I use a combination of sweet and hot paprika (2 tsp/10 mL sweet and 1 tsp/5 mL hot) but if you like heat, use 2 tsp (10 mL) hot paprika. If you are averse to heat, stick with sweet paprika.

Nutrients Per Serving

Calories	198
Protein	26.2 g
Carbohydrates	9.3 g
Fat (Total)	6.1 g
Saturated Fat	2.2 g
Monounsaturated Fat	2.6 g
Polyunsaturated Fat	1.0 g
Dietary Fiber	3.0 g
Sodium	288 mg
Cholesterol	79 mg

EXCELLENT SOURCE OF vitamins A, B_6, B_{12} and K, folate, phosphorus and zinc.

GOOD SOURCE OF potassium, magnesium and iron.

SOURCE OF vitamin C and calcium.

CONTAINS a moderate amount of dietary fiber.

- **Large (approx. 5 quart) slow cooker**

2 oz	chunk bacon, diced	60 g
2 lbs	trimmed pork shoulder or blade (butt) roast, patted dry (see Tips, left)	1 kg
2	onions, thinly sliced on the vertical	2
3	carrots, peeled and sliced	3
4	cloves garlic, minced	4
1 tsp	dried thyme	5 mL
2	bay leaves	2
½ tsp	sea salt	2 mL
½ tsp	cracked black peppercorns	2 mL
2 tbsp	tomato paste	30 mL
2 cups	chicken stock	500 mL
1 tbsp	paprika, dissolved in 3 tbsp (45 mL) cider vinegar (see Tips, left)	15 mL
8 cups	thinly sliced (chiffonade) stemmed collard greens (about 1 bunch) (see Tips, see page 77)	2 L
	Hot pepper sauce, optional	
	Cider vinegar, optional	

1. In a skillet over medium-high heat, cook bacon until browned and crisp. Using a slotted spoon, transfer to slow cooker stoneware.

2. Add pork and brown on all sides, about 10 minutes. Transfer to slow cooker stoneware.

3. Reduce heat to medium. Add onions and carrots to pan and cook, stirring, until carrots are softened, about 7 minutes. Add garlic, thyme, bay leaves, salt and peppercorns and cook, stirring, for 1 minute. Stir in tomato paste. Add chicken stock and bring to a boil. Cook, stirring, for 1 minute, scraping up all brown bits in the pan. Transfer to slow cooker stoneware. Stir well.

Make Ahead

Complete Steps 1 and 3, adding bacon to vegetable mixture after it has been completed. Cover and refrigerate mixture for up to 2 days. When you are ready to cook, add 1 tbsp (15 mL) additional oil to a skillet and brown pork (Step 2). Complete the recipe.

4. Cover and cook on Low for 6 to 8 hours or on High for 3 to 4 hours, until meat is tender. Add paprika solution and stir well. Add collard greens, in batches, completely submerging each batch in the liquid before adding another. Cover and cook on High for 30 minutes, until collards are tender. Discard bay leaves. Pass hot pepper sauce and additional vinegar at the table, if desired.

Mindful Morsels

Garlic is more than a flavor-enhancer for many dishes. It may also help to keep LDL ("bad") cholesterol under control and protect against certain types of cancer.

Natural Wonders

Saturated, Trans and Omega-3 Fats

There is probably no area of nutrition more fraught with controversy than the association among fat intake, blood cholesterol levels and cardiovascular disease. Traditional wisdom asserts that a high intake of saturated fats and cholesterol and a low intake of omega-3 and omega-6 fatty acids increases the risk for heart disease. This conclusion has been based on large overview surveys of individual populations, such as the Seven Countries Study conducted by Ancel Keys, which eventually led to general approval for the so-called "Mediterranean diet." Like most studies of its kind, it identified differences among populations in the types of fats consumed.

However, in a pooled analysis of 11 cohort studies and randomized controlled trials, published in the *Annals of Nutrition and Metabolism* in 2009, researchers concluded that although informative, such studies provide an overview that may produce at best a fuzzy picture. Their review, which looked more deeply into individual populations, revealed different results: only two constants — the consumption of trans fats increased the risk for cardiovascular disease and the consumption of omega-3 fats lowered it. They also concluded, "there is probably no direct relation between total fat intake and the risk of CHD (coronary heart disease)." Their strongest piece of evidence for this conclusion was the results of the Women's Health Initiative, which showed that 8 years on a low-fat diet did not reduce the incidence of CHD.

Extrapolating their findings to daily eating, it is clear that trans fats, which are found in many prepared/packaged foods, should be avoided at all costs, omega-3 fats, which are most abundant in fatty fish, such as salmon and trout, should be consumed as often as possible and the overall amount of fat in your diet isn't likely to be a problem, so long as it is good quality natural fat. If you shun processed food you aren't likely to consume trans fats, unless you use a non-butter spread or shortening. When shopping, always check the label. You won't really know what a food contains unless you read it carefully.

Kale-Spiked Sausages and Beans

Here's a very simple yet delicious dish that is a perfect weeknight meal. Chorizo makes the flavors authentically Spanish or Portuguese, but I've also used homemade leek sausage purchased from a Greek butcher, with splendid results.

Makes 6 servings

Can Be Halved
(see Tips, page 224)

Tip

Cook 2 cups (500 mL) dried beans yourself (see Basic Beans, page 284) or use 2 cans (each 14 to 19 oz/398 to 540 mL) no-salt added beans, rinsed and drained.

Make Ahead

Complete Step 1. Cover mixture, ensuring it cools promptly (see Making Ahead, page 16), and refrigerate for up to 2 days. When you're ready to cook, complete the recipe.

Nutrients Per Serving

Calories	415
Protein	27.5 g
Carbohydrates	46.6 g
Fat (Total)	14.1 g
Saturated Fat	4.2 g
Monounsaturated Fat	6.7 g
Polyunsaturated Fat	2.2 g
Dietary Fiber	12.3 g
Sodium	533 mg
Cholesterol	35 mg

EXCELLENT SOURCE OF vitamins A, C, B_6 and K, folate, phosphorus, magnesium, potassium and iron.

GOOD SOURCE OF zinc.

SOURCE OF vitamin B_{12} and calcium.

CONTAINS a very high amount of dietary fiber.

- **Large (approx. 5 quart) slow cooker**

1 tbsp	olive oil	15 mL
2	onions, finely chopped	2
2	stalks celery, diced	2
1 lb	fresh pork sausage, such as chorizo or Italian, removed from casings	500 g
4	cloves garlic, minced	4
½ tsp	cracked black peppercorns	2 mL
4 cups	cooked white beans, such as cannellini (see Tip, left)	1 L
1 cup	chicken stock	250 mL
4 cups	packed chopped kale (about 1 bunch)	1 L
2 tbsp	red wine vinegar	30 mL

1. In a large skillet, heat oil over medium-high heat. Add onions, celery and sausage and cook, stirring, until sausage is no longer pink, about 7 minutes. Add garlic and peppercorns and cook, stirring, for 1 minute. Stir in beans and chicken stock and bring to a boil, scraping up brown bits from bottom of pan.

2. Transfer to slow cooker stoneware. Cover and cook on Low for 6 hours or on High for 3 hours, until hot and bubbly. Add kale, in batches, stirring to submerge before adding the next batch. Cover and cook on High about 15 minutes, until kale is tender. Stir in vinegar and serve.

Mindful Morsels

When buying garlic, do not succumb to the impressive visual appeal of elephant garlic. Although both plants belong to the same family, elephant garlic is closer to leeks on the flavor scale. To achieve similar pungency and nutrient punch, you would likely need to use an entire head (at least!) instead of the 4 cloves called for in this recipe.

Natural Wonders

Kale

A member of the cabbage family, kale has been called "the king of the crucifers." Because it has been identified as a superfood, kale has become very trendy and is frequently found on restaurant menus, particularly in salads made from baby kale. In addition to baby kale, there are three varieties of kale that are regularly consumed: curly, black (which goes under a variety of names, including dinosaur or lacinto/Tuscan kale) and less common (at least for now) red kale.

Kale is a bitter green, which means it is more nutritious than those that are milder-tasting. If you prefer more timid flavors, I recommend cooking it. Kale is a particularly nutrient-dense vegetable. It is high in vitamins such as A, C and K, and provides a wide range of minerals such as calcium, manganese, copper and iron. Kale has one of the highest oxygen radical absorbance capacity (ORAC) scores of any vegetable, which means it is an antioxidant powerhouse. It provides a wide range of phytonutrients such as the carotenes beta-carotene, lutein and zeaxanthin, as well as anti-cancer and heart-protecting glucosinolates, and indoles, which apparently protect against breast, colon and cervical cancer.

Kale's ability to help prevent cancer is well recognized; less known is the possibility that it may actually work to slow down the growth of existing tumors. Kale contains sulfur and provides a substance called sulforaphane, which according to one study, published in the *Journal of Nutrition*, helps to stop breast cancer from growing. Sulforaphane also boosts your body's ability to detoxify, disposing of chemicals such as free radicals, which might damage DNA.

If you are lactose intolerant, it is worth adding leafy greens such as kale to your diet because while not as rich in the nutrient as dairy products, they do provide a reasonable amount of calcium.

Home-Style Pork and Beans

There is nothing fancy about this dish — it's real down-home cooking that is simply delicious. Serve it with a big salad and robust red wine. This is a great recipe for a tailgate or Super Bowl party.

Makes 6 servings

Can Be Halved
(see Tips, page 224)

Tips

The nutritional analysis on this recipe was done using conventional mustard and ketchup, both of which are extremely high in sodium. Together these condiments contribute 491 mg of the sodium in a serving of this recipe. I recommend using low-sodium versions of both these products. In the case of mustard, it is extremely easy to make your own, without salt.

When using any condiment, always check the label to make sure it is gluten-free.

Nutrients Per Serving

Calories	516
Protein	21.0 g
Carbohydrates	68.6 g
Fat (Total)	19.2 g
Saturated Fat	10.2 g
Monounsaturated Fat	12.4 g
Polyunsaturated Fat	4.3 g
Dietary Fiber	14.6 g
Sodium	950 mg
Cholesterol	25 mg

EXCELLENT SOURCE OF folate, phosphorus, magnesium, potassium, iron and zinc.
GOOD SOURCE OF vitamins B$_6$, B$_{12}$ and calcium.
SOURCE OF vitamins A, C and K.
CONTAINS a very high amount of dietary fiber.

• **Medium to large (3½ to 6 quart) slow cooker**

2 cups	dried white beans such as great Northern or navy, soaked, drained and rinsed (see Basic Beans, page 284)	500 mL
½ cup	pure maple syrup	125 mL
½ cup	grainy mustard (see Tips, left)	125 mL
½ cup	ketchup	125 mL
½ cup	tomato paste	125 mL
1 tsp	cracked black peppercorns	5 mL
½ tsp	salt	2 mL
8 oz	pork belly or chunk bacon (see Tip, right)	250 g
3	onions, finely chopped	3
4	cloves garlic, minced	4

1. In a saucepan, combine rinsed beans with 6 cups (1.5 L) fresh cold water. Bring to a boil over medium heat. Reduce heat and simmer until beans are just tender to the bite but not fully cooked, about 30 minutes. Scoop out 1½ cups (375 mL) of the cooking liquid and set aside. Drain beans and set aside, discarding remaining liquid.

2. In a large measuring cup, combine maple syrup, mustard, ketchup, tomato paste, peppercorns, salt and ½ cup (125 mL) of the bean cooking liquid. Stir well and set aside.

3. In slow cooker stoneware, place half the pork. Add half the onions and garlic, sprinkling evenly over bottom of stoneware. Add half of the beans and remaining pork. Repeat with remaining onion, garlic and beans. Pour tomato mixture evenly over top.

4. Cover and cook on Low for 8 hours or on High for 4 hours, adding more bean cooking liquid, if necessary to keep beans moist, until beans are tender and mixture is hot and bubbly.

Tip

If you are using pork belly, cut it into two equal pieces. If bacon, slice it thinly.

Make Ahead

Complete Step 1, retaining enough cooking liquid to cover the cooked beans. Cover and refrigerate for up to 2 days. When you're ready to cook, drain the beans, reserving 1½ cups (375 mL) of the cooking liquid, and continue with the recipe.

Mindful Morsels

When buying deli meats such as sausages and bacon, it goes without saying that you need to avoid potentially harmful additives (see page 226) such as synthetic nitrates. These substances, which contain heavy metals, are potentially carcinogenic. They differ from natural nitrates, such as celery juice or sea salt, which may also be used to preserve food. High quantities of natural nitrates are found in many foods and many people mistakenly link them with their man-made relative. Dietary nitrates have an important role in the production of nitric oxide, a compound with health promoting properties, not the least of which is helping to maintain healthy blood pressure levels.

Natural Wonders

Healthy Fats for Cooking

As we learn more about fat, it is becoming increasingly obvious that most of the cooking oils we commonly consume are bad for us. This includes vegetable oils such as corn, soy, "vegetable," sunflower, canola, and safflower oil as well as hydrogenated oils, which have been identified as harmful for some time. These oils have been refined, bleached and chemically treated. They have been processed using solvents and other undesirable chemicals so they will have a higher smoke point and a longer shelf life. They also contain an unhealthy ratio of omega-6 to omega-3 fatty acids. Among other concerns, these oils have been linked with chronic inflammation, which is a precursor to many diseases.

The default fat in this book is olive oil. I use it most often because it is a stable oil with a mild flavor and acceptable smoke point. The Olive Oil Council claims that extra virgin olive oil has a smoke point of 410°F (205°C), the temperature at which it burns, creating harmful toxins. I take a more cautious approach. I treat extra virgin olive oil as if it has a smoke point of 350°F (180°C) and use it for medium-heat cooking, such as softening vegetables. However, alternatives such as clarified butter, ghee, coconut oil, beef tallow or pure lard are all healthy fats. They are also safe for cooking at higher heats. (Clarified butter has a smoke point of 480°F/249°C; beef tallow is 400°F/200°C and lard is 375°F/190°C). When buying any oil, look for a dark-colored glass bottle. Oil is susceptible to light and fatty acids appear to pull some compounds from plastic bottles.

Perhaps surprisingly, old-fashioned animal fats are actually healthy alternatives to refined cooking oils. If they fit the flavor profile of your dish, feel free to use pure lard, beef tallow, chicken fat (schmaltz) or duck or goose fat. Make a serious effort to ensure it is from pasture-raised animals. Do not use packaged lard. It is made from the fat of poorly raised animals and as a result is too high in omega-6 fatty acids. It is also likely to be hydrogenated, which means it contains deadly trans fats. I buy lard from my butcher, who renders it from the fat of pasture-raised pigs. It keeps well in the freezer.

Sausage-Spiked Chickpeas with Yogurt

It's hard to believe that a dish so simple to make can taste so delicious. This is the perfect combination of ingredients — they seem to work synergistically, each enhancing the flavor of the others. The slightly sour tang of the yogurt makes a particularly nice finish.

Makes 6 servings

Can Be Halved
(see Tips, below)

Tips

If you are halving this recipe, be sure to use a small (approx. 1½ to 3 quart) slow cooker.

If you're looking for some "wow" factor, make this recipe using merguez sausage, a North African specialty made with lamb and seasoned with harissa. The flavor is fantastic. It is also great made with chorizo, or even Italian sausage.

Nutrients Per Serving

Calories	473
Protein	25.4 g
Carbohydrates	46.6 g
Fat (Total)	21.6 g
Saturated Fat	6.4 g
Monounsaturated Fat	9.2 g
Polyunsaturated Fat	2.7 g
Dietary Fiber	10.2 g
Sodium	575 mg
Cholesterol	45 mg

EXCELLENT SOURCE OF vitamins B$_6$ and K, folate, phosphorus, magnesium, potassium, iron and zinc.

GOOD SOURCE OF vitamin C and calcium.

SOURCE OF vitamin A.

CONTAINS a very high amount of dietary fiber.

- **Medium to large (3½ to 5 quart) slow cooker**

1 tbsp	olive oil	15 mL
1 lb	spicy sausage, removed from casings (see Mindful Morsels, page 226)	500 g
2	onions, finely chopped	2
1 tbsp	ground cumin	15 mL
2 tbsp	tomato paste	30 mL
1	can (28 oz/796 mL) no-salt added tomatoes including juice	1
1 cup	chicken stock or water	250 mL
1	potato, peeled and shredded	1
3 cups	cooked chickpeas	750 mL
½ cup	plain yogurt	125 mL
¼ cup	finely chopped parsley leaves	60 mL

1. In a skillet, heat oil over medium-high heat. Add sausage and onions and cook, stirring and breaking up with a spoon, until sausage is cooked through, about 7 minutes. Add cumin and cook, stirring, for 1 minute. Stir in tomato paste. Add tomatoes with juice and stock and bring to a boil, scraping up brown bits from bottom of pan.

2. Transfer to slow cooker stoneware. Stir in potato and chickpeas. Cover and cook on Low for 6 to 8 hours or on High for 3 to 4 hours, until hot and bubbly. To serve, ladle into bowls, top with yogurt and garnish with parsley.

more information on page 226

Make Ahead

Complete Step 1. Cover mixture, ensuring it cools promptly (see Making Ahead, page 16), and refrigerate for up to 2 days. When you're ready to cook, complete the recipe.

Mindful Morsels

Most of the sodium in a serving of this recipe (504 mg) comes from the sausage. The nutritional analysis was done using deli sausage because that was the only kind for which nutrient data was available. To reduce the amount of sodium in any recipe containing sausage, make your own with no salt added, or buy from a butcher who doesn't add much salt. It's always important to buy sausage from a butcher you trust. Preferably, it should be made from pasture-raised meat. Also, check to make sure it's gluten-free.

Natural Wonders

Healthy Sausage

Sausage is one of those foods that, in my opinion, has been unjustly demonized because of what the fast-food industry has done to it. Sausage has a noble tradition. It was consumed in ancient civilizations such as Greece and Rome, providing those societies with a tasty and convenient method for utilizing all the edible parts of an animal. Sausage making is a backbone of the tradition we now identify as "nose-to-tail eating," an environmentally driven strategy for creating a culture of sustainable agriculture.

About ten years ago, I spent a week in Michoacán, Mexico, cooking with Diana Kennedy, the esteemed doyenne of Mexican cuisine. I remember our sausage-making session vividly. We made two kinds of chorizo, one that might be described as "regular" and a much more (at least in my experience) exotic green chorizo, which in addition to pasture-raised pork and the requisite seasonings, contained copious amounts of leafy herbal greens, such as cilantro, parsley and Swiss chard. Diana's accompanying talk on the Mexican tradition of chorizo was inspiring: it was an artisanal process, from soaking the meat in wine and spices and stuffing it into appropriately prepared pig intestines, to tying it with natural plant fibers. In Mexico, they have been making chorizo since the beginning of the eighteenth century. Every locale has its unique recipes and today there is passionate rivalry among the regions about whose is the best.

Sadly, these products bear little resemblance to the sausages most people in the industrialized world eat today. For starters, the meat is likely to be feedlot-raised and of poor quality. It almost certainly contains problematic additives such as MSG, high-fructose corn syrup and artificial flavorings and fillers, including gluten. Synthetic nitrate, which differs from natural nitrates, and contains potentially carcinogenic heavy metals, has probably been used as a preservative.

All of which is to say that when buying sausage, purchase it from a butcher you trust. Mine sells only high-quality, pasture-raised meat. His sausage is guaranteed to be gluten-free and made from his own combinations of meat, including fat, and seasonings, in the classic artisanal style. It is delicious.

Moroccan-Style Lamb with Raisins and Apricots

This classic tagine-style recipe, in which lamb is braised in spices and honey, is an appetizing combination of savory and sweet. I like to serve it with gluten-free quinoa, which adds a new world twist to this Middle Eastern dish.

Makes 8 servings

Can Be Halved
(see Tips, below)

Tips

If you are halving this recipe, be sure to use a small (1½ to 3½ quart) slow cooker.

I prefer a peppery base in this dish to balance the sweetness of the apricots and raisins, so I usually use a whole teaspoon (5 mL) of cracked black peppercorns in this recipe. But I'm a pepper lover, so use your own judgment.

Nutrients Per Serving

Calories	253
Protein	25.9 g
Carbohydrates	21.8 g
Fat (Total)	5.7 g
Saturated Fat	1.8 g
Monounsaturated Fat	4.1 g
Polyunsaturated Fat	0.8 g
Dietary Fiber	2.0 g
Sodium	295 mg
Cholesterol	81 mg

EXCELLENT SOURCE OF vitamin B$_{12}$, potassium and zinc.

GOOD SOURCE OF vitamin B$_6$, phosphorus, magnesium and iron.

SOURCE OF vitamins A and K and folate.

CONTAINS a moderate amount of dietary fiber.

- Medium to large (3½ to 5 quart) slow cooker

1 to 2 tbsp	olive oil	15 to 30 mL
2 lbs	trimmed stewing lamb, cut into 1-inch (2.5 cm) cubes	1 kg
1	onion, finely chopped	1
1 tbsp	minced gingerroot	15 mL
1 tbsp	ground cumin (see Tip, page 235)	15 mL
1 tsp	ground coriander	5 mL
1 tsp	grated lemon zest	5 mL
½ tsp	salt	2 mL
½ tsp	cracked black peppercorns (approx.) (see Tip, left)	2 mL
1	piece (1 inch/2.5 cm) cinnamon stick	1
½ cup	chicken stock	125 mL
1 tbsp	freshly squeezed lemon juice	15 mL
1 tbsp	liquid honey	15 mL
	Salt, optional	
1 cup	dried apricots, chopped	250 mL
½ cup	raisins	125 mL
½ cup	finely chopped cilantro leaves	125 mL

1. In a skillet, heat 1 tbsp (15 mL) of the oil over medium-high heat. Add lamb, in batches, and cook, stirring, adding more oil if necessary, until browned, about 4 minutes per batch. Transfer to slow cooker stoneware.

2. Reduce heat to medium. Add onion to pan and cook, stirring, until softened. Add ginger, cumin, coriander, lemon zest, salt, peppercorns and cinnamon stick and cook, stirring, for 1 minute. Add stock and bring to a boil.

3. Transfer to slow cooker stoneware. Stir well. Cover and cook on Low for 6 to 8 hours or on High for 3 to 4 hours, until lamb is tender. Add lemon juice and honey and stir well. Season to taste with salt, if using. Stir in apricots and raisins. Cover and cook on High for 20 minutes, until fruit is warmed through. Garnish with cilantro. Discard cinnamon stick.

more information on page 229

Moroccan-Style Lamb with Raisins and Apricots

Make Ahead

Heat 1 tbsp (15 mL) of the oil and complete Step 2. Cover and refrigerate overnight or for up to 2 days. When you're ready to cook, either brown the lamb as outlined in Step 1 or add it to the stoneware without browning. Stir well and continue with Step 3.

Natural Wonders

Apricots

In addition to providing a hint of exotic flavor, the apricots in this recipe deepen its nutritional value by adding vitamin A, potassium and iron. They also provide soluble, as well as insoluble fiber (see Natural Wonders, page 94). This tasty fruit also contains a wide variety of carotenoids, powerful antioxidants that have been linked to various health benefits (see Natural Wonders, page 99). Enjoying apricots in a stew has an added benefit because their beta-carotene becomes more available to the body when they are cooked.

Dried apricots are available year-round. They are convenient because they can be easily transported and they make a very nutritious snack. Drying removes their high water content and concentrates the nutrients, which means that bite for bite, dried apricots are

more nutritious than fresh. It makes sense to have them on hand for those times when fresh fruit isn't an option. However, because dried fruits are concentrated, they also contain more calories and sugar than those that are fresh. One other thing to watch for — most dried apricots are treated with sulfur dioxide, which maintains their bright orange color but can trigger allergic reactions or an attack of asthma in people sensitive to sulfur. I prefer to buy sulfur-free versions at a natural foods store.

Spanish-Style Pork and Beans

Here's a dish that is as delicious as the best Boston baked beans but even more nutritious. Salt pork is replaced with pork shoulder and nutrient-dense kale is added just before the dish has finished cooking. This is a generous serving (approximately 2 cups/500 mL) so it doesn't need much to complete it — perhaps a small green salad sprinkled with shredded carrots to add color to the meal.

Makes 8 servings

Can Be Halved
(see Tips, below)

Tips

If you are halving this recipe, be sure to use a small (2 to 3½ quart) slow cooker.

When preparing kale, chop off the stem, then fold the leaf in half and remove the thickest part of the vein that runs up the center of the leaf.

If you don't have kale you can substitute an equal quantity of spinach or Swiss chard.

• Large (approx. 5 quart) slow cooker

2 tbsp	olive oil, divided	30 mL
2 lbs	trimmed boneless pork shoulder, cut into bite-size pieces	1 kg
3	onions, finely chopped	3
4	cloves garlic, minced	4
2 tsp	dried oregano, crumbled	10 mL
½ tsp	salt	2 mL
½ tsp	cracked black peppercorns	2 mL
1 cup	dry white wine or chicken stock	250 mL
2 tsp	sherry vinegar or white wine vinegar	10 mL
1	can no-salt added (28 oz/796 mL) tomatoes, including juice, coarsely chopped	1
4 cups	cooked white kidney beans	1 L
2 tsp	hot or mild paprika dissolved in 2 tbsp (30 mL) dry white wine or water	10 mL
8 cups	coarsely chopped, stemmed kale, about 2 bunches (see Tips, left)	2 L

1. In a skillet, heat 1 tbsp (15 mL) oil over medium-high heat. Add pork, in batches, and cook, stirring, adding more oil as necessary, until browned, about 5 minutes per batch. Transfer to slow cooker stoneware.

2. Reduce heat to medium. Add onions to pan and cook, stirring, until softened, about 3 minutes. Add garlic, oregano, salt and peppercorns and cook, stirring, for 1 minute. Add wine and vinegar and cook, stirring, for 1 minute. Add tomatoes with juice and bring to a boil. Transfer to slow cooker stoneware. Add beans and stir well.

3. Cover and cook on Low for 8 hours or on High for 4 hours, until pork is very tender (it should be falling apart).

4. Add paprika solution and stir well. Add kale, in batches, stirring well after each addition, until it begins to wilt. Cover and cook on High for 30 minutes, until kale is tender. Serve immediately.

Nutrients Per Serving

Calories	400
Protein	37.2 g
Carbohydrates	43.9 g
Fat (Total)	9.3 g
Saturated Fat	2.4 g
Monounsaturated Fat	4.7 g
Polyunsaturated Fat	1.6 g
Dietary Fiber	11.2 g
Sodium	272 mg
Cholesterol	72 mg

EXCELLENT SOURCE OF vitamins A, C, B$_6$ and K, folate, phosphorus, magnesium, potassium, iron and zinc.

GOOD SOURCE OF vitamin B$_{12}$ and calcium.

CONTAINS a very high amount of dietary fiber.

Make Ahead

Heat 1 tbsp (15 mL) of the oil and complete Step 2. Cover and refrigerate overnight or for up to 2 days. When you're ready to cook, either brown the pork as outlined in Step 1 or add it to the stoneware without browning. Stir well and continue with Steps 3 and 4.

Natural Wonders

Pork

Contemporary farming has changed the way we think about pork. Not only is the fat in pork mostly unsaturated, when pigs are pastured, they are leaner and their fat contains more valuable omega-3 fatty acids. At least one study indicates that the meat of pasture-raised pigs will also contain significantly higher amounts of nutrients such as vitamin E and selenium.

This makes pork, eaten in moderation, a nutritious food choice. (Even the fat in "conventionally raised" pork is healthier than traditional wisdom suggests. Only 45% of "conventionally raised" pork fat is saturated, and that part contains stearic acid, a fatty acid that scientists are interested in studying because they think it might help lower blood cholesterol.)

Pastured pigs forage for plants such alfalfa and clover, which also provide chlorophyll, the precursor to the higher levels of omega-3 fatty acids. According to pig farmer Walter Jeffries, even though they are not ruminants, they also consume grass, which they can digest properly and thrive on.

Like all meat, pork is high in protein, which helps the body to build and repair tissues and produce the antibodies necessary to battle infection. It also contains a wide range of nutrients, such as iron, pantothenic acid, zinc and vitamins B_6 and B_{12}. Pork is also one of the best food sources of thiamine, a B vitamin that supports your nervous system and helps to keep you energized.

Pork Belly with Flageolets

This is, quite simply, pork and beans for gourmands. Made with luscious pork belly, which melts into the mélange and falls apart after cooking, and flageolets, the Rolls-Royce of legumes, it is the ne plus ultra of rustic cooking. Just add a tossed green salad, and, perhaps, an appropriate bottle of wine.

Makes 8 servings

Can Be Halved
(see Tips, page 224)

Tip

To soak the flageolets, combine them in a saucepan with 6 cups (1.5 L) cold water. Bring to a boil over medium heat and boil rapidly for 3 minutes. Turn off element and let stand for 1 hour. Or soak overnight in cold water. Drain and rinse thoroughly under cold running water. If you have difficulty digesting legumes, add 2 tbsp (30 mL) cider vinegar to the soaking water.

Nutrients Per Serving

Calories	495
Protein	17 g
Carbohydrates	34.1 g
Fat (Total)	32.7 g
Saturated Fat	11.3 g
Monounsaturated Fat	15.4 g
Polyunsaturated Fat	3.5 g
Dietary Fiber	12.7 g
Sodium	239 mg
Cholesterol	46 mg

EXCELLENT SOURCE OF vitamin A, phosphorus, potassium and iron.

GOOD SOURCE OF vitamin B$_{12}$.

SOURCE OF vitamins C, B$_6$ and K, folate, calcium, magnesium and zinc.

CONTAINS a very high amount of dietary fiber.

• **Medium to large (3½ to 5 quart) slow cooker**

2 cups	dried flageolets, soaked and drained (see Tip, left)	500 mL
1 lb	boneless pork belly	500 g
1 tbsp	olive oil	15 mL
2	onions, finely chopped	2
2	carrots, peeled and diced	2
2	stalks celery, diced	2
4	cloves garlic, minced	4
1 tsp	dried thyme	5 mL
1 tsp	dried rosemary	5 mL
½ tsp	salt	2 mL
½ tsp	cracked black peppercorns	2 mL
1 cup	dry white wine	250 mL
¼ cup	tomato paste	60 mL
2 cups	chicken stock	500 mL

1. Place pork belly in slow cooker stoneware.

2. In a skillet, heat oil over medium heat. Add onions, carrots and celery and cook, stirring, until softened, about 7 minutes. Add garlic, thyme, rosemary, salt and peppercorns and cook, stirring, for 1 minute. Add flageolets and toss until well coated with mixture. Add wine and tomato paste, bring to a boil and boil for 2 minutes. Stir in chicken stock.

3. Transfer to slow cooker stoneware. Cover and cook on Low for 8 hours or on High for 4 hours, until beans are very tender.

Make Ahead

Complete Step 2. Cover and refrigerate mixture for up to 2 days. When you're ready to cook, complete the recipe.

Mindful Morsels

In addition to being delicious, the flageolets in this recipe, like all legumes, provide valuable minerals such as potassium, magnesium, phosphorus, manganese, iron and zinc.

Natural Wonders

Salad

Completing a meal with salad is an excellent way to ensure that you consume an adequate amount of valuable fiber. But it's also a technique for adding nutrients to your diet. Among other nutrients, romaine lettuce contains vitamins A and C and folate. For an even greater nutritional hit, use dark green or red loose leaf lettuce, which provides far more antioxidants, and add a bit of bitter green such as radicchio or arugula. In general terms, the more bitter the green, the more nutritious it is. Arugula, for instance, provides more vitamin E, folate, magnesium and calcium than most greens used in salads, and it is loaded with antioxidants. Adding dark leafy greens, such as spinach and parsley, bumps up the vitamin K content, in particular, and a sprinkling of toasted whole sesame seeds helps to provide much-needed calcium. Add sliced bell peppers, chopped scallions, a few radishes — whatever captures your fancy — and you have a bowl brimming with a colorful array of vitamins, minerals and phytonutrients, all of which will work together to keep you healthy.

Pork Chili with Black-Eyed Peas

If you're tired of beef-based chilies with red beans, try this equally delicious but lighter version. It makes a great potluck dish or the centerpiece for a casual evening with friends. For a special occasion, serve with hot gluten-free cornbread.

Makes 8 servings

Can Be Halved
(see Tips, below)

Tips

If you are halving this recipe, be sure to use a small (2½ to 3½ quart) slow cooker.

For this quantity of beans, use 2 cans (14 to 19 oz/ 398 to 540 mL) drained and rinsed no-salt added black-eyed peas, or soak and cook 2 cups (500 mL) dried beans yourself (see Basic Beans, page 284).

Many butchers sell cut-up pork stewing meat, which is fine to use in this recipe.

Nutrients Per Serving

Calories	406
Protein	37.6 g
Carbohydrates	39.3 g
Fat (Total)	10.8 g
Saturated Fat	3.0 g
Monounsaturated Fat	5.6 g
Polyunsaturated Fat	1.6 g
Dietary Fiber	10.6 g
Sodium	365 mg
Cholesterol	79 mg

EXCELLENT SOURCE OF vitamins C, B$_6$, B$_{12}$ and K, folate, phosphorus, magnesium potassium, iron and zinc.

SOURCE OF vitamin A and calcium.

CONTAINS a very high amount of dietary fiber.

• **Large (approx. 5 quart) slow cooker**

4 cups	cooked black-eyed peas (see Tips, left)	1 L
2 tbsp	olive oil, divided	30 mL
4 oz	chunk bacon, diced	125 g
2 lbs	trimmed pork shoulder or blade (butt), cut into 1-inch (2.5 cm) cubes, and patted dry (see Tips, left)	1 kg
2	onions, finely chopped	2
2	stalks celery, thinly sliced	2
4	cloves garlic, minced	4
2 tsp	ground cumin (see Tip, right)	10 mL
2 tsp	ground coriander (see Tip, right)	10 mL
2 tsp	dried oregano, crumbled	10 mL
1 tsp	cracked black peppercorns	5 mL
½ tsp	salt	2 mL
1	piece (2 inches/5 cm) cinnamon stick	1
1	can (15 oz/425 g) no-salt added crushed tomatoes	1
1 cup	chicken stock	250 mL
1	red bell pepper, seeded and diced	1
1	green bell pepper, seeded and diced	1
1 to 2	chipotle peppers in adobo sauce, minced	1 to 2
	Sour cream	
	Finely chopped red onion	
	Shredded Monterey Jack cheese	

1. In a skillet, heat 1 tbsp (15 mL) of the oil over medium-high heat. Add bacon and cook, stirring, until browned and crisp, about 4 minutes. Using a slotted spoon, transfer to slow cooker stoneware. Add pork, in batches, and cook, stirring, until browned, about 4 minutes per batch. Transfer to stoneware as completed.

2. Reduce heat to medium. Add remaining tbsp (15 mL) of oil to pan. Add onions and celery and cook, stirring, until softened, about 5 minutes. Add garlic, cumin, coriander, oregano, peppercorns, salt and cinnamon stick and cook, stirring, for 1 minute. Add tomatoes and chicken stock and boil for 1 minute, scraping up brown bits.

For best results, toast and grind the cumin and coriander seeds yourself. Place seeds in a dry skillet over medium heat and cook, stirring, until fragrant, about 3 minutes. Using a mortar and pestle or a spice grinder, pound or grind as finely as you can.

Make Ahead

Complete Step 2. Cover and refrigerate mixture for up to 2 days. When you're ready to cook, complete the recipe.

3. Transfer to stoneware. Stir in peas. Cover and cook on Low for 6 hours or on High for 3 hours. Stir in red and green bell peppers and chipotles. Cover and cook on High for about 20 minutes, until peppers are tender. Discard cinnamon stick. Garnish with any combination of sour cream, onion and/or cheese.

Mindful Morsels

For various reasons, it is usually best to cook dried beans from scratch rather than using the canned variety. However, canned beans, which are almost as nutritious as those cooked-from-scratch, can be an excellent alternative. The sodium content may be high so buy those with no salt added (even the reduced sodium ones are pretty high in sodium). Also, the cans may be lined with bisphenol A (BPA), a potential toxin, so look for brands with BPA-free cans.

Natural Wonders

Vitamin B_{12}

The pork in this recipe is an excellent source of vitamin B_{12}, which works in conjunction with other substances to help the body develop red blood cells and nerve cells, among other functions. Along with vitamin B_6 and folate, B_{12} has been linked with lower homocysteine levels, which have been associated with a reduced risk of heart attack and stroke. Although it is unusual, a B_{12} deficiency can cause pernicious anemia, a condition where the body cannot make an adequate supply of red blood cells. Taken together, vitamins B_6, B_{12} and folate work in concert to recycle artery-clogging homocysteine into methionine, an essential amino acid that helps your body to perform many important functions. Moreover, although researchers don't understand why it works, a recent study reported that a combination of B_{12} and folate taken after a stroke reduces the incidence of subsequent hip fractures.

The body stores B_{12}, which means you don't need to consume it on a regular basis. However, recent studies suggest it can be depleted more quickly than was previously thought. A B_{12} deficiency may affect a substantial number of infants in the developing world and as many as 22% of Americans over the age of 65. As we age, our bodies may absorb this vitamin less efficiently due to declining levels of stomach acid.

Because it is found naturally only in animal products, those most at risk for a B_{12} deficiency often eat little or no meat, do not consume fortified foods and do not take supplements. One study of mothers who followed a macrobiotic diet found that their breast milk contained insufficient levels of this vitamin. A long-term lack of B_{12} may be linked with chronic anxiety and depression and even lead to neurological damage. Meat, fish, shellfish, turkey, eggs and milk are the most common sources. Vegans need to consume vitamin B_{12} in fortified foods, such as breakfast cereals, or by taking supplements.

Spicy Lamb with Chickpeas

Here's a dish with robust flavor that will delight even your most discriminating guests. Serve over hot quinoa, and open a good Rioja for a perfect accompaniment.

Makes 8 servings

Can Be Halved
(see Tips, below)

Tips

If you are halving this recipe, be sure to use a small (2 to 3½ quart) slow cooker.

For the best flavor, toast and grind the cumin and coriander yourself, rather than buying the ground versions. Place seeds in a dry skillet over medium heat, stirring until fragrant, about 3 minutes. Using a mortar and pestle or a spice grinder, pound or grind as finely as you can.

Nutrients Per Serving

Calories	336
Protein	31.1 g
Carbohydrates	34.5 g
Fat (Total)	9.0 g
Saturated Fat	2.3 g
Monounsaturated Fat	4.8 g
Polyunsaturated Fat	1.0 g
Dietary Fiber	7.3 g
Sodium	381 mg
Cholesterol	84 mg

EXCELLENT SOURCE OF vitamins A and B$_{12}$, folate, phosphorus, magnesium, potassium, iron and zinc.
GOOD SOURCE OF vitamin B$_6$.
SOURCE OF vitamins C and K and calcium.
CONTAINS a very high amount of dietary fiber.

• **Medium to large (3½ to 5 quart) slow cooker**

1 tbsp	ground cumin (see Tips, left)	15 mL
2 tsp	ground coriander (see Tips, left)	10 mL
1 tsp	ground turmeric	5 mL
1 tsp	cracked black peppercorns	5 mL
¼ tsp	salt	1 mL
1 tsp	finely grated lime zest	5 mL
2 tbsp	freshly squeezed lime juice	30 mL
2 lbs	trimmed stewing lamb, cut into 1-inch (2.5 cm) cubes	1 kg
2 tbsp	olive oil, divided	30 mL
2	onions, finely chopped	2
2	carrots, diced	2
2	parsnips, peeled and diced	2
4	cloves garlic, minced	4
2 tbsp	minced gingerroot	30 mL
4	black cardamom pods, crushed	4
1	piece (2 inches/5 cm) cinnamon stick	1
6	whole cloves	6
½ tsp	salt	2 mL
½ tsp	cracked black peppercorns	2 mL
1	can (28 oz/796 mL) no-salt added tomatoes, including juice, coarsely chopped	1
1 cup	chicken or vegetable stock	250 mL
3 cups	cooked chickpeas, mashed (see Tips, right)	750 mL
1 tsp	Aleppo pepper (see Tips, right)	5 mL
¼ tsp	cayenne pepper	1 mL

1. In a bowl, combine cumin, coriander, turmeric, 1 tsp (5 mL) peppercorns, ¼ tsp (1 mL) salt and lime zest and juice. Stir well. Add lamb and toss to coat. Cover and set aside in refrigerator for 4 hours or overnight.

2. Pat lamb dry. In a skillet, heat 1 tbsp (15 mL) of the oil over medium heat. Add lamb, in batches, and cook, stirring, until lightly browned, about 4 minutes per batch. Transfer to slow cooker as completed.

Tips

You can cook your own chickpeas (see Basic Beans, page 284) or use canned chickpeas, with no salt added, rinsed and drained.

Aleppo pepper is a mild Syrian chile pepper. It is increasingly available in specialty shops or well-stocked supermarkets. If you don't have it, substitute another mild chile powder such as ancho or New Mexico, or add another $\frac{1}{4}$ tsp (1 mL) cayenne.

Make Ahead

Complete Steps 1 and 3. Cover and refrigerate overnight. When you're ready to cook, complete the recipe.

3. Add remaining tbsp (15 mL) oil to pan. Add onions, carrots and parsnips and cook, stirring and scraping up brown bits, until carrots are softened, about 7 minutes. Add garlic, ginger, cardamom, cinnamon stick, cloves, salt and peppercorns and cook, stirring, for 1 minute. Add tomatoes with juice and chicken stock and bring to a boil, scraping up brown bits from bottom of pan. Transfer to stoneware. Stir in chickpeas.

4. Cover and cook on Low for 8 hours or on High for 4 to 5 hours, until meat is very tender. Stir in Aleppo and cayenne. Cover and cook on High for 10 minutes.

Mindful Morsels

The Aleppo and chile pepper in this recipe provide capsaicin (see Natural Wonders, page 89). One Dutch study found that people who consumed capsaicin (in supplement form) before a meal consumed less fat and fewer calories.

Natural Wonders

Lamb: A Sustainable Meat Choice

Lamb is not a popular meat in North America and that's a shame because properly prepared, it is at least as delicious as comparable cuts of beef. It is also very nutritious and, if you are buying your meat at a supermarket because you don't have access to a good butcher, there is an excellent chance that you can purchase lamb that has been pasture-raised and is antibiotic free. Just look for New Zealand Spring Lamb, which is widely available. Although naturally raised meat may, in some cases be difficult to find and more costly than feedlot-produced meat, it is better for your health. Some evidence suggests that grass-fed lamb has 14% less fat and 8% more protein than grain-fed lamb.

Lamb is the meat from a sheep that is less than a year old. (If the animal is older than a year, its meat is called mutton, which has a much stronger flavor that many people find unappealing.) Lamb is an excellent source of high quality protein (a 3-ounce serving of cooked lean lamb provides 43% of the RDA of high-quality protein, weighed against only 7% of the calories), vitamin B_{12}, and the mineral zinc (a 3-ounce serving provides 30% of the DV of this important nutrient). It is also one of the best food sources of carnitine, an amino acid that helps your body transform fat into energy, among other functions. (A 2013 study that suggested a connection between the carnitine in meat and heart disease has been robustly questioned on several fronts. Other research shows that taking carnitine in supplement form is very beneficial to people with heart disease.) Lamb also provides the B vitamins niacin and riboflavin as well as trace elements of minerals such as selenium, manganese and copper.

Natural Wonders

Micronutrients

Most of us take our ability to function for granted, but to maintain good health you need to provide your body with good nutrition. There are two basic categories of nutrients, macronutrients (protein, carbohydrates and fat), which provide energy in the form of calories, and micronutrients (vitamins, minerals and the more-recently discovered phytonutrients) which work together to maintain your metabolism, performing thousands of different jobs, from repairing damaged tissues and fighting infections to building bones. While most people in the developed world are not at risk for consuming too few calories, a diet that is high in refined/processed foods is likely to be low in micronutrients.

In developed societies, few people suffer from deficiency diseases that are obvious because a variety of foods are available year-round and many foods are fortified with vitamins and/or minerals to compensate for identified shortages. However, in the past disease states resulting from inadequate micronutrient intake were more evident. Two of the best-known examples are scurvy and beriberi. During the age of exploration, sailors developed scurvy because they didn't have access to fresh fruit or vegetables and as a result suffered from an acute absence of vitamin C. In the 19th century, when polishing (refining) rice became popular, people who depended on this grain to fulfill their dietary needs often developed an illness characterized by a debilitating lack of energy. Eventually, scientists realized that thiamine (vitamin B_1) is removed from rice when it is polished and the people who were ill were suffering from a deficiency of this nutrient.

These are extreme cases: To some extent your body can adjust micronutrient availability to meet its needs. In a lecture delivered in 2005, micronutrient expert Alan Shenkin noted that the body has a number of complex mechanisms "that move micronutrients around to ensure they are in the correct place and in the correct concentration". For instance, he cited studies that show after 8 to 12 hours of elective surgery blood levels of zinc and iron fall and those of copper rise, a situation that lasts for several days and is directed toward ensuring that at each phase of illness the body has "the right concentration of each micronutrient in the right tissue or body fluid."

Although your body may be able to juggle existing supplies of micronutrients to meet specific needs over the short term, it can't manufacture them in sufficient amounts to keep you well over the span of a lifetime. In recent years it has become increasingly clear that inadequate amounts of micronutrients are linked with the so-called "diseases of civilization," such as heart disease, diabetes, osteoporosis and various types of cancer. The poor quality of energy-dense (relatively high calorie), nutrient-poor processed foods, which, unfortunately, constitute a significant part of the North American diet have been linked with these diseases. On the other hand, many large-scale epidemiological studies have demonstrated connections between micronutrient consumption (for example, certain antioxidants) and specific health benefits, such as improved eye health.

That's why this book (among others) stresses eating food that is nutrient dense. When consuming food, it's important to be aware of how much nutrition it provides in relation to its caloric count. When assessing food (and recipe) quality, you want a positive ratio in favor of nutrients. Based on USDA data, consider, for instance, that 1 medium carrot provides 25 calories, 1% of the DV. At the same time that carrot provides 204% of the DV for vitamin A; 10% of the DV for vitamin K, and 6% each of potassium and vitamin C, in addition to a smattering of other nutrients. Traditional nutrient analysis doesn't track the phytonutrients in foods but carrots are also rich in carotenoids such as beta-carotene. Foods providing ample amounts of these compounds have been linked with a reduced risk of many types of cancer, among other benefits.

On the other hand, a small serving of unsalted potato chips (100 g) provides 537 calories, 27% of the recommended daily calorie consumption. While it also provides a positive ratio of vitamin C (52%) on most other macronutrients its performance is poor: compared to those noted in the carrots, 0% of vitamins K and A and 17% of potassium.

Viewed from this perspective, it seems clear that people who consume large amounts of processed foods may be at risk for deficiency diseases, as well as obesity. Processed foods are energy (calorie) dense but light on most vitamins, minerals (except for sodium) and phytonutrients. When you consume a diet rich in micronutrients, which are found in abundance in whole foods, these compounds work together to keep your body in optimal health, preventing disease and helping you to enjoy life to the fullest.

Mixed Vegetables in Spicy Peanut Sauce

Vegetarian Mains

Mixed Vegetables in Spicy Peanut Sauce

Here's one way to get kids to eat their vegetables, so long as they don't have peanut allergies — cook them in a spicy sauce made from peanut butter and add a garnish of chopped roasted peanuts. All you need to add is some steaming rice or brown rice noodles.

Makes 8 servings

Can Be Halved
(see Tips, page 246)

Tip

I always have a bag of frozen green beans in the freezer because they can be conveniently added to slow cooker recipes. They contain valuable nutrients: vitamins C and K, a selection of the B vitamins, including folate, and the minerals manganese, iron and magnesium. They also contain fiber.

Nutrients Per Serving

Calories	241
Protein	9.3 g
Carbohydrates	22.7 g
Fat (Total)	14.9 g
Saturated Fat	2.1 g
Monounsaturated Fat	7.7 g
Polyunsaturated Fat	4.4 g
Dietary Fiber	6.5 g
Sodium	290 mg
Cholesterol	0 mg

EXCELLENT SOURCE OF vitamins A, B₆ and K, folate and magnesium.

GOOD SOURCE OF vitamin C, potassium, phosphorus and zinc.

SOURCE OF calcium and iron.

CONTAINS a very high amount of dietary fiber.

- **Medium to large (3½ to 5 quart) slow cooker**

1 tbsp	olive oil	15 mL
2	onions, finely chopped	2
6	medium carrots, peeled and thinly sliced (about 4 cups/1 L)	6
4	stalks celery, diced (about 2 cups/500 mL)	4
2 tbsp	minced gingerroot	30 mL
4	cloves garlic, minced	4
½ tsp	cracked black peppercorns	2 mL
1 cup	vegetable stock	250 mL
3 cups	frozen sliced green beans (see Tips, left and right)	750 mL
½ cup	smooth natural peanut butter	125 mL
2 tbsp	gluten-free reduced-sodium soy sauce	30 mL
2 tbsp	freshly squeezed lemon juice	30 mL
1 tbsp	pure maple syrup	15 mL
2 tsp	Thai red curry paste (see Tips, right)	10 mL
4 cups	shredded napa cabbage	1 L
2 cups	bean sprouts	500 mL
½ cup	finely chopped green onions, white part only	125 mL
½ cup	chopped dry roasted peanuts	125 mL

1. In a large skillet, heat oil over medium heat. Add onions, carrots and celery and cook, stirring, until softened, about 7 minutes. Add ginger, garlic and peppercorns and cook, stirring, for 1 minute. Transfer to slow cooker stoneware. Add vegetable stock and stir well.

2. Add green beans and stir well. Cover and cook on Low for 6 hours or on High for 3 hours, until vegetables are tender.

Tips

If you prefer, substitute fresh green beans for the frozen. Blanch in boiling water for 4 minutes after the water returns to a boil and add to the slow cooker along with the cabbage.

Check the label to make sure your curry paste doesn't contain unwanted additives, such as gluten.

Make Ahead

This dish can be partially prepared before it is cooked. Complete Step 1. Cover and refrigerate overnight or for up to 2 days. When you're ready to cook, continue with Steps 2 and 3.

3. In a bowl, beat together peanut butter, soy sauce, lemon juice, maple syrup and red curry paste until blended. Add to slow cooker stoneware and stir well. Add napa cabbage, in batches, stirring until each batch is submerged in liquid. Cover and cook for 10 minutes, until heated through. Stir in bean sprouts. Garnish each serving with a sprinkle of green onions, then peanuts.

Variation

Add 2 cups (500 mL) cooked broccoli florets along with the cabbage.

Mindful Morsels

One Harvard study found that women who ate a handful of nuts or 2 tbsp (30 mL) of peanut butter at least five times a week were 20% less likely to develop type-2 diabetes.

Natural Wonders

Pure Maple Syrup

Recent research suggests that pure maple syrup is loaded with beneficial compounds, which may be anti-inflammatory. It also may be beneficial to people managing type-2 diabetes because these substances appear to inhibit the process of converting carbohydrates to sugars. Pure maple syrup also contains a smattering of nutrients. According to research provided by Canadian maple syrup producers, a $1/4$ cup (60 mL) serving is an excellent source of manganese and riboflavin, a B vitamin that helps your body to metabolize food, among other benefits. It is also a good source of zinc and a source of magnesium, calcium and potassium. It also provides a range of active antioxidants. When purchasing maple syrup it's wise to look for more deeply colored grades, which are actually less expensive than the lighter versions. The darker the maple syrup, the higher its antioxidant activity.

Ratatouille

Ratatouille makes a great accompaniment to roast meat or, if you're a vegetarian, served over baked tofu. I also think it's delicious on its own.

Makes 8 servings

Can Be Halved
(see Tips, below)

Tips

If you are halving this recipe, be sure to use a small (2 to 3½ quart) slow cooker.

Be sure to rinse the salted eggplant thoroughly after sweating. Otherwise it may retain salt and your ratatouille will be too salty.

I use Italian San Marzano tomatoes in this recipe. They are richer and thicker and have more tomato flavor than domestic varieties. If you are using a domestic variety, add 1 tbsp (15 mL) tomato paste along with the tomatoes.

Nutrients Per Serving

Calories	121
Protein	3.1 g
Carbohydrates	17.5 g
Fat (Total)	5.6 g
Saturated Fat	0.8 g
Monounsaturated Fat	3.8 g
Polyunsaturated Fat	0.7 g
Dietary Fiber	5.1 g
Sodium	300 mg
Cholesterol	0 mg

EXCELLENT SOURCE OF vitamins C and K and potassium.
GOOD SOURCE OF vitamin B$_6$, folate and magnesium.
SOURCE OF vitamin A, phosphorus and iron.
CONTAINS a high amount of dietary fiber.

- **Large (approx. 5 quart) slow cooker**
- **Preheat oven to 400°F (200°C)**
- **Rimmed baking sheet, ungreased**

2	medium eggplant (each about 12 oz/375 g), peeled and cut into 1-inch (2.5 cm) cubes	2
2 tbsp	coarse sea or kosher salt	30 mL
3 tbsp	olive oil, divided	45 mL
4	medium zucchini (about 1½ lbs/750 g total), peeled and thinly sliced	4
2	cloves garlic, minced	2
2	onions, thinly sliced	2
1 tsp	herbes de Provence	5 mL
½ tsp	salt	2 mL
½ tsp	cracked black peppercorns	2 mL
8 oz	mushrooms, sliced	250 g
1	can (28 oz/796 mL) tomatoes, including juices, coarsely chopped	1
2	green bell peppers, cubed (½ inch/1 cm)	2
½ cup	chopped parsley or basil leaves	125 mL

1. In a colander over a sink, combine eggplant and salt. Toss to ensure eggplant is well coated and let stand for 30 minutes to 1 hour. Rinse thoroughly under cold running water. Lay a clean tea towel on a work surface. Working in batches over the sink and using your hands, squeeze liquid out of eggplant. Transfer to the tea towel. When batches are complete, roll the towel up and press down to remove remaining liquid. Transfer eggplant to baking sheet and toss with 1 tbsp (15 mL) of the olive oil. Spread evenly on baking sheet. Cover with foil and bake in preheated oven until soft and fragrant, about 15 minutes. Remove from oven and transfer to slow cooker stoneware.

2. Meanwhile, heat 1 tbsp (15 mL) of the oil over medium-high heat. Add zucchini and cook, stirring, for 6 minutes. Add garlic and cook, stirring, until zucchini is soft and browned, about 1 minute. Transfer to a bowl. Cover and refrigerate.

Complete Steps 1 through 3. Cover and refrigerate stoneware and zucchini mixture separately overnight. The next day, continue with Step 4.

3. Reduce heat to medium. Add remaining 1 tbsp (15 mL) of oil. Add onions and cook, stirring, until softened, about 3 minutes. Add herbes de Provence, salt and peppercorns and cook, stirring, about 1 minute. Add mushrooms and toss until coated. Stir in tomatoes with juice and bring to a boil. Transfer to stoneware.

4. Cover and cook on Low for 6 hours or on High for 3 hours, until vegetables are tender. Add green peppers, reserved zucchini mixture and parsley and stir well. Cover and cook on High for 25 minutes, until peppers are tender and zucchini is heated through.

Mindful Morsels

Researchers are studying nasunin, a powerful antioxidant found in eggplant, which appears to protect cells and joints from free radical damage. Nasunin appears to have cancer-protective properties and may also help to reduce the risk of cancer and rheumatoid arthritis.

Natural Wonders

Zucchini

Zucchini is a member of the summer squash family. While not a nutrient-dense vegetable, it is low in calories (a 1-cup/250 mL serving has only 27 calories) and provides small amounts of a variety of nutrients, such as manganese, vitamin C, magnesium and potassium. However, zucchini excels in phytonutrients that help to keep your eyes healthy, particularly the carotenoids lutein and zeanxanthin (see page 81). One study in the journal *Archives of Ophthalmology*, for instance, linked those antioxidants with a lower risk of getting cataracts. Since these phytonutrients are concentrated in the skin of the vegetable, it makes sense to purchase organic zucchini and leave the skin on when cooking. Avoiding "conventional" zucchini also makes sense because much of it is genetically modified.

Mushroom and Chickpea Stew with Roasted Red Pepper Coulis

I often serve this delicious stew to non-vegetarians who scrape the bowl. Topped with the luscious coulis, it is quite divine. Add a green salad or steamed asparagus, in season.

Makes 6 servings

Can Be Halved
(see Tips, below)

Tips

If you are halving this recipe, be sure to use a small (1½ to 3½ quart) slow cooker.

For slightly more exotic flavor, substitute 1 bulb fennel, trimmed, cored and thinly sliced on the vertical for the celery.

Nutrients Per Serving

Calories	239
Protein	10.6 g
Carbohydrates	36.6 g
Fat (Total)	7.2 g
Saturated Fat	1.0 g
Monounsaturated Fat	4.8 g
Polyunsaturated Fat	1.0 g
Dietary Fiber	9.4 g
Sodium	376 mg
Cholesterol	0 mg

EXCELLENT SOURCE OF vitamins A, C, and K, folate, potassium and iron.
GOOD SOURCE OF vitamin B$_6$, phosphorus, magnesium and zinc.
SOURCE OF calcium.
CONTAINS a very high amount of dietary fiber.

- **Medium to large (3½ to 5 quart) slow cooker**
- **Food processor**

1 tbsp	olive oil	15 mL
2	onions, finely chopped	2
2	carrots, peeled and diced	2
4	stalks celery, thinly sliced	4
4	cloves garlic, minced	4
1 tbsp	ground cumin (see Tips, page 270)	15 mL
1 tsp	ground turmeric	5 mL
½ tsp	each salt and cracked black peppercorns	2 mL
8 oz	cremini mushrooms, thinly sliced	250 g
1	can (28 oz/796 mL) no-salt added diced tomatoes, including juice	1
2 cups	cooked chickpeas (see Basic Beans, page 284)	500 mL

Roasted Red Pepper Coulis

2	roasted red bell peppers	2
3	oil-packed sun-dried tomatoes, drained and chopped	3
2 tbsp	extra virgin olive oil	30 mL
1 tbsp	balsamic vinegar	15 mL
10	fresh basil leaves	10

1. In a skillet, heat oil over medium heat. Add onions, carrots and celery and cook, stirring, until vegetables are tender, about 7 minutes. Add garlic, cumin, turmeric, salt and peppercorns and cook, stirring, for 1 minute. Add mushrooms and toss until coated. Add tomatoes with juice and bring to a boil. Transfer to slow cooker stoneware.
2. Add chickpeas and stir well. Cover and cook on Low for 6 hours or on High for 3 hours, until hot and bubbly.
3. *Roasted Red Pepper Coulis:* In food processor fitted with the metal blade, combine roasted peppers, sun-dried tomatoes, oil, vinegar, and basil. Process until smooth. Ladle stew into bowls and top with coulis.

Make Ahead

This dish can be partially prepared before it is cooked. Complete Step 1. Cover and refrigerate overnight or for up to 2 days. When you're ready to cook, continue with Steps 2 and 3 .

Mindful Morsels

A serving of this stew is an excellent source of potassium, about half of which is provided by the chickpeas and tomatoes. However, most of the remainder is provided by the onions, carrots, celery and mushrooms, reinforcing the message that consuming lots of vegetables ensures an adequate supply of this nutrient.

Natural Wonders

Combining Fiber-Rich Foods to Lower Cholesterol

If you're watching your blood cholesterol levels, enjoy dishes that contain a variety of high-fiber and cholesterol-lowering foods. One Canadian study shows that combining fiber-rich foods may boost their individual effect. The study showed that a high-fiber diet combined with other foods known to have cholesterol-lowering properties, such as tofu, can control blood cholesterol levels as effectively as drugs.

Researchers tested a diet that included vegetables such as okra and eggplant, soy protein, legumes, nuts and plant sterol-enriched margarine. It was more than three times as effective in lowering cholesterol as a diet low in saturated fat, a traditional approach. Moreover, it was almost as effective as a low (saturated) fat diet combined with a cholesterol-lowering drug, called a statin. It is well documented that statins may have unpleasant side effects, ranging from nausea to type-2 diabetes and, in rare and unusual circumstances, serious health conditions such as extreme muscle damage. A 2013 study published online in *JAMA Ophthalmology* found that people who used statins for an average of two years increased their risk of developing cataracts by 9 to 27%.

Although these might be acceptable risks if you were at high risk for heart disease, the assumption that high levels of LDL ("bad") cholesterol are linked with atherosclerosis and heart disease in people with no history of heart disease has been questioned for many years. Most compelling, about 75% of people who have heart attacks have normal cholesterol levels. A 2013 *New York Times* article on Fred Kummerow, the scientist who first identified the problems with trans fats, highlighted his recent research, which links heart disease with the process of oxidation, rather than elevated LDL. Another article in the fall 2005 issue of the *Journal of American Physicians and Surgeons* made a case against the link between elevated LDL on heart disease, suggesting that oxidized LDL is far more likely to be a factor and that "a person's antioxidant status is a far more important determinant than LDL levels." Citing two studies published in January 2005 in the *New England Journal of Medicine*, the author reinforced the connection between inflammation and heart disease, and concluded that any success statins have demonstrated in lowering the risk of heart disease is linked to their anti-inflammatory effect rather than their ability to lower lipids. Many plant foods are anti-inflammatory and a diet of specific high-fiber foods now has a proven track record in lowering cholesterol. In my books, a dietary approach to managing cholesterol has obvious benefits over drug therapy.

New Age Succotash

I call this dish "new age" because it uses edamame, or soybeans, instead of traditional lima beans. I've also bumped up the flavor with paprika, and finished with a smattering of mouthwatering roasted red peppers. I like to serve this with steamed asparagus, in season.

Makes 8 servings

Can Be Halved
(see Tips, below)

Tips

If you are halving this recipe, be sure to use a small (1½ to 3½ quart) slow cooker.

Make sure your edamame are organically grown. Most of the soybeans grown in North America are genetically modified.

Nutrients Per Serving

Calories	207
Protein	10.7 g
Carbohydrates	33.5 g
Fat (Total)	5.7 g
Saturated Fat	0.8 g
Monounsaturated Fat	2.2 g
Polyunsaturated Fat	1.9 g
Dietary Fiber	7.6 g
Sodium	267 mg
Cholesterol	0 mg

EXCELLENT SOURCE OF vitamins A, C and K, folate and potassium.
GOOD SOURCE OF vitamin B$_6$, magnesium, phosphorus, iron and zinc.
SOURCE OF calcium.
CONTAINS a very high amount of dietary fiber.

- **Medium to large (3½ to 5 quart) slow cooker**

1 tbsp	olive oil	15 mL
2	onions, finely chopped	2
4	stalks celery, diced	4
2	carrots, peeled and diced	2
4	cloves garlic, minced	4
1	sprig fresh rosemary or 2 tsp (10 mL) dried rosemary leaves, crumbled	1
½ tsp	salt	2 mL
½ tsp	cracked black peppercorns	2 mL
1	can (28 oz/796 mL) no-salt-added tomatoes, including juice, coarsely chopped	1
1½ cups	vegetable stock	375 mL
4 cups	frozen shelled edamame	1 L
2 tsp	paprika, dissolved in 2 tbsp (30 mL) water	10 mL
4 cups	corn kernels, thawed if frozen	1 L
2	roasted red bell peppers, diced	2
½ cup	finely chopped parsley leaves	125 mL

1. In a skillet, heat oil over medium heat. Add onions, celery and carrots and cook, stirring, until softened, about 7 minutes. Add garlic, rosemary, salt and peppercorns and cook, stirring, for 1 minute. Stir in tomatoes with juice and vegetable stock and bring to a boil. Transfer to slow cooker stoneware.

2. Add edamame and stir well. Cover and cook on Low for 8 hours or on High for 4 hours, until mixture is hot and bubbly. Stir in paprika solution. Add corn, roasted red peppers and parsley and stir well. Cover and cook on High for 15 minutes, until corn is tender and mixture is heated through.

Variation

Spicy Succotash: For a livelier dish, stir in 1 can (4.5 oz/ 127 mL) mild green chiles along with the red peppers.

more information on page 250

Mindful Morsels

A serving of this succotash provides over 100% of the DV for both vitamin A and vitamin K.

Natural Wonders

Organic Soybeans

If you follow nutrition news, you've been hearing a lot about soy. One day it's being touted as a panacea for almost all that ails us, the next we're being told to avoid it at all costs. What are confused consumers to do?

In general terms, the concerns around soy focus on a couple of issues. First, most of the soybeans produced in North America are grown from genetically modified seeds. How soy products are made is also problematic; for starters, many contain worrisome additives and, unless it is cold-pressed, soy oil is highly processed and probably contains trans fats.

Soy supplements versus whole soy foods is another concern. Evidence suggests that taking isoflavones (a phytochemical contained in soy) in supplement form may have a negative effect on hormone-dependent breast cancer, and there is speculation that soy itself may contain compounds that encourage existing breast cancers to grow. Soy contains phytoestrogens, which some believe encourage tumor growth in women with estrogen-sensitive breast cancer. However, these substances are extremely weak and their effect is likely mitigated when consumed in a whole food. In fact, most large studies have found that regular consumption of soy is linked with reduced rates of breast cancer, and in 2012 the American Cancer Society came out on the side of consuming soy. Their nutrition guidelines for cancer survivors state that eating soy foods such as tofu, miso and soy milk may lower the risk of breast and some other cancers. However, many of the claims related to soy's cardiovascular benefits and its supposed ability to ease women's transition to menopause and reduce the risk of osteoporosis have not been proven.

One thing there is little doubt about is that soybeans themselves are extremely nutritious. Soybeans provide a complete protein and are an excellent source of potassium, calcium, iron, folate and niacin, a good source of thiamine and a source of riboflavin and zinc. They are low in saturated fat, cholesterol-free, and a source of omega-3 fatty acids (see pages 169 and 219 for more on omega-3 fatty acids). As noted, most of the soybeans grown in North America have been genetically modified, so be sure to look for those that are organically grown. If using soy products make sure they have been made from organic soybeans.

Vegetable Chili

Here's a chili that is loaded with flavor and nutrients. Garnish with any combination of roasted red peppers, diced avocado, finely chopped red onions and cilantro, or a good dollop of Avocado Topping (see page 148). This is a generous serving (2 cups/500 mL) so it is a meal in itself. If you feel like extending the range of nutrients, add a simple green salad for a great weekday meal.

Makes 6 servings

Can Be Halved
(see Tips, page 254)

Tips

If you don't have leeks, substitute 2 yellow onions, finely chopped.

If you prefer a more peppery chili use up to 1 tsp (5 mL) of cracked black peppercorns in this recipe.

You can substitute your favorite chili powder blend for the ancho or New Mexico chili powder. Just check to make sure it is gluten-free.

Nutrients Per Serving

Calories	254
Protein	11.3 g
Carbohydrates	49.2 g
Fat (Total)	3.8 g
Saturated Fat	0.5 g
Monounsaturated Fat	2.0 g
Polyunsaturated Fat	1.0 g
Dietary Fiber	10.9 g
Sodium	94 mg
Cholesterol	0 mg

EXCELLENT SOURCE OF vitamins A, B$_6$, C and K, folate, potassium and iron.
GOOD SOURCE OF calcium, phosphorus, magnesium and zinc.
CONTAINS a very high amount of dietary fiber.

- **Large (approx. 5 quart) slow cooker**

1 tbsp	olive oil	15 mL
2	large leeks, white and green parts only, cleaned and thinly sliced (see Tips, left)	2
4	stalks celery, diced	4
4	carrots, peeled and diced	4
4	cloves garlic, minced	4
2 tsp	dried oregano, crumbled	10 mL
½ tsp	cracked black peppercorns (see Tips, left)	2 mL
1 tbsp	ground cumin (see Tips, page 270)	15 mL
1	can (28 oz/796 mL) no-salt added tomatoes, including juice, coarsely chopped	1
2 cups	cooked red kidney or pinto beans (see Basic Beans, page 284)	500 mL
1 tbsp	ancho or New Mexico chili powder, dissolved in 2 tbsp (30 mL) freshly squeezed lemon juice (see Tips, left)	15 mL
2 cups	corn kernels	500 mL
2	green bell peppers, diced	2
1	jalapeño or chipotle pepper in adobo sauce, diced	1
	Sour cream, optional	

1. In a skillet, heat oil over medium heat. Add leeks, celery and carrots and cook, stirring, until carrots are softened, about 7 minutes. Add garlic, oregano, peppercorns and cumin and cook, stirring, for 1 minute. Add tomatoes with juice and bring to a boil.

2. Transfer to stoneware. Stir in beans. Cover and cook on Low for 6 hours or on High for 3 hours, until vegetables are tender.

3. Meanwhile, add chili powder solution to stoneware and stir well. Add corn, bell peppers and jalapeño and stir well. Cover and cook on High for 20 to 30 minutes, until peppers are tender. Ladle chili into bowls. Top with sour cream, if using.

more information on page 253

Vegetable Chili

Make Ahead

Complete Step 1. Cover and refrigerate for up to 2 days. When you're ready to cook, complete the recipe.

Mindful Morsels

Although soaking beans before cooking them helps to alleviate the gas problem by leaching out the fermentable sugars, flatulence may still be an undesirable side effect — a result of their high fiber content. Fortunately there are techniques for mitigating this problem. One way to reduce abdominal discomfort is to introduce legumes into your diet gradually, eating more easily digested varieties such as split peas and lentils and increasing the quantities slowly so your body can adapt over time. You should also avoid eating legumes along with other gas-producing vegetables such as cabbage, cauliflower, broccoli and Brussels sprouts.

Indian cooks, who have been making dal for centuries, know a thing or two about limiting the potential consequences of eating legumes. They often season their lentils with spices that aid digestion, such as gingerroot or asafetida. In Mexico, where beans are a dietary staple, epazote, a pungent and bitter-tasting herb, is thought to do the trick. Another technique is to add a pinch of baking soda to the water in which the dried legumes are soaked. Finally, a digestive enzyme such as Beano can help to break down the fiber, making it easier to digest.

Natural Wonders

Soaking Legumes

When cooking legumes from scratch, it is crucial to soak them thoroughly. While legumes are a wonderful source of nutrition, some (kidney, navy and black beans are the worst offenders) are likely to contain sugars known as oligosaccharides, which are difficult to digest. A good soak eliminates most of these problematic substances (see Mindful Morsels, above).

However, like whole grains, legumes may also contain "anti-nutrients," substances such as phytates, which prevent your body from absorbing some of the valuable nutrients they contain. As a result, I recommend "souring" legumes before cooking them, by soaking them overnight or for up to 2 days in a cider vinegar solution (about 1 tbsp/15 mL apple cider vinegar to 4 cups/1 L warm water). Studies show that this eliminates or significantly reduces the phytates in these foods. Another option is to use sprouted legumes, which are available in natural food stores and well-stocked supermarkets, or to sprout them yourself.

Squash and Black Bean Chili

Flavored with cumin and chili powder, with a hint of cinnamon, this luscious chili makes a fabulous weeknight meal. This is a generous serving. Just add a tossed green salad, relax and enjoy.

Makes 6 servings

Can Be Halved
(see Tips, below)

Tips

If you are halving this recipe, be sure to use a small (1½ to 3½ quart) slow cooker.

Try substituting coconut oil for the olive oil. It adds a hint of coconut flavor to this chili that is quite appealing.

Check the label to make sure your chili powder does not contain gluten.

Add the chipotle pepper if you like heat and a bit of smoke.

Nutrients Per Serving

Calories	227
Protein	10.2 g
Carbohydrates	44.1 g
Fat (Total)	3.1 g
Saturated Fat	0.4 g
Monounsaturated Fat	1.8 g
Polyunsaturated Fat	0.6 g
Dietary Fiber	9.9 g
Sodium	434 mg
Cholesterol	0 mg

EXCELLENT SOURCE OF vitamins A and C, folate, magnesium, potassium and iron.
GOOD SOURCE OF vitamins B_6 and K, calcium and phosphorus.
SOURCE OF zinc.
CONTAINS a very high amount of dietary fiber.

• **Medium to large (3½ to 5 quart) slow cooker**

1 tbsp	olive oil	15 mL
2	onions, finely chopped	2
4	cloves garlic, minced	4
1 tsp	dried oregano	5 mL
1 tsp	ground cumin (see Tips, page 270)	5 mL
½ tsp	salt	2 mL
1	piece (3 inches/7.5 cm) cinnamon stick	1
1	can (28 oz/796 mL) no-salt added tomatoes, including juice, coarsely chopped	1
2 cups	cooked black beans	500 mL
4 cups	cubed (1 inch/2.5 cm) peeled butternut squash	1 L
2 tsp	chili powder (see Tips, left)	10 mL
2	green bell peppers, diced	2
1	can (4.5 oz/127 mL) chopped mild green chiles	1
1	finely chopped chipotle pepper in adobo sauce, optional	1
	Finely chopped fresh cilantro leaves	

1. In a skillet, heat oil over medium heat. Add onions to pan and cook, stirring, until softened, about 3 minutes. Add garlic, oregano, cumin, salt and cinnamon stick and cook, stirring, for 1 minute. Add tomatoes with juice and bring to a boil. Transfer to slow cooker stoneware. Add beans and squash and stir well.

2. Cover and cook on Low for 6 hours or on High for 3 hours, until squash is tender.

3. Scoop a little of the cooking liquid into a small bowl and add the chili powder. Stir until dissolved. Add to stoneware along with bell peppers, chiles and chipotle pepper, if using. Cover and cook on High for 20 minutes, until bell pepper is tender. Discard cinnamon stick. When ready to serve, ladle into bowls and garnish with cilantro.

Make Ahead

Complete Step 1. Cover and refrigerate overnight or for up to 2 days. When you're ready to cook, complete the recipe.

Variation

Squash and Black Bean Chili con Carne: Add 1 lb (500 g) lean ground beef along with the onions. Cook, stirring, until meat is no longer pink, about 6 minutes. Drain off fat and continue with Step 2.

Mindful Morsels

The beans in this recipe contain non-heme iron, the kind obtained from vegetarian sources. It is not as effectively absorbed by the body as heme iron (which is found in meat). Consume non-heme iron with vitamin C, such as that provided by the tomatoes and peppers in this recipe, to improve absorption.

Natural Wonders

Phytonutrients and Cancer

The vegetables in these recipes contain a wide range of phytonutrients — carotenoids, isoflavones and lycopene, among others — which may help your body fight certain types of cancer. Studies show that people who regularly consume fruits and vegetables may reduce their risk of cancers of the esophagus, stomach, colon, lung and ovaries, among others. And there is evidence to suggest that specific vegetables help to protect against different types of cancer. For instance, the lycopene in tomatoes appears to reduce the risk of prostate cancer and/or its progression. Carrots and dark leafy green vegetables have been linked with lower rates of lung cancer, and cruciferous vegetables, such as broccoli, cabbage and cauliflower, appear to reduce the risk of colon cancer.

Many spices and herbs have potent anticarcinogenic properties, as well. So far, all the studies have been done in laboratories, but spices and herbs as diverse as basil, bay leaf, ginger, juniper berries, lemongrass, marjoram, mint, tamarind, vanilla and turmeric, to name just a few, have shown potential as cancer fighters and preventatives. More research is needed before we fully understand the relationship between cancer and the consumption of fruits, vegetables, spices and herbs, but in the meantime, it's advisable to eat the recommended 7 to 10 servings a day and to spice them up as much as makes you happy.

Smoky Butternut Hominy Chili

Adding chipotle peppers to this chile gives it an enticing smoky flavor. Add the smoked paprika only if you really like the flavor of smoke. This makes a delicious meal and, with the combination of hominy (a whole grain) and beans, provides a complete protein. You might want to add a green salad to complete the meal.

Makes 6 to 8 servings

Can Be Halved
(see Tips, below)

Tips

If you are halving this recipe, be sure to use a small (1½ to 3 quart) slow cooker.

Chipotle chiles are pretty powerful, so unless you're a heat seeker, err on the side on caution and use only one. Include a bit of the sauce, which adds flavor in addition to heat.

Nutrients Per Serving

Calories	180
Protein	6.4 g
Carbohydrates	32.1 g
Fat (Total)	4.2 g
Saturated Fat	0.6 g
Monounsaturated Fat	2.7 g
Polyunsaturated Fat	0.6 g
Dietary Fiber	7.0 g
Sodium	249 mg
Cholesterol	0 mg

EXCELLENT SOURCE OF vitamin A, folate and potassium.

GOOD SOURCE OF vitamins C and K, magnesium and iron.

SOURCE OF vitamin B$_6$, calcium, phosphorus and zinc.

CONTAINS a very high amount of dietary fiber.

- **Large (approx 5 quart) slow cooker**

2 tbsp	olive oil	30 mL
2	onions, finely chopped	2
4	stalks celery, diced	4
2	carrots, peeled and diced	2
6	cloves garlic, minced	6
1 tbsp	ground cumin (see Tips, page 270)	15 mL
1 tbsp	dried oregano	15 mL
1 tsp	ground allspice	5 mL
½ tsp	salt	2 mL
½ tsp	cracked black peppercorns	2 mL
1	piece (2 inches/5 cm) cinnamon stick	1
1	can (28 oz/ 796 mL) no-salt-added tomatoes, including juice, coarsely chopped	1
3 cups	cubed (1 inch/2.5 cm) peeled butternut squash	750 mL
2 cups	cooked black beans	500 mL
1	can (15 oz/425 g) hominy, drained and rinsed (see Mindful Morsels, right)	1
1 to 2	chipotle chiles in adobo sauce, minced (see Tips, left)	1 to 2
	Smoked paprika, optional	

1. In a skillet, heat oil over medium heat. Add onions, celery and carrots and cook, stirring, until softened, about 7 minutes. Add garlic, cumin, oregano, allspice, salt, peppercorns and cinnamon stick and cook, stirring, for 1 minute. Stir in tomatoes with juice and bring to a boil, breaking up with a spoon. Remove from heat.

2. In slow cooker stoneware, combine squash, beans and hominy. Add tomato mixture and stir well. Cover and cook on Low for 6 hours or on High for 3 hours, until squash is tender. Stir in chile(s) and smoked paprika to taste, if using. Cover and cook on High for 10 minutes to meld flavors.

Make Ahead

Complete Step 1. Cover and refrigerate mixture for up to 2 days. When you're ready to cook, complete the recipe.

Natural Wonders

Complex Carbohydrates

Virtually all of the carbohydrates in this recipe are contributed by the vegetables (onions, squash and tomatoes) and the beans and the hominy, all of which are healthy complex carbohydrates. Most nutritionists agree that complex carbohydrates, such as legumes and whole grains, should be a dietary staple of healthy eating. North Americans get about half their calories from carbohydrates. The problem is, about half those carb calories come from refined foods, such as white bread, fast food snacks and baked goods. Research links a steady diet of refined carbs with an increase in diabetes and cardiovascular disease, among other illnesses.

On the other hand, a diet rich in good carbs, such as fruits, vegetables and whole grains, can significantly benefit your health. For instance, participants in the Harvard Nurses' Study who ate three servings of whole grains, or more, a day reduced their risk of heart attack by 35%. And a 2008 study published in the *Journal of the American College of Nutrition* concluded that people who ate the most beans were 22% less likely to be obese. So it's not surprising that the Harvard School of Public Health recommends "whenever possible, replace highly processed grains, cereals and sugars with minimally processed whole-grain products." As Dr. Walter Willet writes in his book *Eat, Drink and Be Healthy*, along with beans, these are the kinds of carbohydrates that should form the keystones of a healthy diet.

Indian Peas and Beans

Simple, yet delicious, this Indian-inspired dish makes a great weeknight dinner, served with gluten-free flatbread, such as Yogurt Flatbread (page 62) and a cucumber salad. It also makes a nice addition to a multi-dish Indian meal.

Makes 6 servings

Can Be Halved
(see Tip, page 266)

Tips

Can sizes vary. If your supermarket carries 19-oz (540 mL) cans of diced tomatoes with no salt added, by all means substitute for the 14 oz (398 mL) called for in the recipe.

I always have a bag of frozen green beans in the freezer. They contain valuable nutrients: vitamins K and C, a selection of the B vitamins, including folate, and the minerals manganese, iron and magnesium. They also contain fiber.

Nutrients Per Serving

Calories	190
Protein	10.3 g
Carbohydrates	32.7 g
Fat (Total)	3.2 g
Saturated Fat	0.4 g
Monounsaturated Fat	2.0 g
Polyunsaturated Fat	0.5 g
Dietary Fiber	6.0 g
Sodium	21 mg
Cholesterol	0 mg

EXCELLENT SOURCE OF folate and potassium.

GOOD SOURCE OF vitamin K, magnesium and iron.

SOURCE OF vitamins A, C and B_6, calcium, phosphorus and zinc.

CONTAINS a very high amount of dietary fiber.

- **Medium to large (3½ to 5 quart) slow cooker**

1 cup	yellow split peas, rinsed	250 mL
1 tbsp	cumin seeds	15 mL
2 tsp	coriander seeds	10 mL
1 tbsp	olive oil or extra virgin coconut oil	15 mL
2	onions, finely chopped	2
4	cloves garlic, minced	4
1 tbsp	minced gingerroot	15 mL
1 tsp	ground turmeric	5 mL
1 tsp	cracked black peppercorns	5 mL
2	bay leaves	2
1	can (14 oz/398 mL) no-salt-added diced tomatoes, including juice (see Tips, left)	1
2 cups	vegetable stock	500 mL
2 cups	frozen sliced green beans	500 mL
¼ tsp	cayenne, dissolved in 1 tbsp (15 mL) freshly squeezed lemon juice	1 mL
1 cup	coconut milk, optional	250 mL
½ cup	finely chopped cilantro leaves	125 mL

1. In a large saucepan, combine peas with 6 cups (1.5 L) cold water. Bring to a boil and boil rapidly for 3 minutes. Remove from heat and set aside for 1 hour. Rinse thoroughly under cold water, drain and set aside.

2. In a large dry skillet over medium heat, toast cumin and coriander seeds, stirring, until fragrant and cumin seeds just begin to brown, about 3 minutes. Immediately transfer to a mortar or a spice grinder and grind. Set aside.

3. In same skillet, heat oil over medium heat. Add onions and cook, stirring, until softened, about 3 minutes. Add garlic, ginger, turmeric, peppercorns, bay leaves and reserved cumin and coriander and cook, stirring, for 1 minute. Add tomatoes with juice and reserved split peas and bring to a boil. Transfer to slow cooker stoneware.

Make Ahead

This dish can be partially prepared before it is cooked. Complete Steps 1 through 3. Cover and refrigerate overnight or for up to 2 days. When you're ready to cook, continue with Step 4.

4. Add vegetable stock and green beans and stir well. Cover and cook on Low for 8 hours or on High for 4 hours, until peas are tender. Stir in cayenne solution and coconut milk, if using. Add cilantro and stir well. Cover and cook on High for 20 minutes, until heated through. Discard bay leaves.

Mindful Morsels

For centuries, many of the spices and herbs used to season Indian food, such as curries, have been thought to have antibacterial qualities. As we learn more about the phytonutrients in food, it seems that many actually do have those qualities.

Natural Wonders

Turmeric

In culinary terms, turmeric, which gives curry powder blends their vibrant orangey-yellow color, and is often described as "poor man's saffron," is a modest spice. It has a slightly peppery flavor, is a tad bitter, and works quietly in the background of a dish, adding subtle hints of earthiness. But in terms of its nutraceutical ability turmeric packs a real wallop. Its anti-inflammatory abilities have been long recognized. Now as we learn more about phytonutrients, turmeric has emerged as an antioxidant superstar.

The magic ingredient in turmeric is curcumin, which numerous studies show may be as effective as some drugs in reducing inflammation and fighting the progression of a wide range of cancers — breast, colon, prostate and skin cancer, among others.

Curcumin has also been identified as having the potential to prevent and possibly slow the progression of Alzheimer's disease. Not only does it appear to guard against age-related memory decline and mental acuity, but studies also suggest that this powerful antioxidant may be able to break up plaque and inhibit the formation of destructive protein fragments in the brain, a process that precedes Alzheimer's disease. So far, it's only been tested on mice but the Alzheimer's Disease Research Center at UCLA is beginning human trials.

Curcumin's strong anti-inflammatory power also means it has tremendous potential in treating arthritis. In fact, at least one study has demonstrated its potential ability to ease knee pain associated with arthritis just as well as ibuprofen does. Another study concluded it was as effective as a powerful NSAID in easing the arthritis symptoms associated with rheumatoid arthritis. Several studies have indicated that turmeric and curcumin may also be an effective treatment for inflammatory bowel diseases, such as Crohn's disease and ulcerative colitis.

Red Beans and Greens

Few meals could be more healthful than this delicious combination of hot leafy greens over flavorful beans. I like to make this with collard greens but other dark leafy greens such as kale work well, too. The smoked paprika makes the dish more robust but it isn't essential.

Makes 6 to 8 servings

Can Be Halved
(see Tip, page 266)

Tip

The smoked paprika adds a nice but of smoky flavor to this dish. Use hot (for some added spice) or sweet to suit your taste. To make sure it is smoothly incorporated into the beans, scoop about 2 tbsp (30 mL) of the bean cooking liquid into a small bowl and stir in the paprika until smooth, then stir the mixture back into the beans.

Nutrients Per Serving

Calories	218
Protein	13.3 g
Carbohydrates	37.8 g
Fat (Total)	2.7 g
Saturated Fat	0.4 g
Monounsaturated Fat	1.3 g
Polyunsaturated Fat	0.7 g
Dietary Fiber	11.8 g
Sodium	172 mg
Cholesterol	0 mg

EXCELLENT SOURCE OF vitamins A and K, folate, magnesium, potassium and iron.
GOOD SOURCE OF vitamins C and B$_6$, calcium, phosphorus and zinc.
CONTAINS a very high amount of dietary fiber.

• **Medium to large (3½ to 5 quart) slow cooker**

2 cups	dried kidney beans	500 mL
1 tbsp	olive oil	15 mL
2	large onions, finely chopped	2
2	stalks celery, finely chopped	2
4	cloves garlic, minced	4
1 tsp	dried oregano	5 mL
1 tsp	dried thyme	5 mL
½ tsp	salt	2 mL
½ tsp	cracked black peppercorns	2 mL
¼ tsp	ground allspice or 6 whole allspice, tied in a piece of cheesecloth	1 mL
2	bay leaves	2
4 cups	vegetable stock	1 L
1 tsp	smoked paprika (optional)	5 mL

Greens

2 lbs	greens, thoroughly washed, stems removed and chopped	1 kg
	Butter or butter substitute	
1 tbsp	balsamic vinegar	15 mL
	Salt and freshly ground black pepper	

1. Soak beans according to either method in Basic Beans (see page 284). Drain and rinse and set aside.

2. In a skillet, heat oil over medium heat. Add onions and celery and cook, stirring, until softened, about 5 minutes. Add garlic, oregano, thyme, salt, peppercorns, allspice and bay leaves and cook, stirring for 1 minute. Transfer to slow cooker stoneware. Add beans and vegetable stock.

3. Cover and cook on Low for 8 to 10 hours or on High for 4 to 5 hours, until beans are tender. Stir in smoked paprika, if using.

4. *Greens:* Steam greens until tender, about 10 minutes for collards. Toss with butter or butter substitute and balsamic vinegar. Season with salt and pepper to taste. Add to beans and stir to combine. Serve immediately.

more information on page 262

Make Ahead

Complete Steps 1 and 2. Cover and refrigerate overnight. The next day, continue cooking as directed.

Mindful Morsels

According to the USDA, dried red beans (the smaller the better) have one of the highest antioxidant capacities of any food. Red beans contain molybdenum, an essential trace element that enhances your body's enzymatic activity.

Natural Wonders

Glycemic Index

The Glycemic Index (GI) is a measure of how quickly a food is broken down and digested and, in turn, how much that food will raise blood sugar levels. Foods that contain carbohydrate have the greatest impact on blood sugar, followed by protein-rich foods. Fat does not affect blood sugar levels. Foods with a high GI release glucose quickly, prompting a strong insulin response and providing short-lived bursts of energy. Those that are low on the GI release glucose more slowly, providing sustained energy.

The GI of a food can be influenced by many factors. In experimental models a food's GI has been modified by what it is eaten with. This includes fat, protein, fiber, acids, such as vinegar or lemon juice, the fluids consumed with the food, the sodium content and the cooking method. For example, the GI of a food is lowered when the food is eaten as part of a mixed meal. The GI of a bagel is lower when it is eaten with peanut butter (fat, fiber and protein) and/or a piece of fruit (fiber), or an egg (fat and protein).

Another determinant of a food's glycemic rating may be the degree to which its carbohydrates have been processed. For instance, the more finely ground a grain, the higher its glycemic rating. The GI rating of foods can be used as a dieting tool because foods that are low on the glycemic index tend to keep you from feeling hungry longer.

The GI alone cannot be relied on for choosing nutritious foods. Some foods like watermelon have a high GI but don't provide a lot of carbohydrate in a typical serving so their impact on blood sugar isn't significant. On the other hand, "less healthy" foods can have a lower GI, which, may seem positive. However, ice cream (GI 38), chocolate bars (GI 51) and regular soft drinks (GI 63), have low to moderate GI values but tend not to be nutrient dense.

Ultimately, lower GI diets reflect better diet quality. They are likely based on whole fruits, vegetables, whole grains, nuts and seeds, pulses, meats, fish, poultry and dairy foods. Whether this dietary pattern is based on governmental guidelines or specific dietary guidelines such as Mediterranean or Paleo, nutrient-dense, whole foods predominate in low GI diets. Their ability to lower the risk of certain diseases may be due to the lower carbohydrate and sugar content, lower blood glucose and insulin levels following meals, or their greater phytonutrient and micronutrient (vitamins and minerals) content.

Research supports this. Dietary patterns based on lower-GI, nutrient-dense foods, such as the ones in theses recipes are associated with healthier body weights, lower rates of many cancers including breast, prostate, colorectal and pancreatic cancer, lower rates of cardiovascular disease and lower postprandial blood glucose as well as insulin levels.

Poached Eggs on Spicy Lentils

This delicious combination is a great cold-weather dish. Add the chiles if you prefer a little spice and accompany with warm gluten-free Indian bread, such as Yogurt Flatbread (page 62), and hot white rice. The Egg and Lentil Curry (see Variation, below) is a great dish for a buffet table or as part of an Indian-themed meal.

Makes 6 servings

Can Be Halved
(see Tip, page 266)

Tip

To poach eggs: In a deep skillet, bring about 2 inches (5 cm) lightly salted water to a boil over medium heat. Reduce heat to low. Break eggs into a measuring cup and, holding the cup close to the surface of the water, slip the eggs into the pan. Cook until whites are set and centers are still soft, 3 to 4 minutes. Remove with a slotted spoon.

Nutrients Per Serving

Calories	323
Protein	16.8 g
Carbohydrates	31.6 g
Fat (Total)	15.8 g
Saturated Fat	9.0 g
Monounsaturated Fat	4.3 g
Polyunsaturated Fat	1.2 g
Dietary Fiber	6.4 g
Sodium	168 mg
Cholesterol	182 mg

EXCELLENT SOURCE OF vitamin K, folate, phosphorus, potassium and iron.

GOOD SOURCE OF vitamins A, B_6 and B_{12}, magnesium and zinc.

SOURCE OF vitamin C and calcium.

CONTAINS a very high amount of dietary fiber.

• **Medium (approx. 4 quart) slow cooker**

1 tbsp	olive oil	15 mL
2	onions, finely chopped	2
1 tbsp	minced garlic	15 mL
1 tbsp	minced gingerroot	15 mL
1 tsp	ground coriander	5 mL
1 tsp	ground cumin	5 mL
1 tsp	cracked black peppercorns	5 mL
1 cup	red lentils, rinsed	250 mL
1	can (28 oz/796 mL) no-salt-added tomatoes with juice, coarsely chopped	1
2 cups	vegetable stock	500 mL
1 cup	coconut milk	250 mL
	Salt	
1	long green chile pepper or 2 Thai bird's-eye chiles, finely chopped, optional	1
6	eggs	6
¼ cup	finely chopped parsley leaves	60 mL

1. In a large skillet, heat oil over medium heat. Add onions and cook, stirring, until softened, about 3 minutes. Add garlic, ginger, coriander, cumin and peppercorns and cook, stirring, for 1 minute. Add lentils, tomatoes with juice and vegetable stock and bring to a boil. Transfer to slow cooker stoneware.

2. Cover and cook on Low for 6 hours or on High for 4 hours, until lentils are tender and mixture is bubbly. Stir in coconut milk, salt, to taste, and chile pepper, if using. Cover and cook for 20 to 30 minutes until heated through.

3. When ready to serve, ladle into soup bowls and top each serving with a poached egg (see Tip, left). Garnish with parsley.

Variation

Egg and Lentil Curry: Substitute 4 to 6 hard-cooked eggs for the poached. Peel them and cut into halves. Ladle the curry into a serving dish, arrange the eggs on top and garnish.

more information on page 265

Poached Eggs on Spicy Lentils

Natural Wonders

Phytonutrients

Legumes, along with all other plant foods, provide a variety of phytonutrients, such as antioxidants, which are beneficial compounds in plant foods. Unlike vitamins and minerals, phytonutrients are not considered essential for health, but they do help to make the difference between simply surviving and thriving.

Phytonutrients help to promote health and play an important role in reducing the risk for chronic disease. For example, in one 2011 study that investigated the antioxidant capacity of specific fruits, vegetables and legumes, researchers found not only that legumes are antioxidant-rich but also that by combining a legume with a fruit, for instance, the total antioxidant capacity of both foods was increased. In other words, pairing the foods created synergy in their antioxidant capacity. This emphasizes the importance of eating a variety of plant foods, not only at each meal but also throughout the day, to ensure that you get the most out of this teamwork.

Gingery Red Lentils with Spinach and Coconut

I love this recipe! The red lentils and shredded potato melt into the sauce, creating a luscious texture and the flavors are so appealing, even non-vegetarians will lap it up. It makes a great main course; this makes a generous serving, so you won't need to add much if you are using it as a main course. It's perfect served over brown rice. It also makes a beautiful substitute for dal as part of an Indian meal, where you can extend the number of servings to at least 12.

Makes 6 servings

Can Be Halved
(see Tips, below)

Tip

If you are halving this recipe, be sure to use a small (1½ to 3 quart) slow cooker.

Make Ahead

Complete Step 1. When you're ready to cook, complete the recipe.

Nutrients Per Serving

Calories	279
Protein	12.7 g
Carbohydrates	36.3 g
Fat (Total)	11.2 g
Saturated Fat	7.6 g
Monounsaturated Fat	2.2 g
Polyunsaturated Fat	0.7 g
Dietary Fiber	8.2 g
Sodium	275 mg
Cholesterol	0 mg

EXCELLENT SOURCE OF vitamins A, B$_6$ and K, folate, phosphorus, magnesium, potassium and iron.
GOOD SOURCE OF zinc.
SOURCE OF vitamin C and calcium.
CONTAINS a very high amount of dietary fiber.

• **Medium to large (3½ to 5 quarts) slow cooker**

1 tbsp	olive or coconut oil	15 mL
2	onions, finely chopped	2
2	stalks celery, diced	2
2	carrots, peeled and diced	2
4	cloves garlic, minced	4
2 tbsp	minced gingerroot	30 mL
2 tsp	ground cumin	10 mL
2 tsp	ground turmeric	10 mL
½ tsp	salt	2 mL
½ tsp	cracked black peppercorns	2 mL
1 cup	red lentils, rinsed	250 mL
3 cups	vegetable stock	750 mL
1	potato, peeled and shredded	1
1 cup	coconut milk	250 mL
¼ tsp	cayenne pepper	1 mL
1 lb	fresh spinach leaves, or 1 package (10 oz/300 g) fresh or frozen spinach, thawed and drained if frozen, stems removed and coarsely chopped	500 g

1. In a skillet, heat oil over medium heat. Add onions, celery, carrots and cook, stirring, until carrots are softened, about 7 minutes. Add garlic, ginger, cumin, turmeric, salt and peppercorns and cook, stirring, for 1 minute. Add lentils and toss to coat. Add vegetable stock and bring to a boil.

2. Transfer to slow cooker stoneware. Stir in potato. Cover and cook on Low for 8 hours or High for 4 hours, until lentils are very tender and slightly puréed.

3. In a small bowl, combine 1 tbsp (15 mL) of the coconut milk and cayenne. Stir until blended. Add to stoneware along with remaining coconut milk and spinach. Cover and cook on High for 20 minutes until spinach is wilted and flavors meld. Serve immediately.

Natural Wonders

Legumes as a Source of Protein

Dried beans, peas, chickpeas and lentils provide low-fat vegetable protein, and as such are an ideal staple for vegan and vegetarian diets. However, they do not contain the entire range of essential amino acids that would allow them to be classified as a "complete" protein. Vegans and vegetarians should ensure that they also eat adequate amounts of grains and cereals, seeds and nuts in addition to legumes every day to obtain the complete range of amino acids.

For example, until recently, nutrition experts thought it was necessary to eat incomplete proteins in the same meal; the classic example is rice and beans. Rice has adequate amounts of methionine but lacks lysine, and beans have plenty of lysine but are low in methionine; eating them together would provide the essential amino acids in a similar manner as would eating a complete protein, such as an egg.

We now know, however, that whenever a food containing protein is eaten its amino acids enter a reservoir called the amino acid pool, and the body can draw on that pool, as needed, to build new proteins. As long as you eat a variety of foods throughout the day, the amino acids go in to this pool, and your body can get what it needs when it needs it. Foods with incomplete proteins include legumes, nuts and seeds and most grains, amaranth, buckwheat and quinoa being notable exceptions.

In order for the foods to complement each other, they must be consumed throughout the day, and eaten consistently, day after day to provide the full range of essential amino acids.

Spinach Dal with Millet

Dal is one of my favorite ethnic comfort foods. Usually served as one of several small dishes at an Indian meal, dal is very versatile. It also makes a delicious side to accompany grilled or roasted chicken or meat. I often enjoy it as a main course, accompanied by a tossed salad, which is what this generous serving size reflects. If you are serving this as a side dish or as part of an Indian meal, expect it to serve at least 10 people.

Makes 6 servings

Can Be Halved
(see Tips, below)

Tips

If you are halving this recipe, be sure to use a small (2 to 3½ quart) slow cooker.

If using fresh spinach, be sure to remove the stems, and if it has not been pre-washed, rinse it thoroughly in a basin of lukewarm water.

Nutrients Per Serving

Calories	318
Protein	15.3 g
Carbohydrates	57.9 g
Fat (Total)	4.2 g
Saturated Fat	0.6 g
Monounsaturated Fat	2.2 g
Polyunsaturated Fat	1.0 g
Dietary Fiber	10.4 g
Sodium	59 mg
Cholesterol	0 mg

EXCELLENT SOURCE OF vitamins A, B$_6$ and K, folate, phosphorus, magnesium, potassium and iron.
GOOD SOURCE OF vitamin C, calcium and zinc.
CONTAINS a very high amount of dietary fiber.

- **Large (approx. 5 quart) slow cooker**

1 tbsp	olive oil	15 mL
2	onions, finely chopped	2
4	cloves garlic, minced	4
1 tbsp	minced gingerroot	15 mL
1 tsp	ground turmeric	5 mL
½ tsp	cracked black peppercorns	2 mL
2	bay leaves	2
1 tbsp	ground cumin (see Tips, page 270)	15 mL
2 tsp	ground coriander	10 mL
1	can (28 oz/796 mL) no-salt added tomatoes, including juice, coarsely chopped	1
3 cups	vegetable stock	750 mL
1 cup	red lentils, rinsed	250 mL
1 cup	millet, rinsed	250 mL
¼ tsp	cayenne, dissolved in 2 tbsp (30 mL) freshly squeezed lemon juice	1 mL
	Salt, optional	
1 lb	fresh spinach, stems removed, or 1 package (10 oz/300 g) fresh or frozen spinach, thawed and drained if frozen (see Tips, left)	500 g
	Coconut milk or plain yogurt, optional	
¼ cup	finely chopped cilantro leaves	60 mL

1. In a skillet, heat oil over medium heat. Add onions and cook, stirring, until softened, about 3 minutes. Add garlic and ginger and cook, stirring, for 1 minute. Add turmeric, peppercorns, bay leaves, cumin and coriander and cook, stirring, for 1 minute. Add tomatoes with juice and bring to a boil.

2. Transfer to slow cooker stoneware. Add vegetable stock, lentils and millet and stir well. Cover and cook on Low for 6 hours or on High for 3 hours, until lentils are tender.

Make Ahead

This dish can be partially prepared before it is cooked. Complete Step 1. Cover and refrigerate overnight or for up to 2 days. When you're ready to cook, continue with Step 2.

3. Stir in cayenne solution and add salt to taste, if necessary. Add spinach, in batches, stirring after each batch until all the leaves are submerged in the liquid. Cover and cook on High for 20 minutes, until spinach is tender. Discard bay leaves. Transfer to a large serving bowl, drizzle with coconut milk, if using, and garnish with cilantro.

Mindful Morsels

A serving of this dal is an excellent source of fiber, providing 42% of the DV. The lentils provide 3.9 grams and the millet 3.1 grams of this valuable nutrient, with the tomatoes and spinach making up the remainder.

Natural Wonders

Folate

It's long been known that pregnant women with a folate deficiency are more likely to give birth prematurely or to have a baby with a low birth weight or a neural tube defect. As a result, food manufacturers have been supplementing grain products with this nutrient for many years. But new information from the Harvard Nurses' Study suggests that an adequate supply of folate has more broad-ranging effects. Consumption of folate helps to prevent high blood pressure and keeps homocysteine levels under control, protecting blood vessels from plaque. There also appears to be a link between folate intake and a reduced risk of colon cancer, especially for women with a family history of the disease. And Finnish researchers found a link between the consumption of folate and a reduced risk of depression. Folate also works with vitamin B_6 and B_{12} to improve mental acuity. At least one study showed that adequate levels of this nutrient slowed cognitive decline in older people (see Natural Wonders, page 54).

On the other hand, taking too much folate in the form of supplements has been linked with negative effects. These warnings also apply to fortified foods, such as breakfast cereals and pasta, which are a major source of this nutrient for many people. One study published in the *American Journal of Clinical Nutrition* linked taking folate supplements with an increased risk of breast cancer, and other studies have connected it with increased risk of other kinds of cancer.

As always, the safest bet is to consume your nutrients in food, not supplements. Good food sources of folate are leafy greens, legumes such as lentils, globe artichokes, broccoli, asparagus and orange juice.

Eggplant Lentil Ragoût

This is a delicious combination of flavors and textures. Just add a green salad for a satisfying meal.

Makes 6 servings

Can Be Halved
(see Tips, below)

Tips

If you are halving this recipe, be sure to use a small (1½ to 3 quart) slow cooker.

If time is short, blanch the eggplant pieces for a minute or two in heavily salted water then rinse and continue with Step 1.

For the best flavor, toast cumin seeds and grind them yourself. Place seeds in a dry skillet over medium heat and cook, stirring, until fragrant about 3 minutes. Immediately transfer to a spice grinder or mortar and grind finely.

Nutrients Per Serving

Calories	191
Protein	9.6 g
Carbohydrates	28.8 g
Fat (Total)	5.3 g
Saturated Fat	0.7 g
Monounsaturated Fat	3.6 g
Polyunsaturated Fat	0.7 g
Dietary Fiber	6.3 g
Sodium	198 mg
Cholesterol	0 mg

EXCELLENT SOURCE OF folate and iron.
GOOD SOURCE OF vitamin B$_6$, phosphorus, magnesium and potassium.
SOURCE OF vitamins C and K and zinc.
CONTAINS a very high amount of dietary fiber.

- **Medium (approx. 4 quart) slow cooker**

1	medium eggplant (about 1 lb/500 g) peeled, cubed (2 inch/5 cm) and sweated (see Tips, left)	1
	Coarse sea or kosher salt	
2 tbsp	olive oil, divided (approx.)	30 mL
2	onions, finely chopped	2
4	cloves garlic, minced	4
1 tbsp	ground cumin (see Tips, left)	15 mL
1 tsp	finely grated lemon zest	5 mL
½ tsp	salt	2 mL
½ tsp	cracked black peppercorns	2 mL
1 cup	brown or green lentils, rinsed	250 mL
3 cups	vegetable stock	750 mL
1 tbsp	freshly squeezed lemon juice	15 mL
½ cup	finely chopped dill fronds	125 mL

1. In a colander over a sink, place eggplant. Sprinkle liberally with salt. Toss to ensure eggplant is well coated and let stand for 30 minutes to 1 hour. Rinse thoroughly under cold running water. Lay a clean tea towel on a work surface. Working in batches over the sink and using your hands, squeeze liquid out of eggplant. Transfer to the tea towel. When batches are complete, roll the towel up and press down to remove remaining liquid (see Tips, left).

2. In a skillet, heat oil over medium-high heat. Add sweated eggplant, in batches, and cook until browned, adding more oil as necessary.

3. Add onions to pan, adding more oil, if necessary, and cook, stirring, until softened, about 3 minutes. Add garlic, cumin, lemon zest, salt and peppercorns and cook, stirring, for 1 minute. Add lentils and toss until coated.

4. Transfer to slow cooker stoneware. Stir in stock. Cover and cook on Low for 6 to 8 hours or on High for 3 to 4 hours, until lentils are tender. Stir in lemon juice and dill.

Make Ahead

Complete Steps 1, 2 and 3, adding 1 cup (250 mL) of the stock to the lentil mixture. Cover and refrigerate for up to 2 days. When you're ready to cook, add remaining stock and complete the recipe.

Mindful Morsels

Studies show that as part of an overall healthy diet that includes many anti-inflammatory foods, legumes can help to lower markers of inflammation such as C-reactive protein (CRP) and complement C3. High levels of these inflammatory markers have been linked with a variety of chronic illnesses, including several cancers, arthritis, cardiovascular disease, obesity and diabetes.

Natural Wonders

Supplements vs the Real Thing

A serving of this dish is a source of vitamin C, a powerful antioxidant that reduces the risk of heart disease and certain cancers, among other benefits. Vitamin C is one of the most commonly consumed supplements, but, like all nutrients, it is preferable to obtain it from foods.

Nature doesn't produce nutrients in isolated form, the way they appear in supplements, but in combinations that work together to promote health and prevent disease. Every food is composed of fats, carbohydrates and protein (the macronutrients) plus countless vitamins, minerals, enzymes and phytonutrients. Any food contains so many nutrients it would be impossible to reproduce all of them in a supplement. And plants are highly complex collections of compounds that work in synergy with each other in ways that manufactured products can't even begin to duplicate.

However, there are many reasons why even people who consume a healthy diet may need to take nutritional supplements. To name just three: over the past four decades agribusiness practices have reduced the nutrient content of "conventionally" grown plant foods from 30 to 70%; prescribed pharmaceuticals may deplete the body's supply of specific nutrients; and ongoing exposure to environmental toxins (which, sad to say, may work together synergistically like the nutrients in foods) have likely increased our need for dietary supplements. Once a specific nutrient deficiency has been identified, supplementation is, obviously, the most effective way to address it.

On the other hand, although we still have a lot to learn about how nutrients work, studies are sending early warning signals about supplements. For instance, concern has been raised about vitamin E, beta-carotene and isoflavones in supplement form. New research is also beginning to show that the protective effect of phytonutrients is produced by the intakes found in foods, not the larger doses provided by supplements. This is a bit of a conundrum. In a perfect world — one in which you eat the right combination of organically grown produce, pasture-raised meat and sustainably caught fish and seafood, manage to avoid environmental pollution, exercise regularly and have no chronic healthy problems, diet is probably enough. Otherwise, some degree of supplementation may be necessary.

Vegetable Curry with Lentils and Spinach

Serve this delicious curry for dinner with warm gluten-free Indian bread such as Yogurt Flatbread (page 62). This makes a large serving, slightly more than 2 cups (500 mL) so it's a meal in itself.

Makes 6 servings

Can Be Halved
(see Tips, below)

Tips

If you are halving this recipe, be sure to use a small (1½ to 3½ quart) slow cooker.

If using fresh spinach, be sure to remove the stems, and if it has not been pre-washed, rinse it thoroughly in a basin of lukewarm water.

Nutrients Per Serving

Calories	361
Protein	13.5 g
Carbohydrates	56.1 g
Fat (Total)	11.5 g
Saturated Fat	7.6 g
Monounsaturated Fat	2.3 g
Polyunsaturated Fat	0.7 g
Dietary Fiber	12.0 g
Sodium	94 mg
Cholesterol	0 mg

EXCELLENT SOURCE OF vitamins A, C, B$_6$ and K, folate, magnesium, potassium, phosphorus and iron.

GOOD SOURCE OF calcium and zinc.

CONTAINS a very high amount of dietary fiber.

• **Large (approx. 5 quart) slow cooker**

1 tbsp	olive oil or extra virgin coconut oil	15 mL
2	onions, finely chopped	2
4	carrots, peeled and thinly sliced (about 1 lb/500 g)	4
4	parsnips, peeled, tough core removed and thinly sliced (about 1 lb/500 g)	4
4	cloves garlic, minced	4
1 tbsp	minced gingerroot	15 mL
2 tsp	ground turmeric	10 mL
2 tsp	ground cumin (see Tips, page 270)	10 mL
1 tsp	ground coriander (see Mindful Morsels, right)	5 mL
1	piece (2 inches/5 cm) cinnamon stick	1
½ tsp	cracked black peppercorns	2 mL
2 cups	vegetable stock	500 mL
	Salt, optional	
2	sweet potatoes, peeled and thinly sliced (about 1 lb/500 g)	2
1 cup	brown or green lentils, picked over and rinsed	250 mL
1	long red chile pepper, finely chopped, or ½ tsp (2 mL) cayenne pepper, dissolved in 1 tbsp (15 mL) lemon juice	1
1 lb	fresh spinach, stems removed, or 1 package (10 oz/300 g) spinach leaves, thawed and drained if frozen, coarsely chopped (see Tip, left)	500 g
1 cup	coconut milk	250 mL

1. In a skillet, heat oil over medium heat. Add onions, carrots and parsnips and cook, stirring, until vegetables are tender, about 6 minutes. Add garlic, ginger, turmeric, cumin, coriander, cinnamon stick and peppercorns and cook, stirring, for 1 minute. Add vegetable stock and bring to a boil. Season to taste with salt, if using, and transfer to slow cooker stoneware. Add sweet potatoes and lentils and stir well.

Make Ahead

This dish can be partially prepared before it is cooked. Complete Step 1. Cover and refrigerate overnight or for up to 2 days. When you're ready to cook, continue with Step 2.

2. Cover and cook on Low for 6 hours or on High for 3 hours, until lentils are tender. Add chile pepper and stir well. Add spinach, in batches, stirring after each batch until all the leaves are submerged in the liquid, then coconut milk. Cover and cook on High for 20 minutes, until spinach is wilted and flavors have blended. Discard cinnamon stick.

Mindful Morsels

Coriander seed, which is likely to be a component of curry powder, is well known as a treatment for a wide variety of digestive problems. Now research is confirming this traditional wisdom. For instance, one study found that the symptoms of people suffering from irritable bowel syndrome (IBS) who were given a treatment containing coriander were three times more likely to see improvement than those given a placebo.

Natural Wonders

Spicy Antioxidants Love Company

A curry is actually a spicy stew, not a dish seasoned with curry powder. In fact, most Indian cooks make their own curry seasoning (or powder) using a blend of spices that complements their recipe ingredients. Most include turmeric, which gives commercially blended curry powder its bright yellow color, and coriander seeds, which have a light lemon flavor. Cinnamon is often added for sweetness and cumin adds a pungent note. Chile peppers add heat. All these spices contain antioxidants, which have been linked with a range of health benefits. Moreover, when researchers in India studied the antioxidant ability of individual seasonings such as cinnamon, pepper, ginger, garlic and onion alone, and then together, they found the combination produced greater health benefits.

If you are interested in learning more about the healing power of spices, be sure to read Dr. Bharat Aggarwal's book *Healing Spices*. Dr. Aggarwal, a biochemist, is an authority on the therapeutic uses of spices. In his book he highlights scientific research that has linked the consumption of spices to the prevention and treatment of more than 150 health conditions ranging from heart disease and cancer to chronic conditions such as arthritis and type-2 diabetes.

Creamy Polenta with Corn and Chiles

Sides and Sauces

Creamy Polenta with Corn and Chiles

In my opinion, polenta is a quintessential comfort food. I love it as side dish, where it is particularly apt at complementing robust stews, or as a main course topped with a traditional pasta sauce. This version, which contains the luscious combination of corn and chiles, also works as a main course on its own. I like to serve it with a tossed salad, sliced tomatoes with vinaigrette or some marinated roasted peppers, all of which would add a panoply of valuable nutrients to the meal.

Makes 6 servings

Can Be Halved
(see Tips, below)

Tips

If you are halving this recipe, be sure to use a small (1½ to 3½ quart) slow cooker.

I have not added salt to this polenta because the cheese contains a significant amount of sodium.

If you have trouble digesting cornmeal, see Mindful Morsels, page 61.

Nutrients Per Serving

Calories	221
Protein	13.1 g
Carbohydrates	24.6 g
Fat (Total)	8.3 g
Saturated Fat	4.9 g
Monounsaturated Fat	2.4 g
Polyunsaturated Fat	0.6 g
Dietary Fiber	2.9 g
Sodium	466 mg
Cholesterol	24 mg

EXCELLENT SOURCE OF calcium and phosphorus.

GOOD SOURCE OF vitamin B_{12}, magnesium, potassium and zinc.

SOURCE OF vitamins A, C and B_6, folate and iron.

CONTAINS a moderate amount of dietary fiber.

- **Medium to large (3½ to 5 quart) slow cooker**
- **Greased slow cooker stoneware**

3 cups	skim milk or non-dairy alternative	750 mL
2	cloves garlic, minced	2
1 tsp	finely chopped fresh rosemary leaves or ½ tsp (2 mL) dried rosemary leaves, crumbled	5 mL
	Freshly ground black pepper	
¾ cup	coarse stone-ground yellow cornmeal	175 mL
1 cup	corn kernels	250 mL
1 cup	shredded Monterey Jack cheese	250 mL
½ cup	freshly grated Parmesan cheese	125 mL
1	can (4.5 oz/127 mL) diced mild green chiles, drained	1

1. In a large saucepan over medium heat, bring milk, garlic, rosemary, and black pepper to taste, to a boil. Gradually add cornmeal, in a steady stream, whisking to remove all lumps. Continue whisking until mixture begins to thicken and bubbles like lava, about 5 minutes. Add corn, Monterey Jack and Parmesan cheeses and chiles and mix well. Transfer to slow cooker stoneware.

2. Cover and cook on Low for 2 hours, until mixture is firm and just beginning to brown around the edges.

Natural Wonders

Corn

Although we tend to think of corn as a vegetable, field corn, the kind that is dried and transformed into products such as hominy, cornmeal and grits, is actually a grain. Just make an effort to find products that are GMO-free, such as artisanal grits, because most of the field corn grown in North America is genetically modified.

Cornmeal, from which polenta is made, is produced when the kernels are dried and ground. Most of the cornmeal sold in supermarkets is finely ground, refined and enriched. In the process of refining, most of the B vitamins, fiber, iron and healthful phytonutrients are removed from the grain, although iron may subsequently be returned through fortification. The most nutritious and tastiest form of the grain is stone-ground, which is processed the old-fashioned way, with water-powered millstones. Stone-ground cornmeal, which is available in well-stocked supermarkets and natural food stores, retains the bran and the germ during processing and has more texture and flavor than steel-ground varieties. Whole-grain yellow cornmeal contains more than twice as much magnesium, phosphorus and zinc and significantly more potassium and selenium than the de-germed variety.

So long as it has not been genetically modified (the jury has not even been called into session on that case, I'm sorry to say), corn is definitely a very healthful grain. When researchers tested the antioxidant activity of some grains, corn had the highest ranking by far. Corn contains a range of antioxidants and different varieties highlight different nutrients. For instance, yellow corn is particularly high in the carotenoids lutein and zeaxanthin and blue corn provides anthocyanins. Take extra care when storing whole grain cornmeal. Because the germ contains healthful fats, among other nutrients, it spoils relatively quickly and should be stored in the refrigerator or freezer.

Slow-Cooked Polenta

Polenta, the Italian version of cornmeal mush, is a magnificent way to add whole grains to your diet. When properly cooked, it is a soothing comfort food that functions like a bowl of steaming mashed potatoes, the yummy basis upon which more elaborate dishes can strut their stuff. Grits (see Variation, below), which are more coarsely ground than cornmeal, are even more delicious if you can find artisanal versions being produced in the southern U.S. Whole-grain polenta made from non-GMO corn (see 277) makes a fabulous gluten-free replacement for pasta and it delicious topped with traditional tomato-based sauces, such as Syracuse Sauce (page 300) or Caramelized Onion Sauce (page 303), which would really bump up and round out the nutrients in a typical serving.

Makes 6 servings

Tips

Depending upon your preference, you can cook polenta directly in the slow cooker stoneware or in a 6-cup (1.5 L) baking dish. If you are cooking directly in the stoneware, I recommend using a small (maximum 3½ quart) slow cooker, lightly greased. If you are using a baking dish, you will need a large (minimum 5 quart) oval slow cooker.

If you have trouble digesting cornmeal, see Mindful Morsels, page 61.

Nutrients Per Serving

Calories	107
Protein	3.5 g
Carbohydrates	19.8 g
Fat (Total)	1.7 g
Saturated Fat	0.3 g
Monounsaturated Fat	0.6 g
Polyunsaturated Fat	0.6 g
Dietary Fiber	3.5 g
Sodium	197 mg
Cholesterol	13 mg

SOURCE OF vitamins B_6 and B_{12}, folate, phosphorus, magnesium, potassium, iron and zinc.

CONTAINS a moderate amount of dietary fiber.

- **Medium to large (3½ to 6 quart) slow cooker (see Tips, left)**

4 cups	chicken or vegetable stock or water	1 L
¼ tsp	salt	1 mL
¼ tsp	freshly ground black pepper	1 mL
1¼ cups	coarse stone-ground yellow cornmeal	300 mL

1. In a saucepan over medium heat, bring stock, salt and pepper to a boil. Add cornmeal in a thin stream, stirring constantly.

2. *Direct method:* Transfer mixture to prepared slow cooker stoneware (see Tips, left). Cover and cook on Low for 1½ hours.

3. *Baking dish method:* Transfer mixture to prepared baking dish (see Tips, left). Cover with foil and secure with a string. Place dish in slow cooker stoneware and pour in enough boiling water to come 1 inch (2.5 cm) up the sides of the dish. Cover and cook on Low for 1½ hours.

Variations

Creamy Polenta: Substitute 2 cups (500 mL) milk or non-dairy alternative for 2 cups (500 mL) of the liquid in the recipe above. If desired, stir in ½ cup (125 mL) finely chopped fresh parsley and/or 2 tbsp (30 mL) freshly grated Parmesan cheese, after the polenta has finished cooking.

Slow-Cooked Grits: Substitute an equal quantity of stone-ground grits for the cornmeal.

Cheesy Baked Grits: Substitute an equal quantity of stone-ground grits for the cornmeal. Complete Step 1. Remove from heat and stir in 2 cups (500 mL) shredded Cheddar or Jack cheese and 2 beaten eggs. You can also add a finely chopped roasted red pepper or half of a chipotle pepper in adobo sauce, if you prefer. Stir well and transfer to a greased 6-cup (1.5 L) baking dish.

Make Ahead

Complete Step 1. Transfer to a container, cover and refrigerate overnight or for up to 2 days. When you're ready to cook, continue with Step 2.

Mindful Morsels

A study published in *Nutrition, Metabolism and Cardiovascular Diseases* concluded that eating whole grains benefits cardiovascular health. People who consumed on average 2.5 daily servings of whole grains, such as stone-ground cornmeal or grits, reduced their risk of heart disease and stroke by 21%, compared with those who consumed only 0.2 servings.

Natural Wonders

Whole Grains are Whole Foods

Although we've long known that whole grains, such as stone-ground cornmeal and grits, hominy, buckwheat, and brown rice, are good for us, until fairly recently, significant components of their health benefits were being overlooked. Research by Dr. Rui Hai Liu of Cornell University has shown that the phytonutrients in whole grains are much more powerful than previously recognized.

Traditionally, scientists only studied the "free" forms of phytonutrients, such as phenolics, which are quickly absorbed by the bloodstream. Dr. Liu and his colleagues found almost all the phenolics in whole grains are in "bound" form, which means they must be digested before they can be absorbed. Consequently, the antioxidant activity of whole grains had traditionally been greatly underestimated. This may help to explain why diets high in whole grains appear to be protective against diseases such as diabetes and heart disease, as well as colon, breast and prostate cancer.

Consider, for instance, that clinical trials using isolated supplements, such as fiber, have not consistently shown a reduction in colon cancer, although populations eating high-fiber whole grains have lower rates of the disease. When researchers combined data from 40 studies, they concluded that people who consumed large amounts of whole grains reduced their cancer risk by 34% when compared with those who ate small quantities.

Dr. Liu believes that the wholeness of the food is exactly what gives it cancer-fighting power. The healthful benefits of whole grains are derived from the interaction of all the nutrients they contain.

Whole grains contain other compounds such as lignans, saponins and phytoestrogens, which, along with fiber have been linked with reduced cancer risk. Over 80% of these protective substances are found in the bran and the germ, which are removed when the grain is refined.

Cheesy Grits

I just love good grits — by good I mean those that are stone-ground, preferably from an heirloom variety of corn, which ensures it has not been genetically modified. Seasoned with cheese and chile (see Variation, below), they are so delicious I can make a meal out of grits alone.

Makes 4 servings

Tip

If you have trouble digesting grits and other types of cornmeal, see Mindful Morsels, page 61.

- 4-cup (1 L) baking dish, lightly greased
- Large (approx. 5 quart) oval slow cooker

1 tbsp	olive oil	15 mL
1	onion, finely chopped	1
4	cloves garlic, minced	4
½ tsp	cracked black peppercorns	2 mL
2 cups	chicken or vegetable stock	500 mL
½ cup	stone-ground grits (see Natural Wonders, right)	125 mL
1½ cups	shredded old Cheddar cheese, divided	375 mL

1. In a large skillet, heat oil over medium heat. Add onion and cook, stirring, until softened, about 3 minutes. Add garlic and peppercorns and cook, stirring, for 1 minute. Add stock and bring to a boil. Gradually add grits, stirring constantly, until smooth and blended. Continue cooking and stirring until grits are slightly thickened, about 4 minutes. Stir in 1 cup (250 mL) of the cheese. Transfer to prepared baking dish. Cover tightly with foil and secure with a string.

2. Place in slow cooker stoneware and pour in enough boiling water to come 1 inch (2.5 cm) up the sides of the dish. Cover and cook on Low for 8 hours or on High for 4 hours. Stir well and let stand uncovered for 2 to 3 minutes to absorb any liquid.

3. Meanwhile, preheat broiler. Sprinkle remaining cheese over top of grits and place under broiler until melted and lightly browned.

Variation

Chile-Spiked Cheesy Grits: If you like a little heat, finely mince 1 chipotle chile in adobo sauce. Stir in along with the peppercorns.

Nutrients Per Serving

Calories	307
Protein	14.4 g
Carbohydrates	22.0 g
Fat (Total)	19.0 g
Saturated Fat	9.6 g
Monounsaturated Fat	6.7 g
Polyunsaturated Fat	0.9 g
Dietary Fiber	2.1 g
Sodium	347 mg
Cholesterol	54 mg

EXCELLENT SOURCE OF calcium and phosphorus.

GOOD SOURCE OF zinc.

SOURCE OF vitamins A, B_6, B_{12} and K, folate, magnesium, potassium and iron.

CONTAINS a moderate amount of dietary fiber.

Natural Wonders

Grits

Grits are representative of regional American cooking, where they reside as a kind of *éminence grise* of Southern comfort food. Bland tasting (in an extremely appealing way) they act as a culinary canvas upon which legions of chefs and home cooks have created mouthwatering masterpieces using ingredients such as bacon, cheese, sausage, peppers and, of course, shrimp. (Shrimp 'n' Grits, page 162, is a classic of Southern cuisine.) In recent years, more and more farmers, such as Glen Roberts of Anson Mills in South Carolina, have resurrected heirloom varieties of corn and are transforming them into an array of glorious grits, produced using artisanal methods. These fabulous foodstuffs have, in turn, inspired chefs, so it's not surprising that in many ways grits have become emblematic of cooking in the New South. Today, talented chefs — too many to mention — are going back to basics and recreating Southern cuisine from the ground up, and cooking with grits has become part of that process.

Grits are the coarsest grind of whole corn. Real grits bear very little resemblance to their refined relatives, which have always been an American supermarket staple south of the Mason-Dixon line. Firstly, they are stone-ground, crushed between millstones and ground the old-fashioned way, with the power of water. They are one of the whole-grain forms of field corn and although they can be difficult to find, they are worth the extra effort, not only for their flavor but also for their nutritional profile. Unlike conventional refined grits, many are made from heirloom varieties of corn and are not genetically modified. They also maintain the bran and germ layers, which is where almost all the nutrients are housed in the plant.

Stone-ground grits contain a good range of minerals such as magnesium, potassium and selenium and are particularly high in antioxidants. For best flavor and nutrition, look for coarse texture and dark flecks of germ and bran scattered throughout. Because the germ is loaded with healthful unsaturated oils, grits are very perishable, so buy from a source with high turnover. Store grits in an airtight container, in the refrigerator for up to 2 months or in the freezer for up to 6 months.

Brown and Wild Rice with Bay Leaves

This recipe was inspired by one developed by the late film producer and cook Ismail Merchant, which used plain long-grain brown rice. I have found that a combination of wild and brown rice produces excellent results in the slow cooker and makes a great pairing with many dishes, particularly grilled salmon or braised vegetables. This makes a generous serving (approximately 1 cup/250 mL) of rice.

Makes 4 servings

Tip

You can buy prepackaged combinations of brown and wild rice or make your own, using equal portions of each. I have also made this using ¼ cup (60 mL) each long-grain and wild rice and ½ cup (125 mL) French red rice from the Camargue, with excellent results.

● **Small (2 to 3½ quart) slow cooker**

2 tbsp	butter or olive oil	30 mL
4	bay leaves	4
½ tsp	cracked black peppercorns	2 mL
2½ cups	chicken or vegetable stock	625 mL
1 cup	long-grain brown and wild rice mixture (see Tip, left)	250 mL

1. In a saucepan over low heat, melt butter. Add bay leaves and peppercorns and cook, stirring, for 1 minute. Add stock and bring to a boil. Stir in rice. Return to a boil and boil for 1 minute. Transfer to slow cooker stoneware.

2. Place a clean tea towel folded in half (so you will have 2 layers) over top of stoneware to absorb moisture. Cover and cook on Low for 6 hours or on High for 3 hours, until rice is tender and liquid is absorbed. Remove and discard bay leaves.

Mindful Morsels

The mother of an old friend used to say that you can always identify a good cook based on whether or not she (sic) added a bay leaf or two to dishes such as soups and stews. Now that we know more about the healing power of herbs and spices, you can add health benefits as well as culinary skill to the mix. More than 80 active beneficial compounds have been identified in this innocuous leaf, which is an antioxidant powerhouse.

Nutrients Per Serving

Calories	255
Protein	5.7 g
Carbohydrates	39.4 g
Fat (Total)	7.9 g
Saturated Fat	3.8 g
Monounsaturated Fat	1.8 g
Polyunsaturated Fat	0.4 g
Dietary Fiber	3.1 g
Sodium	140 mg
Cholesterol	28 mg

GOOD SOURCE OF phosphorus.
SOURCE OF vitamins A, B_6 and B_{12}, potassium and iron.
CONTAINS a moderate amount of dietary fiber.

Natural Wonders

Brown Rice

While white rice is eaten in copious quantities around the world, brown rice is significantly more nutritious. For starters, it contains more fiber ($^1/_2$ cup/125 mL white rice provides 0.3 grams of dietary fiber, while you will get 1.5 grams from the same quantity of brown rice). Moreover, most of that fiber is insoluble fiber, which may protect against some cancers, while helping to keep LDL ("bad") cholesterol low. A substance called y-oryzanol, which is found in rice bran oil, is used to treat high cholesterol, as well as symptoms of menopause.

A half cup (125 mL) serving of brown rice is also an excellent source of manganese, a mineral that helps your body utilize key nutrients and keeps your bones healthy. Rice also supplies varying degrees of minerals such as magnesium, selenium, phosphorus, zinc, copper, thiamine and niacin, as well as valuable phytonutrients. Recent research suggests that brown rice is rich in beneficial antioxidants, particularly phenolic compounds (found in many fruits and vegetables), which have been shown to protect against cardiovascular disease. Because it also contains essential oils, which become rancid at room temperature, brown rice should be stored in the refrigerator in an airtight container.

Brown rice is high in phytates, which can be hard to digest. If you have difficulty digesting grains, give your rice a good soak (about 8 hours) before cooking, preferably in acidulated water (see Natural Wonders, page 31). Discard the soaking water and rinse well. Or use sprouted rice, which is available in natural foods stores.

Basic Beans

Loaded with nutrition and high in fiber, dried beans are one of our most healthful edibles. And the slow cooker excels at transforming them into potentially sublime fare. It is also extraordinarily convenient. Put presoaked beans into the slow cooker before you go to bed and in the morning they are ready for whatever recipe you intend to make.

Makes approx. 2 cups (500 mL) cooked beans, about 4 servings

Tip

If you have difficulty digesting legumes, add 2 tsp (10 mL) cider vinegar or lemon juice to the water when soaking dried beans.

Nutrients Per Serving (½ cup/125 mL serving)

Calories	154
Protein	10.5 g
Carbohydrates	27.6 g
Fat (Total)	0.6 g
Saturated Fat	0.1 g
Monounsaturated Fat	0.0 g
Polyunsaturated Fat	0.3 g
Dietary Fiber	8.0 g
Sodium	2 mg
Cholesterol	0 mg

EXCELLENT SOURCE OF folate and iron.

GOOD SOURCE OF phosphorus, magnesium and potassium.

SOURCE OF vitamin K.

CONTAINS a very high amount of dietary fiber.

● **Medium to large (3½ to 5 quart) slow cooker**

1 cup	dried white beans (see Tip, left)	250 mL
3 cups	water	750 mL
	Garlic, optional	
	Bay leaves, optional	
	Bouquet garni, optional	

1. *Long soak:* In a bowl, combine beans and water. Soak for at least 6 hours or overnight. Drain and rinse thoroughly with cold water. Beans are now ready for cooking.

2. *Quick soak:* In a pot, combine beans and water. Cover and bring to a boil. Boil for 3 minutes. Turn off heat and soak for 1 hour. Drain and rinse thoroughly under cold water. Beans are now ready to cook.

3. *Cooking:* In slow cooker stoneware, combine 1 cup (250 mL) presoaked beans and 3 cups (750 mL) fresh cold water. If desired, season with garlic, bay leaves or a bouquet garni made from your favorite herbs tied together in a cheesecloth. Cover and cook on Low for 10 to 12 hours or overnight or on High for 5 to 6 hours, until beans are tender. Drain and rinse. If not using immediately, cover and refrigerate. The beans are now ready for use in your favorite recipe.

Variations

Substitute any dried bean (for instance, red kidney beans, pinto beans, white navy beans), chickpeas or split yellow peas for the white beans. Soybeans and chickpeas take longer than other legumes to cook. They will likely take the full 12 hours on Low (about 6 hours on High).

Dried Lentils: These instructions also work for lentils, with the following changes: Unless you have problems digesting legumes, they do not need to be presoaked. If you have problems digesting legumes, presoak or use sprouted lentils, which are available in natural food stores. Reduce the cooking time to about 6 hours on Low.

Tips

This recipe may be doubled or tripled to suit the quantity of beans required for a recipe.

Once cooked, legumes should be covered and stored in the refrigerator, where they will keep for 4 to 5 days. Cooked legumes can also be frozen in an airtight container. They will keep frozen for up to 6 months.

Natural Wonders

Nutrients in Legumes

Although the nutrient content varies among the different types of lentils, dried beans, chickpeas and peas, all these foodstuffs share some common nutritional characteristics. A typical serving of legumes is high in dietary fiber (you can expect $1/2$ cup/125 mL of any cooked legume to provide, on average, about 7 grams of fiber in total and 1 to 2 grams of soluble fiber), a good source of low-fat vegetable protein, and low in both sugar and sodium. All provide valuable micronutrients in varying degrees. These include

- the B vitamins thiamine (B_1) and folate;
- minerals such as potassium, magnesium, manganese, copper, iron, zinc and phosphorus; and
- phytonutrients, such as antioxidants.

Legumes are also a natural appetite suppressant; because they are digested slowly and cause a low, sustained increase in blood sugar, eating legumes can delay the onset of hunger and make it easier to control appetite.

However, since legumes contain substances that are hard to digest, it is crucial to soak them before cooking, preferably with the addition of a little acid, which has been shown to draw out problematic compounds (see page 253).

Butterbeans Braised with Celery

This is an adaptation of a recipe developed by Greek cooking expert Diane Kochilas. It's a traditional way of cooking gigantes, the large dried lima beans that feature in a variety of Greek dishes. You can buy them at stores specializing in Greek provisions or substitute slightly smaller lima beans instead. This makes a wonderful side for grilled or roasted fish, meat or vegetables and is a great dish for a buffet. Stirring the beans a few times before serving encourages a lusciously creamy texture.

Makes 6 servings

Can Be Halved
(see Tips, page 292)

Tip

To soak the beans, bring them to a boil in 4 cups (1 L) water over medium heat. Boil rapidly for 3 minutes. Cover, turn off element and let stand for 1 hour. Drain and rinse under cold running water. Using your hands, pop the beans out of their skins. Discard skins and cook as per Step 1.

Nutrients Per Serving

Calories	170
Protein	8.1 g
Carbohydrates	25.3 g
Fat (Total)	5.1 g
Saturated Fat	0.7 g
Monounsaturated Fat	3.4 g
Polyunsaturated Fat	0.7 g
Dietary Fiber	8.1 g
Sodium	290 mg
Cholesterol	0 mg

EXCELLENT SOURCE OF vitamin K, folate and potassium.
GOOD SOURCE OF vitamins A, C and B$_6$, magnesium and iron.
SOURCE OF calcium, phosphorus and zinc.
CONTAINS a very high amount of dietary fiber.

- **Medium (approx. 3½ quart) slow cooker**

1 cup	dried butterbeans, lima beans or gigantes, soaked, drained and popped out of their skins (see Tip, left)	250 mL
2 tbsp	olive oil	30 mL
1	whole bunch celery, with leaves, diced	1
6	cloves garlic, minced	6
½ tsp	salt	2 mL
½ tsp	cracked black peppercorns	2 mL
1	bay leaf	1
¼ cup	tomato paste	60 mL
1½ cups	water	375 mL
1 cup	finely chopped parsley leaves	250 mL
¼ cup	freshly squeezed lemon juice	60 mL
	Extra virgin olive oil	

1. In a large pot of water, cook soaked beans until tender to the bite (you do not want them to be fully cooked), about 20 minutes. Drain and transfer to slow cooker stoneware.

2. Meanwhile, in a skillet, heat oil over medium heat. Add celery and garlic and cook, stirring, until celery is softened, about 5 minutes. Add salt, peppercorns and bay leaf and cook, stirring, for 1 minute. Stir in tomato paste. Add water and bring to a boil.

3. Transfer to slow cooker stoneware. Stir well. Cover and cook on Low for 6 hours or on High for 3 hours, until beans are meltingly tender. Stir in parsley. Cover and cook on High for 15 minutes. Stir in lemon juice and adjust seasoning, adding more lemon juice if desired. Stir well. Remove and discard bay leaf. Drizzle with olive oil and serve warm.

more information on page 288

Make Ahead

Complete Steps 1 and 2. Cover and refrigerate for up to 2 days. When you're ready to cook, complete the recipe.

Mindful Morsels

I like to use tomato paste in recipes because it adds an intense hit of tomato flavor. However, check the label to make sure the brand you are using doesn't contain gluten. I buy mine at my neighborhood natural foods store. It contains only organic tomatoes and salt.

Natural Wonders

Minerals

Legumes provide valuable minerals, such as potassium, magnesium, phosphorus, manganese, iron and zinc, all of which perform various functions in your body. These nutrients are among those most likely to be severely diminished in the process of refining foods, such as grains. For instance, white wheat flour has about 15% of the magnesium, and not much more than 20% of the zinc, potassium and iron found in whole-grain wheat flour.

All minerals are important to keep your body functioning properly, and each benefits your body in different ways. They often work together to keep you healthy. Both potassium and magnesium help to keep your blood pressure under control and have, in various studies, been linked with reduced risk of ischemic stroke (80% of strokes are ischemic, which means they are caused by a blood clot). Both minerals also play a role in keeping your bones and teeth strong, with some assistance from manganese and phosphorus. And magnesium is a well-known partner of calcium. These minerals team up to keep bones strong and your nerves relaxed.

Even minerals we don't think about much play important roles in keeping your body running smoothly. Boron supports bone health and helps to keep your muscles free from pain. Chromium helps your body to use glucose, which is particularly important for people with diabetes. Iodine keeps your thyroid functioning properly and silicon works to keep the fluids in your body balanced. Zinc has many functions, not the least of which is helping to keep your immune system strong and maintaining taste acuity, which means that it supports the way your taste buds help you enjoy the foods you eat.

Down-Home Tomatoes with Okra

This is a great side dish. A particularly mouthwatering combination of flavors, it makes a perfect accompaniment to grilled meat, fish or seafood. Leftovers make a delicious filling for an omelet.

Makes 6 servings

Can Be Halved
(see Tips, below)

Tips

If you are halving this recipe, be sure to use a small (approx. 1½ to 2 quart) slow cooker.

Okra has a great flavor but becomes unpleasantly sticky when overcooked. Choose young okra pods 2 to 4 inches (5 to 10 cm) long that don't feel sticky to the touch (if sticky, they are too ripe). Gently scrub the pods and cut off the top and tail. Okra can also be found in the freezer section of the grocery store. Thaw before adding to the slow cooker.

Nutrients Per Serving

Calories	101
Protein	4.4 g
Carbohydrates	12.2 g
Fat (Total)	4.6 g
Saturated Fat	1.1 g
Monounsaturated Fat	2.7 g
Polyunsaturated Fat	0.5 g
Dietary Fiber	3.0 g
Sodium	339 mg
Cholesterol	6 mg

EXCELLENT SOURCE OF vitamins C and K.

GOOD SOURCE OF potassium.

SOURCE OF vitamins A and B$_6$, folate, calcium, phosphorus, magnesium, iron and zinc.

CONTAINS a moderate amount of dietary fiber.

- **Medium (approx. 3½ quart) slow cooker**

1 tbsp	olive oil	15 mL
4 oz	chunk bacon, diced (see Tip, page 291)	125 g
1	onion, finely chopped	1
2	cloves garlic, minced	2
½ tsp	salt	2 mL
½ tsp	cracked black peppercorns	2 mL
1	can (28 oz/796 mL) no-salt-added tomatoes including juice	1
1	green bell pepper, seeded and diced	1
2 cups	sliced (½ inch/1 cm) okra, about 12 oz (375 g) (see Tips, left)	500 mL

1. In a skillet, heat oil over medium-high heat. Add bacon and cook, stirring, until nicely browned, about 4 minutes. Using a slotted spoon, transfer to slow cooker stoneware. Add onion and cook, stirring, until softened, about 3 minutes. Add garlic, salt and peppercorns and cook, stirring, for 1 minute. Add tomatoes with juice and bring to a boil. Transfer to slow cooker stoneware.

2. Cover and cook on Low for 6 hours or on High for 3 hours, until hot and bubbly. Add bell pepper and okra. Cover and cook on High for about 30 minutes, until okra is tender.

more information on page 291

Down-Home Tomatoes with Okra

Be sure to use bacon made from pigs that have been pastured. It is higher in omega-3 fatty acids, which are provided by the plants, such as clover and alfalfa, which the pigs forage. Also ensure that it is free from additives and synthetic nitrates.

Mindful Morsels

Most of the fat in bacon is unsaturated. However, there is no reason to be concerned about saturated fat so long as you consume it in moderation (like everything). Much of the bad news about saturated fat in the past was really directed at trans fats because earlier research didn't properly distinguish between the two. There is new research with robust data showing that saturated fats are not the bad guys we once thought they were and that the association between saturated fats and heart disease are minimal to non-existent (see page 191).

Natural Wonders

Glutathione

The okra in this recipe provides glutathione, an antioxidant that supports the immune system and assists your body with eliminating toxins, such as drugs and other chemicals. Glutathione has been called the most important antioxidant because it is produced by your body and actually resides within your cells, where it is well positioned to neutralize free radicals. Consequently, studies show that it has the potential to help your body fight virtually any disease. Research indicates that used medically, glutathione has helped people battling even serious illness such as cancer and AIDS.

Many foods provide glutathione and if you are eating a healthy diet, you probably have enough. However, one study published in the *Lancet* indicated not only that glutathione declines as we age, but also that people who are ill may be deficient in this nutrient. There are a couple of things you can do to keep your glutathione levels up: exercise regularly to boost your immune system and eat lots of fresh fruits and vegetables, as well as pasture-raised meats. Foods that are rich in sulfur, such as those belonging to the allium family (onions, garlic, leeks and shallots) and cruciferous vegetables (collard greens, kale and watercress to name three) help your body to produce glutathione. Eating foods rich in folate, vitamins B_6 and B_{12} also help to maintain levels. Your body uses the amino acids glutamine, glycine and cysteine, along with selenium to support glutathione production. Without adequate amounts of cysteine, your body will be limited in the amount of glutathione it can produce. The best food sources of this amino acid are dairy foods, but it is also found in egg yolks, cruciferous vegetables, onions and garlic. Good mineral-rich bone broth provides glycine (see Natural Wonders, page 205). Selenium is found in tuna, halibut, cod, sardines, shrimp, lamb and Brazil nuts.

Glutathione is an enzyme antioxidant and as such it can't be taken orally as a supplement because its enzymes will be degraded by stomach acid.

Hoppin' John with Collard Greens

In the American South, where it is served over rice with a liberal dash of local hot sauce, this is a traditional New Year's dish. At my house it often appears as a side to roast pork, but it also makes a main course on its own, accompanied by a bowl of mixed whole-grain rice.

Makes 8 servings

Can Be Halved
(see Tips, below)

Tips

If you are halving this recipe, be sure to use a small (approx. 1½ to 2 quart) slow cooker.

I've served this over a combination of brown, black and red varieties of rice, and it's particularly delicious.

- Medium (approx. 4 quart) slow cooker

2 cups	black-eyed peas, soaked, drained and rinsed (see Tip, right)	500 mL
2 oz	chunk bacon, diced	60 g
2	large onions, finely chopped	2
4	stalks celery, finely chopped	4
4	cloves garlic, minced	4
1 tsp	dried thyme leaves	5 mL
½ tsp	salt	2 mL
½ tsp	cracked black peppercorns	2 mL
2	bay leaves	2
4 cups	chicken or vegetable stock	1 L
½ tsp	cayenne pepper, optional	2 mL
8 cups	collard greens, stems removed, chopped	2 L
1 tbsp	apple cider vinegar	15 mL
	Butter	
	Salt and freshly ground black pepper	

1. In a skillet over medium-high heat, cook bacon until browned and crisp, about 3 minutes. Drain on paper towel and set aside. Reduce heat to medium.

2. Add onions and celery to pan and cook, stirring, until celery is softened, about 5 minutes. Add garlic, thyme, salt, peppercorns and bay leaves and cook, stirring, for 1 minute. Transfer to slow cooker stoneware. Add peas, stock and reserved bacon.

3. Cover and cook on Low for 8 hours or on High for 4 hours, until peas are tender. Stir in cayenne, if using. Remove and discard bay leaves.

4. Meanwhile, in a vegetable steamer, steam greens until tender, about 10 minutes. Toss with cider vinegar and butter. Season with salt and pepper to taste. Add to pea mixture and stir to combine. Serve immediately.

Nutrients Per Serving

Calories	210
Protein	13.1 g
Carbohydrates	32.7 g
Fat (Total)	3.8 g
Saturated Fat	1.9 g
Monounsaturated Fat	2.2 g
Polyunsaturated Fat	1.0 g
Dietary Fiber	10.2 g
Sodium	291 mg
Cholesterol	14 mg

EXCELLENT SOURCE OF vitamins A and K, folate, phosphorus, magnesium and iron.

GOOD SOURCE OF vitamin B_6, potassium and zinc.

SOURCE OF vitamins C and B_{12} and calcium.

CONTAINS a very high amount of dietary fiber.

Tip

For this quantity of black-eyed peas, use 1 can (14 to 19 oz/398 to 540 mL) drained and rinsed black-eyed peas with no salt added, or soak and cook 1 cup (250 mL) dried black-eyed peas (see Basic Beans, page 284).

Vegan and Vegetarian Alternatives

For vegans, omit bacon and use 2 tbsp (30 mL) olive oil to soften the vegetables. Toss the greens with a butter substitute. Vegetarians may use 4 slices of meatless bacon strips, chopped.

Mindful Morsels

Thyme is one of the most common kitchen spices — so common, in fact, that we add it to many dishes without giving it a second thought. However, this somewhat self-effacing plant contains the volatile oil thymol, which is an extremely powerful antiseptic. Researchers have found that this substance can calm coughing fits associated with bronchitis. Among other benefits, it also "kills germs on contact," as a commercial for the mouthwash Listerine, which contains thymol, touted.

Natural Wonders

Quercetin

The onions and peas in this recipe (along with apples, pears and leafy greens such as green cabbage, kale, parsley and dill) are among the common food sources of quercetin, a powerful antioxidant with some unique qualities. Quercetin is a flavonoid. This group of phytonutrients apparently works to keep blood cholesterol levels under control and prevent plaque from forming in your arteries, among other benefits. Quercetin has specifically been shown to reduce the pain and swelling associated with prostate problems and to lower blood pressure in people with mild hypertension. It also acts as a natural antihistamine. In laboratory tests, it has prevented mast cells from creating and releasing histamine. As a result, quercetin has shown promise in reducing allergy symptoms. Quercetin works to strengthen the body's immune system, and several studies indicate that it has anti-inflammatory properties, which makes it useful in treating symptoms associated with conditions such as rosacea and eczema.

Fennel Braised with Tomatoes

Here's a perfectly luscious side dish that makes a great companion for grilled or roasted fish and meats or a splendid topping for rice. The gratin variation, which adds a fancy finish and nice texture, is particularly attractive on a buffet table.

Makes 6 servings

Can Be Halved
(see Tips, below)

Tips

If you are halving this recipe, be sure to use a small (approx. $1\frac{1}{2}$ to 2 quart) slow cooker.

If the outer sections of your fennel bulb seem old and dry, peel them with a vegetable peeler before using. *To prepare fennel:* Chop off the top shoots (which resemble celery) and discard. If desired, save the feathery green fronds to use as a garnish. Cut in half lengthwise. Remove core and thinly slice on the vertical.

Nutrients Per Serving

Calories	100
Protein	2.3 g
Carbohydrates	14.2 g
Fat (Total)	4.8 g
Saturated Fat	0.7 g
Monounsaturated Fat	3.3 g
Polyunsaturated Fat	0.5 g
Dietary Fiber	4.6 g
Sodium	264 mg
Cholesterol	0 mg

GOOD SOURCE OF vitamin C and potassium.
SOURCE OF vitamins A and B$_6$, folate, calcium, phosphorus, magnesium and iron.
CONTAINS a high amount of dietary fiber.

- **Medium (approx. $3\frac{1}{2}$ quart) slow cooker**
- **Parchment paper**

2 tbsp	olive oil	30 mL
1	onion, thinly sliced on the vertical	1
3	bulbs fennel, cored and thinly sliced on the vertical (see Tips, left)	3
4	cloves garlic, minced	4
$\frac{1}{2}$ tsp	salt	2 mL
$\frac{1}{2}$ tsp	cracked black peppercorns	2 mL
1	can (14 oz/398 mL) no-salt added diced tomatoes including juice	1
	Fennel fronds, optional	

1. In a large skillet, heat oil over medium heat. Add onion and fennel and cook, tossing, until fennel begins to brown, about 5 minutes. Add garlic, salt and peppercorns and cook, stirring, for 1 minute. Add tomatoes with juice and bring to a boil.

2. Transfer to slow cooker stoneware. Place a large piece of parchment over the mixture, pressing it down to brush the food and extending up the sides of the stoneware so it overlaps the rim.

3. Cover and cook on Low for 6 hours or on High for 3 hours, until fennel is tender. Lift out parchment and discard, being careful not to spill the accumulated liquid into the sauce. Garnish with fennel fronds, if using.

Variation

Fennel and Tomato Gratin: After the fennel has finished cooking, preheat broiler. Scoop out about $\frac{1}{4}$ cup (60 mL) of the cooking liquid and set aside. In a bowl, combine $\frac{1}{2}$ cup (125 mL) each dry gluten-free bread crumbs and finely grated Parmesan cheese and $\frac{1}{4}$ tsp (1 mL) finely grated lemon zest. Sprinkle evenly over fennel and drizzle with reserved cooking liquid. Place under broiler until cheese melts and top is browned. Garnish with fennel fronds, if desired.

Tip

I like to use parchment when cooking this dish because it doesn't contain much liquid. Creating a tight seal ensures that none evaporates and that the vegetables are well basted in their own juices.

Natural Wonders

Fennel

Fennel is an interesting plant, not only for its enticing mild licorice flavor but also because its various parts have different culinary roles. The bulb is a vegetable, the leafy fronds function as a herb and the seeds (produced when the fronds flower) are a spice.

Florence fennel (often incorrectly identified by greengrocers as anise) is the variety used as a vegetable. The plant is a member of the Apiaceae family, which also includes parsley, cumin, caraway, aniseed and dill. Fennel is very low in calories. One cup (250 mL) of sliced fennel provides only 27 calories (1% DV) and 17% of the DV of vitamin C, 10% of potassium, 8% of manganese, 6% of folate and a smattering of other nutrients, such as calcium, iron, magnesium and various B vitamins. It also provides 2.7 g of dietary fiber (11% DV) and valuable antioxidants such as quercetin (see page 293) and rutin.

When using fennel, don't discard the fronds. They make a wonderful garnish and can be added to salads. As I write, fennel pollen, which is extracted from the flowers, is very trendy in chef circles. It you're looking for hard-core medicinal benefits, look no further than fennel seed (see page 155). These pungent nuggets, which are a mainstay of popular spice blends such as curry powder and ras-el-hanout, contain some powerful phytonutrients such as anethole, a volatile oil, which studies show acts as a phytoestrogen.

Basic Tomato Sauce

Not only is this sauce tasty and easy to make, it is also much lower in sodium than prepared sauces. It keeps covered for up to 1 week in the refrigerator and can be frozen for up to 6 months, so it is worth preparing a batch (or two) and keeping it on hand, frozen, for use in a variety of recipes.

Makes about 8 cups (2 L)

Can Be Halved
(see Tips, page 300)

Tip

If you are in a hurry, you can soften the vegetables on the stovetop. Heat oil in a skillet. Add onions and carrots and cook, stirring, until carrots are softened, about 7 minutes. Add garlic, thyme and peppercorns and cook, stirring, for 1 minute. Transfer to slow cooker stoneware. Add tomatoes with juice and continue with Step 2.

Nutrients Per Serving (2 cups/500 mL approx. sauce)

Calories	152
Protein	4.4 g
Carbohydrates	29.1 g
Fat (Total)	3.5 g
Saturated Fat	0.5 g
Monounsaturated Fat	2.5 g
Polyunsaturated Fat	0.4 g
Dietary Fiber	5.4 g
Sodium	88 mg
Cholesterol	0 mg

EXCELLENT SOURCE OF vitamins A and C and potassium.

GOOD SOURCE OF vitamin K, calcium and iron.

SOURCE OF vitamin B_6 and folate.

CONTAINS a high amount of dietary fiber.

• **Medium to large (3½ to 5 quart) slow cooker**

1 tbsp	olive oil	15 mL
2	onions, finely chopped	2
2	carrots, peeled and diced	2
6	cloves garlic, minced	6
1 tsp	dried thyme	5 mL
½ tsp	cracked black peppercorns	2 mL
2	cans (each 28 oz/796 mL) no-salt added tomatoes, including juice, coarsely chopped	2
	Salt, optional	

1. In slow cooker stoneware, combine olive oil, onions and carrots. Stir well to ensure vegetables are coated with oil. Cover and cook on High for 1 hour, until vegetables are softened. Add garlic, thyme and peppercorns. Stir well. Stir in tomatoes with juice.

2. Place a tea towel folded in half (so you have two layers) over top of stoneware to absorb moisture. Cover and cook on Low for 6 to 8 hours or on High for 3 to 4 hours, until sauce is thickened and flavors are melded. Season to taste with salt, if using.

Mindful Morsels

One advantage to making your own tomato sauce is that it is much lower in sodium than prepared versions. One-half cup (125 mL) of prepared tomato sauce may contain as much as 700 milligrams of sodium. One-half cup (125 mL) of this sauce with no added salt contains approximately 22 milligrams of sodium.

Natural Wonders

Tomatoes

Low in calories, tomatoes are extremely nutritious. They contain vitamins A and C, potassium and folate and are loaded with phytonutrients. Tomatoes contain carotenoids: beta-carotene, alpha-carotene and lutein, which are important nutrients for eye health, and lycopene, a powerful antioxidant with cancer-fighting properties. Consumption of lycopene may help prevent colon, stomach, breast and lung cancers. Research suggests that lycopene may also protect against heart disease and atherosclerosis, and help to keep your skin from showing its age.

Tomato sauce is one of the best ways to consume lycopene because cooking tomatoes, especially with oil, makes this nutrient more available to the body. Since your body can't produce lycopene, you need to eat foods rich in this phytonutrient to obtain the benefits, and because lycopene is fat soluble, it needs to be consumed with a bit of dietary fat to be absorbed by your body.

A number of studies link the consumption of tomato products with a significantly reduced risk (about one-third) of prostate cancer. Interestingly, for many years researchers thought that the lycopene in tomatoes was exclusively responsible for this ability. However recent laboratory studies show that another compound in tomatoes, the saponin alpha-tomatine, was even more effective at stopping aggressive prostate cancer in its tracks. It is another example of why consuming nutrients in food, not supplements, is the ideal strategy.

Mushroom Tomato Sauce

One way of adding variety to your diet is by expanding the kinds of grains you use with sauces traditionally served with pasta. I like to serve this classic sauce over polenta or grits. It also makes a nice topping for roasted spaghetti squash or even paper-thin slices of raw zucchini. To significantly boost the health promoting impact of the tomatoes, accompany your dish with a platter of steamed broccoli (see page 307).

Makes 6 servings

Can Be Halved
(see Tips, page 300)

Tip

For an easy and delicious meal, make this sauce ahead of time and refrigerate. Prepare 1 batch of Slow-Cooked or Creamy Polenta (see page 278), and just before you are ready to serve, reheat Mushroom Tomato Sauce. To serve, spoon polenta onto a warm plate and top with the sauce. Sprinkle with parsley and grated Parmesan, if desired.

Nutrients Per Serving
(1 cup/250 mL sauce)

Calories	73
Protein	2.8 g
Carbohydrates	11.9 g
Fat (Total)	2.4 g
Saturated Fat	0.3 g
Monounsaturated Fat	1.7 g
Polyunsaturated Fat	0.3 g
Dietary Fiber	2.8 g
Sodium	233 mg
Cholesterol	0 mg

EXCELLENT SOURCE OF vitamin K.

GOOD SOURCE OF vitamin C and potassium.

SOURCE OF vitamins A and B$_6$, folate, calcium, phosphorus, magnesium, iron and zinc.

CONTAINS a moderate amount of dietary fiber.

- **Medium to large (3½ to 5 quart) slow cooker**

1 tbsp	olive oil	15 mL
1	onion, finely chopped	1
2	stalks celery, diced	2
4	cloves garlic, minced	4
1 tbsp	finely chopped fresh rosemary or 2 tsp (10 mL) dried rosemary leaves, crumbled	15 mL
½ tsp	salt	2 mL
½ tsp	cracked black peppercorns	2 mL
8 oz	cremini mushrooms, sliced	250 g
½ cup	dry white wine or chicken or vegetable stock	125 mL
1 tbsp	tomato paste	15 mL
1	can (28 oz/796 mL) no-salt added tomatoes, including juice, coarsely chopped	1
½ cup	finely chopped parsley leaves	125 mL
	Crushed hot pepper flakes, optional	

1. In a skillet, heat oil over medium heat. Add onion and celery and cook, stirring, until celery is softened, about 5 minutes. Add garlic, rosemary, salt and peppercorns and cook, stirring, for 1 minute. Add mushrooms and toss to coat. Add wine and cook for 1 minute. Stir in tomato paste and tomatoes with juice and bring to a boil. Transfer to slow cooker stoneware.

2. Place a tea towel folded in half (so you will have two layers) over top of the stoneware to absorb moisture. Cover and cook on Low for 6 hours or on High for 3 hours, until hot and bubbly. Stir in parsley and pepper flakes, if using.

Make Ahead

This dish can be partially prepared before it is cooked. Complete Step 1. Cover and refrigerate overnight or for up to 2 days. When you're ready to cook, continue with Step 2.

Variation

Double Mushroom Tomato Sauce: Soak 1 package ($^1/_2$ oz/ 14 g) dried porcini mushrooms in 1 cup (250 mL) hot water for 20 minutes. Drain, reserving soaking liquid, pat dry and chop finely. Add soaked mushrooms to pan along with peppercorns and replace wine with an equal quantity of the mushroom soaking liquid.

Mindful Morsels

Not only are the mushrooms in this recipe very low in calories, they are also a good source of potassium, which helps control blood pressure, and zinc, which helps the immune system to function.

Natural Wonders

Rosemary

Rosemary is a highly aromatic herb with a very robust flavor. It is widely used, particularly in Italian and Provençal cooking. Rosemary adds an enticing pine-like flavor to many dishes and, in my opinion, is especially delicious with tomatoes. It also combines well with lemon, orange or mint, and is often used along with classic French herbs such as parsley, sage and thyme.

But rosemary is much more than a tasty accent to food. Among other talents, it is a powerful antioxidant that can boost your immune system, improve your circulation (by preventing blood platelets from clumping) and perk up your digestion. Due to its unique combination of the antioxidants rosmarinic and carnosic acid, and carnosol, it can also thwart carcinogens. Multiple laboratory studies have confirmed that rosemary is effective against cancers such as leukemia and breast cancer.

Rosemary has also been shown to have strong skin-protective abilities, which may help to slow the aging process, among other benefits. It guards the skin from harmful UV radiation, as well as from certain carcinogens linked with skin cancer. One study indicated that a skin cream containing rosemary was significantly helpful in treating severe dermatitis. It has also been shown to reduce the pain and inflammation associated with arthritis. And, it may be helpful in controlling type-2 diabetes. One laboratory study indicated that rosemary was as effective as a drug in lowering blood sugar levels in people with diabetes.

Syracuse Sauce

Serve this rich and delicious sauce over hot gluten-free pasta or polenta for a great Italian-themed dinner. Add a simple green salad, with an abundance of red or dark green lettuce (see Natural Wonders, page 233) to round out the nutritional components of the meal. Serving it over a nutritious base, such as Slow-Cooked Polenta (page 278) or roasted spaghetti squash will also add valuable nutrients to your meal.

Makes 6 servings

Can Be Halved
(see Tips, below)

Tips

If you are halving this recipe, be sure to use a small (1½ to 3½ quart) slow cooker

You can't taste the anchovies in this sauce, but they add depth to the flavor. If you're a vegetarian, you can omit the anchovies and enhance the flavor of this sauce by adding 1 tbsp (15 mL) brown rice miso (which is gluten-free) along with the parsley.

Nutrients Per Serving (1¼ cups/300 mL approx. sauce)

Calories	136
Protein	3.2 g
Carbohydrates	19.9 g
Fat (Total)	6.1 g
Saturated Fat	0.9 g
Monounsaturated Fat	4.3 g
Polyunsaturated Fat	0.7 g
Dietary Fiber	4.6 g
Sodium	312 mg
Cholesterol	1 mg

EXCELLENT SOURCE OF vitamins C and K.
GOOD SOURCE OF vitamin A and potassium.
SOURCE OF vitamin B$_6$, folate, calcium, magnesium and iron.
CONTAINS a high amount of dietary fiber.

• **Medium to large (3½ to 5 quart) slow cooker**

1	large eggplant, peeled and cut into 2-inch (5 cm) cubes	1
1 tsp	salt	5 mL
2 tbsp	olive oil, divided (approx.)	30 mL
2	onions, finely chopped	2
4	cloves garlic, minced	4
4	anchovy fillets, finely chopped (see Tips, left)	4
1	can (28 oz/796 mL) no-salt-added tomatoes, including juice, coarsely chopped	1
1 tbsp	tomato paste	15 mL
2	roasted red bell peppers, diced	2
½ cup	black olives, pitted and chopped (about 20 olives)	125 mL
½ cup	finely chopped parsley leaves	125 mL
2 tbsp	capers, drained and minced	30 mL
	Cooked gluten-free pasta or polenta	

1. In a colander over a sink, combine eggplant and salt. Toss and let stand for 30 minutes. Rinse thoroughly under cold running water. Lay a clean tea towel on a work surface. Working in batches over the sink and using your hands, squeeze liquid out of the eggplant. Transfer to the tea towel. When batches are complete, roll the towel up and press down to remove remaining liquid.

2. In a skillet, heat 1 tbsp (15 mL) of the oil over medium heat. Add sweated eggplant, in batches, and cook until browned, adding more oil as necessary. Transfer to slow cooker stoneware.

3. Add onions to pan, adding oil, if necessary, and cook, stirring, until softened, about 3 minutes. Add garlic and anchovies and cook, stirring, for 1 minute. Add tomatoes with juice and tomato paste and bring to a boil. Transfer to slow cooker stoneware.

recipe continued on page 302

4. Place a clean tea towel folded in half over top of the stoneware to absorb moisture. Cover and cook on Low for 6 hours or on High for 3 hours, until hot and bubbly. Add roasted peppers, olives, parsley and capers. Stir well. Cover and cook on High for 20 minutes, until heated through.

Mindful Morsels

A serving of this sauce provides 100% of the daily value of vitamin C. Two-thirds comes from the red peppers.

Natural Wonders

Antioxidants

While enjoying this tasty sauce think of it as a potent antioxidant cocktail that is helping your body defend itself against aging, cancer, heart disease and numerous other diseases. Antioxidants are a group of phytonutrients that are found in a wide variety of fruits, vegetables, spices and herbs. In general terms, they protect your body against the harmful effects of free radicals, much like rust proofing protects your car from rust. Think about what happens when you leave a sliced apple exposed to air. That browning is called oxidation and when it happens to your cells, it causes serious damage. Oxidative stress plays a major role in the development of chronic disease, from macular degeneration to Alzheimer's. The antioxidants in food help your body to fight this process.

The best-known antioxidants are vitamins C and E and beta-carotene, but minerals such as selenium and manganese also pack significant antioxidant punch. The list of known antioxidants is very long — polyphenols and flavonoids are two you have likely heard of, but you are not likely to be familiar with many others, such as carbazole alkaloids, punicic acid and carnosol. Scientists are only beginning to learn about antioxidants, and new ones are constantly being discovered. Researchers are invariably surprised by their apparent power to fight disease.

Whole foods contain unique combinations of phytonutrients and these various substances work together to fight disease, which is why it's important to consume as wide a variety of foods as possible. While consumption of cruciferous vegetables, such as broccoli and cauliflower, has been long been linked with reduced risk of cancer, thanks to compounds such as isothiocyanates and indole-3-carbinol, the antioxidants in other vegetables also seem to have a protective effect against this disease. For instance, eggplant is rich in phenolic compounds, which also help to keep cholesterol under control, onions contain the flavonoid quercetin, which is also a powerful inflammatory, and tomatoes and bell peppers contain lycopene, which may also protect against heart disease. Interestingly, research suggests that the antioxidants in food work together as part of the whole food. Some recent studies indicate that taking antioxidants as single agents does not produce similar benefits, emphasizing yet again the importance of a healthy diet.

Caramelized Onion Sauce with Arugula

I love the bittersweet flavor of caramelized onions, but on the stovetop caramelizing onions is a laborious process. In the slow cooker, caramelizing onions requires almost no attention. Serve this luscious sauce over gluten-free whole-grain pasta, roasted spaghetti squash, polenta, or even a bowl of steaming grits. Complete the meal with a salad of dark green lettuce, some torn radicchio and a couple of handfuls of shredded carrots for splashes of healthy color.

Makes 6 servings

Can Be Halved
(see Tips, page 306)

Tip

If you prefer, soften the onions on the stovetop. Heat the oil over medium heat in a skillet. Add the onions and cook, stirring, until softened, about 5 minutes. Transfer to stoneware and continue with Step 2.

Nutrients Per Serving (1½ cups/375 mL sauce)

Calories	175
Protein	5.5 g
Carbohydrates	27.5 g
Fat (Total)	6.3 g
Saturated Fat	0.9 g
Monounsaturated Fat	4.1 g
Polyunsaturated Fat	0.9 g
Dietary Fiber	5.1 g
Sodium	138 mg
Cholesterol	2 mg

EXCELLENT SOURCE OF vitamins A and K and potassium.
GOOD SOURCE OF vitamins C and B$_6$, folate, calcium and magnesium.
SOURCE OF phosphorus, iron and zinc.
CONTAINS a high amount of dietary fiber.

- **Medium to large (3½ to 5 quart) slow cooker**

2 tbsp	olive oil	30 mL
6	onions, thinly sliced on the vertical (about 3 lbs/1.5 kg)	6
1 tsp	granulated or coconut sugar	5 mL
1 tsp	cracked black peppercorns	5 mL
4	anchovy fillets, finely chopped, or 1 tbsp (15 mL) brown rice miso	4
3 cups	Basic Tomato Sauce (page 296)	750 mL
2	bunches arugula, stems removed and chopped (see Variation, below)	2

1. In slow cooker stoneware, combine olive oil and onions. Stir well to coat onions thoroughly. Cover and cook on High for 1 hour, until onions are softened (see Tip, left).

2. Add sugar and peppercorns and stir well. Place two clean tea towels each folded in half (so you will have four layers) over top of stoneware to absorb the moisture. Cover and cook on High for 4 hours, stirring two or three times to ensure that the onions are browning evenly and replacing towels each time.

3. Remove towels, add anchovies and stir well to ensure they are well coated with oil and integrated into the onions. Add tomato sauce and arugula and stir well to blend. Cover and cook on High for 15 minutes, until mixture is hot and flavors have blended.

Variation

If you prefer a smoother sauce, combine the arugula with 1 cup (250 mL) of the tomato sauce in a food processor and pulse several times until the arugula is finely chopped and integrated into the sauce. Add to the onion mixture along with the remaining sauce.

more information on page 305

Caramelized Onion Sauce
with Arugula

Mindful Morsels

One serving of this sauce is an excellent source of vitamin K. Studies link consumption of vitamin K with increased bone density in women and fewer hip fractures in members of both sexes (for more about vitamin K, see Natural Wonders, page 193).

Natural Wonders

Arugula

Often identified as rocket (its European name) this member of the cabbage family has an appealingly bitter yet spicy flavor. In recent years it has become quite popular and additional varieties, such as baby and wild arugula (as well as tasty little arugula microgreens), are increasingly available.

Arugula is a particularly nutrient dense salad green. One cup (250 mL) provides a mere 5 calories and 28% of the DV of vitamin K, which helps your body to absorb calcium, among other benefits. It also provides a smattering of other nutrients from dietary fiber to vitamin A, folate, calcium, manganese, iron, magnesium and potassium, among others. Like all greens, arugula provides a goodly amount of chlorophyll, which helps your body to eliminate toxins and fight inflammation.

Arugula is also loaded with phytonutrients and has more antioxidants than most salad greens. For instance, it provides the carotenoids beta-carotene, lutein and zeaxanthin, which are particularly important for eye health (see page 81). Because it is a member of the cruciferous family (which includes broccoli and cabbage) it is a recognized cancer fighter. The glucosinolates in these vegetables have strong anticancer properties. If you are cooking arugula (it is a lovely addition to pasta sauce, such as Caramelized Onion Sauce with Arugula) it's important not to boil it; boiling dramatically reduces its glucosinolate content). However, some evidence also suggests that gentle cooking with the addition of a bit of fat, helps your body to better utilize its full nutritional power.

Best-Ever Bolognese Sauce

This version of the hearty Italian meat sauce combines beef, pork and pancetta with traditional vegetables and robust porcini mushrooms. Traditionally the sauce develops flavor from long, slow simmering, making it perfect for the slow cooker. This makes a large batch and the servings are generous. It is wonderful to have on hand. If it is too large, freeze half or make half a batch. Serve it over a small portion of gluten-free pasta, Slow-Cooked Polenta (page 278) or roasted spaghetti squash, and add some steamed broccoli to maximize the nutritional punch (see Natural Wonders, page 307).

Makes 12 servings

Can Be Halved
(see Tips, below)

Tips

If you are halving this recipe, be sure to use a small (2 to 3½ quart) slow cooker.

Bolognese sauce should be thick. Placing the tea towels over the top of the slow cooker absorbs generated moisture that would dilute the sauce.

Nutrients Per Serving
(1¼ cups/300 mL approx. sauce)

Calories	192
Protein	3.0 g
Carbohydrates	9.0 g
Fat (Total)	11.6 g
Saturated Fat	4.2 g
Monounsaturated Fat	5.5 g
Polyunsaturated Fat	0.9 g
Dietary Fiber	1.8 g
Sodium	223 mg
Cholesterol	40 mg

EXCELLENT SOURCE OF vitamin A.
GOOD SOURCE OF vitamin B$_{12}$, potassium and zinc.
SOURCE OF vitamins C, B$_6$ and K, folate, calcium, phosphorus, magnesium and iron.

• **Medium to large (3½ to 5 quart) slow cooker**

1	package (½ oz/14 g) dried porcini mushrooms	1
1 cup	hot water	250 mL
1 tbsp	olive oil (approx.)	15 mL
2 oz	chunk pancetta, diced	60 g
1 lb	lean ground beef	500 g
8 oz	ground pork or chicken	250 g
2	onions, diced	2
2	stalks celery, diced	2
2	carrots, peeled and diced	2
4	cloves garlic, minced	4
1 tbsp	dried Italian seasoning	15 mL
2	bay leaves	2
½ tsp	salt	2 mL
½ tsp	cracked black peppercorns	2 mL
½ tsp	ground cinnamon	2 mL
1 cup	dry red wine	250 mL
1	can (28 oz/796 mL) no-salt added tomatoes, including juice, coarsely chopped	1
¼ cup	tomato paste	60 mL

1. In a bowl, combine dried mushrooms and hot water. Let stand for 30 minutes. Drain through a fine sieve, reserving liquid. Pat mushrooms dry with paper towel and chop finely. Set liquid and mushrooms aside.

2. Meanwhile, in a large skillet, heat oil over medium-high heat. Add pancetta and cook, stirring, until browned, about 3 minutes. Using a slotted spoon, transfer to slow cooker stoneware. Add more oil to pan if necessary. (You should have about 1 tbsp/15 mL.) Add beef, pork, onions, celery and carrots and cook, stirring, until carrots have softened and meat is no longer pink, about 7 minutes.

Complete Steps 1, 2 and
3. Cover mixture, ensuring
it cools promptly (see
Making Ahead, page 16), and
refrigerate for up to 2 days.
When you're ready to cook,
complete the recipe.

3. Add garlic, Italian seasoning, bay leaves, salt, peppercorns, cinnamon and reserved dried mushrooms and cook, stirring, for 1 minute. Add wine, bring to a boil and boil, stirring and scraping up brown bits from bottom of pan, for 2 minutes. Add reserved mushroom liquid.

4. Transfer to slow cooker stoneware. Add tomatoes with juice and stir well. Stir in tomato paste. Place two clean tea towels each folded in half (so you will have four layers) over top of stoneware to absorb moisture. Cover and cook on Low for 6 hours or on High for 3 hours.

Mindful Morsels

When buying tomato paste, look for those that contain only organic tomatoes and salt. I buy mine at my local natural foods store. Commercial brands are not likely to be as unadulterated.

Natural Wonders

Food Synergy

The more we learn about the nutrients in food, the more we understand that their relationships with your body and among themselves influence their effectiveness. Different nutrients interact with different organs, tissues and cells, and studies are now showing that the components of foods interact with each other, creating benefits that are more than the sum of their individual parts.

For instance, while tomatoes and broccoli have both been identified as cancer fighters, tomatoes rely on lycopene to do this job and broccoli uses glucosinolates, along with other substances. A study published in the *Journal of Nutrition* shows that rats fed broccoli and tomatoes together had less tumor growth than those eating a diet containing either food alone. Another study done by Britain's Institute of Food Research combined broccoli and chicken. Chicken is high in the mineral selenium, and broccoli contains sulforaphane, both of which have cancer-fighting properties. Researchers found the combination of broccoli and chicken was up to 13 times more powerful than when either food was consumed alone. Other studies have also shown, for instance, that a bowl of mixed berries had more cardioprotective power than the same-size bowl of a single berry. The vinegar in sushi rice can reduce the glycemic impact of the rice by as much as 35%. And a squirt of fresh lemon juice on spinach or other leafy greens makes the iron in these foods more bioavailable.

While this represents an exciting direction in nutritional science, we've known about aspects of nutrient synergy for quite a while. For instance, without fat your body can't absorb the fat-soluble vitamins A, D, E and K, as well as antioxidant carotenoids. That means, for instance, adding a drizzle of extra virgin olive oil to cooked tomatoes increases the availability of their lycopene.

Turkey, Mushroom and Chickpea Sauce

Kids always want seconds of this lip-smacking sauce, which is delicious over roasted spaghetti squash, chunky gluten-free pasta, brown rice, polenta, or even quinoa, whose new world origins resonate with turkey. This makes a very generous serving, so you don't need to add anything else.

Makes 6 servings

Can Be Halved
(see Tips, page 306)

Tips

If you don't have a mortar or a spice grinder, place the toasted fennel seeds on a cutting board and use the bottom of a wine bottle or measuring cup to grind them.

If you don't have hot paprika, use regular paprika instead with a pinch of cayenne.

Nutrients Per Serving
(1¾ cups/425 mL approx.)

Calories	260
Protein	19.0 g
Carbohydrates	26.5 g
Fat (Total)	9.6 g
Saturated Fat	2.2 g
Monounsaturated Fat	4.2 g
Polyunsaturated Fat	2.2 g
Dietary Fiber	5.7 g
Sodium	977 mg
Cholesterol	60 mg

EXCELLENT SOURCE OF vitamins C and B₆ and potassium.

GOOD SOURCE OF vitamins A and K, folate, magnesium, phosphorus, iron and zinc.

SOURCE OF calcium.

CONTAINS a high amount of dietary fiber.

• **Medium to large (3½ to 5 quart) slow cooker**

½ tsp	fennel seeds (see Tips, left)	2 mL
1 tbsp	olive oil	15 mL
1 lb	ground turkey	500 g
2	onions, minced	2
4	stalks celery, diced	4
2	cloves garlic, minced	2
1 tsp	dried oregano, crumbled	5 mL
1 tsp	sea salt	5 mL
½ tsp	cracked black peppercorns	2 mL
8 oz	cremini mushrooms, trimmed and quartered	250 g
1	can (28 oz/796 mL) tomatoes, including juice, coarsely chopped	1
1 cup	vegetable, chicken or turkey stock	250 mL
2 cups	cooked chickpeas, drained and rinsed (see Tips, page 237)	500 mL
2 tsp	hot paprika (see Tips, left) dissolved in 1 tbsp (15 mL) lemon juice	10 mL
1	red bell pepper, diced	1

1. In a dry skillet over medium heat, toast fennel seeds, stirring, until fragrant, about 3 minutes. Immediately transfer to a mortar or a spice grinder and grind (see Tips, left). Set aside.

2. In same skillet, heat oil over medium heat. Add turkey, onions and celery and cook, stirring, until celery is softened and no hint of pink remains in the turkey, about 6 minutes. Add fennel seeds, garlic, oregano, salt and peppercorns and cook, stirring, for 1 minute. Add mushrooms and toss to coat. Add tomatoes with juice and stock and bring to a boil. Transfer to slow cooker stoneware. Add chickpeas and stir well.

3. Cover and cook on Low for 6 hours or on High for 3 hours, until mixture is hot and bubbly. Add paprika solution and stir well. Add bell pepper and stir well. Cover and cook on High for 20 minutes, until pepper is tender.

Make Ahead

This dish can be partially prepared before it is cooked. Complete Steps 1 and 2. Cover and refrigerate overnight or for up to 2 days. When you're ready to cook, continue with Step 3.

Mindful Morsels

Almost 500 mg of the sodium in this recipe comes from using standard versions of prepared foods, specifically, prepared vegetable broth, chickpeas and tomatoes. If you're concerned about your intake of sodium, use homemade stock with no added salt (see Homemade Chicken Stock, page 116, or Basic Vegetable Stock, page 120), canned tomatoes with no salt added, and cook dried chickpeas from scratch (see Basic Beans, page 284).

Natural Wonders

Protein Sources

About one-third of the calories in this recipe come from protein. Our bodies need protein and it's not difficult to obtain an adequate supply of this macronutrient eating an average North American diet unless you're a vegetarian. However, it is wise to pay attention to the source of the protein you consume, particularly if you are watching fat calories, and are concerned about saturated fat.

Take red meat, for example. Three ounces (90 g) of grain-fed (not pasture-raised) beef top sirloin provides about 28 grams of protein and 3.1 grams of saturated fat. Compare that to the same quantity of skinless turkey breast, which delivers about 27 grams of protein and only 1 gram of saturated fat. That's a comparable amount of protein and a third of the saturated fat. The ground turkey in one serving of this recipe, which combines white and dark meat, which is higher in fat, contains 13.2 grams of protein and 1.7 grams of saturated fat. So, if you are watching your fat calories, it's a good food choice.

The chickpeas are another source of protein. The chickpeas in one serving of this recipe provide 2.6 grams of protein and a mere 0.1 gram of saturated fat. However, the quality of that protein, which is classified as incomplete protein, is not as high as the protein in meat. Meat is a complete protein, which means it contains all the essential amino acids in amounts needed to support health and well-being. Legumes don't contain the full range of amino acids and will need to be combined with other foods to create a complete protein.

Basmati Rice Pudding

Desserts

Basmati Rice Pudding

The cardamom in this pudding provides an irresistible Indian flavor. I like to serve it at room temperature, but it also works warm or cold and I love having leftovers in the refrigerator for an afternoon snack. This makes a generous serving, so if you have enjoyed a substantial meal, you will likely want to reduce the quantity.

Makes 6 servings

Tip

Virtually all of the sodium in this recipe (65 mg) comes from the milk and occurs naturally in that food.

- **Small (maximum 3½ quart) slow cooker**
- **Lightly greased slow cooker stoneware**

4 cups	whole milk or fortified rice milk	1 L
⅓ cup	evaporated cane juice sugar	75 mL
2 tsp	ground cardamom	10 mL
¾ cup	brown basmati rice, rinsed	175 mL
½ cup	chopped unsalted pistachio nuts	125 mL

1. In a large saucepan over medium heat, bring milk to a boil, stirring often. Add sugar and cardamom. Remove from heat and stir in rice. Transfer to prepared slow cooker stoneware.

2. Place a tea towel folded in half (so you will have two layers) over top of stoneware to absorb moisture. Cover and cook on High for 3 hours, until rice is tender and pudding is creamy. Transfer to a serving bowl and cool to room temperature. Garnish with pistachios, dividing equally.

Mindful Morsels

Sprinkling the pudding with pistachios adds small amounts of fiber, calcium, folate, potassium and vitamin B_6, among other nutrients.

Nutrients Per Serving

Calories	271
Protein	8.9 g
Carbohydrates	37.4 g
Fat (Total)	10.6 g
Saturated Fat	3.6 g
Monounsaturated Fat	3.8 g
Polyunsaturated Fat	1.6 g
Dietary Fiber	2.1 g
Sodium	66 mg
Cholesterol	16 mg

GOOD SOURCE OF calcium, phosphorus and potassium.

SOURCE OF vitamins A, B_6, B_{12} and K, folate, magnesium, iron and zinc.

Natural Wonders

Evaporated Cane Juice Sugar

For many years I have wondered why nutritionists dismissed sugar made from evaporated cane juice because they claimed that, like white sugar, it was completely devoid of nutrients. After all, molasses, which is the by-product of making refined white sugar, has always been identified as a source of nutrients and that liquid is an integral part of the sugar cane plant. Blackstrap molasses, the most nutritious version, provides minerals such as potassium, magnesium, calcium and iron, and has traditionally been viewed as a health food. Presumably, those nutrients don't vanish into thin air in the process of producing raw cane sugar.

Now I'm pleased to see that various groups are taking a second look at sugar cane and its unrefined products and have concluded that even though it is high in calories it does have some nutritional value.

Raw cane sugar is made by boiling sugar cane juice down until all the liquid evaporates. Evaporated cane juice retains complex sugars, minerals and molasses and it is less likely to cause cavities than refined white sugar. Although there is no official USDA nutrient data, the unrefined sugar that results contains trace amounts of vitamins and minerals (thiamine, riboflavin, niacin, calcium, iron, magnesium, phosphorus and potassium, among others). However, the real nutritional value is probably found in its phytonutrients. Evaporated cane juice sugar appears to be rich in antioxidants such as flavonoid and phenolic compounds. One of the few laboratory studies that exists concluded that these compounds have the potential to be beneficial to health and useful for therapeutic applications.

Since we do know that the substances in whole foods work together synergistically to create nutritional benefits far beyond the sum of their parts, I've bet my money on raw

cane sugar and have been using it for many years. However, one problem with the product is that it's difficult to identify the real thing. Some manufacturers label products as raw cane sugar that have not actually been made from evaporated cane juice. As always, you need to read labels carefully or trust your instincts and search out traditional products. In India, where it is known as jaggery, they've been making raw cane sugar for at least two thousand years. Mexican piloncillo, which is sold in solid cones, is likely to be another good choice. Pricier options include Sucanat® or Rapadura®.

Pumpkin Rice Pudding

The combination of flavors and the chewy but crunchy texture of this luscious pudding make it hard to resist.

Makes 8 servings

Tips

Cook 1 cup (250 mL) raw rice to get the 2 cups (500 mL) of cooked rice required for this recipe.

If you prefer, use 1½ tsp (7 mL) pumpkin pie spice instead of the cinnamon, nutmeg and cloves.

- Small to medium (2 to 3½ quart) slow cooker
- Greased slow cooker stoneware

2 cups	cooked brown rice (see Tips, left)	500 mL
1½ cups	pumpkin purée (not pie filling)	375 mL
1 cup	dried cranberries or dried cherries	250 mL
1 cup	evaporated skim milk	250 mL
½ cup	packed muscovado or other evaporated cane juice sugar	125 mL
2	eggs	2
1 tsp	ground cinnamon (see Tips, left)	5 mL
½ tsp	grated nutmeg	2 mL
¼ tsp	ground cloves	1 mL
	Toasted chopped pecans, optional	
	Vanilla-flavored yogurt or cultured coconut milk, optional	

1. In prepared slow cooker stoneware, combine rice, pumpkin purée and cranberries.
2. In a bowl, whisk together milk, sugar, eggs, cinnamon, nutmeg and cloves until smooth and blended. Stir into pumpkin mixture. Cover and cook on High for 3 hours, until pudding is set. Serve warm, garnished with toasted pecans and a dollop of yogurt, if using.

Mindful Morsels

Finishing this pudding with a sprinkling of toasted pecans adds more than taste and texture to the dish. Pecans contain beneficial fats, fiber and iron, among other nutrients.

Nutrients Per Serving

Calories	224
Protein	6.2 g
Carbohydrates	47.5 g
Fat (Total)	2.0 g
Saturated Fat	0.7 g
Monounsaturated Fat	0.7 g
Polyunsaturated Fat	0.4 g
Dietary Fiber	3.4 g
Sodium	68 mg
Cholesterol	48 mg

EXCELLENT SOURCE OF vitamin A.

GOOD SOURCE OF vitamin K, magnesium and potassium.

SOURCE OF calcium, phosphorus and iron.

CONTAINS a moderate amount of dietary fiber.

Natural Wonders

Cinnamon

A staple in North American kitchens, cinnamon is inextricably linked with fond memories of indulgent desserts. Now researchers are telling us that this delightful spice may actually be good for us. Long known to have benefits as a digestive, cinnamon bark contains essential oils that have been associated with a range of health benefits, from easing inflammation to inhibiting the growth of pathogens. Israeli research indicates that cinnamon extract stalls the growth of the ulcer-causing bacteria *Helicobacter pylori*, and other scientists have found it dramatically undermined the power of the potentially life threatening *E. coli* bacteria.

Cinnamon is also a powerful antioxidant. In fact, some research suggests it may have more antioxidant activity than almost any other spice. Other studies indicate that cinnamon may also have a role in controlling diabetes. One study showed that consuming less than $\frac{1}{2}$ tsp (2 mL) of cinnamon a day reduced blood sugar levels, triglycerides and cholesterol in people with type-2 diabetes. And if that isn't enough, recent research found that just the smell of cinnamon may make you smarter. In one study, subjects who inhaled cinnamon or chewed cinnamon-flavored gum demonstrated improved cognitive function.

Be aware, though, that the cinnamon in your cupboard is not likely to be real or Ceylon cinnamon, which is sweeter than the more common cassia. In culinary terms there is not a great deal of difference between the two. However, cassia has much more coumarin, a substance that acts as a natural blood thinner.

Coconut Rice Pudding with Flambéed Bananas

It is hard to believe that something this easy to make can taste so delicious. Whenever I make this, temptation strikes — I fantasize about not sharing it and eating the whole thing myself.

Makes 8 servings

Tip

To toast coconut: Spread on a baking sheet and place in a preheated 350°F (180°C) oven, stirring once or twice, for 7 to 8 minutes.

- Small to medium (2 to 3½ quart) slow cooker
- Lightly greased slow cooker stoneware

¾ cup	short-grain brown rice	175 mL
1	can (14 oz/400 mL) coconut milk	1
1 cup	water	250 mL
½ cup	coconut sugar	125 mL
1 tsp	almond extract	5 mL
Pinch	sea salt	Pinch

Banana Topping

3 tbsp	butter	45 mL
3 tbsp	coconut sugar	45 mL
4	bananas, sliced	4
¼ cup	amaretto liqueur	60 mL
¼ cup	toasted shredded unsweetened coconut (see Tip, left)	60 mL

1. In prepared slow cooker stoneware, combine rice, coconut milk, water, sugar, almond extract and salt. Cover and cook on High for 3 to 4 hours, until rice is tender. Uncover and stir well. Serve hot or transfer to a bowl, cover tightly and chill for up to 2 days.

2. *Banana Topping:* In a skillet over medium heat, combine butter and sugar. Cook, stirring, until butter melts and mixture is smooth. Add bananas and cook, stirring, until tender, about 5 minutes. Sprinkle amaretto evenly over top and, standing well back, ignite. Allow liqueur to burn off. To serve, spoon pudding into bowls, top with bananas and garnish with toasted coconut.

Vegan Alternative

Substitute an equal quantity of non-hydrogenated margarine or butter substitute for the butter.

Nutrients Per Serving

Calories	356
Protein	3.0 g
Carbohydrates	51.0 g
Fat (Total)	17.0 g
Saturated Fat	13.4 g
Monounsaturated Fat	1.6 g
Polyunsaturated Fat	0.3 g
Dietary Fiber	3.1 g
Sodium	49 mg
Cholesterol	11 mg

GOOD SOURCE OF magnesium, potassium and iron.

SOURCE OF vitamins C and B_6, folate, phosphorus and zinc.

CONTAINS a moderate amount of dietary fiber.

The toasted coconut in this recipe is used as a garnish to add flavor and texture. Although the quantity is too small to add any significant nutrient punch, if you were consuming a more substantial amount, you could expect to add fiber, iron and zinc to your meal, not to mention all the healthy benefits of coconut oil (see page 91), which coconut also provides.

Natural Wonders

Bananas

Available year-round, bananas are one of our most healthful and versatile fruits. They make a great addition to breads, muffins and morning smoothies as well as a delicious snack on their own. A good source of vitamin B_6, which helps to strengthen the nervous system among other benefits, bananas also contain vitamin C, manganese and magnesium and are one of the best food sources of potassium. An average banana provides 422 mg of potassium and about 1 mg of sodium, an extraordinary ratio, if you consider that people who are extremely health conscious recommended consuming potassium and sodium in a 5 to 1 ratio. Numerous studies indicate that eating a healthy diet that contains foods high in potassium and low in sodium reduces the risk of high blood pressure.

Bananas are also a source of fiber (an average banana has about 3 grams of fiber, providing 12% of the DV). Some of the fiber is pectin, a soluble fiber that is very soothing to the digestive track and helps to keep your bowels functioning smoothly. Bananas also contain a phytonutrient called fructooligosaccharide. It's a prebiotic, which means it feeds the beneficial bacteria in your gut. Among their jobs, these healthy bacteria help your body absorb nutrients, such as calcium. Not only does eating bananas increase the ability to absorb calcium, the potassium they contain helps to prevent its loss in your urine, a definite win-win.

In addition, research suggests that bananas may be an especially potent force in battling kidney cancer. One study published in the *International Journal of Cancer* found that women who ate bananas four to six times a week reduced their chances of developing this disease by 50%.

Indian Banana Pudding

This traditional Indian pudding has an unusual thickener: dried split peas. Exotic and delicious, it has a light banana flavor enhanced with sweet dates and the texture of crunchy toasted almonds.

Makes 8 servings

Tip

To toast almonds: Spread in a single layer on an ungreased baking sheet. Bake at 350°F (180°C), stirring once, until lightly browned, about 5 minutes.

- **Small (approx. 3½ quart) slow cooker**
- **Greased slow cooker stoneware**
- **Food processor or blender**

½ cup	yellow split peas, soaked according to Quick Soak method (see Basic Beans, page 284) and drained	125 mL
1 tbsp	minced gingerroot	15 mL
¼ cup	evaporated cane juice sugar	60 mL
1	can (14 oz/400 mL) coconut milk	1
½ tsp	almond extract	2 mL
1 tsp	ground cardamom	5 mL
2	ripe bananas, peeled and chopped	2
¼ cup	finely chopped pitted soft dates, preferably Medjool	60 mL
½ cup	toasted slivered almonds, divided	125 mL
	Whipped cream, optional	

1. In a food processor or blender, combine soaked peas, ginger, sugar and ¹/₂ cup (125 mL) of the coconut milk. Process until puréed. Add remaining coconut milk, almond extract and cardamom and blend. Pour into prepared slow cooker stoneware.

2. Place a tea towel folded in half (so you will have two layers) over top of stoneware to absorb moisture. Cover and cook on High for 3 hours, until peas are tender and mixture begins to thicken. Stir in bananas. Replace folded towel and cook on High for 30 minutes.

3. Remove stoneware from casing and, using a wooden spoon, beat mixture vigorously. Fold in dates and half the almonds. Transfer to a serving bowl. Cover and refrigerate until thoroughly chilled, about 1¹/₂ hours. Garnish with remaining almonds and serve with a dollop of whipped cream, if using.

Nutrients Per Serving

Calories	252
Protein	6.2 g
Carbohydrates	28.6 g
Fat (Total)	14.4 g
Saturated Fat	9.4 g
Monounsaturated Fat	3.0 g
Polyunsaturated Fat	1.1 g
Dietary Fiber	3.0 g
Sodium	12 mg
Cholesterol	0 mg

GOOD SOURCE OF magnesium, potassium and iron.
SOURCE OF vitamin B₆ and phosphorus.
CONTAINS a moderate amount of dietary fiber.

Mindful Morsels

The dates in this pudding add sweetness, fiber and a range of minerals, including potassium.

Natural Wonders

Almonds

The almonds in this recipe deliver more than flavor and texture; they also provide significant nutritional punch. Although many people shy away from eating nuts because they are high in fat, most of the fat in almonds is monounsaturated fat, which has long been linked with keeping cholesterol under control. In fact, studies have linked eating almonds with improved cholesterol levels, and one study published in 2002 showed that people with elevated cholesterol could significantly reduce their levels of LDL ("bad") cholesterol by consuming almonds. Other studies have linked the consumption of almonds with helping to keep weight under control.

One ounce of almonds (28 g/about 23 whole almonds) provides 162 calories (8% DV), 7.4 mg vitamin E (37% DV), 0.3 mg riboflavin (17% DV), 0.6 mg manganese (32% DV) and 75.7 mg magnesium (19% DV), among other nutrients. They also provide 6 g of protein and 3.4 g (14% DV) of fiber. In other words, almonds make an extremely nutrient-dense snack or addition to dishes, such as dessert.

Almonds are one of the best food sources of vitamin E, an antioxidant that protects cells against free radical damage and helps prevent some chronic diseases. Research indicates that most people in North America do not get enough of this valuable nutrient. Observational studies have linked vitamin E intake with a lower incidence of heart disease, although this has been questioned because studies utilizing vitamin E supplements did not show any benefit. Unfortunately, there does not seem to be much research focused on intake of vitamin E from food. One study did show that people who consumed the recommended daily intake (30 IU) of vitamin E reduced the likelihood that they would develop age-related macular degeneration by about 20%.

Cornmeal Pudding

This is a terrific old-fashioned dessert. Traditionally known as "Indian pudding," likely because the natives introduced the early settlers to cornmeal, it is great comfort food. It is also very versatile. It is delicious served with fresh berries, a dollop of whipped cream or cultured coconut milk.

Makes 8 servings

Can Be Halved
(see Tip, page 325)

Tips

The nutrient analysis on this recipe was done using 2% milk. If you are counting calories, use skim milk instead, but be aware that it does not contain any beneficial conjugated linoleic acid (CLA). If you prefer a richer flavor, use whole milk.

Most of the sodium in this recipe is from naturally occurring sodium in food (57 mg from the milk; 24 mg from the butter; and 41 mg from the molasses). If you are watching your sodium intake, omit the added salt, which provides 72 mg per serving.

Nutrients Per Serving

Calories	231
Protein	6.8 g
Carbohydrates	28.1 g
Fat (Total)	10.4 g
Saturated Fat	5.1 g
Monounsaturated Fat	2.7 g
Polyunsaturated Fat	0.6 g
Dietary Fiber	1.5 g
Sodium	204 mg
Cholesterol	94 mg

GOOD SOURCE OF vitamins A and B$_{12}$, calcium, magnesium and potassium.
SOURCE OF vitamin B$_6$, folate, phosphorus, iron and zinc.

- **Small (maximum 3½ quart) slow cooker**
- **Greased slow cooker stoneware**

4 cups	milk or non-dairy alternative (see Tips, left and Variation)	1 L
⅔ cup	stone-ground cornmeal	150 mL
3	eggs, beaten	3
¼ cup	butter	60 mL
½ cup	fancy molasses	125 mL
1 tsp	ground ginger	5 mL
1 tsp	ground cinnamon	5 mL
1 tsp	freshly grated nutmeg	5 mL
¼ tsp	sea salt	1 mL

1. In a saucepan, heat milk over medium heat, stirring often to prevent scorching, until boiling. Gradually whisk in cornmeal in a steady stream. Cook, stirring, until mixture begins to thicken and bubbles like lava, about 5 minutes. Remove from heat.

2. In a small bowl, combine eggs with about ½ cup (125 mL) of the hot cornmeal, beating until combined. Gradually return to pot, mixing well. Stir in butter, molasses, ginger, cinnamon, nutmeg and salt. Transfer to prepared stoneware.

3. Place a tea towel folded in half (so you will have two layers) over top of stoneware to absorb moisture. Cover and cook on High for 3 hours, until set. Spoon into individual serving bowls and top with fresh berries, vanilla ice cream or a dollop of whipped cream, if using.

Variations

Dairy-Free Cornmeal Pudding: I have made a dairy-free version of this pudding, with excellent results. Substitute equal quantities of almond milk and coconut oil for the milk and butter, respectively.

Fruit-Studded Cornmeal Pudding: About half an hour before the pudding has finished cooking, stir in ½ cup (125 mL) dried cherries, cranberries or raisins.

Grits Pudding: Substitute an equal quantity of stone-ground grits for the cornmeal.

This recipe provides 206 mg of calcium and is a good source of that nutrient, which we usually associate with healthy bones. But among its other benefits, this essential mineral can also help your body to counteract stress. Some research indicates that an adequate supply of dietary calcium helps keep blood pressure, which tends to rise in stressful situations, under control.

Natural Wonders

Milk

Milk is one of the best food sources of calcium and a good source of protein. The milk in one serving of Cornmeal Pudding, for example, provides 4.0 grams of protein. Milk is often derided in contemporary society, but there is little doubt that drinking milk can have significant health benefits beyond the contribution that calcium makes to preventing osteoporosis. If you are lucky enough to live in an area where you can purchase raw organic milk from grass-fed cows, you have access to something approaching a health food. Milk also provides vitamin A and is one of the few food sources of vitamin D. And, if the cows are grass-fed, it will also provide a significant amount of beneficial omega-3 fats.

Many people avoid drinking milk because whole milk is high in saturated fat. However, contrary to traditional wisdom, one 2012 study in the *American Journal of Clinical Nutrition* actually linked the consumption of the saturated fat specific to dairy products with a reduced risk of cardiovascular disease. Research also indicates that people who regularly consume dairy products are likely to be slimmer than those who avoid them and that people on calorie controlled diets are likely to lose weight faster, especially around the abdomen, if they drink milk. One study found that women who consumed at least three daily servings of dairy reduced their risk of becoming obese by 80%.

In addition to weight control, drinking milk may also play a role in managing diabetes. One study published in the *Journal of the American Medical Association*, linked young adults' consumption of milk with a significant reduction in insulin resistance. Another study, which examined the diets of 37,000 middle-aged women, concluded that those who consumed the most dairy were the least likely to develop type-2 diabetes.

Although people who suffer from arthritis are often told to avoid dairy, at least one study linked the consumption of milk with a reduced risk of gout, a type of arthritis. Milk, when not the fat-free or skim versions, is a major food source of conjugated linoleic acid (CLA), which has been identified as a nutraceutical with bioactive properties. Studies done on animals suggest that CLA may be anticarcinogenic and reduce fat to lean body mass ratio, among other benefits.

The Ultimate Baked Apples

These luscious apples, simple to make yet delicious, are the definitive autumn dessert. If you feel like gilding the lily, serve them with a dollop of whipped cream, coconut whipped cream or cultured coconut.

Makes 8 servings

Tips

In my experience the vast percentage of walnuts sold in supermarkets have already passed their peak. Taste before you buy. If they are not sweet, substitute an equal quantity of pecans.

To toast walnuts: Spread in a single layer on an ungreased baking sheet. Bake at 350°F (180°C), stirring once, until lightly browned, about 7 minutes.

- Large (minimum 5 quart) oval slow cooker

½ cup	chopped toasted walnuts (see Tips, left)	125 mL
½ cup	dried cranberries, sweetened with juice	125 mL
2 tbsp	coconut sugar	30 mL
1 tsp	grated orange zest	5 mL
8	apples, cored	8
1 cup	pure pomegranate juice	250 mL

1. In a bowl, combine walnuts, cranberries, sugar and orange zest. To stuff the apples, hold your hand over the bottom of the apple and, using your fingers, tightly pack core space with filling. One at a time, place filled apples in slow cooker stoneware. Drizzle pomegranate juice evenly over tops.

2. Cover and cook on Low for 6 hours or on High for 3 hours, until apples are tender.

3. Transfer apples to a serving dish and spoon cooking juices over them. Serve hot.

Mindful Morsels

The walnuts in this recipe provide 0.66 mg of omega-3 fatty acids. They also contribute 0.5 grams of fiber per serving.

more information on page 324

Nutrients Per Serving

Calories	173
Protein	1.5 g
Carbohydrates	33.8 g
Fat (Total)	5.2 g
Saturated Fat	0.5 g
Monounsaturated Fat	0.7 g
Polyunsaturated Fat	3.6 g
Dietary Fiber	3.6 g
Sodium	6 mg
Cholesterol	0 mg

SOURCE OF vitamins C and B$_6$, folate, magnesium and potassium.

CONTAINS a moderate amount of dietary fiber.

Natural Wonders

Apples

Most of us grew up taking it on faith that an apple a day keeps the doctor away. Now scientists are confirming the truth of this maxim and explaining the reasons why. Although it varies among varieties, one medium apple contains about 95 calories (5% DV), provides 4.4 g of dietary fiber (17% DV), and 8.4 mg of vitamin C (14% DV), as well as a smattering of other vitamins and minerals such as vitamins K and B_6, riboflavin, niacin, folate, potassium, managanese, magnesium and copper.

However, it's the range of phytonutrients in apples that most interests researchers today. Apples are an antioxidant powerhouse. Among commonly consumed fruits, their antioxidant activity is second only to cranberries.

Consider quercetin, for instance. This flavonoid is a potent antioxidant, which in laboratory studies has shown promise in preventing cancer, among other benefits (see page 293). It has also been shown to be helpful in treating conditions such as atherosclerosis and high cholesterol, so not surprisingly, the consumption of quercetin has been linked with a reduced risk of heart disease.

Apples also contain other significant amounts of other phytonutrients such as phenolic compounds. The phytonutrient combination in apples has been shown to prevent breast cancer in animals and inhibit the growth of colon cancer cells in laboratories. In fact, a review of 85 studies, published in *Nutrition Journal*, linked eating apples, in comparison with other fruits, with a reduced risk of heart disease, cancer and type-2 diabetes.

Unfortunately, though, apples have not escaped the dark side of agribusiness. Supermarket apples may taste good but their ability to fight cancer and other diseases may be limited. In her book *Eating on the Wild Side*, Jo Robinson writes that over the years we have been breeding the nutrients out of apples. Shockingly, one 2003 survey showed that wild apples were much more nutritious than cultivated varieties. For instance Golden Delicious apples had fifteen times fewer phytonutrients when measured against a wild variety. She suggests actively seeking out heirloom varieties, most likely to be found at farmers' markets or on roadside stands, because they are probably more nutritious. If you are shopping in the supermarket, she provides a list of the most nutritious common varieties, which includes Braeburn, Cortland, Discovery, Gala, Granny Smith, Honeycrisp, McIntosh and Red Delicious. Unless you are purchasing a green or russet variety, she recommends choosing the reddest apples, which are likely to have most phytonutrients because they have had more exposure to direct sunlight.

Poached Pears in Chocolate Sauce

Nothing could be simpler than these pears poached in a simple sugar syrup enhanced with vanilla and a hint of cinnamon. The fruit is delicious on its own, but if, like me, you enjoy gilding the lily, add the chocolate sauce, which is very easy to make.

Makes 6 to 8 servings

Can Be Halved
(see Tip, below)

Tip

If you are halving this recipe, be sure to use a small (approx. 1½ to 3½ quart) slow cooker.

Nutrients Per Serving

Calories	253
Protein g	1.8 g
Carbohydrates	45.6 g
Fat (Total)	8.6 g
Saturated Fat	6.0 g
Monounsaturated Fat	0.2 g
Polyunsaturated Fat	0.1 g
Dietary Fiber	4.9 g
Sodium	9 mg
Cholesterol	0 mg

SOURCE OF vitamins C and K, potassium and iron.

CONTAINS a high amount of dietary fiber.

- **Medium to large (3½ to 5 quart) slow cooker**

	Finely grated zest of 1 lemon	
2 tbsp	freshly squeezed lemon juice	30 mL
6	large firm pears, such as Bosc or Bartlett, peeled, cored and cut into quarters on the vertical	6
½ cup	unpasteurized liquid honey	125 mL
1	piece (2 inches/5 cm) cinnamon stick	1
1 tsp	vanilla extract	5 mL

Chocolate Sauce

½ cup	coconut cream	125 mL
1 tbsp	coconut sugar	15 mL
4 oz	bittersweet chocolate, chopped	125 g

1. In a large bowl, combine 4 cups (1 L) water and lemon juice. After preparing the pears immediately drop them into the lemon juice solution. (This will prevent the fruit from turning brown.)

2. In slow cooker stoneware, combine 2 cups (500 mL) water, honey, cinnamon stick, vanilla and lemon zest. Stir well. Drain pears and add to stoneware. Cover and cook on Low for 6 hours or on High for 3 hours, until pears are tender. Transfer pears and liquid to a large bowl. Cover and chill thoroughly.

3. *Chocolate Sauce:* When you're ready to serve, combine cream, sugar and chocolate in a saucepan or microwave-safe bowl. Cook over low heat, stirring constantly, until melted, or microwave on High for 1½ minutes, then stir well.

4. To serve, using a slotted spoon, transfer pears to a plate and top with chocolate sauce.

more information on page 327

Poached Pears in Chocolate Sauce

There is a great deal of conflicting information on whether honey is a healthful sweetener. Many nutritionists feel that honey, like all other sweeteners, has absolutely no nutritional value and should be avoided because it will cause your blood sugar levels to rise. However, unpasteurized honey has a long history of efficacy in folk medicine, where it has been used as an immune system booster, antiviral and anti-inflammatory. In the U.K., honey has been studied extensively as a topical treatment for antibiotic-resistant skin infections. Bees feed on a wide variety of plants and as a result, honey contains valuable phytonutrients and enzymes. Common sense indicates that pasteurization is likely to destroy these substances. Whether honey should be fed to infants is, however, controversial, so check with your physician before doing so.

Natural Wonders

Chocolate

In recent years, chocolate has acquired something of a reputation as a health food. It is rich in antioxidants and provides a smattering of minerals, including magnesium, potassium, phosphorus, zinc, iron, copper and manganese. Many studies suggest that consuming chocolate is good for heart health, among other benefits.

Cacao is the healthful substance in chocolate. It contains flavonols, antioxidants, which, among other functions, protect the lining of the arteries so they can produce beneficial nitric oxide. This substance keeps arteries clear, which facilitates blood flow and helps to keep blood pressure low by dilating or relaxing blood vessels. It also prevents platelets from becoming sticky, which keeps clots from forming, reducing the risk of stroke. One Canadian study indicated that people who consumed chocolate once a week were 22% less likely to have a stroke. Be aware that dark chocolate, which contains a higher percentage of cacao is more healthful than milk chocolate. The greater the cacao mass, the more flavonols, which means you can consume less (keeping calories in check) and still reap the nutritional benefits.

Just for the record, white chocolate is a misnomer. Because it contains no cacao, it is not chocolate.

Gingery Pears Poached in Green Tea with Goji Berries

I love the combination of ginger, pears and goji berries in this light but delicious dessert. Sprinkle with toasted almonds for a perfect finish to a substantial meal.

Makes 4 to 6 servings

Can Be Halved
(see Tips, page 332)

Tips

When poaching, use firmer pears, such as Bosc, for best results.

I prefer a strong ginger taste in these pears, but some might feel it overpowers the taste of the pears. Vary the amount of ginger to suit your preference.

Make Ahead

This dessert should be made early in the day or the night before so it can be well chilled before serving.

Nutrients Per Serving

Calories	178
Protein	1.9 g
Carbohydrates	45.8 g
Fat (Total)	0.1 g
Saturated Fat	0 g
Monounsaturated Fat	0 g
Polyunsaturated Fat	0 g
Dietary Fiber	4.0 g
Sodium	28 mg
Cholesterol	0 mg

GOOD SOURCE OF vitamin A.

SOURCE OF vitamins C and K and iron.

CONTAINS a high amount of dietary fiber.

- Small (approx. 3 quart) slow cooker

2 cups	boiling water	500 mL
2 tbsp	green tea leaves	30 mL
2 tbsp	grated gingerroot (see Tips, left)	30 mL
½ cup	unpasteurized liquid honey	125 mL
1 tsp	grated lemon zest	5 mL
4	firm pears, such as Bosc, peeled, cored and cut into quarters lengthwise	4
½ cup	organic dried goji berries	125 mL
	Toasted sliced almonds, optional	
	Vanilla-flavored yogurt or cultured coconut milk, optional	

1. In a pot, combine boiling water and green tea leaves. Cover and let steep for 5 minutes. Strain through a fine sieve into slow cooker stoneware.

2. Add ginger, honey and lemon zest and stir well. Add pears. Cover and cook on Low for 4 hours or on High for 2 hours, until pears are quite tender. Add goji berries and cook on High for 15 minutes, until puffed and soft. Transfer to a serving bowl, cover and chill thoroughly. Serve garnished with toasted almonds and a dollop of yogurt, if using.

Mindful Morsels

While pears do not contain a large amount of any nutrient, they do provide a smattering of valuable nutrients which, when combined with other nutrient-dense foods, can have an impact on your daily nutrient intake. One pear provides 6.2 g of vitamin C (about 10% DV) and 6.7 g of vitamin K (about 8% DV) a bit of potassium (176 mg, about 6% DV) and copper (0.1 mg, about 6% DV). It also provides 4.6 g of fiber (about 18% DV). When you consider that a pear contains only 86 calories, which is about 4% of the recommended daily intake, it makes for a pretty good equation.

As a fruit, pears have a low glycemic index (33) and glycemic load (4) partly due to the fiber content but also because of their fructose.

Natural Wonders

Tea

Tea has a long history as a tonic and has been used in folk medicine to cure a wide variety of ailments. In recent years, researchers have taken a great deal of interest in the health benefits of this popular beverage, especially the green variety (and its relative, less common white tea). As the least processed teas, green and white teas are the richest in antioxidant catechins, a type of polyphenol also found in garlic, some fruits, and red wine, among other consumables. These substances are thought to be at the heart of the health benefits associated with drinking tea. Your body metabolizes them quickly so they can immediately go to work combating the free radicals associated with the development of conditions such as cancer and cardiovascular disease.

People who drink green tea regularly appear to reduce their risk of infections, likely because catechin is a potent antibacterial. The polyphenols in green tea appear to inhibit the growth of early stage prostate cancer cells and may help prevent prostate cancer from spreading. They may also help in controlling other types of cancer. At least one laboratory study has liked drinking green tea with maintaining a healthy weight, but it has been suggested that drinking the necessary quantity might be challenging under ordinary circumstances. On the other hand a British study, conducted in association with Neal's Yard Remedies, found that drinking even a small amount of white tea inhibited enzyme action that breaks down substances in the skin leading to aging. The same kind of inflammation that is associated with wrinkles is also characteristic of rheumatoid arthritis and some types of cancer, the researchers noted.

Although green and white teas are the best source of catechins, other varieties of tea have slightly different phytonutrients and may be equally good for you as well. A study published in the *Journal of Food Science* in 2009, looked at the polysaccharides in black tea and concluded they may be beneficial in controlling diabetes. Another 2012 study published in the *Archives of Internal Medicine* found that people who drank two to three cups of black tea a day had lower blood pressure levels by an average of two to three points, which researchers considered significant. Chinese studies found that male tea drinkers were about half as likely to develop stomach or esophageal cancer than men who didn't drink much tea. On the other side of the world, Harvard researchers concluded that all varieties of tea, when combined with soy, were even more effective in fighting prostate cancer than tea alone. Given all the positive news about tea, it makes sense to add the beverage to your diet, especially if it replaces less healthy drinks such as soda or fruit drinks loaded with added sugar.

Cranberry-Spiked Applesauce

Not only do the cranberries add nutrients, they also make this dessert a lovely shade of dusky rose. It's delicious and pretty enough to serve to guests. A dollop of whipped cream or whipped coconut cream turns it into a celebratory dish.

Makes 8 servings

Can Be Halved
(see Tips, page 332)

Tips

Do not peel or core the apples or remove the seeds. To avoid pesticide residue be sure to use organic apples.

You can also purée the mixture in a food processor. However, do so very carefully because the sauce is hot and the gas in the liquid will cause it to expand, possibly over the top of the container and, if you are close enough, on to your face, causing a potentially serious burn. If you are using a food processor, divide the mixture into three batches for processing and stand well back when you turn it on.

- **Small to medium (2 to 3½ quart) slow cooker**
- **Large sieve**

6	large apples, quartered	6
½ cup	cranberries	125 mL
	Finely grated zest and juice of 1 orange	
2 tbsp	water	30 mL
2 tbsp	unpasteurized liquid honey (approx.)	30 mL

1. In slow cooker stoneware combine apples, cranberries, orange zest and juice and water. Cover and cook on Low for 6 hours or on High for 3 hours, until apples look like they have melted and cranberries have popped. Using an immersion blender (see Tips, left) purée.

2. Place sieve over a large bowl and add mixture. Using a wooden spoon, push sauce through. Discard residue. Stir in honey, adding more, if necessary, to taste.

Mindful Morsels

I love the rosy color and burst of tart flavor cranberries add to this applesauce. However, in addition to being very flavorful, cranberries are packed with powerful antioxidants, such as plant phenols, which help your body fight a variety of diseases. And, yes, if you are prone to urinary tract infections, cranberries are a good preventative. They work to keep bacteria from sticking to the urinary tract.

Nutrients Per Serving

Calories	96
Protein	0.6 g
Carbohydrates	25.1 g
Fat (Total)	0.2 g
Saturated Fat	0 g
Monounsaturated Fat	0 g
Polyunsaturated Fat	0.1 g
Dietary Fiber	1.9 g
Sodium	1 mg
Cholesterol	0 mg

SOURCE OF vitamin C and potassium.

Natural Wonders

Fruit

Fruit is at the center of the sugar wars because it is high in fructose. Consequently, it is often mistakenly compared to products such as soda, which contain high fructose corn syrup (a different compound) and have been linked to obesity. At its most basic, among other problems, the high fructose content in products such as soda causes blood sugar to spike, whereas the fructose in fruit does not do so because it is low on the glycemic index and is balanced by fiber and other nutrients.

Nevertheless, I continue to come across supposedly informed people who advise against eating fruit. That's why I was delighted to come across an article published in *The Journal of the American Medical Association* debunking the myth that fruit should be avoided. Based on a review of current research, lead author Dr. David Ludwig of the Harvard School of Public Health, concluded there is no association between the sugar consumed in fruit and any adverse health effects.

At its most basic, whole fruits contain a panoply of healthful nutrients, such as vitamins, minerals and antioxidants, which benefit the body in a myriad of ways. They also provide varying amounts of fiber, which can act like a prebiotic, encouraging the growth of healthy bacteria in your gut, in addition to slowing down digestion. As a result, the sugars in fruit are absorbed slowly, ensuring that your blood sugar won't surge. Another benefit of consuming whole foods such as fruit, which are digested slowly, is that you feel full longer.

In fact, contrary to much conventional wisdom, Dr. Ludwig linked increased fruit consumption with lower body weight and a lower risk of diseases associated with obesity. As he writes, "observational studies report inverse associations between fruit consumption and body weight or risk of obesity-related diseases."

Maple Sugar Quince

This is an elegant and delicious dessert that is also low in calories. Making it with Calvados, a French apple brandy, adds richness and depth to the flavor, but it is good made with apple cider, as well. I love to add a drizzle of pure maple syrup when serving, but that's not necessary.

Makes 6 servings

Can Be Halved
(see Tips, below)

Tips

If you are halving this recipe, use a small (approx. 2 quart) slow cooker.

Calvados is a strongly flavored apple brandy. Using it in this recipe will produce fragrant, slightly boozy quinces. Topped with a dollop of whipped cream or coconut whipped cream, it makes an ideal special occasion dessert.

If you prefer, drizzle with maple syrup before serving.

Don't take short cuts on the timing. Quinces require a full 8 hours (or longer) on Low heat to develop their deep, rich flavor.

- **Small to medium (2 to 3½ quart) slow cooker**
- **Large piece of parchment paper**

4	quinces, peeled and cut into wedges (about 8 per quince)	4
¼ cup	apple cider or Calvados (see Tips, left)	60 mL
3 tbsp	pure maple sugar	45 mL
	Finely chopped walnuts, optional	
	Pure maple syrup, optional	

1. Arrange quinces over bottom of slow cooker stoneware. Pour cider evenly over top. Sprinkle evenly with maple sugar. Place parchment over the mixture, pressing it down to brush the food and extending up the sides of the stoneware so it overlaps the rim. Cover and cook on Low for 8 hours or on High for 4 hours, until quinces are tender and have turned pink.

2. Lift out parchment and discard, being careful not to spill the accumulated liquid into the fruit. Serve warm or at room temperature, with a sprinkling of walnuts and a drizzle of maple syrup, if using. This is also delicious served cold.

Mindful Morsels

I like to finish this dessert with a generous sprinkling of walnuts. In addition to omega-3 fatty acids, walnuts provide vitamin B_6, magnesium and potassium and contain arginine, an essential amino acid. Walnuts are also bursting with plant sterols, which help lower cholesterol, and, like all nuts and seeds, are high in fiber. Numerous studies show a strong link between the consumption of nuts and reduced rates of coronary artery disease. For instance, a 2013 study conducted by Brigham and Women's Hospital in Boston concluded that people who regularly consumed nuts were 11% less likely to die from cancer and 29% less likely to die from heart disease. And, they were slimmer, too. So enjoy a small handful of nuts every day — they will definitely help keep the doctor away.

Nutrients Per Serving

Calories	75
Protein	0.4 g
Carbohydrates	19.8 g
Fat (Total)	0.1 g
Saturated Fat	0.0 g
Monounsaturated Fat	0.0 g
Polyunsaturated Fat	0.1 g
Dietary Fiber	1.8 g
Sodium	5 mg
Cholesterol	0 mg

SOURCE OF vitamin C, potassium and iron.

Natural Wonders

Quince

The quince is a fruit with a long and honorable tradition. You have likely seen its delicate blossoms captured in Japanese art and eaten it with cheese as the flavorful orange-hued jelly known as membrillo. Some believe that the biblical apple was actually a quince. The tree is native to the Middle East, where quinces often appear in savory dishes as well as those that are sweet. I've purchased quince vinegar in Turkey. In North America, quinces were quite widely cultivated in the past and commonly made into preserves, but during the last century these lovely trees have all but disappeared from view. Today, thanks to farmers who are striking a quiet blow for biodiversity, the quince is making a slow but steady comeback.

Much larger than apples or pears (the two fruits they most resemble in appearance; in fact, a quince might be described as a yellow apple trying to become a pear), a typical quince weighs about 8 ounces (250 g) but individual fruits can weigh as much as a pound (500 g) or more. Quinces are unusual because, unlike most fruits, they need to be cooked. Raw, they are white fleshed, hard and tasteless but when cooked slowly they are transformed into soft, fragrant drops that are a lovely shade of apricot-tinged pink.

Quinces are nutrient-dense. An average fruit provides 131 calories (7.5% DV) while delivering 34.5 mg of vitamin C (57.5% DV) 452.5 mg of potassium (12.5% DV), 1.5 mg of iron (10% DV), and 18.5 mg of magnesium (5% DV), in addition to a smattering of numerous other nutrients. Quinces are rich in phytonutrients such as tannins, the source of its tart taste. Two tannins in particular, catechin and epicatechin, are thought to have cancer-fighting abilities.

Quinces are also rich in pectin, a kind of soluble fiber that becomes gel-like in the intestinal tract, slowing down the passage of food and delaying the release of glucose into the bloodstream. Research indicates that consuming pectin also reduces blood cholesterol levels and may help to keep triglycerides low. It may also protect against certain types of cancers. Pectin is also being studied for its value as prebiotic, a substance that encourages the growth of healthy bacteria in the intestinal tract.

Goji-Spiked Quince

Quinces are a fabulous winter fruit that are made for the slow cooker because they demand cooking. Raw, the quince is a tough, fibrous ball. Softened by slow cooking, it turns a beautiful shade of pink and melts in your mouth, releasing a panoply of complex flavors. Serve warm or at room temperature.

Makes 4 to 6 servings

Can Be Halved
(see Tips, below)

Tips

If you are halving this recipe, use a small (approx. 2 quart) slow cooker.

Don't take short cuts on the timing. Quinces require a full 8 hours (or longer) on Low heat to develop their deep, rich flavor.

- **Small to medium (2 to 4 quart) slow cooker**

½ cup	unpasteurized liquid honey	125 mL
	Zest and juice of 1 orange	
¼ cup	water	60 mL
4	quinces (about 2 lbs/1 kg), peeled, cored and sliced	4
½ cup	organic dried goji berries	125 mL
	Whipped cream, whipped coconut cream or mascarpone	

1. In slow cooker stoneware, combine honey, orange zest and juice and water. Stir well. Add quinces and stir well. Cover and cook on Low for 8 hours or on High for 4 hours, until quinces are tender and turn pink. Add goji berries and cook on High for 15 minutes, until puffed and soft.

2. To serve, top with whipped cream, whipped coconut cream or a dollop of mascarpone.

Mindful Morsels

If you're concerned about age-related macular degeneration (the major cause of vision loss in older people; see page 81), and you don't like eating carrots, try substituting fruit instead. One study published in the *Archives of Ophthalmology* reported that people who consumed three or more servings of fruit a day lowered their risk of the disease by 36% compared with participants who ate less than 1.5 daily servings of fruit.

Nutrients Per Serving

Calories	182
Protein	1.9 g
Carbohydrates	46.9 g
Fat (Total)	0.1 g
Saturated Fat	0 g
Monounsaturated Fat	0 g
Polyunsaturated Fat	0.1 g
Dietary Fiber	3.3 g
Sodium	30 mg
Cholesterol	0 mg

GOOD SOURCE OF vitamins A and C.
SOURCE OF potassium and iron.
CONTAINS a moderate amount of dietary fiber.

Natural Wonders

Goji Berries

If you haven't heard about goji berries, a supposed superfood, you've likely been living under a rock. In recent years these slightly bitter berries, which are usually sold dried, have become extremely popular. These days, products such as goji-spiked snack bars and goji juice seem to be ubiquitous, largely because the berries' health-promoting properties are legendary.

Goji berries originate in China, where their annual harvest is celebrated with a festival. Although interest in this fruit has spread around the world, virtually all goji berries are still grown in China. Perhaps not surprisingly, they have been widely used in traditional Chinese medicine for centuries to treat a variety of ailments ranging from diabetes to malaria.

Goji berries are known for being nutrient-dense. A twenty-eight gram (1 oz) serving (about $1/4$ cup/60 mL) contains 100 calories (5% DV). It provides 3 grams of fiber; 140% of the DV for vitamin A; 20% of the DV for vitamin C and 10% of the DV for iron, in addition to a smattering of other vitamins and minerals.

While there is little scientific support for some of the health claims associated with goji berries, they are reputedly loaded with antioxidants, particularly carotenoids such as beta-carotene, lutein, beta-cryptoxanthin and lycopene. When grown in optimal conditions they are supposedly one of the best food sources of glyconutrients, plant carbohydrates that do important work promoting clear communication among your cells and helping them to function optimally. I recommend enjoying goji berries as a tasty and nutritious fruit that can add a variety of nutrients to your diet, rather than going whole hog. Also, be sure to buy those that are certified organic.

Diabetes Food Values

The diabetes food values for all the recipes were prepared by Info Access (1988) Inc.

Info Access is a Canadian firm of registered dietitians and computer experts specializing in computer-assisted nutrient analysis, assessing more than 4,000 recipes annually for a broad range of international clients. The Nutritional Accounting System component of the CBORD Menu Management System is used, as well as the Canadian Nutrient File, augmented as necessary with data from other reliable sources.

Info Access has also been involved with the assignment of food choice values in Canada, acting as the consulting firm assigning values for the Canadian Diabetes Association. The U.S. determinations in the following chart were based on Exchange List Guidelines for Recipe/Food Label Calculations, Page 174, Diabetes Medical Nutrition Therapy, The American Dietetic Association/American Diabetes Association, 1997.

While the U.S. and Canadian diabetes assignment methodologies are similar, there are some variations in the approaches taken and the base values used that account for the observed differences. In the U.S. System, dietary fiber is generally not deducted from total carbohydrate (except for high fiber cereals); thus carbohydrate choices may be higher with the U.S. assignments. Vegetables (up to 5 g carbohydrate) are considered "free" in Canada, whereas vegetable assignments are made in the U.S. In the U.S., the Starch Exchange assumes 1 g fat per choice; in Canada the same assignment assumes no fat. Consequently fat assignments may be higher in Canada. In the U.S., half meat and fat exchanges are not allowed; in Canada, half values may be assigned for these choices. Thus, there may be some rounding changes introduced.

For those of you using the carbohydrate counting approach for meal planning the carbohydrate and fiber values are provided with each recipe.

Recipes	Page No.	Canadian Diabetes Association Values	American Diabetes Association Values
Artichoke and White Bean Spread (1/12 of recipe = 1/4 cup/60 mL)	48	1/2 Carbohydrate, 1/2 Meat, 1/2 Fat	1/2 Starch, 1 Vegetable, 1 Fat
Avocado Topping (1/12 of recipe = 2 tbsp/30 mL)	148	1/2 Fat	1/2 Fat
Basic Beans (1/4 of recipe)	284	1 Carbohydrate, 1 Meat	1 1/2 Starches, 1 Very Low-Fat Meat
Basic Tomato Sauce (1/4 of recipe = 2 cups/500 mL)	296	1 Carbohydrate, 1 Fat	1 1/2 Starches, 1 Fat
Basic Vegetable Stock (1/12 of recipe = 1 cup/250 mL)	120	1 Extra	1 Free

In this chart the term "meat" represents meat or meat alternatives/substitutes (foods with a similar amount of protein, fat and calories), in keeping with guidelines of both the American Diabetes Association and the Canadian Diabetes Association.

Recipes	Page No.	Canadian Diabetes Association Values	American Diabetes Association Values
Basmati Rice Pudding (⅙ of recipe)	312	2½ Carbohydrates, 1 Fat	½ Whole Milk, 1 Starch, 1 Other, 1 Fat
Beef and Chickpea Curry with Spinach (¼ of recipe)	203	1½ Carbohydrates, 4 Meat	2 Starches, 2 Vegetables, 4 Low-Fat Meat, ½ Fat
Beet Soup with Lemongrass and Lime (⅛ of recipe)	95	½ Carbohydrate, ½ Fat	1 Carbohydrate, ½ Fat
Best-Ever Bolognese Sauce (⅟₁₂ of recipe)	306	2 Meat, 1 Fat	2 Vegetables, 1 Medium-Fat Meat, 1½ Fat
Bistro Fish Soup (⅟₁₀ of recipe)	156	1 Carbohydrate, ½ Meat, 1½ Fat	1 Starch, 2 Vegetables, 2 Fat
Black Sticky Rice Congee with Coconut (⅙ of recipe)	28	2½ Carbohydrates, 3 Fat	1 Starch, ½ Fruit, 1 Other, 3 Fat
Braised Tomato Topping (⅛ of recipe)	46	1½ Fat	1½ Fat
Braised Veal with Pearl Onions and Sweet Green Peas (⅙ of recipe)	212	4½ Meat	2 Vegetables, 5 Very Low-Fat Meat, 1 Fat
Breakfast Rice (¼ of recipe)	22	5 Carbohydrates, 1 Fat	2 Starches, 1 Fruit, 2 Other, ½ Fat
Brown and Wild Rice with Bay Leaves (¼ of recipe)	282	2½ Carbohydrates, 1½ Fat	2½ Starches, 1 Fat
Buckwheat Meatballs in Tomato Sauce (⅛ of recipe)	208	½ Carbohydrate, 2 Meat, ½ Fat	½ Starch, 2 Vegetables, 1 Medium-Fat Meat, 1½ Fat
Butterbeans Braised with Celery (⅙ of recipe)	286	1 Carbohydrate, 1 Meat, 1 Fat	1½ Starches, 1 Vegetable, 1 Fat
Butternut Chili (⅙ of recipe)	180	1½ Carbohydrates, 3 Meat, ½ Fat	2 Starches, 2 Vegetables, 2 Medium-Fat Meat
Caldo Verde (⅛ of recipe)	77	1½ Carbohydrates, ½ Meat	1½ Starches, 2 Vegetables, ½ Fat
Caper-Studded Caponata (⅛ of recipe = ¼ cup/60 mL)	40	½ Fat	1 Vegetable, ½ Fat
Caramelized Onion Dip (⅛ of recipe = ¼ cup/60 mL)	38	1½ Fat	1 Vegetable, 1½ Fat
Caramelized Onion Sauce with Arugula (⅙ of recipe 1½ cups/375 mL)	303	1 Carbohydrate, 1½ Fat	1 Starch, 2 Vegetables, 1 Fat
Caribbean Fish Stew (⅛ of recipe)	172	3 Meat	2 Vegetables, 3 Very Low-Fat Meat
Caribbean Pepper Pot (⅙ of recipe)	176	1½ Carbohydrates, 4 Meat	1½ Starches, 2 Vegetables, 4 Low-Fat Meat, 1 Fat
Cheesy Grits (¼ of recipe)	280	1 Carbohydrate, 2 Meat, 2 Fat	1 Starch, 1 Vegetable, 1 Medium-Fat Meat, 2½ Fat

Recipes	Page No.	Canadian Diabetes Association Values	American Diabetes Association Values
Chicken Cassoulet (⅛ of recipe)	126	1 Carbohydrate, 3 Meat	1 Starch, 1 Carbohydrate, 2 Lean Meat
Chili with Black Beans and Grilled Chicken (⅙ of recipe)	124	1 Carbohydrate, 2 Meat	1½ Starches, 2 Vegetables, 2 Low-Fat Meat
Chilled Sorrel Soup (⅙ of recipe)	104	1 Fat	2 Vegetables, 1 Fat
Chocolate Atole (⅙ of recipe)	30	2½ Carbohydrates	1 Starch, 1½ Other, ½ Fat
Chunky Black Bean Chili (⅛ of recipe)	200	1 Carbohydrate, 4 Meat, 1 Fat	1½ Starches, 2 Vegetables, 4 Low-Fat Meat, 1 Fat
Cioppino (⅛ of recipe)	154	3½ Meats	2 Vegetables, 4 Very Lean Meat
Coconut Rice Pudding with Flambéed Bananas (⅛ of recipe)	316	3 Carbohydrates, 3½ Fat	1 Starch, 1 Fruit, 1 Other, 3½ Fat
Cornmeal Pudding (⅛ of recipe)	320	2 Carbohydrates, 1½ Fat	½ 1% Milk, ½ Starch, 1 Other, 1½ Fat
Cranberry-Spiked Apple Sauce (⅛ of recipe)	330	1½ Carbohydrates	1½ Fruit
Creamy Coconut Grouper (⅛ of recipe)	174	1 Carbohydrate, 3 Meat, 1 Fat	½ Starch, 2 Vegetables, 3 Low-Fat Meat, 1 Fat
Creamy Morning Millet with Apples (⅙ of recipe)	20	3 Carbohydrates	2 Starches, 1 Other
Creamy Parsnip, Parsley Root and Butterbean Soup (⅛ of recipe)	82	1 Carbohydrate, ½ Fat	1 Starch, 2 Vegetables
Creamy Polenta with Corn and Chiles (⅙ of recipe)	276	1½ Carbohydrates, 1 Meat, 1 Fat	½ Skim Milk, 1 Starch, 1 Low-Fat Meat, 1 Fat
Creamy Sunchoke Soup (⅙ of recipe)	102	½ Carbohydrate, 1 Fat	1 Starch, 2 Vegetables, 1 Fat
Cumin-Spiked Lentil Soup with Eggplant and Dill (⅛ of recipe)	80	1 Carbohydrate, 1 Meat	1 Starch, 2 Vegetables, ½ Fat
Curried Parsnip Soup with Green Peas (⅛ of recipe)	86	1 Carbohydrate, 1½ Fat	1 Starch, 2 Vegetables, 1½ Fat
David's Dream Cholent (1/12 of recipe)	184	1½ Carbohydrates, 4 Meat, 3 Fat	1½ Starches, 2 Vegetables, 4 Medium-Fat Meat, 2½ Fat
Down-Home Tomatoes with Okra (⅙ of recipe)	289	1 Fat	2 Vegetables, 1 Fat
Easy "Paella" (¼ of recipe)	128	2½ Carbohydrates, 6 Meat	3 Starches, 2 Vegetables, 5 Low-Fat Meat

In this chart the term "meat" represents meat or meat alternatives/substitutes (foods with a similar amount of protein, fat and calories), in keeping with guidelines of both the American Diabetes Association and the Canadian Diabetes Association.

Recipes	Page No.	Canadian Diabetes Association Values	American Diabetes Association Values
Eggplant Lentil Ragoût (⅙ of recipe)	270	1 Carbohydrate, 1 Meat, 1 Fat	1½ Starches, 2 Vegetables, ½ Fat
Fennel Braised with Tomatoes (⅙ of recipe)	294	1 Fat	2 Vegetables, 1 Fat
Flavorful Fish Stock (1/12 of recipe = 1 cup/250 mL)	118	1 Extra	1 Free
French Basil Chicken (⅛ of recipe)	134	3 Meat	2 Vegetables, 3 Low-Fat Meat
Gingery Carrot Soup with Orange and Parsley (⅛ of recipe)	98	½ Carbohydrate, ½ Fat	½ Fruit, 2 Vegetables, ½ Fat
Gingery Pears Poached in Green Tea with Goji Berries (⅙ of recipe)	328	3 Carbohydrates	1½ Fruit, 1½ Other, ½ High-Fat Meat
Gingery Red Lentils with Spinach and Coconut (⅙ of recipe)	266	1½ Carbohydrates, 1 Meat, 1½ Fat	Very Low-Fat Meat, 2 Fat
Goji-Spiked Quince (⅙ of recipe)	334	3 Carbohydrates	1½ Fruit, 1½ Other
Greek-Style Beef with Eggplant (⅛ of recipe)	192	½ Carbohydrate, 1½ Meat, 1 Fat	1 Carbohydrate, 1 Lean Meat, 2 Fat
Hearty Beef Stock (1/12 of recipe)	114	1 Extra	1 Free
Homemade Chicken Stock (1/12 of recipe = 1 cup/250 mL)	116	1 Extra	1 Free
Homemade Mushroom Stock (1/12 of recipe = 1 cup/250 mL)	119	1 Extra	1 Free
Home-Style Pork and Beans (⅙ of recipe)	222	2 Meat, 2 Fat	2 Starches, 2 Vegetables, 1½ Other, 2 Medium-Fat Meat, 1½ Fat
Hoppin' John with Collard Greens (⅛ of recipe)	292	1 Carbohydrate, 1 Meat	1½ Starches, 1½ Vegetables, 1 Low-Fat Meat
Indian Banana Pudding (⅛ of recipe)	318	1½ Carbohydrates, ½ Meat, 2½ Fat	1 Starch, 1 Fruit, 2½ Fat
Indian Peas and Beans (⅙ of recipe)	258	1½ Carbohydrates, 1 Meat	1½ Starches, 2 Vegetables, ½ Fat
Indian-Spiced Beef with Eggplant (⅙ of recipe)	196	1 Carbohydrate, 4 Meat, 1½ Fat	½ 1% Milk, ½ Starch, 2 Vegetables, 4 Medium-Fat Meat, 1 Fat
Indian-Style Chicken with Puréed Spinach (⅛ of recipe)	140	4½ Meat	2 Vegetables, 4 Lean Meats
Kale-Spiked Sausages and Beans (⅙ of recipe)	220	2 Carbohydrates, 3 Meat	2 Starches, 2 Vegetables, 3 Medium-Fat Meat

Recipes	Page No.	Canadian Diabetes Association Values	American Diabetes Association Values
Leafy Greens Soup (⅛ of recipe)	106	½ Carbohydrate, ½ Fat	½ Starch, 2 Vegetables, ½ Fat
Maple Sugar Quince (⅙ of recipe)	332	1 Carbohydrate	1 Fruit
Maple-Sweetened Congee (¼ of recipe)	26	4 Carbohydrates, 1 Fat	1 Starch, 1 Fruit, 2 Other, 1 Fat
Mediterranean Beef Ragoût (⅛ of recipe)	186	3 Meat, ½ Fat	2 Vegetables, 3 Medium-Fat Meat
Mediterranean-Style Mahi-Mahi (¼ of recipe)	158	6 Meat	2 Vegetables, 6 Low-Fat Meat
Mexican Meatballs (⅛ of recipe)	206	½ Carbohydrate, 3 Meat, 2½ Fat	½ Starch, 2 Vegetables, 3 Medium-Fat Meat, 2 Fat
Miso Mushroom Chicken with Chinese Cabbage (⅙ of recipe)	144	1 Carbohydrate, 3 Meat	1 Starch, 2 Vegetables, 3 Very Low-Fat Meat, 1 Fat
Mixed Mushroom Soup (¹⁄₁₀ of recipe)	70	½ Fat	2 Vegetables, ½ Fat
Mixed Vegetables in Spicy Peanut Sauce (⅛ of recipe)	242	½ Carbohydrate, 1 Meat, 2 Fat	2 Vegetables, 1 Other, 1 Medium-Fat Meat, 2 Fat
Moroccan-Style Chicken with Prunes and Quinoa (⅛ of recipe)	130	2½ Carbohydrates, 2 Meat	1½ Starches, 1 Fruit, 2 Lean Meat
Moroccan-Style Lamb with Raisins and Apricots (⅛ of recipe)	227	1 Carbohydrate, 3 Meat	1½ Fruit, 4 Very Low-Fat Meat
Mushroom and Chickpea Stew with Roasted Red Pepper Coulis (⅙ of recipe)	246	1 Carbohydrate, ½ Meat, 1 Fat	2 Starches, 2 Vegetables, 1 Fat
Mushroom Lentil Soup (⅛ of recipe)	72	1½ Carbohydrates, 1 Meat	1½ Starches, 2 Vegetables, 1 Very Low-Fat Meat
Mushroom Tomato Sauce (⅙ of recipe = ¾ cup/175 mL)	298	½ Fat	2 Vegetables, ½ Fat
Nettle and Asparagus Soup (⅙ of recipe)	100	1½ Fat	½ Starch, 2 Vegetables, 1½ Fat
New Age Squash Succotash (⅛ of recipe)	248	1½ Starches, 2 Vegetables, 1 Fat	1½ Starches, 2 Vegetables, 1 Fat
New World Leek and Potato Soup (⅛ of recipe)	66	1½ Carbohydrates, 1½ Fat	1½ Starches, 2 Vegetables, 1½ Fat
Onion-Braised Brisket (⅛ of recipe)	182	6 Meat, 2 Vegetables	5 Low-Fat Meat, ½ Fat

In this chart the term "meat" represents meat or meat alternatives/substitutes (foods with a similar amount of protein, fat and calories), in keeping with guidelines of both the American Diabetes Association and the Canadian Diabetes Association.

Recipes	Page No.	Canadian Diabetes Association Values	American Diabetes Association Values
Onion-Braised Shrimp (¼ of recipe)	170	4½ Carbohydrates, 3 Meat	1 Starch, 2 Vegetables, 3 Very Low-Fat Meat, ½ Fat
Onion-Soused Beans (⅛ of recipe = ¼ cup/60 mL)	50	½ Meat, ½ Fat	1 Starch, 1 Vegetable, ½ Fat
Oven-Baked Kale Chips (5 chips)	58	1 Fat	1 Fat
Pepper Pot Soup (⅛ of recipe)	88	1 Carbohydrate, 2½ Fat	1½ Starches, 2 Vegetables, 2 Fat
Peppery Turkey Casserole (⅛ of recipe)	137	1½ Carbohydrates, 2 Meat	1½ Starches, 1 Vegetable, 2 Lean Meat
Persian-Style Beef with Split Peas (⅛ of recipe)	194	½ Carbohydrate, 3½ Meat, ½ Fat	½ Starch, 1 Vegetable, 3 Medium-Fat Meat
Poached Eggs on Spicy Lentils (⅙ of recipe)	263	1 Carbohydrate, 2 Meat, 2 Fat	1½ Starches, 2 Vegetables, 1 Medium-Fat Meat, 2 Fat
Poached Halibut with Dill Hollandaise (⅛ of recipe)	160	3 Meat, 1½ Fat	3 Medium-Fat Meat
Poached Pears in Chocolate Sauce (⅛ of recipe)	325	3 Carbohydrates, 1½ Fat	1½ Fruit, 1½ Other, 1½ Fat
Poached Salmon with Sorrel Sauce (⅛ of recipe)	168	5 Meat	5 Medium-Fat Meat
Polenta Crostini (1/36 of recipe)	60	1 Extra	1 Free
Pork Belly with Flageolets (⅛ of recipe)	232	1 Carbohydrate, 2 Meat, 5 Fat	1½ Starch, 1 Vegetable, 2 Medium-Fat Meat, 4 Fat
Pork Chili with Black-Eyed Peas (⅛ of recipe)	234	1½ Carbohydrates, 4 Meat	2 Starches, 2 Vegetables, 4 Very Low-Fat Meat, 1 Fat
Pork with Pot Likker (⅛ of recipe)	218	3 Meat	2 Vegetables, 3 Very Low-Fat Meat, 1 Fat
Pumpkin Rice Pudding (⅛ of recipe)	314	3 Carbohydrates	1 Starch, 1 Fruit, 1 Other
Ratatouille (⅛ of recipe)	244	½ Carbohydrate, 1 Fat	1 Carbohydrate, 1 Fat
Ratatouille (Side dish: ½ Portion – 1/16 of recipe)	244	½ Fat	½ Fat
Red Beans and Greens (⅛ of recipe)	260	1½ Carbohydrates, 1 Meat	1½ Starches, 2 Vegetables, 1 Low-Fat Meat
Ribs with Hominy and Kale (⅛ of recipe)	216	½ Carbohydrate, 2½ Meat	½ Starch, 2 Vegetables, 2 Medium-Fat Meat
Salty Almonds with Thyme (1/16 of recipe = 2 tbsp/30 mL)	35	½ Meat, 1½ Fat	1 Medium-Fat Meat, 1 Fat

Recipes	Page No.	Canadian Diabetes Association Values	American Diabetes Association Values
Santorini-Style Fava Spread (⅛ of recipe = ¼ cup/60 mL)	55	1 Carbohydrate, ½ Meat, 2½ Fat	1 Starch, 1 Vegetable, 2½ Fat
Sausage-Spiked Chickpeas with Yogurt (⅙ of recipe)	224	2 Carbohydrates, 3 Meat, 2 Fat	2½ Starches, 2 Vegetables, 2 Medium-Fat Meat, 2 Fat
Shrimp 'n' Grits (¼ of recipe)	162	2 Carbohydrates, 2 Meat, 1 Fat	2½ Starches, 1 Vegetable, 2 Medium-Fat Meat
Slow-Cooked Polenta (⅙ of recipe)	278	1 Carbohydrate, ½ Fat	1½ Starches
Smoky Butternut Hominy Chili (⅛ of recipe)	256	1 Carbohydrate, 1 Fat	1½ Starches, 2 Vegetables, ½ Fat
Southwestern Turkey Chowder (⅛ of recipe)	68	2 Carbohydrates, 2 Meat	2½ Starches, 2 Vegetables, 1 Low-Fat Meat
Spanish-Style Pork and Beans (⅛ of recipe)	230	1½ Carbohydrates, 4 Meat	2 Starches, 2 Vegetables, 4 Very Low-Fat Meat, ½ Fat
Spicy Cashews (⅟₁₆ of recipe = 2 tbsp/30 mL)	34	½ Carbohydrate, 1½ Fat	½ Starch, 1½ Fat
Spicy Lamb with Chickpeas (⅛ of recipe)	236	1½ Carbohydrates, 3½ Meat	1½ Starches, 2 Vegetables, 3 Very Low-Fat Meat, 1 Fat
Spicy Peanut Chicken (⅛ of recipe)	142	½ Carbohydrate, 4½ Meat	½ Starch, 1 Vegetable, 4 Lean Meat, 1 Fat
Spicy Tamari Almonds (⅟₁₆ of recipe = 2 tbsp/30 mL)	36	½ Meat, 1½ Fat	1 Medium-Fat Meat, 1 Fat
Spinach Dal with Millet (⅙ of recipe)	268	2½ Carbohydrates, 1 Meat	3 Starches, 2 Vegetables, ½ Fat
Squash and Black Bean Chili (⅙ of recipe)	254	1½ Carbohydrates, 1 Meat	2 Starches, 2 Vegetables
Steel-Cut Oats (¼ of recipe)	24	1 Carbohydrate	1 Starch
Summer Borscht (⅟₁₀ of recipe)	112	1 Fat	2 Vegetables, 1 Fat
Sumptuous Spinach and Artichoke Dip (⅟₁₂ of recipe = ¼ cup/60 mL)	43	1 Meat	1 Medium-Fat Meat
Sweet Potato Coconut Curry with Shrimp (¼ of recipe)	165	1½ Carbohydrates, 3 Meat	2 Starches, 1 Vegetable, 3 Lean Meat
Syracuse Sauce (⅙ of recipe)	300	½ Carbohydrate, 1 Fat	½ Starch, 2 Vegetables, 1 Fat
Tagine of Chicken with Apricots (⅛ of recipe)	132	1 Carbohydrate, 4 Meat, 1½ Fat	1 Fruit, 2 Vegetables, 4 Low-Fat Meat, 1½ Fat

In this chart the term "meat" represents meat or meat alternatives/substitutes (foods with a similar amount of protein, fat and calories), in keeping with guidelines of both the American Diabetes Association and the Canadian Diabetes Association.

Recipes	Page No.	Canadian Diabetes Association Values	American Diabetes Association Values
Texas-Style Chili con Carne (⅛ of recipe)	198	½ Carbohydrate, 3½ Meat	1 Starch, 2 Vegetables, 3 Low-Fat Meat, ½ Fat
Thai-Style Coconut Fish Curry (⅛ of recipe)	152	3 Meat	½ Starch, 1 Vegetable, 3 Lean Meat
Thai-Style Pumpkin Soup (⅛ of recipe)	90	½ Carbohydrate, 1½ Fat	½ Starch, 1 Vegetable, 1½ Fat
The Ultimate Baked Apples (⅛ of recipe)	322	2 Carbohydrates, 1 Fat	2 Fruit, 1 Fat
Turkey Chili with Black-Eyed Peas (⅛ of recipe)	148	1 Carbohydrate, 3 Meat	1 Starch, 2 Vegetables, 4 Very Low-Fat Meat
Turkey, Mushroom and Chickpea Sauce (⅙ of recipe)	308	1 Carbohydrate, 2 Meat	1 Starch, 2 Vegetables, 2 Lean Meat, ½ Fat
Two-Bean Soup with Pistou (⅛ of recipe)	92	1½ Carbohydrates, 1 Meat, 1 Fat	2 Starches, 1 Low-Fat Meat, 1 Fat
Two-Bean Turkey Chili (⅛ of recipe)	146	1 Carbohydrate, 3 Meat	1 Starch, 1 Carbohydrate, 3 Very Lean Meat
Veal Goulash (⅛ of recipe)	210	3 Meat	2 Vegetables, 3 Low-Fat Meat
Vegetable Chili (⅙ of recipe)	251	2 Carbohydrates, 1 Fat	2½ Starches, 2 Vegetables, ½ Fat
Vegetable Curry with Lentils and Spinach (⅙ of recipe)	272	2½ Carbohydrates, 1 Meat, 1½ Fat	3 Starches, 2 Vegetables, 1½ Fat
Vegetable Gumbo (⅙ of recipe)	109	1 Carbohydrate, ½ Fat	1 Starch, 2 Vegetables, ½ Fat
Vichyssoise with Celery Root and Watercress (⅛ of recipe)	74	2½ Fat	2 Vegetables, 2 ½ Fats
Warm Black Bean Salsa (1/12 of recipe = ¼ cup/60 mL)	52	½ Carbohydrate, 1 Meat, ½ Fat	1 Starch, 1 Medium-Fat Meat
Yogurt Flatbread (1/30 of recipe)	62	½ Carbohydrate, ½ Fat	½ Starch
Zesty Braised Beef with New Potatoes (⅛ of recipe)	189	1 Carbohydrate, 3 Meat, ½ Fat	1 Starch, 2 Vegetables, 3 Medium-Fat Meat

Library and Archives Canada Cataloguing in Publication

Finlayson, Judith, author
    The healthy slow cooker : 135 gluten-free recipes for health and wellness / Judith Finlayson. — Second edition.

Includes index.
ISBN 978-0-7788-0479-6 (pbk.)

1. Electric cooking, Slow. 2. Gluten-free diet—Recipes. 3. Cookbooks. I. Title.

TX827.F555 2014   641.5'884   C2013-908428-2

Selected Resources

Books and Articles

Aggarwal, Bharat B. with Yost, Debora. *Healing Spices: How to Use 50 Everyday and Exotic Spices to Boost Health and Beat Disease* (Sterling, New York, 2011)

Boon, Heather and Smith, Michael. *55 Most Common Medicinal Herbs: The Complete Natural Medicine Guide (Second Edition)* (Robert Rose Inc., Toronto, 2009)

Colpo, Anthony. "LDL Cholesterol: "Bad" Cholesterol, or Bad Science?" (*Journal of American Physicians and Surgeons,* Fall, 2005)

Daley, Cynthia A. et al. "A review of fatty acid profiles and antioxidant content in grass-fed and grain-fed beef" (*Nutrition Journal,* 2010)

Daniel, Kaayla. Why Broth is Beautiful: Essential Roles for Proline, Glycine and Gelatin http://www.westonaprice.org/food-features/why-broth-is-beautiful

Fallon, Sally with Enig, Mary. G. Ph.D. *Nourishing Traditions: The Cookbook that Challenges Politically Correct Nutrition and the Diet Dictocrats (Revised Second Edition)* (New Trends Publishing, Inc. Washington, DC. 2001)

Liu, Rui Hai, "Health benefits of fruit and vegetables are from additive and synergistic combinations of phytochemicals" *(American Journal of Clinical Nutrition,* September, 2003)

McCullough, Fran. *The Good Fat Cookbook.* (Scribner, 2003)

Mozaffarian, Dr. Dariush (Ed.) *The Truth About Vitamins and Minerals: Choosing the Nutrients You Need to Stay Healthy* (Harvard Health Publications, 2012)

Pratt, Steven, M.D. and Matthews, Kathy. *Superfoods: Fourteen Foods That Will Change Your Life* (HarperCollins, 2004)

Reader's Digest. *Foods That Harm, Foods That Heal: An A-Z Guide to Safe and Healthy Eating (Revised Edition)* (The Reader's Digest Association, 2004)

Robinson, Jo. *Eating on the Wild Side: The Missing Link to Optimum Health.* (Little, Brown and Company, New York, 2013)

Shenkin, Alan. "The key role of micronutrients" (*Clinical Nutrition,* 2006)

Siebecker, Allison. Traditional bone broth in modern health and disease. http://www.townsendletter.com/FebMarch2005/broth0205.htm

Skeaff, C. Murray and Miller, Jody. "Dietary Fat and Coronary Heart Disease: Summary of Evidence from Prospective Cohort and Randomised Controlled Trials" (*Annals of Nutrition and Metabolism.* 2009)

Taubes, Gary. *Good Calories, Bad Calories: Challenging the Conventional Wisdom on Diet, Weight control, and Disease.* (Alfred A. Knopf, New York, 2007)

Willett, Walter C. M.D. *Eat, Drink and Be Healthy: The Harvard Medical School Guide to Healthy Eating* (Free Press, 2001)

Wood, Rebecca. *The New Whole Foods Encyclopedia: A Comprehensive Resource for Healthy Eating* (Penguin Books, 1999)

Yeager, Selene and the Editors of Prevention. *The Doctors Book of Food Remedies* (Rodale, 1998)

Websites

American Institute for Cancer Research (www.aicr.org)

Harvard School of Public Health, The Nutrition Source (www.hsph.harvard.edu/nutritionsource)

Livestrong.com

National Agricultural Library, US Department of Agriculture (www.nutrition.gov)

National Cancer Institute (www.nci.nih.gov)

National Institutes of Health (www.nih.gov)

Nutritiondataself.com

The World's Healthiest Foods (www.whfoods.com)

Index